DATE DUE			

Trials of Desire

TRIALS OF DESIRE
Renaissance Defenses of Poetry

Margaret W. Ferguson

Yale University Press

New Haven and London

801.951
F38 π
124204
ajn.1983

Published with the assistance of the Elizabethan Club of Yale University from the foundation established in memory of Oliver Baty Cunningham of the Class of 1917, Yale College.

Designed by Nancy Ovedovitz and set in Caledonia type by Ro-Mark Typographic Company, Inc.
Printed in the United States of America by Edwards Brothers, Inc., Ann Arbor, Mich.

Library of Congress Cataloging in Publication Data

Ferguson, Margaret W., 1948–
  Trials of desire.

  Bibliography: p. 238–49.
  Includes index.
  Contents: An apology for defenses—Joachim du Bellay—Torquato Tasso—Sir Philip Sidney—Conclusion.
  1. Poetics—Early works to 1800. 2. Criticism—History—16th century. I. Title.
PN1035.F4   1983   801′.951   82-8525
ISBN 0-300-02787-7   AACR2

  10   9   8   7   6   5   4   3   2   1

For my mother
Mary Anne Ferguson

Life is not intellectual, or critical, but sturdy.
Ralph Waldo Emerson

Contents

Acknowledgments

"Debt gives all things life," says Rabelais's Panurge; in a practical as well as a metaphysical sense, debt gave life to this book. A Morse Fellowship from Yale University allowed me to begin research; a summer grant from the National Endowment for the Humanities helped me write the chapter on Tasso. I am grateful to those who recommended me for these fellowships. I am also grateful to the staffs of the Sterling, Beinecke, and Cross Campus libraries at Yale for valuable help in my research. For permission to reprint essays which appeared, in quite different forms, in their journals, I thank the editors of *PMLA* and *Boundary 2*. I thank also the editors of the Yale University Press for allowing me to use material which originally appeared in a volume edited by Joseph H. Smith entitled *The Literary Freud: Mechanisms of Defense and the Poetic Will*.

Like the dialogic defenses it studies, this book cannot in any simple sense be considered the product or property of an individual consciousness. While I take full responsibility for any errors in the following pages, I do not take full credit for whatever is valuable in them. My friends, family, and students are in a real sense coauthors of this book. Moreover, the very shape of its argument owes a great deal to those persons who listened to chapters that were presented as lectures at the following institutions: the University of Texas at Austin, Princeton University, New York University, Smith College, Columbia University, and the State University of New York at Buffalo. I thank the colleagues who invited me to lecture, and those many persons whose questions and suggestions expanded my knowledge of my topic. I am also grateful for having had the chance to present informal work-in-progress talks to the Marxist Literary Group at Yale and to the Forum on Psychiatry and the Humanities at the Washington School of Psychiatry; dialogue with members of both groups sharpened my theoretical perspective on defensive discourse. The experience of explaining my ideas to actual audiences definitively marked my meditations on a question that preoccupies all of the authors studied in this book: What is the difference between speaking to an audience one can see and writing for an invisible reader?

My attempts to answer this question were aided not only by those who responded to my talks, but also by those many friends who read and commented on draft versions of the manuscript: Alex Beam, Harold Bloom, Paul Bové, Donald Cheney, Kim Elliman, Angus Fletcher, Thomas Greene, John Guillory, Miriam Hansen, John Hollander, Michael Holquist, Daniel Javitch, Barbara Johnson, Constance Jordan, David Marshall, Richard McCoy, Humphrey Morris, Glenn Most, David Quint, Maria Ruegg, Meredith Skura, Joseph H. Smith, Gordon Williams, and Paolo Valesio. I also owe a great debt of gratitude to Jean Edmunds, who typed and retyped much of the manuscript with intelligence and patience; to Miranda Johnson and Daniel Kiefer, who did superb work as my research assistants; to Ellen Graham of the Yale University Press, who gave me encouragement and much shrewd advice; and to Anne Mackinnon, who edited the manuscript with remarkable skill and thoughtfulness. Barbara Packer read all my chapters in all their versions, and repeatedly rescued me from the Slough of Despond. Throughout the years of this book's making, Jean and Stephen Carr provided intellectual and emotional support; I thank them, and Lucy and Tom Allen, for keeping me sane. I also thank Rima Brauer, with whom I worked through many of my ideas on defense. My debt to my mother, Mary Anne Ferguson, is too many-faceted to describe; it is signaled by the dedication.

"Imagine to yourself another world in which everyone lends and everyone owes, where all are debtors and all are lenders," says Rabelais's Panurge, asking us to envision a world not unlike Thomas More's *Utopia*, in which the concept of private property is abolished. In Panurge's version of Utopia, "no one will be a usurer, nor a glutton, nor a miser, nor a refuser." For sharing his ideas with me unstintingly, and for helping me understand the specifically political dimension of Renaissance defenses of poetry, I thank Richard Halpern. Without the pleasure of his company and the benefit of his critical wit, I would never have finished this book.

Note on Texts and Translations

My quotations from Renaissance works are taken, whenever possible, from recent and readily available scholarly editions. Two of these editions—Henri Chamard's of Du Bellay's *La Deffence et illustration de la langue françoyse* and Ezio Raimondi's of Tasso's *Dialoghi*—do not modernize spelling and punctuation. Readers should therefore be prepared for inconsistencies of orthography and accent marks in passages cited from Du Bellay's *Deffence* and from a dialogue by Tasso discussed in chapter three, *Il Gonzaga overo del piacere onesto.* Readers should also be aware that textual problems abound in the works treated in this book, and that the editions I use reflect critical judgments about an author's original intention.*
My notes address some of the questions that arise from the fact that Sidney's *Defence of Poetry* was published posthumously in two somewhat different versions, and also from the fact that Tasso revised his works obsessively and was rarely willing or able to give unqualified approval to the printed versions of them.

All editors are interpreters, and those who modernize the spelling of Renaissance texts are also, in some sense, translators. As a comparatist, I value various kinds of translation that make it easier for a twentieth-century reader to encounter a sixteenth-century text. In a fundamental way, my book is about our need to rely on translation if we are to communicate across temporal and cultural barriers. But my study of defensive discourse is also about the difficulty of translation and the opacities that translation at once effaces and creates. To honor such opacities in a graphic way, I have adopted the rather cumbrous procedure of providing, in the body of my

*My text for Tasso's *Apologia in difesa della "Gerusalemme Liberata"* is the one established by Cesare Guasti and reprinted in Bruno Maier's edition of Tasso's *Opere*, volume five; for Sidney's *Defence of Poetry*, I use the text in Katherine Duncan-Jones's and Jan Van Dorsten's edition of *Miscellaneous Prose of Sir Philip Sidney*. See bibliography for details.

text, both the original and an English translation of most quotations from foreign-language texts. Unless otherwise indicated, translations are my own; they often, of necessity, constitute interpretations, and they make no claim to elegance.

A final note: I spell *defense* with an *s*, in the American fashion, except when I quote from those texts, mainly British, that spell it with a *c*. For this erratic practice, I make no apologies.

I

An Apology for Defenses

Never explain, never apologize.
> —attributed to Benjamin Jowett

Alone among the major disciplines, literary theory has been mainly a branch of apologetics.
> —M. H. Abrams

Jowett's legendary advice to Oxford students embarking on careers in the British Empire may seem an odd epigraph for a book on defenses of poetry.[1] One of my purposes in writing this book, however, is to question the ideological presuppositions which underlie Jowett's aphorism. By exploring a general territory of defensive discourse through readings of exemplary Renaissance texts, I hope, moreover, to suggest some reasons why Jowett's rule has historically been honored more in the breach than in the observance, not only by poets and critics, but also by theologians, historians, scientists, and diplomats.

Let me explain my polemical purpose more fully by drawing a connection between the Victorian don's formula and the argument made by a modern American critic in the essay from which my second epigraph is taken. In that essay, entitled "Belief and the Suspension of Disbelief," M. H. Abrams asks why literary theorists have so often argued about the nature and function of literature "on a terrain selected by the opposition"—by Plato, for instance, who constructed that notorious scene in the *Republic* where "poetry and her friends" are put on trial by the philosopher and sentenced to banishment before being allowed to make a speech of defense.[2] Phrasing Abrams's question another way, we could ask: Why has literary theoretical explanation so often, throughout Western history, taken the form of apology, defense, excuse, or justification, types of discourse which presuppose the existence of an accusation? This book will suggest some answers to that question, answers quite different from those which Abrams gave in 1957. Abrams's aim was to call for an end to apologetic literary theory and to plead for an approach that would consider poetry "as poetry and not another thing."[3] My aim, in contrast, is to suggest that, for

1

literary critics, an escape from apologetics is neither wholly desirable nor, more to the point, possible. Consider Jowett's rule once again. Who, if anyone, is in a position to heed its advice? Only those who possess absolute power, or absolute confidence in their power and their right to it, could even think of taking the proscription seriously. It might be objected that Jowett surely did not mean to be interpreted literally. He stated his rule, however, without nuance or qualification; that is one reason why it is so often quoted. Moreover, however he intended his words to be understood by his original audience of upper-class English students, it seems fair to regard his formula as a powerful expression of distaste for the verbal acts of apology and explanation.[4] In its form as well as in its content, the rule denigrates the value of discourses which rely, as apology characteristically does, on interpretive explanation and qualification of one's views.[5] What links Jowett's aphorism with Abrams's expression of desire for an end of apologetic criticism is the shared ideal of existence in a realm where one can avoid explaining oneself to foreigners—those who may not understand, much less approve of, one's words or deeds.

The historical fate of the British Empire challenges the idea that explaining oneself to literal and figurative foreigners is an unnecessary activity. The authors studied in this book also challenge that idea, for they suggest that apologizing is necessary not only for those who lack power, but also for those who seek to gain and maintain it, both at home and abroad. They further suggest that to argue "on a terrain selected by the opposition" need not involve an admission of inferiority, as both Abrams and Jowett imply; after all, Socrates not only put poets on the defensive in the *Republic*, but also undertook the task of justifying the virtues of philosophy in the *Apology*. The example of Socrates, which was extremely important for Renaissance authors, reminds us that the word *apology* derives from a Greek word that means "a speech in defense" (from *apo*, "away," and *logia*, "speaking");[6] it retains this meaning in common English usage until at least the nineteenth century, though starting in the late sixteenth century it is also used, albeit often ambiguously, to denote a regretful acknowledgment of a fault.[7] Even when Renaissance authors clearly employ the term in its older, "Greek" sense, however, they implicitly acknowledge the necessity of admitting, if not error, then at least the possibility of being misunderstood.[8] Indeed Renaissance authors of defenses are deeply concerned with theoretical as well as practical problems of understanding, interpretation, and translation. This concern underlies their frequent use of a type of story known, significantly, as the apologue. From the Greek *apologos*, meaning "story" or "fable," the term came to be generally used in the Renaissance for didactic allegories like those of Aesop's fables. But for Renaissance defenders of poetry, there was a special conceptual link between the Greek terms *apologos* and *apologia*, a link suggested not only by the fact that both terms were sometimes translated as "apologie" in sixteenth-century English, but also by a Platonic text that was crucial to Renaissance justifications of poetry.[9]

In Book 10 of the *Republic*, Plato uses *apologia* three times and *apologos* once; he deliberately exploits the verbal similarity between the two terms to illuminate the philosopher's role—or roles—in a complex scene of trial. "Since we have brought up the subject of poetry again," Socrates says in 607b, "let it be our apology that it was then fitting for us to send it away from the city on account of its character."[10] Reading this passage in the light of Allan Bloom's argument that all uses of the term "apologia" in the *Republic* allude to the historical event of Socrates' trial, we see that Plato casts his teacher here in the role of defendant *vis à vis* "poetry and her friends"— which is a nicely ironic reminder that one of Socrates' actual accusers, Meletus, was said to have been particularly offended by Socrates' derogatory remarks about the poets.[11] In a dramatic comment on the "true facts" of the case from the philosopher's perspective, Plato goes on, in Book 10, to make poetry the defendant and Socrates the accuser who also claims to possess the power of a judge. Is this a rhetorical gesture of revenge on Plato's part? I think it is, for there is an obvious parallel between the fate of silence Socrates imposes on poetry and the fate of death the Athenian court imposed on him. But Plato adds several ironic twists to his revised version of the trial. His Socrates mercifully suggests that poetry's banishment need not be eternal: she may reenter the republic, perhaps, when she "has made an apology in lyrics or some other meter" (607d). This gesture of mercy is, however, immediately undermined: Socrates not only gives poetry no chance to speak in self-defense, but proposes to drown out her voice altogether with a philosophic "counter-charm," which guarantees the failure of her persuasive apology even if it could—in some hypothetical future time—be articulated. "As long as [she's] not able to make [her] apology, when we listen to [her], we'll chant this argument we are making to ourselves as a counter- charm to this love, which is childish and belongs to the many" (608a).

Plato's Socrates is not content with merely preventing poetry from speaking; shortly after this passage, he offers his own version of a speech that will appeal to "the many." This speech, which translates the philosopher's esoteric concepts about the nature of justice into a form comprehensible—on some level—by ordinary citizens, is the famous Myth of Er. Socrates calls this myth an apologos (614b), and he presents it, significantly, as a replacement for the story in Homer's *Odyssey* traditionally known as the Apologue of Alcinous: the story which Odysseus tells about his adventures in the underworld to Alcinous, king of the Phaeacians (*Odyssey* 9–12).[12] There is a richly ironic significance to Plato's rhetorical move here—a move which substitutes the philosopher's vision of the afterlife for the poet's and, in so doing, provides a more rational notion of justice than Homer does. For the Myth of Er is not only a product of the philosopher's battle with Homer, but also of his continuing battle with those citizens of Athens who unjustly preferred Homer—both as an educator and as an entertainer— to Socrates. The Myth of Er, Plato's apologos, may indeed be read on one level as a deliberate attempt to redress the injustice perpetrated by the historical audience which had heard but not rightly appreciated Socrates' *Apology*. Renaissance authors, as we shall see, frequently follow Plato's lead in resorting to apologues as tools of defense. And even if they use their apologues, as Sir Philip Sidney does, to argue against Plato's views on poetry, they share his desire to be appreciated—by an audience composed of the many as well as the few.

Because the apology or defense is a mode of discourse that both springs from and attempts to remedy failures of communication, this study of apologetic discourse may provide a useful perspective on problems that face modern intellectuals as they attempt to cross and at the same time define the boundaries among various disciplines. To suggest further reasons why the genre of the defense is worth studying (not to mention defining: in what sense can we speak of a *genre* of the defense at all?), I would like in this introductory chapter to offer a brief apology for defenses, modeling my project, in part, on J. L. Austin's in "A Plea for Excuses." Like Austin, I propose not to "treat" my subject exhaustively or systematically, but rather to show why it is worth studying, and how it may be studied.[13] By suggesting a preliminary mapping of a general field of inquiry which might be constituted by the literary defense (and not only those by poets and critics), I hope to give both a theoretical and a historical perspective on the Renaissance texts which are taken, in this book, as case studies in the art of rhetorical defense: Joachim du Bellay's *La Deffence et illustration de la langue françoyse* (1549); Torquato Tasso's *Apologia in difesa della "Gerusalemme"* (1585); and Sir Philip Sidney's *Defence of Poesie*, alternatively entitled *Apologie for Poetrie* (written ca. 1581; published 1595). These texts have not previously been analyzed in conjunction with each other, in part because critics have rarely focused their attention on the defense as a special class of writing. A study which crosses the boundaries between national literary traditions, as well as numerous other boundaries which critics normally use to classify texts, can raise some new questions about these defenses, two of them famous and one of them (Tasso's) "strangely neglected" (to borrow Lucky Jim's phrase for his highly obscure research topic). The questions include the following: Why do certain authors choose to cast their theoretical statements about literature in the form of a defense? How does this form affect the expression of theoretical views? How does it illuminate (and shape) authors' conceptions of their audience? What is the social character of the prosecution to which the defense replies?

To ask these questions, much less to answer them, is to focus attention on the peculiarities of the defense as a mode of discourse. Austin's essay provides a useful model here, for his effort to define a putative field of study called "excuses"—a field which overlaps with that of literary defenses in some interesting ways—starts from the Wittgensteinian premise that phenomena which appear "ordinary" may in truth be odd enough to merit philosophical scrutiny. Excuses, for Austin, are examples of something so familiar it must be made strange to become interesting. "The production of excuses," he remarks, "has always bulked . . . large among human activities"; but this very largeness, he suggests, is both a reason for studying excuses and a challenge to the analytic mind, which gains knowledge by breaking things into smaller ones, "drawing the coverts of the microglot [and] hounding down the minutiae."[14] Austin's essay, like Freud's *Psychopathology of Everyday Life*, is in fact an exercise in what Paul Ricoeur calls "the hermeneutics of suspicion."[15] It is also a witty and serious homage to a Viennese thinker whose investigations in many ways parallel Freud's: "The aspects of things that are most important for us are hidden because of their simplicity and familiarity," Wittgenstein wrote; "One is unable to notice something—because it is always before one's eyes."[16]

Like excuses in ordinary language, literary defenses are "always before our eyes." Indeed one might go further and suggest that both spoken and written defenses are like the poor: they are always with us, they are rarely observed attentively, and they often cause (as well as reflect) discomfort. Excuses, Austin writes, "are cases where there has been some abnormality or failure" (pp. 179–80) or, one might add, where someone thinks there has been some abnormality or failure. Whether they occur at a cocktail party, during a murder trial, or in a piece of writing, defensive verbal acts signal the breach of some social code of behavior. For this very reason, however, they may lay claim to our interest; as Austin argues, "the abnormal will throw light on the normal, will help us penetrate the blinding veil of ease and obviousness that hides the mechanisms of the natural successful act" (p. 180). He also argues, less directly, that the study of abnormal cases may call our definitions of the normal into question.

The defense certainly eludes, and therefore potentially illuminates, the categories which critics normally use to classify types of discourse. Indeed, for reasons that will be enumerated in the following pages, the defense can best be described as a "boundary creature"—a metaphor Freud uses to describe the ego.[17] Consider first the boundary between spoken and written discourse, which is blurred by a type of writing that presents itself as if it were a speech given in a court of law. Renaissance authors frequently make this "as if" a locus of theoretical concern, as they meditate on the similarities and differences between a written defense and an oratorical performance. Sidney's *Defence*, for instance, at once exploits and questions the fiction it creates by its imitation of the classical forensic or judicial oration; the fiction is that the writer is an orator addressing an audience present to his view.[18] For an author like Sidney, an aristocrat who published none of his works except, significantly, a defense of his uncle Leicester, the form of the defense itself has complex ideological implications having to do with the writer's relation to a court very different from the ones in which classical orators argued their cases.

Authors writing at the dawn of the Age of Print understandably use the form of the defense to express various and contradictory attitudes toward the relation between oral and written discourse and, in Du Bellay's case in particular, between the vernacular language and the ancient ones which the Renaissance scholar had to learn through texts. It is important to note, however, that for the ancients, too, the defense as a mode of discourse occupied a problematic border territory between speech and writing. Early in the *Apology*, Plato describes a peculiarity of Socrates' defensive situation which makes it resemble that of the writer. Remarking that he is "an utter foreigner to the manner of speech here"—that is, to the conventions of court oratory and, by implication, sophistic rhetoric in general—Socrates asks permission to use "the same words" (*tôn autôn logôn*) he has previously employed in the open marketplace.[19] But he cannot quite have his wish, for in the court, a closed and unfree place, he must address a kind of interlocutor whom he has never before addressed directly. Not all his accusers, he says, are present; there are some who are absent and whose names he does not even know, unless "one of them happens to be a writer of comedies" (*Apology* 18c–d). This allusion to Aristophanes, who had repeatedly attacked Socrates in his plays, dramatizes a parallel between Socrates and later defenders of discourses which offended social conventions: the defendant addresses a prosecution which includes texts as well as people. The defendant in such a trial often finds, as Socrates does, that the opponents "are most difficult to cope with; for it is not even possible to call any of them up here and cross-examine [them]"; rather, as Socrates laments, " I am compelled in making my defense to fight, as it were, absolutely with shadows [*skiamachein*] and to cross-question when nobody answers" (18d).

In representing the last public speech Socrates made before his death, Plato depicts his master confronting a version of the problem which inevitably confronts the writer, who not only addresses people who do not answer, but also presents his own thoughts in a dead form, one that fixes the thought and prevents it from answering to future readers' queries. In the *Phaedrus*, Socrates criticizes the written word in terms which seem designed (by Plato) to recall the image of Socrates defending himself in the court which sentenced him to death and, except for that simulacrum of his voice preserved in Plato's text, to silence. The dialectical speaker, Socrates tells Phaedrus, "plants and sows in a fitting soul intelligent words which are able to help themselves and him who planted them, which are not fruitless, but yield seed from which there spring up in other minds other words capable of continuing the process forever" (276e–77a). In contrast to the dialectical speaker, the writer as Plato portrays him is a weak "husbandman" and progenitor; he sows his seeds "through a pen with words which cannot defend themselves by argument and cannot teach the truth effectually" (276c). Like the painter's products, the writer's words merely seem like living beings, for "if one asks them a question, they preserve a solemn silence" (275d). This silence is what causes the written word to be both dangerous (it can get into the hands of "those who have no interest in it") and vulnerable: for "every word, when once it is written . . . knows not to whom to speak or not to speak; when ill-treated or unjustly reviled it always needs its father to help it; for it has no power to protect or help itself" (275d). The Greek verb *boetheo*, translated in these passages as "defend," "protect," or "help," has both military and medical connotations; in the *Phaedo* (88e) it is used to describe the way Socrates "rescued" a discredited argument about the immortality of soul. In that passage, as in the ones quoted above from the *Phaedrus*, the issue of defending the truth (rescuing it by bringing "auxiliary forces," or medicines) is clearly linked to the problem which Socrates' death posed for his disciples. The burden of defending the master's words falls on men like Phaedo, who recounts Socrates' last sayings, and Plato, who must somehow use that black fluid called ink to keep Socrates' words alive.

In the Platonic dialogues, the distinction between spoken and written language stands in a complex and highly dialectical relation to the distinction between the philosopher, who uses words to defend the truth, and the poet and the sophistic orator, who use words to defend actions and causes that are not necessarily either true or just.[20] Without purporting to unravel the tangled web of analogies Plato draws to associate a bad kind of speech with both the orator and the poet, a bad kind of writing with the orator, and a good kind of writing and speech with the philosopher, I do want to remark that two modern commentators have given diametrically opposed analyses of the "speech versus writing" question in the Platonic dialogues. The contrast between Jacques Derrida's "La Pharmacie de Platon" and Eric Havelock's *A Preface to Plato* in fact supports my hypothesis that the activity of verbal defense, as Plato defines and practices it, raises rather than answers questions about the boundary between speech and writing. Derrida argues that Plato defends the philosopher and his *logos* against the threat posed by the Sophist by claiming that there is a qualitative difference between a speech grounded in truth (the transcendental *logos*) and sophistical imitations, which, according to Derrida, Plato associates with the "bastard" version of speech given in writing.[21] Derrida's argument is based on a reading of the *Phaedrus*, a dialogue that Havelock perplexingly ignores in his fascinating book about the meaning of Plato's war on poetry. Derrida, however, appears not to have read Havelock's argument that Plato's attack on the poets in the *Republic* is not only a defense of philosophical discourse, but also a defense which could have been made only in a society where writing was becoming increasingly important as a means of education.[22]

Havelock sees Plato's attack on poetry as a crucial strategy in the philosopher's attempt to take control of the Greek system of education dominated by the Homeric rhapsode. In attacking the poet, Plato is defending a kind of language and thought which had as its enabling condition a historical change in communication. The spread of literacy in Greece that occurred in the late fifth and early fourth centuries was the precondition for, if not the cause (certainly not the acknowledged cause) of, Plato's critique of poetry; poetry represents an oral method of teaching and of conceiving information which, according to Havelock, Plato wanted to replace with a teaching whose means and ends involved the articulation of universal, timeless propositions.[23] Such propositions could only be understood by a literate audience weaned of its love for the rhapsodic or dramatic performance, which constituted a type of education (*paideia*) based on memorization and identification.[24]

The difference between Havelock's and Derrida's perspectives on Plato dramatizes the defensive dimension of Plato's own discourse and the complexity of his attempt to define that discourse in contrast both to the Sophist's and to the poet's verbal arts. Renaissance authors were deeply interested in showing that Plato was himself involved in cultural struggles for power, and they read him not only as a theorist but also as a practitioner of defense. They looked with particular attention at his paradoxical arguments about the relation between speech and writing, for they saw that Socrates, the teacher who, like Christ, never wrote, had failed to defend his life with his speech but nevertheless lived in the "majestic silence" of Plato's text. (For a discussion of Sidney's view of Plato as a writer seeking to usurp the throne of the poets, see Chapter 4, below.)

If the defense as a mode of discourse has historically raised questions about the boundary between speech and writing, it has also traditionally blurred a boundary that was as important to Plato as it is to many modern critics: the boundary between theoretical (disinterested) uses of language and pragmatic (self-interested) ones. Plato depicts the philosopher, in the *Gorgias*, as a person who serves the truth rather than himself; he attacks the rhetorician as a person who uses words "for the purpose of defending [his] own guilt, or that of his parents or friends or children, or his country when guilty" (480b–c). Plato's severely ethical perspective (which Aristotle, among others, attempts to challenge) also informs some recent critical discussions of rhetoric.[25] In an interesting essay on Sidney's *Astrophil and Stella*, Richard Lanham attacks Sidney for using art for purposes of "impure persuasion," that is, for egotistical aims (in this case, erotic designs on a lady).[26] Lanham takes the phrase "impure persuasion" from Kenneth Burke; paradoxically, however, Lanham uses the phrase to attack a phenomenon which Burke finds morally disturbing, to be sure, but which he nevertheless insists that the critic, and everyone else, must accept as a truth: all discourse is to some degree "motivated" by the author's desire for personal advantage, economic, political, or sexual.[27] Some kinds of discourse may approach (or seem to approach) the ideal of "pure persuasion" (which, as Burke very well knows, is an inherently contradictory phrase, "pure" meaning no persuasion at all), but it is a delusion to forget that "pure persuasion in the absolute sense exists nowhere."[28]

Because the defense as a form calls attention to the existence of rhetorical motives, it provides a useful perspective on the issue which preoccupies Burke, the issue of the different kinds and degrees of advantage that the writer of a work may seek to gain. One might well borrow Burke's notion of a scale running from "impure" to "pure" motives to classify various historical examples of defenses. At one end of the scale we could place a text like the second poem of Ovid's *Tristia*, a defense of the *Ars Amatoria* which had been accused of teaching immorality to the women of Rome. The *Ars* was a major cause of Ovid's banishment to Tomis, on the Black Sea; his defense of it is manifestly a plea to the Emperor Augustus for a reversal of the harsh sentence.[29] A text like Apuleius's *Apologia*, the funny and fascinating defense Apuleius presented in court in response to accusations that he had won his rich wife by using poetry and magic, might be placed somewhere on the middle of the scale; though the charges against him were serious, Apuleius seems, as one translator remarks, "to have felt quite secure as to the issue, and to have flung himself with great glee into a contest which afforded him such capital opportunities for displaying his wit, his learning, and his powers of rhetoric."[30] Finally, at the purer end of the scale, we could locate works like Gorgias's *Defense of Helen*,[31] or Defoe's apologetic preface to *Moll Flanders*, or Chesterton's *Defense of Nonsense* (1922). Defoe's preface is particularly interesting because it plays ironically with clichés of defensive rhetoric; Defoe alludes to the advocates for the stage and their "great argument to persuade people that their plays are useful" before offering a similar "great argument" for his own narrative's moral usefulness: "There is not a wicked action of any part of it but is first or last rendered unhappy or unfortunate."[32] Like Flaubert, who stages in *Madame Bovary* a comic but nevertheless serious trial of fiction in which the pharmacist, Homais, plays the defense lawyer and the priest, Bournisien, plays the prosecutor, Defoe exposes the tendency inherent in the defense to become parodic and reflectively critical of constraining conventions—including those of the defense.[33] Rhetoric turning a wryly critical eye on itself—this is one aspect of what Burke means by "purer" types of persuasion, types where there is an element of "self-interference" in the author's pursuit of advantage. But as we shall see in Sidney's case, an ironic interference with egotistical aims may be inextricably linked to ardent pursuit of personal desires. Ovid's case presents the other side of the same coin: his blatantly self-serving rhetorical product is also a subtle, and highly influential, meditation on theoretical issues of intentionality and interpretation. (See below, Chapter 4, for a discussion of Ovid's influence on Sidney's *Defence*.)

While it seems to me misleading, in the final analysis, to classify defenses according to a scale which has as one of its hypothetical poles an equation between "pure" writing and writing that manifests neither psychological nor political aims, Burke himself insists that a variety of motives may coexist in any given work; and he also points to a less morally charged way of conceiving degrees of pragmatic motivation in a class of texts. The alternative to the opposition between "pure" and "impure" persuasion is contained in Burke's discussion of classical rhetorical theory, especially in the pages he devotes to the distinction between the epideictic oration, on the one hand, and the types of speech Aristotle called "forensic" and "deliberative," on the other. Epideictic or "display" oratory, also called demonstrative or panegyric, has as its aim praise or abuse (as in a diatribe against a public character, for instance). In contrast to the deliberative speech, "directed towards the future," Burke writes, and "designed to sway an audience on matters of public policy," and also in contrast to the forensic speech aimed at establishing in a jury's mind "the guilt or innocence of an accused person," the epideictic oration characteristically aims not only to persuade, but to delight an audience. It also pleases the speaker, who seeks to win praise for his own eloquence as well as for his subject. Noting that Aristotle considered epideictic the kind of oratory that lends itself best to the written word, Burke allies it to his own notion of "pure persuasion" by describing it as follows:

> Critics must have epideictic in mind who say that eloquence begins in the love of words for their own sake.... [I]ts effects can be savored, hence may profit by a closer, more sustained, scrutiny. Also, since pure display rhetoric comes closest to the appeal of poetic in and for itself, it readily permits the arbitrary selection of topics halfway between rhetoric and poetic. And here even methods originally forensic may be used as artifice. Thus, in the English tradition of love poems written in praise of one's mistress or as mock invective against love, etc., or where the lover pleads the "cause" of his mistress or brings indictments against her, the poet's tactics are not read as he would have them read unless the reader watches their playful adaptation of rhetorical forms to poetic purposes.
> [*A Rhetoric of Motives*, p. 72]

This is clearly an important passage for the student of literary defenses; it reminds us that a work like Sidney's *Defence of Poetry* may have a closer kinship to Erasmus's *Praise of Folly* or to the host of witty defenses of "indefensibles" (baldness, debt, fleas, etc.) which Rosalie Colie discusses in *Paradoxia Epidemica* than it has to a sober treatise like Scaliger's *Poetics*.[34] Modern readers who are accustomed to classifying defenses of poetry as a species of literary criticism or theory should recall that the boundaries between criticism, fiction, and rhetoric were much less distinct in the sixteenth century than they are today. The defense is a signal instance of the Renaissance capacity to create mixed or even "monstrous" genres which contain imitations of various classical forms and bear family resemblances to "new-old" forms like the Erasmian mock-encomium and the *paragone*. That minor but fascinating rhetorical genre (which derives its name from the Italian verb *paragonare*, "to liken") characteristically stages a competition between two nations, two art forms, two languages, or even two poets.[35] Traces of the paragone appear in all the sixteenth-century defenses studied in this book; there are competitions between ancient and modern languages in Du Bellay, between romance and epic in Tasso, and between the poet and cultural rivals such as the historian and philosopher in Sidney. In depicting such contests, the defense illustrates Burke's point that "methods originally forensic may be used as artifice." But the defense also shows that works which contain an "epideictic" dimension need not therefore cease to pursue the aims Aristotle originally associated with forensic and deliberative oratory: establishing guilt or innocence and persuading an audience about issues of public policy.

Renaissance poets knew perfectly well that the public role of the classical orator depended on a democratic or republican form of government; but this knowledge often increased rather than diminished their desire to use poetic means for political ends. The poet as Puttenham describes him in *The Arte of English Poesie*—"a pleader of pleasant causes"—may address less pleasant causes through the means of allegory and indirection available to the courtier.[36] In the cases examined in this book, "poetic purposes" are never purely poetic.

Hence the Renaissance form of the defense necessarily offends those who believe, as Walter Ong does, that a conflation of poetry and rhetoric is a "monster" born in certain unhappy historical periods.[37] O. B. Hardison, Jr., a noted Renaissance scholar, uses similarly charged language when he discusses the "error" of poetic theories which, like Philip Sidney's, maintain that the end of art is to shape readers' actions as well as their minds. "The notion that art must be free of the practical functions for which oratory is responsible," Hardison writes, "allows us to recognize that all human activities have their proper spheres and also that the boundaries of those spheres cannot be overstepped without loss."[38] Such critical views, which invoke the Kantian notion of a disinterested aesthetic realm, suggest that the desire to mark off a space for innocent art is related to the desire for an innocent criticism—one that would approach the ideal of an objective, scientific field of inquiry. Northrop Frye's "Polemical Introduction" to *Anatomy of Criticism* neatly illustrates the connection between these desires. His call for a "scientific" criticism (for which adjective, he says, we may substitute "systematic" or "progressive") goes hand in hand with, and in fact depends on, his belief that literature is a "disinterested use of words" which can be distinguished from "the descriptive or assertive writing which derives from the active will and the conscious mind, and which is primarily concerned to 'say' something."[39]

By virtue of their very existence as textual moments which can be classified neither as disinterested art nor as disinterested critical theory, defenses of poetry—including Frye's own in the "Polemical Introduction"—undermine the notion of an aesthetic realm uncontaminated by rhetoric. But defenses like the ones examined in this book, which reflect on the aims and means of their own discourse, become active rather than passive advocates of what we might call the claims of the ego. "Self-love," Sidney writes at the beginning of his treatise, "is better than any gilding to make that seem gorgeous wherein our selves be parties."[40] When defenses not only inhabit a border territory of "interested rhetoric" but also explore it and attempt to extend its boundaries—by calling attention, for instance, to the desires for personal advantage that motivate philosophers and historians as well as poets—then literary defenses may be usefully compared to those texts in which Freud demystified the ideal of disinterested discourse.

Freud's views on the motives of literary rhetoric are well known: "the writer softens the egotistical character of his daydreams by changes and disguises" (*SE* 9: 153). More significant for my purposes—which include a desire to show how defenses by poets illuminate Freud's writing, as well as vice versa—is the fact that Freud presents the psychoanalyst himself as an artist who "softens and disguises" the workings of his ego (which includes, of course, an unconscious portion). Freud's theoretical elaboration of the relation between the observing and the observed subject (whether that subject is oneself or another) counters the notion that a "human science" can exist in the form envisioned by a critic like Frye, who asserts that "literature is not a subject of study but an object of study: the fact that it consists of words makes us confuse it with the talking verbal disciplines."[41] Contrast this with Freud's description of the relation between observer and observed in *his* science:

> Every science is based on observations and experiences arrived at through the medium of our psychical apparatus. But since *our* science has as its subject that

apparatus itself, the analogy ends here. We make our observations through the medium of the same perceptual apparatus, precisely with the help of the breaks in the sequence of 'psychical' events: we fill in what is omitted by making plausible inferences and translating it into conscious material. [*An Outline of Psychoanalysis, SE* 23: 159]

There is, of course, more than a mere analogy between the analyst's observation of a "psychical apparatus" and the critic's observation of a text: both acts of observation are also productions, translations which substitute one verbal sequence for another. Freud, who developed his theory of interpretation by analyzing his own dreams as well as those of others— indeed by viewing his dreams as the products of the "other" within, the unconscious—points throughout his work to the possibility of error in interpretations made through the medium of our "perceptual apparatus" (*Wahrnehmungsapparat*). "The reproduction of a perception as a presentation is not always a faithful one; it may be modified by omissions, or changed by the merging of various elements." This sentence, from the paper "Negation" (*SE* 19: 238), provides a useful gloss on the notion of interpretation as a "filling in" of "what is omitted." Although Freud insists on the "relative certainty" of psychoanalytic interpretation, it is worth remarking that his defenses of that relative certainty often presuppose a situation in which the analyst can test his conjectures against a patient's responses.[42] It may be true, as Freud insists in his late paper "Constructions in Analyses," that an interpretative error "can do no harm" to a patient (*SE* 23: 261); but the problem becomes more severe when the analyst applies his constructions to a written text which cannot talk back, as Freud does, for instance, when he analyzes the Bible in *Moses and Monotheism*.

It should be clear that I think Freud's metapsychological theory offers useful perspectives on the activity of verbal defense practiced by writers in various fields, including the sciences.[43] Because Freud formulated a complex theory of psychic defense, and because he illuminates certain aspects of this theory by his own practice as a writer, he may serve as an important albeit not entirely reliable guide into the general territory of defensive discourse I attempt to explore in this book—a territory which must be mapped both with reference to modalities of psychic defense and with reference to social pressures on the authorial ego.

Freud uses the term "defence" (the German word, *Abwehr*, has the military but not the legal connotations of the English one) throughout much of his career "as a general designation for all the techniques which the ego makes use of in conflicts which may lead to neurosis" (*SE* 20: 163; for a discussion of the complex development of Freud's concept of defense, see the Appendix, below). The psychoanalytic "theory of defence," as set forth both by Freud and by his American, English, and French followers, is enormously complex;[44] but analysts generally agree that the theory of defense deals with conflicts between the ego and the instincts. "It is against an internal threat that the ego seeks to defend itself," write Laplanche and Pontalis.[45] And Otto Fenichel elaborates the point when he explains that although "the motives of defense are rooted in external influences," "without an intrapsychic institution that represents and anticipates the external world, no defense and no neurosis could arise."[46] No defense in the technical psychoanalytic sense of the term, that is. But Freud's metaphor of *Abwehr* connotes more than a battle between the ego and the instincts. In *Beyond the Pleasure Principle* (1920)—the text in which he calls attention to the inadequacies of the "scientific terms, that is to say . . . the figurative language" that he is obliged to use to describe the "bewildering and obscure processes" of psychic life—he posits the existence of a "protective shield" that defends the individual against *external* stimuli. It seems to me that his discussion of this "protective shield" calls into question the idea of a firm theoretical distinction between internal defensive processes and those directed against threats that originate "outside" the individual.[47] It also seems to me that Freud is most useful as a theorist of verbal defenses when he turns his attention, as he does in *Beyond the Pleasure Principle*, to the general problems of defining and defending one's boundaries.

He begins the "far-fetched speculations" of Chapter IV by assigning to the conscious ego (the system *"Pcpt.-Cs."*) a "position in space": "It must lie on the borderline [*Grenze*] between inside and outside; it must be turned toward the external world and must envelop the other psychical systems" (p. 24). He goes on to "picture" the psyche as a "living vesicle" with a "receptive cortical layer"; the outermost surface of this receptive layer consists of "membrane" (*Rinde*) which has been "baked through" so that it becomes a "protective shield against stimuli" (*Reizschutz*) (pp. 26–27). Freud powerfully indicates the need for this shield by comparing the psyche to "a little fragment of living substance . . . suspended in the middle of an external world charged with the most powerful energies." Without its shield, the organism would perish, and Freud portrays the shield as a sacrificial victim:

> By its death, the outer layer has saved all the deeper ones from a similar fate—unless, that is to say, stimuli reach it which are so strong that they break through the protective shield. Protection against stimuli [*Reizschutz*] is an almost more important function for the living organism than reception of stimuli [*Reizaufnahme*]. [p. 27]

Freud distinguishes between the ego's relation to the external world and its relation to its own "deeper layers" on the grounds that there can be no "protective shield" against internal stimuli: "The excitations in the deeper layers extend into the system directly and in undiminished amount, insofar as certain of their characteristics give rise to feelings in the pleasure-unpleasure series" (p. 29). But this distinction, drawn to support the point that "feelings of pleasure and unpleasure . . . predominate over all external stimuli," is immediately qualified. The ego that lacks a shield against internal threats may, Freud suggests, create one by a substitutive operation:

> [A] particular way is adopted of dealing with any internal excitations which produce too great an increase of unpleasure: there is a tendency to treat them as though they were acting, not from the inside, but from the outside, so that it is possible to bring the shield against stimuli into operation as a means of defence [*Abwehrmittel*] against them. This is the origin of projection, which is destined to play such a large part in the causation of pathological processes. [p. 29]

This passage could be studied as a metapsychological *prise de position* no less complex than that of *Inhibitions, Symptoms and Anxiety*, where Freud tortuously reflects on the problem of whether anxiety is to be regarded as "transformed libido" or as a reaction to situations of external danger.[48] For our purposes the chapter's interest lies in the way it sketches a field of defense which has two frontiers but which is occupied by a creature capable of treating one frontier as though it were the other. We should note, moreover, that the metaphorical operation Freud ascribes to the psyche is very like the one he performs throughout his work when he uses the term "defence" to treat an internal world as though it were an external one.

In the concluding chapter of this book I analyze Freud's own rhetorical practice of defense in the light of his theory about the ego as a "boundary creature." I look in particular at passages in which he defends his territory of psychoanalysis against threats posed both by rebellious disciples (Jung and Adler, for instance) and by members of other cultural disciplines—natural scientists, philosophers, and, last but not least, poets and literary critics. My own practice of reading Freud illustrates that crossing of disciplinary boundaries which is, I believe, an essential feature of the art of defense defined both by Freud and by the Renaissance poet-critics studied in the central chapters of this book: defense, which involves defining one's discursive territory in relation to other writers' claims to authority, always makes one resemble the figure praised by Cicero and attacked by Plato—the orator who roams through many fields of knowledge and claims to find himself "on his own ground" wherever he goes.[49]

By ending this book with Freud, I hope to provoke thought about the defense as an interdisciplinary mode of writing—interdisciplinary both because it has been used, historically, by writers in different fields and because it frequently records (and participates in) power struggles among the various "sciences of humankind." When Sidney and Shelley brood on the poet's place within the body politic of culture, and when they present that body as a battleground torn by civil war among its various members, they anticipate the argument formulated by modern semioticians: "In the study of culture," states a manifesto of the Soviet Tartu group, "the initial premise is that all human activity concerned with the processing, exchange, and storage of information possesses a certain unity. Individual sign systems, though they presuppose immanently organized structures, function only in a unity, supported by one another. None of the sign systems possesses a mechanism which would enable it to function culturally in isolation."[50] The manifesto adds, however, that one must pay special attention to "questions of the hierarchical structure of the languages of culture, of the distribution of spheres among them, of cases in which these spheres intersect or merely border on one another."[51] The form of the defense, I would argue, characteristically points to disputes about "the hierarchical structure of the languages of culture."

This brings me back to M. H. Abrams and his plea for an end to apologetic literary theorizing. Abrams fantasizes about what would have happened if someone other than the meek Glaucon had been present to debate with Socrates in Book 10 of the *Republic*:

> Now look here, Socrates, I see your game. You've got me trapped in a set of premises by which the end is foreordained. But I refuse to consider poetry in a context in which it must aim to do what philosophy can do better. I propose that when we consider poetry, we consider it as poetry and not another thing.[52]

Abrams acknowledges that Aristotle's *Poetics* constituted such an answer to Plato; unfortunately, he says, Aristotle did not argue loudly enough for poetry's value as an autonomous activity, so that "over the centuries Aristotle has been interpreted as refuting or correcting Plato's theory on its own terms. *As a consequence*, literary criticism has been maneuvered into a defensive stance from which it has never entirely recovered" (p. 2; my emphasis). Abrams's view of causality here is a defense; it denies the fact that the malady being described is a historical and social phenomenon which an individual author like Plato does not simply "cause" and which later individuals cannot simply cure by an act of will.[53] Abrams himself sees that the defense of literature is a cultural phenomenon, but he does not want alls to explore the implications of his insight:

> The [critical] positions most strongly defended have shifted, to meet the threat from one another enterprise claiming exclusive access to the kind of truth poetry was supposed to pretend to: philosophy, history, Christian theology and morals, and then, in the seventeenth century, the New Science. But in every age the seemingly positive principles of criticism have been designed for the defense of poetry and usually, as in the Platonic dialogues, on a terrain selected by the opposition. [pp. 2–3]

Abrams's desire for an autonomous sphere of literary activity, a sphere in which poets and critics would be free of the burden of defining and defending themselves in relation to other cultural discourses (as well as culturally powerful institutions and authority figures), is a desire voiced not only by other modern critics, but also by the Renaissance authors studied in this book. Their textual trials all manifest the wish to escape from the scene of trial itself, whether it is figured as a court, a battlefield, a prison, or a "brazen world." Unlike many modern critics, however, the authors studied in the following chapters acknowledge, by the very fact of writing works explicitly titled "defenses," that they are trapped in what Sidney calls a "predicament of relation," a predicament created by the literary artist's or critic's status as a member of a body politic. Moreover, if Du Bellay, Tasso, and Sidney all long for a golden world in which the poet would be master of his own territory, they also share Milton's belief that writers, like other fallen human beings, must engage in struggle with themselves and others to bring forth works which will have power and authority. "Assuredly we bring not innocence into the world," Milton writes in *Areopagitica*, his great defense of free speech; "we bring forth impurity much rather, that which purifies us is trial, and trial is by what is contrary."[54] As they define their desires against what is contrary, Renaissance authors of defenses create arguments and allegorical apologues that support not only Milton's belief in the creative value of trial, but also Wallace Stevens's point in "Notes Toward a Supreme Fiction":

> From this the poem springs: that we live in a place
> That is not our own and, much more, not ourselves
> And hard it is in spite of blazoned days.

II

Joachim du Bellay: The Exile's Defense of His Native Language

The new consciousness of the Renaissance was born not in a perfected and fixed linguistic system but at the intersection of many languages and at the point of their most intense interorientation and struggle.
—Mikhail Bakhtin, *Rabelais and His World*

The little treatise entitled *La Deffence et illustration de la langue françoyse* (1549) represents Joachim du Bellay's first public entrance into the arena of historical struggle Bakhtin describes, the arena located in a border territory where the intersection of many languages, ancient as well as modern, reflected and generated ideological conflict.[1] Throughout his literary career Du Bellay explored this border territory, defining it as a land of Babel, a land of exile, and finally as a textual space occupied—as so many parts of Europe itself were in the sixteenth century—by forces with competing claims to possession.[2] Modern readers have often criticized Du Bellay's treatise for its logical incoherence; a close look at the text and its context suggests, however, that its theoretical inconsistencies are precisely what constitute its value as a product and interpretation of a complex competition among languages.[3]

The Offensive Defense

Est-ce là defense & illustration, ou plustot offense & denigration?—Barthélemy Aneau, *Quintil Horatian*

Like many other defensive enterprises, literary and military, Du Bellay's has aggressive aims. These must be considered, first, in the light of the text's status as a manifesto, a work designed to display the literary and social theories of a group. Along with Ronsard, Baïf, and other young men at the Collège de Coqueret in Paris, Du Bellay belonged to a group known initially as the "Brigade" and later as the "Pléiade."[4] His treatise is in part the expression of a collective poetics, and it should therefore be read as an effort to "illustrate" the Brigade as well as the French language. This effort involves

18

vehement denunciations of previous French authors (the "denigrations" which so offended the contemporary critic Barthélemy Aneau) and equally vehement prescriptions for the "future poet" to whom the treatise is addressed.[5] Like later authors of manifestos, Du Bellay seeks to make room for a new generation of writers; in so doing, he takes what a Russian manifesto calls "a whack at the public taste."[6] He also makes that argument of "self-assertion or self-defense" which small avant-garde societies typically make, according to Renato Poggioli, as they define themselves against "society in the larger sense."[7]

Du Bellay's version of this argument is strongly influenced by the fact that his group at Coqueret was composed chiefly of young noblemen who lacked the property and traditional prerogatives of feudal aristocrats.[8] Though they did not lack traditional upper-class opinions, these were influenced in complex ways by their study of classical texts under Jean Dorat, the humanist philologist who was the principal of Coqueret.[9] Du Bellay's attacks on previous French poets like Marot and Scève, and his failure even to mention the achievements of writers like Villon and Rabelais, no doubt reflect both his upper-class prejudice against lower-class authors and his fervent admiration for the ancients, who constituted, in his eyes, a nobility of letters.[10] One might suggest, indeed, that humanist ideology served Du Bellay and his comrades as a means of reinforcing an elitist social perspective which was threatened by the blurring of class distinctions in sixteenth-century France.[11]

Barthélemy Aneau's reaction to the *Deffence* supports the suggestion that Du Bellay's particular brand of humanist elitism was a weapon in a complex social struggle. As the bourgeois principal of the Collège de la Trinité in Lyons, Aneau was especially irritated by Du Bellay's expressions of scorn for provincial authors and literary academies.[12] This irritation underlies his objection to Du Bellay's very project of defending the French language. The vernacular, in Aneau's view, was alive and well as an instrument of literary expression; it needed no defense from the man he mockingly describes as "a small, foolish personage who mounts on stilts to achieve height" ("un petit personnage nain, qui pour attaindre hault, monte sur eschaces" [p. 3, n. 2]). Equating Du Bellay's rhetorical efforts to achieve a grand style with aspirations to social greatness, Aneau attempts to cut Du Bellay down to his natural size, as it were, by exposing the artifice of his "stilted" language and the shakiness of his social self-image.

In the Préambule to his critical pamphlet, Aneau compares Du Bellay to an orator who offers a speech in praise of Hercules to a man from Laconia. As that man rejects the speech, asking (laconically), "Who is it that blames him?" so Aneau rejects Du Bellay's defense, asking, "Who accuses or has accused the French language? No one, certainly, at least not in writing" ("Qui accuse ou qui a accusée la langue Françoise? Nul certes: au moins par escrit" [p. xi]). The qualification is significant—and also incorrect, since many Catholic theologians and humanist educators (including Du Bellay's own teacher, Jean Dorat) had expressed their low opinion of the vulgar tongue in writing as well as in speech.[13] But even if Aneau polemically overstates his case, he usefully reminds us that the vernacular had been ably defended, as well as illustrated, long before the members of the Brigade took up their pens. He also suggests, rightly, that Du Bellay so desired personal glory that he would create enemies, if none were present, in order to prove his strength. Like Don Quixote, Du Bellay and his comrades sought a field of heroic action which, in Aneau's opinion, no longer existed, if it ever had. To underscore this point, he likens Du Bellay to a "Hercules factitius" who lacks genuine labors and therefore creates imaginary monsters he can easily overcome.[14]

Aneau's image of Du Bellay as a *Hercules factitius* calls attention to a social fact ignored by most modern critics: the *Deffence* was written by a man literally in search of noble labor, a man who belonged, in name and in fantasy, to that "landowning class whose profession was war," but who was forced to earn his living by his pen.[15] Du Bellay was highly ambivalent about the social status of the pen. In the second preface to his first book of poems, the *Olive*, he writes defensively that in producing poetry he follows "the example of many gentle French spirits, even those of my profession, who do not scorn to use both the sword and the pen, despite the false opinion of those who think that such an exercise of letters is a derogation to the estate of the nobility" ("par l'example de plusieurs gentiz espritz françois, mesmes de ma profession, qui ne dedaignent point manier & l'epée & la plume, contre la faulse persuasion de ceux qui pensent tel exercice de lettres deroger à l'estat de noblesse").[16] It should therefore not surprise us to see him doing his best to make a virtue of necessity by making the profession of letters a facsimile of the profession of arms: his project of "illustrating" the French language is in part an aggressive attempt to ennoble the writer who keenly feels that the very labor of writing may represent a derogation of his estate.

In this project, the pen serves both as a figurative substitute for the sword and as a literal means for acquiring the power and property it represents. Du Bellay makes it difficult to distinguish between these two functions, since he dedicates his text to the wealthy kinsman from whom he hoped to gain employment: the Cardinal Jean du Bellay. Although in 1549 the cardinal himself was temporarily unemployed, he had previously served François I as a diplomat to the Papal Court in Rome.[17] Joachim clearly hoped that the new king, Henri II, would allow the cardinal to resume his political labors; he also hoped that the cardinal would look with favor on the young relative who sought to gain glory and patronage by writing a patriotic literary treatise. In pursuit of the double goal of literary fame and economic advancement, Du Bellay not only prefaces his text with a letter to his illustrious kinsman; he also brings the cardinal and his political activities into the very fabric of the *Deffence* through a complex allegory that arises, as we shall see, from both unconscious fantasies and theoretical designs.

In his prefatory letter, he portrays the cardinal as a man of heroic stature, a major actor in the theatre of modern European politics and also in that temporally more ambiguous place he calls "ce grand Theatre Romain": "Veu le personnaige que tu joues au spectacle de toute l'Europe, voyre de tout le monde, en ce grand Theatre Romain," Du Bellay begins (pp. 3–4). Aneau testily objects to this theatrical metaphor, finding it "indecorous" to refer to a nobleman as if he were a "jongleur" and to a royal legation as if it were a "comédie."[18] It is here, moreover, that Aneau specifically reproves Du Bellay for his assumption of a stilted style that makes him seem greater than he is. Aneau thus underscores the threat to social hierarchy implicit in the concept of the world as a stage where persons of various classes may, like actors, change parts. Paradoxically, the bourgeois critic from Lyons is offended by precisely that which, in Du Bellay's rhetoric, expresses an apparently typical middle-class notion: that style rather than birth makes the man.

The political implications of Du Bellay's theatrical metaphor emerge more clearly in the body of the text, particularly in his arguments about the innate equality of various languages and in his insistence—influenced by Reform theologians—that all persons should be free to read the Bible in their native tongues.[19] The liberal aspects of his ideological position are, however, marked and sometimes countered by conservative ones which derive from his desire to preserve or create a sphere for genuinely noble action, literary or political. In the prefatory letter to the cardinal, as in the treatise as a whole, we can observe a conflict between what might be called the old and the new aristocratic souls within Du Bellay's breast. The old one reveres authority and longs for a feudal world where property was "naturally" passed on from father to son. Du Bellay associates this world with his ancestral home in Anjou and, more ambiguously, with ancient Rome, which was for him a symbol for patriarchal authority and landed wealth.[20] The new aristocratic soul, in contrast, is much like that of an ambitious and educated son of the bourgeoisie: it is ambivalent toward authority; it perceives that great men of both ancient and modern times gained power as actors do, by exercising skill and by usurping the places of others; and, finally, it longs for a future that will not repeat but, rather, surpass the past.[21]

The Faustian metaphor of two souls warring within one breast is particularly apt for a poet who wrote both in French and in Latin and who recorded for posterity an intense and troubled dialogue between these two tongues. To understand what is at stake in this dialogue, and to see its complex relation to the battle between what I have called the old and the new aristocratic souls in Du Bellay, we must examine his theory of imitation. This theory offended Aneau and other contemporary readers because it implied that French was in need of enrichment from foreign sources. Commenting on the title of Book 1, Chapter 4, "That the French language is not so poor as many esteem it" ("Que la langue françoyse n'est si pauvre que beaucoup l'estiment"), Aneau says to Du Bellay:

> You are one of those [who don't esteem French] for you do nothing throughout [your] work . . . but induce us to greekicize and latinize in French, always vituperating our form of poetry while attributing to those [ancient languages] all the virtues and praises of good speech and writing; you show the poverty of our language in comparison with those, without remedying [ours] at all or enriching it with a single word, [or] a single virtue, in brief, with nothing but promise and hope, saying that French might be, that it will come, that it will be, etc. But what? when and how? Is this a defense and illustration, or rather an offense and denigration?

> Tu es de ceux là, car tu ne fais autre chose par tout l'oeuvre . . . que nous induire à greciser & latiniser en François, vituperant tousjours nostre forme de poësie, comme vile & populaire, attribuant à iceux [the classics] toutes les vertus & louanges de bien dire & bien escrire, & par comparaison d'iceux monstres la povreté de nostre langue, sans y remedier nullement et sans l'enricher d'un seul mot, d'une seule vertu, ne bref de rien, sinon que de promesse & d'espoir, disant qu'elle pourra estre, qu'elle viendra, qu'elle sera, etc. Mais quoy? quand et comment? Est-ce là defense & illustration, ou plustot offense & denigration? [p. 28, n. 1]

Not only Aneau but Guillaume d'Autelz saw a problem in Du Bellay's emphasis on imitation. In 1550, d'Autelz attacked both Du Bellay's theory in the *Deffence* and his practice of imitating Italian poets in the *Olive*: "I do not share the opinion of those who think that the Frenchman can do nothing by his invention that is worthy of immortality, without the imitation of others" ("Je ne suis pas de l'avis de ceux, qui ne pensent point que le françois puisse faire chose digne de l'immortalité de son invention, sans l'imitation d'autrui").[22] I quote these sixteenth-century critics because nineteenth- and twentieth-century ones have tended to take Du Bellay's patriotic aims as self-evident, without seeing that his very emphasis on imitation constituted, in the eyes of some Frenchmen, a kind of treason, both to the country as a whole and to persons who valued the concept of "invention," that act of making associated with the notion of the individual as a self-contained and self-determining entity. It is important to attend to the criticisms Du Bellay's treatise provoked (to read the *Deffence*, that is, as part of a historical dialogue), for these criticisms direct attention to Du Bellay's own ambivalence about the theory and practice of imitation. When he replies to his critics in the second preface of his *Olive*, for instance, he shows an anxiety about the relation between imitation and invention that pervades the *Deffence* and much of his later work as well. In his writing, he insists, he has not tried to resemble "anyone but myself," and he further asserts that his poems have "much more natural invention than artificial or superstitious imitation" (*OP* 1: 20). As this statement suggests, imitation is not, for Du Bellay, an innocent activity: both as a theory and as a practice, it requires defense.

If Barthélemy Aneau had not been blinded by class resentment, he might have seen that Du Bellay's stress on imitation as a means of "illustrating" the vernacular stems as much from defensive humility as from aggressive hubris. Aneau's own view of the text as a self-glorifying exercise in epideictic oratory—a praise of Hercules written by a man who desires to see himself as a Herculean hero—invites us to note the strong identification between Du Bellay and the object of his theoretical discourse, that native language he personifies as presently poor and weak but capable of future greatness. Aneau, as we have seen, accuses Du Bellay of being among those who do not esteem the vernacular, but he misses the corollary of the point, which is that Du Bellay suffers from a lack of *self*-esteem. This lack generates his desire to emulate persons he wants to see as noble relatives: the ancient Roman authors and the Cardinal Jean du Bellay. Imitation, which may be considered both as a literary act and as a psychic phenomenon related to the defense Freud called "identification," preoccupies Du Bellay not because he does not value original invention, but because he feels himself presently too impoverished to create great works from his "natural" faculty alone.[23] There is, however, a significant tension between the theories of imitation he offers: imitation conceived as emulation of the great—an act of homage made in the hope that reward will ensue—is different from imitation conceived as an act of plundering, of taking another's property for oneself.

Du Bellay's treatise oscillates between presenting imitation as an act of reverent homage and as an act of aggressive theft. Although it is tempting to consider the former view of imitation simply as an idealized or mystified version of the latter one, such an interpretation would reduce the psychological as well as the ideological richness of the text. That richness lies, I think, in the work's articulation of contradictory perspectives on imitation, perspectives that must be analyzed by looking closely not only at the various metaphors Du Bellay employs to define imitation theoretically, but also at his discursive practice of imitating ancient and modern Italian authors. Critics have frequently noted his manifold borrowings from Italian treatises on language, but they have not viewed this practice either as a complex and often contrapuntal dimension of his theory or as an ideologically significant phenomenon.[24] A treatise dedicated to a nobleman serving his monarch's political interests in Rome—which included the appropriation of Italian territory and the enriching of his soldiers with foreign goods—offers us a version of literary plundering that cannot be explained simply in terms of the Renaissance author's supposed lack of concern with literary property rights.[25]

If we turn at this point to an analysis of Du Bellay's theory of imitation, which focuses on the modern writer's relation to the ancients, we can observe a struggle to define literary creation both as a natural mode of invention and as an artificial mode of appropriation. Du Bellay's shifting metaphors for the creative process (metaphors that Aneau regularly accuses of "impropriety"), suggest, however, that the battle represented in the *Deffence* is not only between ancients and moderns, but also among moderns with different national and class allegiances.

Imitation, Invention, and the Voyage between Past and Future

All that Adam had, all that Caesar could, you have and can do. Adam called his house heaven and earth; Caesar called his house, Rome; you perhaps call yours, a cobbler's trade; a hundred acres of ploughed land; or a scholar's garret. Yet line for line and point for point, your dominion is as great as theirs, though without fine names. Build, therefore, your own world.—Emerson, *Nature*

... l'exil est ce temps de la détresse où les dieux ne sont plus et où ils ne sont pas encore.—Maurice Blanchot, *L'Espace littéraire*

Du Bellay's stated aim in *La Deffence* is to "design" or "rough hew" (*ebaucher*) the "edifice" of language that will house the future French poet.[26] The effort to build a home in the vernacular is, however, hindered by the architect's uncertainty about the site to choose and the tools and materials to employ. Moreover, his project is hindered from the outset by his sense that the literary monuments of the ancients seem somehow to occupy the space the French poet desires to fill with works of his own hand. A passage in Book 2, Chapter 12, shows, in emblematic form, the way Du Bellay's designs for the future are marred by his ambivalent admiration for past literary achievement.

The passage begins with vigorously patriotic praise of the French people's moral virtues in general and of the vernacular language in particular. Paradoxically, however, Du Bellay justifies his praise of French by appealing to the authority of Cicero and Virgil, who chose to write in Latin rather than in Greek; he then cites such eminent modern Italians as Petrarch, Boccaccio, and Bembo, who contributed to their vernacular literature despite their talents in Latin (p. 189). Du Bellay describes these authors as having undergone a "conversion" to their "maternal tongue," a formulation that shows his awareness of the religious issues at stake in the turn from Latin, the *sermo patrius* hotly defended by the fathers of the church (the Council of Trent began four years before the *Deffence* was published), to the "vulgar" tongue, which even women and commoners could read.[27] The movement of

Du Bellay's argument thus implies a complex attitude toward authority: the vernacular is praised by means of appeals to ancient and then modern Italian authorities, but the description of the latter hints, through the metaphor of conversion, at questions about the authority of the Roman church that were being raised more openly in France, on the eve of the religious wars, than in Italy.

Having cited two historical examples of a movement toward cultural and linguistic differentiation and away from the notion of a universal and atemporal authority, whether it be that of the Greeks, the Romans, or, implicitly, the Catholic church, Du Bellay would seem to have set the stage for an assertion of relative autonomy for the French writer:[28] if even the Italians had established their independence from their Roman forebears—and they, as Du Bellay remarks, "have much greater reasons for adoring the Latin language than we do"—why should the French poet remain tied to the past? This question underlies Du Bellay's fervid appeal to the French poet to undertake new literary labors, despite the lack of "domestic examples." Such a lack should indeed spark the poet's desire to "be the first to occupy [the place] where others have failed." But this invocation of the possibility of primacy—a possibility Du Bellay elsewhere claims to have realized in his own poetic endeavors—leads to a strange fall in tone and in thought.[29] It is as if Du Bellay's memory takes revenge for the fiction he has just perpetrated, which involves forgetting the examples of native literary innovation offered by writers like Rabelais and Scève. Significantly, however, Du Bellay's assertion that the future French poet has an unoccupied territory at his disposal conjures up the nay-saying ghosts not of native forebears but of ancient, foreign ones: we are free to wonder whether the ancients represent a greater or lesser psychic threat to Du Bellay than do the moderns. In any case, he cannot protect his assertion of primacy from a wave of pessimism:

> Someone (perhaps), already persuaded by the reasons I have alleged, would willingly be converted to his vulgar tongue, if he had some domestic examples. And I say he should more quickly betake himself thereto, to be the first to occupy the place where others have failed. The great Greek and Latin fields are already so full that there remains very little empty space. Already many with an easy pace have reached the goal so much desired. A long time ago the prize was won. But, O God, how much sea remains before we reach the port! How far still is the end of our course!

> Quelqu'un (peut estre) deja persuadé par les raisons que j'ay alleguées, se convertiroit voluntiers à son vulgaire, s'il avoit quelques exemples domestiques. Et je dy que d'autant s'y doit-il plus tost mettre, pour occuper le premier ce à quoy les autres ont failly. Les larges campaignes Greques & Latines sont deja si pleines, que bien peu reste d'espace vide. Ja beaucoup d'une course legere ont attaint le but tant desiré. Long temps y a que le prix est gaigné. Mais, ô bon Dieu, combien de mer nous reste encores, avant que soyons parvenuz au port! combien le terme de nostre course est encores loing! [pp. 190–91]

Du Bellay's rhetoric falls from optimism to pessimism because his vision of a French future is overwhelmed by a vision of the past; the future then reemerges in a bizarre new form. This metamorphosis is complex because a tonal shift occurs before the reader understands its logical basis; indeed, Du Bellay sets up a pattern of expectation that works against his tone. The sentence about the fullness of "les larges campaignes Greques & Latines" does not hinder the initial exhortation to action; on the contrary, it leads us to expect something like this: if the fields of ancient literature are full, the modern poet should clearly turn "to pastures new." We may be surprised that, instead of proceeding to this conclusion, Du Bellay rests for two sentences on a description of the ancients' already completed achievement. With the mention of a sea voyage to be undertaken by the modern poet, however, we feel the point is on its way again. Readers familiar with sixteenth-century literature may even expect Du Bellay to give a Renaissance twist to the traditional metaphor of the sea as poetic task: the ancient country is indeed crowded, but *we* know there are new lands beyond the seas.[30] The repetition of *reste* in the phrases "bien peu reste d'espace vide" and "combien de mer nous reste encores" also leads us to expect a contrast between the ancients' land achievement and the modern poet's sea voyage. By the time we reach the final exclamations, however, we realize that our logical expectations have somehow been foiled. Instead of urging us on to a new endeavor, the rhetoric has been slowing down; by the end we seem to be infinitely further from the goal of writing French poetry that we were at the beginning.

What has happened? The vision of the future is drowned by the past because Du Bellay has blended spatial and temporal metaphors in a way that finally makes the modern poet's goal not a brave new world but a "port" on the very shores where "peu d'espace vide" remains. The apparent contrast between land and sea achievements is undermined because the only land the passage mentions is the ancient fields; the modern poet's voyage is leading him to a port whose only synonym is the "but tant desiré" already achieved by the ancients. During the course of the passage Du Bellay moves from a vision of a future primacy to an evocation of time as a possession of others, a time irremediably over ("Long temps y a que le prix est gaigné"). With an appeal to God that implicitly likens the modern poet's plight to that of the Israelites awaiting entrance to the Promised Land or the Christian awaiting the Eschaton, Du Bellay then turns to a conception of time as seemingly endless.[31] But this view of time, however painful, serves as a defense against the dilemma caused by the presence of powerful ghosts who occupy this graveyard landscape. If one's goal suddenly appears undesirable—like death rather than life—one might well prefer the known pain of voyaging to the unknown fate of arrival. The hope for an immediate accession to primacy and greatness is transformed into a prospect of wandering and exile because the vision of the future passes through the crucible of Du Bellay's ambivalence toward the mighty dead—and toward death itself, that prerequisite for immortality.[32]

The tonal and conceptual shifts of this passage—from exhortation to despair, from a vision of primary achievement to a recognition of secondariness—show an imagination trapped between an unattainable future and an irrecoverable past. The passage also helps us understand why Du Bellay cannot consistently distinguish between invention and imitation. Again and again, his advice to be original tends to slide into advice to imitate. Consider, for example, the following sentence from the chapter entitled "D'inventer des motz, & quelques autres choses que doit observer le poëte Françoys":

> I would warn him who would undertake a great work, that he should not fear to invent, adopt, or compose in imitation of the Greeks some French words, as Cicero boasts of having done in his language.
>
> Je veux bien avertir celuy qui entreprendra un grand oeuvre, qu'il ne craigne point d'inventer, adopter & composer à l'immitation des Grecz quelques motz Françoys, comme Ciceron se vante d'avoir fait en sa Langue. [p. 137]

If Du Bellay slides, here, from the idea of inventing to the idea of imitating (thus repeating the title's movement from "D'invention" to the anticlimactic "quelques autres choses"), he does so in part because he has been seduced by a fallacious concept that Claude-Gilbert Dubois describes concisely: "Le point initial se confond avec le point de plénitude."[33] Poets in various ages have suffered from and fought against the idea that literary power is a function of historical priority; what makes Du Bellay's imaginative involvement with this idea so interesting is his explicitly economic interpretation of it.

Like many other Renaissance theoreticians, he tends to associate power, the ability to move a reader by eloquence, with the notion of *copia*, richness of discourse.[34] But he adopts a distinctly more pessimistic perspective on the possibility of achieving *copia* than Erasmus and other contemporaries did, and his pessimism derives in large part from his sense that the matter of poetic imitation is inherently finite.[35] Du Bellay's dark view of the natural resources, as it were, available to the modern poet, reflects the feudal aristocrat's conception of wealth in terms of land rather than in terms of the manufacture of commodities. "Land," as Perry Anderson remarks, "is a natural monopoly; it cannot be indefinitely extended, only redivided."[36] And as the doctrine of primogeniture states, this inherently limited source of wealth should be passed without "redivision," from father to first-born son. A *fils cadet* like Du Bellay, who was not only orphaned early but raised by an

elder brother who seems to have treated him as shabbily as Oliver treats
Orlando in Shakespeare's *As You Like It*, had strong reasons for equating
wealth with chronological priority.[37] He had equally strong reasons for
desiring to dispossess his elders both at home and abroad, though he also
desired to make this dispossession seem a legitimate act.

His text weaves a web of complex defenses around the equation between
literary power and historical priority. In this web one can discern and name
three threads, intertwined but separable for purposes of exposition: the
organic, the historical, and the linguistic. Each of these defenses is a locus of
contradictions, and together they constitute a serious meditation on a problem that Terence Cave rightly sees as fundamental to Renaissance literary
theory, but which I would argue is also fundamental to the social struggles of
the age: "the contrast (or equivalence) between *copia* as plenitude and *copia*
as copy."[38]

Transplantation and Translation:
The Organic and Historical Defenses

> . . . *higher argument*
> *Remains, sufficient of itself to raise*
> *That name, unless an age too late, or cold*
> *Climate, or years damp my intended wing*
> *Depressed . . .*   —Milton, *Paradise Lost*

Du Bellay's treatise begins with the offensive move characteristic of his
attempts to assert independence from the past. In his first chapter, entitled
"L'Origine des langues," he distinguishes between languages and plants in
order to argue that all languages are inherently equal in value:

> If Nature (of whom a greatly renowned person has not without reason won-
> dered whether we should call her mother or stepmother) had given to men a
> common will and consent, besides the innumerable advantages which would have
> thereby resulted, human inconstancy would not have needed to forge for itself
> so many manners of speaking. This diversity and confusion can rightly be called
> the Tower of Babel. For languages are not born of themselves after the fashion
> of herbs, roots, or trees: some infirm and weak in their nature; the others healthy,
> robust, and more fitted to carry the burden of human conceptions; but all their
> virtue is born in the world of the desire and will of mortals.

> Si la Nature (dont quelque personnaige de grand' renommée non sans rayson a
> douté si on la devoit appeller mere ou maratre) eust donné aux hommes un
> commun vouloir & consentement, outre les innumerables commoditez qui en
> feussent procedées, l'inconstance humaine n'eust eu besoing de se forger tant de
> manieres de parler. Laquéle diversité & confusion se peut à bon droict appeller
> la Tour de Babel. Donc les Langues ne sont nées d'elles mesmes en façon

d'herbes, racines & arbres: les unes infirmes & debiles en leurs espéces: les autres saines & robustes, & plus aptes à porter le faiz des conceptions humaines: mais toute leur vertu est née au monde du vouloir & arbitre des mortelz. [pp. 11–12]

The view that languages are not natural but conventional in origin had been maintained by other French writers, notably by Charles de Bovelles in his *Liber de differentia vulgarium linguarum et Gallici sermonis varietate* (1533) and by Rabelais in *Le Tiers Livre* (1546).[39] Du Bellay's version of this argument, however, directly echoes not a French source but an Italian one: Sperone Speroni's *Dialogo delle lingue* (1542). Indeed to say Du Bellay echoes Speroni is to put the matter too imprecisely: from the sentence about the Tower of Babel to the end of the passage quoted above, Du Bellay translates Speroni's text word for word.[40] This act of translation is itself an interesting gloss on Du Bellay's (and Speroni's) interpretation of the Tower of Babel *topos*: instead of using it as Dante had in the *De vulgari eloquentia*, to symbolize a linguistic fall which is equivalent in moral import to man's original fall in Eden, the Renaissance authors both invoke the Tower to support an implicitly Pelagian view of man's free will.[41] By blaming Nature rather than man for causing the confusion of tongues in the world, the text of the *Deffence* prepares us for an argument in favor of man's capacity to redeem that confusion by an exercise of the *arbitre* or will. In translating Speroni's text, moreover, Du Bellay performatively supports his belief that diversity of tongues need not represent an impediment to understanding, as it did for the original builders of Babel whose inability to communicate with each other was a punishment for hubris.

There is, however, a logical problem in Du Bellay's argument for the arbitrary and hence inherently equal nature of languages. Barthélemy Aneau exposes this problem in his commentary on the title of the first chapter, a commentary which characteristically accuses Du Bellay of promising more than he can deliver. Claiming to contribute to our knowledge of the origins of language, Du Bellay in fact gives us something "vulgar and common," Aneau asserts, something which "a rustic could have said as well," namely that languages arise from man's "fantasy" (p. 11, n. 1). In Aneau's view, there is no real difference between Du Bellay's account of origins and the accounts given by medieval Christian writers: "It would have been just as easy to say that languages derive from Nature and from God," Aneau writes, as to say they derive from human fantasy. Although Aneau misses (perhaps deliberately) the antitraditional thrust of Du Bellay's distinction between a natural origin and a conventional origin of language, his commentary highlights the shakiness of that distinction. For by blaming Nature for giving man the inconstant will which caused linguistic diversity, Du Bellay implicitly accepts the idea of a source that is logically and temporally prior to man. If he does not deny Nature's status as a source, however, he does invoke the authority of an ancient Roman, Pliny the Elder, to call her credentials into question: is she a mother or a stepmother?[42] If she is the latter, then she has a paradoxically conventional nature, the role of stepmother being defined by legal rather than biological ties. We see that the idea of a natural source has not so much been denied as denigrated, in a way that makes room for a relative rise in the status of a secondary shaping power, the fantasy of man.

Du Bellay's denigration of Nature plays an important role in his offensive strategy: it is meant to persuade those who would "praise one language and blame another" that languages do not differ in value according to their place in a natural or God-given hierarchy. Unlike Rabelais and modern linguists, Du Bellay is not concerned with the conventional or arbitrary relation between the sign and the signified; for him, as for Speroni, the notion of an arbitrary origin of language is allied with the notion of an order of things amenable to the exercise of free will. But his views on language and the individual's power to effect changes in the language system are neither so simple nor so sanguine as they appear to be at first. If his initial chapter is designed to persuade the reader that languages were originally equal, it is also designed to defend the author against his own perception that there are *now* inequalities among languages. The major weapon in this defense is the concept of individual labor or *industrie*, the means whereby poverty may be remedied.

"It is true," Du Bellay writes,

> that in the succession of time, some [languages], from having been more carefully regulated, have become richer than others; but this should not be attributed to the felicity of the said languages, but solely to the artifice and industry of men.

> Il est vray que par succession de tens les unes, pour avoir eté plus curieusement reiglées, sont devenues plus riches que les autres: mais cela ne se doit attribuer à la felicité desdites Langues, ains au seul artifice & industrie des hommes. [p. 13]

This passage shows that the distinction between languages and plants, initially introduced to support a belief in the equality of languages, begins to collapse in the face of Du Bellay's admission that history—the "succession de tens"—has indeed made languages separate but *un*equal. The distinction between a natural and an arbitrary origin of language suppresses, temporarily, the problem of origin; but it emerges as soon as he starts to explain the "industrie" required if French is to equal the languages that history has given a head start.

Du Bellay returns to the notion of "industrie" in Book 1, Chapter 3, but only after a significant digression, in Chapter 2, on the injustice done to the French language by those who call it a barbarian tongue. This digression (pp. 15–21) is heavily indebted to Speroni, which is ironic in light of the fact that the chapter accuses the modern Italians as well as the ancient Romans of denigrating French. But if Du Bellay achieves a kind of oblique revenge on the Italians by appropriating Speroni's text for an argument against Italian assumptions of superiority (in the political as well as the literary sphere), he also reveals his anxiety about the concept of appropriation itself, which is here viewed materialistically as the result and cause of imperialist warfare.[43] The Roman invasion of Gaul was a labor of appropriation that deprived the French nobility of their proper status, making them servants rather than masters. Du Bellay associates this deprivation with another: Roman authors (such as Caesar) have stolen from Frenchmen their very memories of great deeds—their history. Because the Gauls and later the Franks did not collect their deeds in writing, "we have almost lost not only the glory of them, but even the memory of them." The Romans' envy, Du Bellay adds, contributed to this loss, for they "as if in a certain conspiracy conspiring against us, weakened, as far as they were able, our warlike glory, whose brilliance they could not endure, and not only have they done us wrong thereby, but, to render us still more contemptible, they have called us brutal, cruel, and barbarous" (pp. 19–20). When one's very self-image has been determined by a conquering nation's texts, when one's *nature* has been defined in a foreign language by others, it is difficult to conceive of appropriation as anything but a denaturing and violent process. As if to ward off this idea, Du Bellay turns in Chapter 3 to a peaceful notion of "industrie," defined now in an agricultural metaphor. It is as if we have gone back (temporarily) from the battle-grounds of Virgil's *Aeneid* to the orderly fields of his *Georgics*.

The distinction made in Chapter 1 between languages as the products of human fantasy and plants as the products of nature collapses completely in Chapter 3; here Du Bellay argues that the French people must "cultivate" the heretofore neglected plant of their language as the Romans, "in the guise of good farmers," first transplanted their language into fertile soil and then pruned the "useless branches," substituting for them new branches "drawn in masterly fashion from the Greek tongue, which quickly were so well grafted and made similar to their trunk that henceforward they appeared no longer adopted but natural" (p. 25).

Du Bellay attempts to soften the contradiction between this argument and the one in the first chapter by insisting that, even if languages are like plants, their relative strength or weakness is the fault of the cultivators, not of the plant itself. The way he makes this point reveals, however, an exile's sense that the land of France itself is a "desert." Moreover, the changes in his perception of the French plant's present stage of growth suggest his inability to locate the root of his language's "default." Arguing that neither the Greek nor the Roman language would have achieved greatness without undergoing a gradual process of "cultivation," he attempts, but fails, to make an analogous case for French:

I can speak similarly of our tongue, which now begins to flower without fructifying; or rather, like a plant and small shoot, has not yet flowered, still less borne all the fruit that it might well produce. That, certainly, does not derive from any defect in the nature thereof, which is as apt to engender as others; the fault lies rather in those who were to guard the plant, and did not cultivate it sufficiently, treating it instead like a wild plant in that same desert where it had begun to live; without ever watering, or pruning, or guarding it from brambles and thorns which shaded it, they have let it grow old and almost die.

Ainsi puys-je dire de nostre Langue, qui commence encores à fleurir sans fructifier, ou plus tost, comme une plante & vergette, n'a point encores fleury, tant se fault qu'elle ait apporté tout le fruit qu'elle pouroit bien produyre. Cela, certainement, non pour le default de la nature d'elle, aussi apte à engendrer que les autres: mais pour la coulpe de ceux qui l'ont euë en garde, & ne l'ont cultivée à suffisance, ains comme une plante sauvaige, en celuy mesmes desert ou elle avoit commencé à naitre, sans jamais l'arrouser, la tailler, ny defendre des ronces & epines qui lui faisoint umbre, l'ont laissée envieillir & quasi mourir. [pp. 24–25]

Is the modern poet to cultivate a young plant, or is he to rescue one that is already old and on the point of dying? Du Bellay's rhetoric slides, once again, from an optimistic to a pessimistic assessment of the French poet's task; and it does so in a way that underscores the identification between the author and the "plant" of his native language. In "La Complainte du desesperé," an autobiographical poem published in 1552, Du Bellay depicts his own temporal dilemma in terms that recall the *Deffence*. His youth, he writes, was blighted by neglect:

Qu'ay-je depuis mon enfance
Sinon toute injuste offence
Senty de mes plus prochains?   [*OP* 4: 92, ll. 121–23]

What have I experienced since childhood, from those nearest to me, except every unjust offense?

The brother who failed to "cultivate" him is clearly the perpetrator of the offense to which these lines allude; Du Bellay goes on to liken his own development to that of a plant which grows in the shade and is "wounded" by winter before it can bear flower or fruit. In this unnatural cycle, "le triste hyver" arrives "devant l'esté de mes ans" ("before the summer of my years").

An argument based on organic metaphors fails to ward off despair either in the *Deffence* or in the "Complainte." In theoretical terms, the problem is that an imitation seen as the "grafting" of stronger branches onto a weaker trunk necessarily reintroduces the concept of a privileged source, which Du Bellay had tried to banish in his first chapter by drawing a firm distinction between languages and plants. With the blurring of this distinction in Chapter 3 comes a parallel blurring of the distinction between invention and imitation: imitation is seen more and more not simply as the means to achieve inventive richness, but as an end in itself. As if impelled by entropy, Du Bellay's theory of labor as cultivation, which implies an individual worker at home on his own ground, turns into a theory of labor as acquisition of the property of others. The metamorphosis is subtle but important, especially when we note that it involves a significant departure from the Italian text used as a source throughout Du Bellay's discussion of "industrie."

In Speroni's *Dialogo delle lingue*—which is in fact a series of dialogues among various speakers—a character based on the historical Bembo defends the vernacular against a classical scholar named Lazaro. Agreeing with his opponent that great poetry cannot be translated without loss of its original eloquence, Bembo advocates "cultivating" the vernacular in order to create works which rival those of the ancients. Later in the dialogue, a character named Peretto takes up the defense of the vernacular against another classical purist, Lascari. Peretto focuses on a different aspect of "la questione della lingua"; unlike Bembo, he is concerned not with poetry but with scientific and philosophical works which, he argues, can and should be translated into the vernacular so they may be freely disseminated to all. Du Bellay borrows freely from the speeches of both Bembo and Peretto, but his argument is less lucid than Speroni's, largely because he does not clearly distinguish the issue of writing vernacular poetry from that of translating prose works. This is significant, since Du Bellay's textual practice shows that, in his case, the two issues *cannot* be separated: he is an aspiring poet presently engaged in translating prose in order to teach the French how to write superior poetry.

His transformation of Speroni's arguments should also be seen in the light of his particular concerns as a member of the French noble class. If he frequently transforms Peretto's arguments for democratic translation into supporting evidence for his own theory of imitation—a theory for the "illustration" of the vernacular that does not appear as such in the Italian text—that transformation reflects an obsession with social status that Speroni, a bourgeois humanist, did not share.[44] Speroni's major theoretical goal is to articulate a theory of invention: Bembo's arguments for cultivating the vernacular and Peretto's arguments for translation as a means of acquiring knowledge are aimed at enhancing the individual author's creative powers. Du Bellay, in contrast, regularly shifts from praising invention to advocating imitation; as we have seen, he cannot rest long on the idea that an individual might fully develop his potential by exercising "industrie" at home. This emphasis on imitation is, in part, a function of class ideology "The categorical objective of noble rule was territory, regardless of the community inhabiting it," writes Perry Anderson. "Land as such, not language, defined the natural perimeters of its power. The feudal ruling class was thus essentially mobile. . . . land is naturally immobile, and nobles had to travel to take possession of it."[45]

If we look again at Du Bellay's development of what I have called his "organic defense," we can see how it serves to legitimize and naturalize imitation as an appropriation of foreign riches. Imitation, as Du Bellay presents it, is a means for acquiring the two desiderata that he associates with invention: a principle of power that he calls *energie* and a rich matter that he calls *copie* and conceives as the possession of encyclopedic knowledge, the "intelligence parfaite des sciences."[46] "That divinity of invention," as he calls it (p. 40), takes the form of energy when he is discussing poetry, with arguments often borrowed from Speroni's Bembo; it takes the form of matter when he is discussing philosophical knowledge, with arguments borrowed from Speroni's Peretto. As I have said, however, he departs from Speroni in his tendency to see invention not as a faculty of mind, but as a piece of portable property that must be acquired through imitation. Although in Book 1, Chapter 4, he declares that French is not "so infertile, that she cannot herself produce some fruit of good invention" (p. 29), he goes on to describe the means for this invention as nothing other than the "cultivation" already defined as a "grafting" of foreign branches onto a native trunk. The argument shows his fundamental sense that the plant of the French language cannot become strong without joining with plants that grow closer, in space or in time, to a source of invention. Moreover, in his eyes the native plant is not merely weak but "scabrous," tainted in some serious way. The metaphors of disease occur later in the treatise, during an invective against "mauvais poëtes Françoys"; the invective, which also refers to French soil as having been "longuement sterile," suggests an almost pathological disgust for the "corrupted flesh" produced in French territory.[47] If he associates this corruption not only with his literary ancestors, the "mauvais poëtes," but also with his biological ones, the noble parents who died and left him in a degraded state, we should not be surprised that he turns, as Tasso and other Renaissance authors also do, to fantasies of replacing his unsatisfactory progenitors with nobler ones.[48] Chief but not alone among these surrogate ancestors are the Romans of antiquity, who possess that richness of invention the modern poet desires. In Chapter 8, Du Bellay clearly expresses his belief that invention, at present, belongs to those who are first-born:

> Just as it was most praiseworthy in the ancients to invent well, so is it most useful [for the moderns] to imitate well; it is especially useful for those whose language is not yet very copious nor rich.
>
> Tout ainsi que ce feut le plus louable aux Anciens de bien inventer, aussi est ce le plus utile de bien immiter, mesmes à ceux dont la Langue n'est encor' bien copieuse & riche. [pp. 45–46]

Because it implies that invention is a "property" of those who came first, the organic defense needs to be supplemented by a historical one that legitimizes the transfer of property from ancient to modern. The organic metaphor of imitation is in fact the basis for a theory of history that views the relation between past and present not as one of rivalry but as a nonviolent, natural succession. History, rather than individual ambition, is responsible for the son's replacing his father; moreover, instead of having to journey to the source of invention, the modern poet need only wait while history "transports," or "transplants," literary power to his present.

In Book 1, Chapter 10, Du Bellay develops the idea of a transportation of literary power into a myth of progress that has a geographical as well as a historical dimension; it is a version of the "translatio studii," that westering movement of civilization explained by Dante's Justinian in *Paradiso* 6.[49] Arguing that France is as worthy a home for philosophy as Greece was, Du Bellay points out that philosophy was not a native product of Greece, that it was, in fact, not the true property of the Greeks at all, but rather something they had borrowed from a prior owner. That owner was the East, the Egypt and India so important to Renaissance hermetic thinkers. The Greeks, who call others barbarians, were themselves crude newcomers compared with the Eastern masters to whom they went for instruction: "les uns aux Indes, pour voir les gymnosophistes, les autres en Egypte, pour emprunter de ces vieux prestres & prophetes ces grandes richesses, dont la Grece est maintenant si superbe" (p. 71).

Du Bellay does not elaborate this myth, and none of his critics has commented on it; but it is clearly related to the same defensive impulse that leads him to undermine Rome's greatness by stressing the Roman authors' debts to their Greek forebears.[50] This defense involves viewing the ancients as no more primary than the modern imitator; it also involves a certain vagueness about the nature of the property transfers that took place between Egyptians and Greeks or between Greeks and Romans. The word *emprunter* ("borrow") delicately avoids the problematic relation between the realm of ideas and that of politics: Alexander conquered the East in the generation after Plato voyaged there to "borrow" ideas, and the Romans conquered Greece while doing her the honor of imitating her philosophers. But if Du Bellay saw any connection between this pattern of "borrowing" ideas and his own country's political designs on Italian territory, he says nothing about it here; instead he evokes a myth of a westering movement which implies that philosophic knowledge has progressed through time and space and will continue to do so, reaching France naturally and inevitably. Another passage in Chapter 10 shows how he uses this myth to displace his own sense of being exiled from a source of richness; combining the historical myth with an organic metaphor, he envisions the French writer welcoming an exiled philosophy to its new home:

> Therefore if the philosophy sown by Aristotle and Plato in the fertile Attic field were replanted in our French plain, it would not be casting it among the

brambles and thorns, where it would become sterile, but would be making it near rather than distant and, instead of a stranger, a citizen of our republic.

Donques si la phylosophie semée par Aristote & Platon au fertile champ Atique etoit replantée en notre pleine Françoyse, ce ne seroit la jeter entre les ronses & epines, ou elle devint sterile: mais ce seroit la faire de loingtaine prochaine, & d'etrangere citadine de notre republique. [pp. 61–62]

The *translatio studii* theory as Du Bellay deploys it posits a progression of poetry, but not a true progress. One might well expect a more hopeful view from Du Bellay, not only because he was a Catholic who believed, ostensibly, in providential history, but because he elsewhere points with pride to the new inventions of Renaissance science—printing, for instance, and that "not less admirable than dangerous" invention, gunpowder (pp. 53–54). It seems, however, that he seeks in history only a defense against his fears that modern poets cannot legitimately equal the ancients. His use of a cyclical view of history to bolster the linear notion of the *translatio studii* shows that his primary concern is not to surpass the ancients but simply to succeed them without a direct confrontation.[51] In Book 1, Chapter 9, a cyclical view of time supports his hope that someday ("quelquefoys") the French language may be as good as the classical ones (p. 54). The possibility of literary succession is guaranteed, Du Bellay argues, by the model of natural succession, the process whereby God's "inviolable law" decrees "to all created things, not to last perpetually, but to pass without ending from one state to the other, the end and corruption of the one being the beginning and generation of the other" ("Dieu . . . a donné pour loy inviolable à toute chose crée de ne durer perpetuellement, mais passer sans fin d'un etat en l'autre, etant la fin & corruption de l'un, le commencement & generation de l'autre" [p. 57]).

The Romans—those whom Du Bellay describes as "the first to occupy that which Nature has not, however, denied to others" ("ceux qui ont occupé les premiers ce que Nature n'ha pourtant denié aux autres" [p. 56]—have now reached the end of their destined cycle; they are, he declares, at their "fin et corruption." A fatal law requires them to give way to the French. Someone, he admits, may object that French is rising to its perfection very slowly indeed; to that (surely self-generated) doubt, however, he replies by invoking, once again, the analogy between languages and plants which he had rejected in Chapter 1:

Every tree which is born, flowers, and bears fruit quickly, also grows old and dies very quickly; and on the contrary, that [tree] lasts for years, which has labored long to throw out its roots.

Tout arbre qui naist, florist et fructifie bien tost, bien tost aussi envieillisse & meure: & au contraire, celuy durer par longues années, qui a longuement travaillé à jeter ses racines. [p. 57]

The historical defense, modest as it is in its efforts to make room for modern poetry, does not succeed in freeing Du Bellay's imagination from the burden of the past. The *translatio studii* and the cyclical theory of "eternal return" both imply that literary power moves through time without being diminished; but elsewhere in the treatise Du Bellay reveals a more pessimistic view. The Romans, he says, enriched their language by imitation so successfully that they made it "*almost* equal the Greek" ("egaller *quasi* à la Greque" [p. 42]; my emphasis); in this formulation, literary history seems to involve a slight but significant decline in linguistic power, a decline signaled by the adverb "almost." The hint of historical pessimism is broadened in the discussion of France's failure to produce an epic (Book 2, Chapter 5). Du Bellay urges the French poet to make an epic effort despite "some infelicity of the present age" ("quelque infelicité de siecle ou nous soyons" [p. 136]).[52]

The historical defense fails to mask Du Bellay's sense that a *translatio* may involve a diminution of power; it also fails because it conceives of the energy or matter of invention as something separate from language. That which can be transported through time and space, from Greece to Rome to France, must be something not changed by the different languages in which it is expressed—or, in Du Bellay's metaphor, "contained." The idea of a transportation or transplantation works best, in fact, when Du Bellay is discussing philosophy or "les Ars et Sciences" considered as a body of knowledge. A difficulty appears when he considers poetry, a kind of discourse in which "ceste divinité d'invention" the ancients possessed "plus que les autres" is inextricably linked to an undefinable, untranslatable "spirit" of language:

> that grandeur of style, magnificence of words, gravity of sentences, audacity and variety of figures, and countless other lights of poetry: in short, that energy and undefinable spirit that is in their writings, and which the Latins would call *genius*.
>
> ceste grandeur de style, magnificence de motz, gravité de sentences, audace & varieté de figures, & mil' autres lumieres de poësie: bref ceste energie & ne scay quel esprit, qui est en leurs ecriz, que les Latins appelleroient *genius*. [p. 40]

The difficulty of separating excellence of thought or content from a quality of style haunts Du Bellay's discussions of philosophy as well as poetry. He argues, for example, that Aristotle's and Plato's greatness derived from the fact that philosophy "truly adopted them as her sons, not because they were born in Greece, but because they had spoken in a high sense and written well of her" ("La philosophie vrayement les a adoptez pour ses filz, non pour estre nez en Grece, mais pour avoir d'un hault sens bien parlé & bien ecrit d'elle" [p. 71]. This argument personifies philosophy and makes her an allegorical double of the cardinal to whom the *Deffence* is addressed, who is throughout the text being encouraged to "adopt" as his son the author who deserves a reward for writing well of him and of France.

Unlike Aristotle and Plato, however—whose power is here located in their high style—Du Bellay has not yet received confirmation of his ability to move and delight. He therefore envies the ancients and continues to grapple with two problems that are left unsolved by what I have called "the historical defense": that the invention he desires cannot simply be transported (or transplanted or translated) from culture to culture because it resides in a quality of style as well as in a knowledge of things; and that some form of overt rivalry with the ancients is unavoidable because literature endures, though empires rise and fall. No "natural" historical process, in other words, will bestow on the modern poet the riches he wants, just as the mere fact of noble birth will not give Du Bellay the power and wealth possessed by his illustrious kinsman. The most complex defense in the text—the linguistic— may be examined in those passages of the *Deffence* which deal directly with Du Bellay's ambivalence toward those who possess property and who prevent him from acquiring it except through an act more violent, and more unnatural, than a transplantation.

The Linguistic Defense: Reverent Iconoclasm

O Apolon! O Muses! prophaner ainsi les sacrées reliques de l'Antiquité?
—Du Bellay, *Deffence*

The first move in the linguistic defense might be described as an effort to leap out of the competitive arena altogether by fleeing dependence on the ancients and on language itself. In Book 1, Chapter 10, Du Bellay laments the time and energy Frenchmen expend on learning ancient languages. The lament becomes a remarkable accusation when he asserts that the principal reason that the French are intellectually inferior to the ancients is the study of the Greek and Latin languages by the French (p. 65). The ancients are cast in the role of fathers who prevent their sons from achieving strength and maturity. Du Bellay's anger, however, is directed not only toward the ancients but toward the moderns who submit to humiliation:

> [We] consume not only our youth in this vain exercise, but as if repenting of having left the cradle and become men, we return again to childhood; and in the space of twenty or thirty years, we do nothing but learn to speak, this man in Greek, this one in Latin, this one in Hebrew.

> [Nous] ne consumons pas seulement nostre jeunesse en ce vain exercice: mais comme nous repentans d'avoir laissé le berseau & d'estre devenuz hommes, retournons encor' en enfance, & par l'espace de xx ou xxx ans ne faisons autre chose qu'apprendre à parler, qui Grec, qui Latin, qui Hebreu. [p. 66]

Feeling himself to be in the degraded position of a perpetual child or servant, Du Bellay strikes out against the tyrannical power of the ancients and their languages. He invokes the Platonic notion of anamnesis, as well as the Pauline distinction between letter and spirit, to voice a protest against foreign languages in Book 1, Chapter 10. The major points are borrowed, paradoxically, from Speroni, but the rhetorical fervor is Du Bellay's own:[53]

> If the affection which we bear to foreign tongues (whatever excellence there may be in them) should prevent this great felicity [the flowering of French poetry], these tongues would be worthy, truly not of envy but of hatred, not of fatigue but of vexation; they would be worthy finally not to be learnt, but recovered by those who have more need of the lively understanding of the spirit than of the sound of dead words.

> Si l'affection que nous portons aux Langues etrangeres (quelque excellence qui soit en elles) empeschoit cete notre si grande felicité [the flowering of French poetry], elles seroint dignes veritablement non d'envie, mais de hayne, non de fatigue, mais de facherie: elles seroint dignes finablement d'estre non apprises, mais reprises de ceux qui ont plus de besoing du vif intellect de l'esprit que du son des paroles mortes. [p. 73]

This passage articulates an aggressive fantasy of "retaking" the ancient languages without the labor of learning them, as if they exist in a kind of prenatal memory reservoir or treasure trove to which the modern poet has access. The fantasy reflects a strong resentment directed not only against the ancients but against words themselves, which are here allied with a realm of death and opposed to the "living intellect of the spirit." The hostility toward words appears also in an earlier passage in Chapter 10, where Du Bellay comes closer than at any other point in the text to advocating the view that writers may turn directly to Nature for inspiration, rather than relying on imitation of foreign texts. Echoing his assertion in Chapter 1 that Nature is equally available to all persons in all times, he writes here that she is "always the same thing in every age, in every province, in every use"; she is therefore "worthy of being known and praised by everyone, in all languages" ("Nature, . . . en tout aage, en toute province, en toute habitude est toujours une mesme chose . . . aussi est elle digne d'estre congneue & loûee de toutes personnes, & en toutes Langues" [p. 63]).

This vision of a universal and universally available Nature does not lead Du Bellay to a theory of imitating natural objects rather than textual ones; on the contrary, it leads to a nostalgic fantasy of easy nonverbal communication. If only human beings could "signify their affections without distinction of words," as birds and fish do, they could avoid that painful burden of dependency which Du Bellay associates with imitating foreign tongues. But the unstated corollary of this argument is that communicating only in one's maternal language is tantamount to communicating as infants do, without any power of speech at all ("sans distinction de paroles"). Hence Du Bellay cannot for long maintain, as he does in this passage, that "we men should do the same thing [as the animals], each one in his language, without having recourse to others" ("nous hommes devrions faire le semblable, chacun avecques sa Langue, sans avoir recours aux autres" [p. 64]). Although the passage provides an important sign of his ambivalence toward the ancients and toward language itself, it also shows why he must leave his mother tongue for repeated battles with those foreign ones which play the roles of brothers and fathers in his psychological drama.[54] Despite his arguments that Nature is equally available to all persons in all times, he wants something Nature cannot provide, something that exists, like a desired woman, in the hands of a rival. "The Arts and the Sciences," he writes, are at the present moment between the hands of the Greeks and the Latins" ("Les Ars & Sciences sont pour le present entre les mains des Grecz & Latins" [p. 67]).[55]

The second move in the linguistic defense is aimed at wresting power and wealth from the ancient authors who presently hold it in their hands. This move consists of an attempt to define a mode of imitation that allows the modern poet both to appropriate qualities of ancient texts and to maintain his own individuality, his proper voice. Imitation therefore is the locus where Du Bellay explores the problem underlying his entire project of making French poetry equal to that of the ancients: the problem of being at once like and unlike the great originals. Michel Deguy neatly formulates the paradoxical demands implied by Du Bellay's theory of imitation: "Do not imitate them in order to be like them; imitate them in order to arrive at the difference of equality" ("Ne les imites pas, pour être comme elles; imite-les pour parvenir à la différence de l'égalité").[56]

By distinguishing an ideal imitator from translators on the one hand and from Neo-Latin imitators on the other, Du Bellay seeks to draw a thin line of theoretical safety between two classes of writer who endanger his project: the "traducteurs," who cannot capture the "je ne scay quoy" unique to each language and who therefore do not sufficiently *resemble* the ancients; and the imitators, the "whitewashers of walls," as he calls them ("reblanchisseurs de murailles" [p. 76]), who refuse to use the vernacular and who therefore do not sufficiently *differentiate* themselves from the ancients. The task Du Bellay gives his ideal imitator looks more and more like a Herculean labor when we see that it involves avoiding two actions the text defines as criminal: that perpetrated by the translators who fail to capture a "genius" located in the words of the ancients, and that perpetrated by the Neo-Latin writers who devote themselves merely to words and thus fail to capture the "idea" of the ancient text.

If, for Du Bellay, the question of imitation in general is associated with issues of crime and punishment, there is a nice irony in the fact that two of his readers accuse him of committing crimes in setting forth his theory of imitation. Barthélemy Aneau finds a "vicious and inconsequential transla-tion" in one of Du Bellay's descriptions of the imitative act, while Henri

Chamard, the modern editor of the *Deffence*, finds Du Bellay's tendency to begin a discussion of imitation and then interrupt it to be an "irritating vice of method."[57] Both critics charge Du Bellay with incoherence. The charge is true, but the text does not therefore deserve the punishment of being dismissed. On the contrary, if we grant that, for Du Bellay, the topic of imitation is itself highly dangerous—like a sacred space that at once fascinates and provokes desires to engage in sacrilegious acts—the incoherence of his exposition may interest rather than irritate us.

Du Bellay himself adopts the role of a priest guarding precious relics when he inveighs against the translators for failing to approach the ancient texts with sufficient reverence: "O Apollo! O Muses! [How can they] so profane the sacred relics of Antiquity?" (p. 41). This rhetorical expression of outrage underscores the distinction Du Bellay draws between poetry and all other forms of discourse. Here he is discussing the translation of poetic texts, and he calls upon the deities of poetry to avenge the crime perpetrated by the translators. Later, however, during a discussion of scientific works, he assumes a radically different stance—a sarcastic, iconoclastic one. He mocks the opponents of translation who, like "venerable Druids," attempt to keep "all the disciplines . . . enclosed within the Greek and Latin books," as if knowledge were a sacred relic "that one is not allowed to touch with one's hand" (pp. 67, 70). But the distinction between poetry and prose does not fully explain Du Bellay's metamorphosis from priest to protestant; as we shall see, this metamorphosis occurs even when he is focusing on poetry alone.

Seeing the objects of poetic imitation as "sacred treasures," Du Bellay oscillates between approaching them reverently and iconoclastically. The reverent approach reveals his longing to identify with the ancient authors in an act of quasi-mystical union. This desire for identification sparks his theoretical emphasis on an ideal of holistic resemblance between ancient and modern texts, an ideal that depends on a distinction between words and an essential spirit beneath them. So long as he maintains the distinction between words, as merely a surface phenomenon, and an essential spirit of a text, Du Bellay avoids the idea that the ancient relic may undergo a significant change in the process of being imitated. When, however, the distinction between words and spirit begins to blur, as it often does in the *Deffence*, we can see Du Bellay becoming an iconoclast. By considering the ancient texts as verbal structures rather than as mysteriously living beings, Du Bellay justifies the notion of imitation as a transformation (or violation) of the original textual material. For the iconoclastic imitator as Du Bellay defines him, power comes from changing the ancient text rather than from merging with it. The text of the *Deffence* shows, however, Du Bellay's profound reluctance to choose between these two concepts of power. Imitation, as he defines it, is at once an act of homage and an act of profanation.

Consider, for example, the passage from Book 1, Chapter 7, where Du Bellay exhorts the French poet not simply to imitate Latin texts, but rather to imitate the Romans' practice of imitating the Greeks:

> Imitating the best Greek authors, transforming themselves into the Greeks, devouring them, and after having well digested them, converting them into blood and nourishment, they proposed the best author as a pattern, each according to his natural bent and according to the argument he wished to elect; they diligently observed all of the rarest and most exquisite virtues of the model author, and treating these virtues as grafts, as I have said before, they grafted and applied them to their own language. By doing this (I say), the Romans built all those beautiful writings, that we praise and admire so strongly.

> Immitant les meilleurs aucteurs Grecz, se transformant en eux, les devorant, & apres les avoir bien digerez, les convertissant en sang & nouriture, se proposant, chacun selon son natural & l'argument qu'il vouloit elire, le meilleur aucteur, dont ilz observoint diligemment toutes les plus rares & exquises vertuz, & icelles comme grephes, ainsi que j'ay dict devant, entoint & apliquoint à leur Langue. Cela faisant (dy-je) les Romains ont baty tous ces beaux ecriz, que nous louons & admirons si fort. [pp. 42–43]

Aneau testily takes Du Bellay to task for the shifting of metaphors in this passage, which he finds an illogical and "vicious" translation, "beginning by *eating*, moving to a middle of *planting*, and ending with *building*, while all the time speaking of the same things" ("translation vicieuse & inconsequente, commençant par *manger*, moyennant par *planter*, & finissant par *bastir*, en parlant tousjours de mesmes choses") [p. 43, n. 2]. But Du Bellay is not, in truth, speaking of "the same things" at all; his metaphors point to radically different conceptions of the relation between imitation and original. Whereas the innutrition metaphor implies a process of total transformation, of appropriation so complete that one entity actually becomes another, the organic and architectural metaphors introduce a concern with the synecdochic relation of part to whole.[58] But this whole, presumably the native "langue," has already been defined by the innutrition metaphor: it is the ancient author, devoured and digested by the imitator. This shifty concept of a whole is what makes the passage so interesting, and the varying metaphors are indeed, as Aneau observes, an offense against "proprieté."

The innutrition metaphor seeks to eradicate any difference between ancient and modern. To do so, it must elide the issue of language. Although in Book 1, Chapter 6, Du Bellay compares the translators who fail to capture a genius in language to painters who can represent a body but not an intangible soul, he shifts in Chapter 7 to a new surface/depth dichotomy by which the ancient author's power is conceived as something corporeal, hence graspable (although only through a violation of the imitated object): the essence the imitator seeks is something deep within the body, not its surface "skin and color," but what a later passage calls "the flesh, the bones, the nerves, and the blood" (p. 100). Cannibalistic overtones? Yes; and the violence is not merely figurative, since it inheres in Du Bellay's fundamental conception of eloquence, the force the imitator desires to take from the original text and make his own. Although earlier Du Bellay had associated this force with a quality of style unique to each language (and hence not translatable), now he attempts to define a paradoxical quality that belongs to language and yet somehow exists beneath or beyond the level of "les mots." His definitions of this quality repeatedly do violence to logic, as Aneau remarks in his commentary on one of Du Bellay's most enigmatic surface/ depth metaphors. This one is combined with an outside/inside opposition to present eloquence as a sword presently covered by a sheath. Aneau explains this as an "improper similitude" in which the sword denotes the power of French letters (on the analogy of the swordlike eloquence of the Scriptures), whereas the sheath denotes "the impolished rudeness of harsh language"— the present condition of French, in Du Bellay's view. But as Aneau points out, the double figure of sword and sheath (which implies two separate material entities) is inadequate to describe the linguistic problem at hand; while a sheath may "cover" a sword, bad language cannot "cover" elo- quence, for eloquence does not exist at all in the presence of bad language (p. 34, n. 4).

As we have seen, Du Bellay's ideal of imitation as a holistic resemblance between two texts (personified as living beings) depends on problematic definitions of a force of language separate from words. A passage in Book 1, Chapter 8, further illuminates the theoretical difficulties Du Bellay encoun- ters in articulating a concept of imitation as a supraverbal transformation:

> But he who wishes to imitate should understand that it is not an easy thing to follow well the virtues of a good author, and almost (as it were) transform oneself into him; for Nature herself has not known how to make even things that seem very similar so alike that they cannot be distinguished by some mark or difference. I say this, because many persons who write in all languages fail to penetrate to the most hidden and interior parts of the author whom they have taken for a model; instead, they apply themselves only to what meets the eye, and amuse themselves with the beauty of words, losing the force of things.

> Mais entende celuy qui voudra immiter, que ce n'est chose facile de bien suyvre les vertuz d'un bon aucteur, & quasi comme se transformer en luy, veu que la Nature mesmes aux choses qui paroissent tressemblables, n'a sceu tant faire, que par quelque notte & difference elles ne puissent estre discernées. Je dy cecy, pour ce qu'il y en a beaucoup en toutes Langues, qui sans penetrer aux plus cachées & interieures parties de l'aucteur qu'ilz se sont proposé, s'adaptent seulement au premier regard, & s'amusant à la beauté des motz, perdent la force des choses. [p. 46]

This passage advocates an imitation that can transcend all difference; by an act of supreme artifice, the imitator will remedy what Nature "n'a sceu tant faire" and will achieve a resemblance beyond Nature's differences.[59] Du Bellay in fact sets up a parallel between two kinds of superficial resemblance. The things that merely appear "tressemblables" in Nature are like the art that resembles its original only on the level of "la beauté des motz." The true resemblance occurs on the deeper level of "la force des choses."

By avoiding or denigrating the role of language, these descriptions of a holistic imitation leave no room for the notion of the imitator's individual identity. Du Bellay tries to remedy this problem by repeatedly insisting that the imitator must use a language different from the ancient author's. Paradoxically, he seems to be recommending difference on the very level of imitation he has defined as superficial: "les motz." A resemblance amounting to identity is to be sought on the level of "les choses." If, however, we look again and more closely at the initial formulation of the innutrition metaphor, we can see that a problem of identity is indeed present but is cast in terms of power rather than in terms of linguistic differentiation:

> Immitant les meilleurs aucteurs Grecz, se transformant en eux, les devorant, & apres les avoir bien digerez, les convertissant en sang & nouriture, se proposant, chacun selon son naturel & l'argument qu'il vouloit elire, le meilleur aucteur. . . . [p. 42]

This tortuous sentence begins with the imitator transforming himself into the ancient author; it then shifts to emphasize the change undergone by the ancient author. Despite the gesture toward mild and civilized free choice in the phrase "chacun selon son naturel & l'argument qu'il vouloit elire," the sentence insists on the imitator's uncanny movement from a total denial of self ("se transformant en eux") to a total assertion of self—an assertion in which the imitator rhetorically recreates the author he had previously devoured ("se proposant . . . le meilleur aucteur"). The syntax forces us to wonder whether the imitated object is logically or temporally *prior* to the imitation.

Even in the holistic concept of imitation, then, there is a tendency toward profanation, reflecting a desire to change or even efface the sacred relic. The imitator-devourer's assertion of power over the ancient text is the rhetorical foundation for the organic and architectural models of imitation. Although it still invests the ancient work with life, the image of imitation as a grafting diffuses the power of the original as a vital organism because it advocates a selection of the ancient author's "vertuz." The brief mention of the imitation as a building completes the transformation of the original text from a holistic being to a structure composed of movable parts.

When the imitated object is seen as an architectural structure, imitation can involve a linguistic process of adapting units of the ancient text to new uses. Du Bellay does not offer much practical advice about imitation, but he does mention the idea of "acclimatizing" classical words, which "will be in our language like strangers in a city, and for whom periphrases will always serve as interpreters" ("seront en notre Langue comme etrangers en une cité: aux quelz toutefois les periphrazes serviront de truchementz" [pp. 59–60]). With the notion of paraphrase, he suggests a view of imitation as interpretation rather than reproduction; but he does not follow this line of thought as far as other classical and Renaissance authors do—authors like Quintilian, who sees periphrasis as a way of rivaling the imitated author; or Vida and Castiglione, who both advocate an interpretive imitation that gives classical words and *topoi* "altra significazione che la lor propria."[60] Nor does he mention the possibility of an imitation that not only changes the ancient source but plays ironically on the change; this is the kind of critically interpretive imitation that we find in many of Du Bellay's own poems.[61] He does not pursue the idea of imitation as an interpretive reordering of the parts of an original text because it threatens to undermine his ideal of holistic resemblance. Although the architectural metaphor of imitation seems effectively to deconstruct that ideal, Du Bellay elaborates the metaphor in a way that shows how deeply he resists the iconoclastic implications of his theory and practice.

The architectural metaphor is most fully developed in a negative context, in the course of an invective against Neo-Latin imitators. Du Bellay attacks them in Book 1, Chapter 11, for their habit of gathering "now a noun, now a verb, from this poet and that orator"; the imitators are pseudomasons who attempt to restore an ancient edifice with as much success as all the king's men had with Humpty-Dumpty:

> But you will never be such good masons . . . that you will be able to restore the form which those good and excellent architects originally gave to their buildings; and if you hope to revive those buildings by gathering their fragments (as Aesculapius did with the members of Hippolytus), you delude yourselves.

> Mais vous ne serez ja si bons massons . . . que leur puissiez rendre celle forme que leur donnarent premierement ces bons & excellens architectes: & si vous esperez (comme fist Esculape des membres d'Hippolyte) que par ces fragmentz recuilliz elles puyssent estre resuscitées, vous vous abusez. [p. 79]

The *Deffence* offers two reasons for the imitators' failure to create a unity ("reduire en un") from the fragments of ancient literature: the modern writers lack the "idea" which gave the original building its true form; and they lack the natural ability to use ancient languages. The historical pessimism of this passage, with its wistful evocation of a lost golden age when everyone sucked eloquence in with "the milk of the nurse," points to a problem that affects not only the Neo-Latin imitators. The invective against them suggests, indeed, that Du Bellay despairs of great literary achievement from any writer who lacks a naturally rich language. It is, after all, not only the Neo-Latin imitators, but Du Bellay himself—the author of Latin and French poems—who expends "pain and industry" on a task he views, in this passage, as hopeless: the restoration of life to fragments of ancient texts, fragments that have "wandered," he says, "through the long course of centuries," and now "cannot be found by anyone" (p. 80).[62]

In the text of the *Deffence*, the architectural metaphor is clearly a double-edged sword: it is used both to define an imitation that successfully reorders and interprets the fragments of ancient originals and to denounce an imitative act that does not and perhaps cannot revive the integral spirit of the original. The metaphor therefore illuminates the tenuous logical status of Du Bellay's distinction between true and false imitators; the distinction does not succeed in separating two classes of modern writers or two linguistic methods. On the contrary, it illustrates Michel Deguy's definition of a contradiction that cannot be dialectically resolved: "les faces d'une même chose sont dites dans leur divergence et antagonisme" ("the faces [or facades or aspects] of a single thing are stated in their divergence and antagonism").[63] If Du Bellay's distinction between true and false imitators ultimately fails to mark a genuine difference, the rhetorical labor of making the distinction is nevertheless important: it testifies to a refusal to conceive of imitation statically, as a set of linguistic rules or procedures. The *Deffence* defines imitation as a relation between texts, an unstable relation in which the balance of power is continually shifting.

In representing this shifting balance of power by a rhetorical practice of moving from one metaphor to another ("translation vicieuse," as Aneau calls it), Du Bellay's text provides a fascinating gloss on Cicero's definition of metaphorical words as "those which are transferred and settled, as it were, in an alien place."[64] The *Deffence* explores the problem of homelessness not only in its thematic focus on journeys between France and Rome, but also in its textual practice of journeying from one metaphor to another—and in the related practice of translating metaphorical formulations from ancient and modern Italian authors. The problem of property in all of its many dimensions is addressed in Du Bellay's concluding chapter, to which I now turn to begin some concluding remarks on the *Deffence*.

The Endless Journey of Exile

Moy chetif ce pendant loing des yeux de mon Prince,
  Je vieillis malheureux en estrange province,
  Fuyant la pauvreté: mais las ne fuyant pas
Les regrets, les ennuys, le travail et la peine
                          —Du Bellay, *Les Regrets*, sonnet 24

The *Deffence*, as we might expect, has not one but two conclusions. The first is the last chapter of Book 2, entitled "Exhortation to the French to Write in Their Language: With Praises of France." The second, a separate chapter entitled "Conclusion of the Entire Work," belongs to the text in the ambiguous way that the Dedicatory Epistle to the Cardinal Jean du Bellay does: both are liminal sets of pages, at once attached to and separate from the body of the *Deffence*. It is no accident that both the Epistle and the Conclusion allude to the actual journey Du Bellay hoped to make with the cardinal, a journey from France to Rome which is the historical analogue to those linguistic journeys described (and illustrated) in the pages of the *Deffence* devoted to imitation.

Let us look at the Conclusion before going back to the Dedicatory Epistle. It begins with a traditional metaphor of the book as a ship, now, at last, reaching a safe harbor:

> Now, thanks to God, we have come safely to port, through many perils and foreign waves. We have escaped from the midst of the Greeks, and by going through the squadrons of the Romans, we have penetrated the breast of our greatly desired France.

> Or sommes nous, la grace à Dieu, par beaucoup de perilz & de flotz etrangers, renduz au port à seureté. Nous avons echappé du millieu des Grecz, & par les scadrons Romains penetré jusques au seing de la tant desirée France. [p. 195]

No sooner has Du Bellay brought us to France, however, than he urges us to embark on a new voyage—to Rome:

> Therefore, Frenchmen, march courageously toward that proud city of Rome; and from her enslaved spoils, ornament your temples and altars (as you have done more than one time before).

> La donq', Françoys, marchez couraigeusement vers cete superbe cité Romaine: & des serves depouilles d'elle (comme vous avez fait plus d'une fois) ornez vos temples & autelz. [pp. 195–96]

These sentences figuratively locate the French reader between two journeys, one to France, the other to Rome, one a metaphor for a past labor—the reading or writing of the *Deffence*—the other a metaphor for a future labor of putting the text's precepts into practice. Both journeys, however, have a similar aim, figured in both cases as an erotic triumph: a "penetration" of France and a rape and pillage of Rome. What, precisely, is the connection between these two journeys? Is one the means to the other's end, in both senses of that word? And how do we relate this paradoxical conclusion to the final sentence of Book 2, which exhorts the reader who is a "friend of the French Muses" to write in his native tongue—that is, not to take journeys— because "it is worth more to be an Achilles among one's own, than a

Diomedes, indeed often a Thersites, among foreigners" ("qu'il vault mieux estre un Achille entre les siens, qu'un Diomede, voyre bien souvent un Thersite, entre les autres" [p. 194])? To answer these questions, we must look back at the Dedicatory Epistle, and at the light it sheds on the theory of imitation set forth in the body of the *Deffence*.

As we saw at the beginning of this chapter, Du Bellay presents the cardinal as a heroic actor in "ce grand Theatre Romain"; he also presents the cardinal as a man engaged in heroic labors which take nearly all of his time. The author of the *Deffence* wants, however, to take some portion of the cardinal's time for himself, and thereby to make the cardinal a spectator to another's act of labor.

> Spying therefore some hour in the little amount of relaxation you take in order to breathe under the heavy weight of French affairs (a burden truly worthy of such robust shoulders, no less than the Heavens were a worthy burden for great Hercules' shoulders), my Muse has made bold to enter into the sacred cabinet of your holy and studious occupations; and there, among so many and rich and excellent *ex-voto* objects, dedicated from day to day to the image of your greatness, [my Muse has ventured] to hang her small and humble offering.

> Epiant donques quelque heure de ce peu de relaiz que tu prens pour respirer soubz le pesant faiz des affaires Francoyses (charge vrayement digne de si robustes epaules, non moins que le Ciel de celles du grand Hercule), ma Muse a pris la hardiesse d'entrer au sacré cabinet de tes sainctes & studieuses occupations: & là, entre tant de riches & excellens voeuz de jour en jour dediez à l'image de ta grandeur, pendre le sien humble & petit. [pp. 5–6]

The cardinal's "sacred cabinet" is the place Du Bellay desires to penetrate with his words: in the symbolic sexual drama of the passage, the cardinal is cast in the role of a woman, with Du Bellay playing a young lover's part: he first spies the cardinal during a moment of leisure, then takes advantage of the seductive opportunity. And in so doing, he at once makes a symbolic act of homage, offering his small *ex-voto* object to a saint's image, and profanes a holy place, entering it boldly and suggesting that others have done so before him.

There is clearly a parallel between what Du Bellay figuratively does to the cardinal and what he later urges the French poet to do to ancient texts. Successful imitators, he writes, must not merely look at surface beauties, but must "penetrate to the most hidden and interior parts of the author they have taken for their model" ("penetrer aux plus cachées & interieures parties de l'aucteur qu'ilz se sont proposé" [p. 46]).

What is the relation between the cardinal's "sacred cabinet," the objects of imitation, and the two places Du Bellay describes, in the conclusion, as a much desired country and a city about to be pillaged? France and Rome seem to be two names for the same object of desire: wealth, literary and

economic. Like a latter-day Jason, Du Bellay sets out to acquire a golden
fleece, and he conflates his economic and literary desires in a way that
prevents us from distinguishing between practical and theoretical aims.
Writing, among other reasons, to gain employment, he designs his text from
beginning to end to flatter the man whose labor involved journeying between France and Rome. Du Bellay knows that the cardinal undertook these
travels with the hope of enriching himself by diplomatically furthering his
king's designs on Italian territory. No wonder, then, that Du Bellay's conclusions suggests that the act of penetrating "la tant desirée France" is intimately linked to pillaging Rome. For Du Bellay, the idea of a future in
France is inconceivable without the idea of a future journey to Rome, the
city of ancient ruins which haunted him both as a humanist poet and as an
impoverished nobleman.

Penetrating the cardinal's "sacred cabinet" is therefore the figurative
expression of a desire to enter the sacred city of Rome, which is also a desire
to gain the literary and literal riches necessary for building a great home in
France. Throughout the treatise, however, Du Bellay shows his fear of being
punished for violating, or desiring to violate, a sacred object, whether it is
conceived as the cardinal's cabinet, the ancient texts, the breast of "la tant
desirée France," or the city of Rome itself. He defends himself against this
fear by attempting to present the act of violation and theft as natural and
legitimate, like the transplantation of plants or a painless blending of es-
sences. He also attempts to reassure himself (and the cardinal) that his
ambitions reflect a desire simply to pay (and be rewarded for paying)
homage rather than a desire to usurp another's place. In the Dedicatory
Epistle, his effort to show the harmlessness of his ambitions appears in his
portraits of himself as a small, humble person in need of the protection of a
paternal hero. He dedicates his book to the "grandeur" of the cardinal's
name (which is, of course, also his own family name) "in order that it may
hide itself (as if beneath the shield of Ajax), from the poisoned arrows of
[Envy,] that old enemy of virtue" (p. 6). Du Bellay goes on, in a stunning
shift from classical to biblical allusion, to compare the cardinal to God, who
protects the weak "beneath the shade of [his] wings." Praying to the cardinal
as David did to the Lord ("sub umbra alarum tuarum protege me" [Psalm
16:8]), Du Bellay presents himself as a humble and adoring supplicant. But
there is more at stake here than flattery; the reverent stance Du Bellay adopts
toward the cardinal, and later toward the ancient authors, is a complex
defense against the guilt engendered by desires for property and power
(including sexual power). The act of writing itself, for Du Bellay, evidently
involves an Oedipal crime of simultaneously usurping the father's place and
joining in erotic union with a forbidden object. The punishment for this
crime is suggested by the sentence which concludes the miniature drama of

the "sacred cabinet": the little book which has boldly entered a holy space becomes a sacrificial offering, an *ex-voto* object left by its owner "to hang . . . humble and small" ("pendre . . . humble et petit") in the father's room (pp. 5–6).

The author who thus figuratively humiliates himself (warding off punishment with self-chastisement) does not, of course, thereby quench his desires for power; on the contrary, he whets them, generating the movement between reverent and iconoclastic postures that we have observed throughout the treatise. The small figure who imitates David praying for protection from the Lord holds a sling in his hands as well as a harp: and the great men he sometimes reveres as lords look, from another perspective, like Goliaths, giants to be conquered.

* * *

Four years after writing the *Deffence*, Du Bellay's desires were apparently fulfilled: he entered the cardinal's sacred cabinet as his secretary, and in that role accompanied him to the sacred city of Rome.[65] What he found there, and what he also found when he returned to France, is recorded in the four collections of poems he published in 1558. These collections, three written in French and one in Latin, might be bound together with the general title, *Patriae desiderium*.[66] Like the poem which does bear that title, many of the lyrics which Du Bellay wrote in Rome analyze the condition of homelessness he calls "eternel exil."[67] This condition is defined in terms of numerous oppositions which signal the modern poet's inability to be at home in a single language, a single country, or a single time. Not only does he write both in French and in Latin, but he writes two apparently antithetical but intimately related vernacular sonnet sequences about Rome. One, *Les Antiquitez de Rome*, focuses on the ancient city; the other, *Les Regrets*, focuses on the modern city, which is repeatedly contrasted with the poet's ancestral home in Anjou. The sequences thus formally elaborate the problem Du Bellay states epigrammatically in lines such as the following, in which the name "Rome" means two different things:

> Nouveau venu qui cherches Rome en Rome,
> Et rien de Rome en Rome n'appercois. . . .   [*Antiquitez*, sonnet 3]
>
> Que Rome n'est plus Rome. . . .   [*Regrets*, sonnet 131]

The paradoxical rhetoric stresses the interpretive effort required of a "nouveau venu" confronted with two texts: the traces of a past Rome and the political and erotic duplicities of the present one. And Du Bellay as reader of this double text expresses a double response to it. In *Les Antiquitez* he employs a high style to mark his awe before the mystery of ancient Rome's greatness and fall; in *Les Regrets* he uses a low style to define a satirical perspective on modern Rome's corruptions. We see, here, yet another instance of the oscillation between defensive reverence and aggressive iconoclasm which we have traced in the *Deffence*. And it is important to note that the opposition between ancient and modern Rome does not fully correspond to that between reverent and critical perspectives; though Du Bellay is considerably more circumspect about attacking forefathers than about attacking contemporaries, in both sequences he demystifies and mystifies Rome, undermines and admires it.[68]

The French sonnets about Rome provide a particularly useful gloss on the rhetoric of the *Deffence* because they define the home as a relational rather than an essential concept. Recording the poet's nostalgic desire both for his ancestral seat in France and for a place in ancient Rome, the city that once nourished literary greatness, the sonnets present exile as both a spatial and a temporal phenomenon; and they define the home negatively, in terms of what it is no longer or what it has not yet become.[69] It is, in short, what one does not at present possess.

When he wrote the *Deffence*, Du Bellay still hoped that a literal journey to Rome could make him like the hero he describes in the text's final sentence: a "Hercule Gallique" drawing his audience behind him with a chain linking their ears to his tongue. This image of a hero-author at once bound to his readers (as Du Bellay hoped to be bound to the cardinal) and leading them powerfully westward, from Greece to Rome to France, is a fantasy worthy of a "Hercules factitius," a poet not willing to accept the brazen world into which he was born.[70] By the end of his actual experience of a *translatio studii*—which involved a journey east, not west, and which did not lead to any golden fleece—Du Bellay no longer imagined himself a Hercules. He compared himself, instead, to Ulysses—or rather, to two figures of Ulysses, the first like Homer's hero, the second more like Tennyson's. The difference between the rhetoric of desire in the *Deffence* and that in Du Bellay's later work might, indeed, be defined in terms of the different views of homecoming offered in sonnets 31 and 130 of *Les Regrets*. In the first poem, often read, like the *Deffence* itself, as an expression of French patriotism, Du Bellay longs to resemble heroes like Ulysses and Jason, who returned home with experiential and material wealth, respectively:

> Heureux qui, comme Ulysse, a fait un beau voyage,
>   Ou comme cestuy la qui conquit la toison,
>   Et puis est retourné, plein d'usage & raison,
>   Vivre entre ses parents le reste de son aage!
> Quand revoiray-je, helas, de mon petit village
>   Fumer la cheminee, & en quelle saison,
>   Revoiray-je le clos de ma pauvre maison,
>   Qui m'est une province, & beaucoup d'avantage?

Plus me plaist le sejour qu'ont basty mes ayeux,
   Que des palais Romains le front audacieux,
   Plus que le marbre dur me plaist l'ardoise fine:
Plus mon Loyre Gaulois, que le Tybre Latin,
   Plus mon petit Lyré, que le mont Palatin,
   Et plus que l'air marin la doulceur Angevine.

Happy is he who made a fine voyage and then returned, as Ulysses did or the man who conquered the golden fleece; filled with experience and wisdom, such voyagers return to live with their families for the rest of their lives. When shall I, alas, again see the chimney smoking in my little village, and in what season shall I again see the vineyard of my poor house, which is a province to me and much more? The abode that my ancestors built pleases me more than the arrogant facades of Roman palaces; I am more pleased by fine slate than by hard marble; more by the Gallic Loire than by the Latin Tiber; more by my small Lyre hill than by the Palatine mount; and more by Angevine sweetness than by sea air.

Ninety-nine poems later Du Bellay again takes up the theme of Ulysses' voyage; this time, however, he looks ironically at the optimism of his own former poem, the product, he implies, of a more naive poetic self. In sonnet 130, moreover, he explicitly confronts the problem that plagued him throughout his life, both as a poor aristocrat and as a late-born poet: he has no true home in either France or Rome, for wherever his journey stops he finds rivals in his place. Unlike Homer's Ulysses, who slew Penelope's suitors and reestablished his property rights, Du Bellay is unsure whether he has either the weapons or the will to do battle with his enemies. Longing for vengeance, he nevertheless suggests that a renewed journey may be the exile's only defense against the disappointment that awaits him at home:

Et je pensois aussi ce que pensoit Ulysse,
   Qu'il n'estoit rien plus doulx que voir encor' un jour
   Fumer sa cheminee, & apres long sejour
   Se retrouver au sein de sa terre nourrice.
Je me resjouissois d'estre eschappé au vice,
   Aux Circes d'Italie, aux Sirenes d'amour,
   Et d'avoir rapporté en France à mon retour
   L'honneur que l'on a s'acquiert d'un fidele service.
Las mais apres l'ennuy de si longue saison,
   Mille souciz mordants je trouve en ma maison,
   Qui me rongent le coeur sans espoir d'allegence.
Adieu donques (Dorat) je suis encor' Romain,
   Si l'arc que les neuf soeurs te misrent en la main
   Tu ne me preste icy, pour faire ma vengence.

And once I thought what Ulysses thought, that there was nothing sweeter than someday to see one's chimney smoking, and to find oneself in the heart of one's native land after long wandering. I rejoiced to have escaped from vice, from the

Circes of Italy, from the Sirens of love, and to have brought back to France, on my return, the honor which one gains from faithful service. But alas, after the ennui of such a long season away from home, I find a thousand gnawing cares in my house, cares which eat away my heart without hope of relief. Adieu then, Dorat, I am still a Roman, unless you lend me here the bow that the nine muses put in your hand, so I may wreak my vengeance.

III

Torquato Tasso: The Trial of Conscience

I thought mine enemies had been but Man,
But spirits may be leagued with them—all Earth
Abandons—Heaven forgets me;—in the dearth
Of such defence the Powers of Evil can—
It may be—tempt me further,—and prevail
Against the outworn creature they assail.
Why in this furnace is my spirit proved,
Like steel in tempering fire?

—Byron, "The Lament of Tasso"

Like Du Bellay's *Deffence*, Tasso's *Apologia in difesa della "Gerusalemme Liberata"* (1585) is a strange and convoluted work that records a poet's effort to defend and define his literary identity. Critics from the Florentine Accademia della Crusca had violently attacked the *Gerusalemme Liberata*, arguing that it was inferior in style and content to Ariosto's *Orlando Furioso*.[1] To defend himself, Tasso had to prove the superiority of his Christian epic to Ariosto's poem, which was, in Tasso's view, ethically and aesthetically confused, an "animal of uncertain nature."[2] Basically, Tasso defines the difference between his and Ariosto's poems in terms of a distinction between epic and romance; he associates epic with Aristotelian principles of formal unity and with political and religious ideas about the value of a single, absolute ruler; he associates romance with "multiple" plots in the aesthetic sphere, with rebellion against political authority, and with polytheistic, pagan values that oppose the doctrines of Christian monotheism.[3] The irony is that his own poem, although much more tightly structured than Ariosto's, is nevertheless a strange blending of romance and epic elements, formal and thematic.[4] Tasso was deeply uneasy about this blending. His critical works and the manifold revisions he made to his epic testify to this uneasiness and suggest that for Tasso, in contrast to Ariosto, the attempt to marry different genres generated psychic as well as theoretical conflicts.[5] Tasso's ambivalence toward the romance elements in his poem was undoubtedly increased by his need to define himself against Ariosto. The *Apologia* dramatizes the

54

way in which the concept of romance represents, for Tasso, a threat no less complex than that which the concept of Rome represents for Du Bellay.

The threat is greatly complicated by the fact that Tasso's father, Bernardo, had written a hundred-canto epic on the Amadis de Gaul legend. Bernardo's *L'Amadigi di Gaula* (1560) had been attacked by men on both sides of the major critical war of late sixteenth-century Italy. The "Ariostisti," who included the Cruscans, disparaged Bernardo as well as his son; but the "Tassisti," who based their aesthetic views on admiration for Virgil's *Aeneid* and for Aristotelian principles of formal unity, also criticized Bernardo's poem, which they rightly saw as resembling Ariosto's digressive romance more than it resembled Tasso's classically structured epic on a Christian theme.[6] Tasso thus found himself in the unhappy position of being genealogically attached to a poet who was held to be in Ariosto's camp. Genealogy is indeed a crucial issue in the *Apologia*. If Tasso broods obsessively on the difficulties of defining father-son relationships, it is because, for him, questions of literal and figurative filiation were necessarily and inextricably linked. I can think of no other major writer in the Western tradition whose identity as a son was more problematically overdetermined than Tasso's. Not only did the historical circumstances of his involvement in the critical battle heighten his anxiety about his relation both to his biological father and to Ariosto; the critical battle defined the competition between Ariosto and Tasso in terms of a larger dispute, characteristic of Renaissance literary theory, about the modern writer's relation to two competing sets of ancestors, medieval and classical.

It was, however, not only the critical battle which shaped Tasso's concern with problems of filial identity. Questions posed by the critics—about obedience to Aristotelian rules, for instance, or about the legitimacy of romance as a genre—were clearly related to the questions about obedience to religious and political authority that preoccupied Italians in the late sixteenth century. These questions were frequently expressed through the familiar metaphor of the state as a "body politic"—a metaphor which was used, as David George Hale observes, "to buttress arguments for and against many kinds of social, political, and religious institutions," ranging from the Athenian polis and the Roman republic to the medieval papacy and the absolutist monarchies of the Renaissance.[7] Tasso's personal and political experience made him unusually sensitive to the ideological conflicts that his age expressed in its various uses of the organic analogy, especially in the version that makes the monarch a paternal "head" who requires absolute obedience from his subjects. As the son of a man who had participated in a rebellion against the paternal authority of the Holy Roman Emperor, as a courtier frequently out of favor with his noble patrons, and, last but not least, as a Christian in post-Trentine Italy who wrote anxious letters to priests he addressed as "Vostra Paternità," Tasso had more than enough reasons to become a serious analyst of what we may call "the family politic."[8]

Tasso's fears of being condemned by the fathers of the church contributed greatly to the doubts he expresses in the *Apologia* about the ethos of romance poetry. When he wrote his reply to the Cruscans in 1585, he had been imprisoned for six years in the Ferrarese fortress of Sant'Anna. He was probably imprisoned not because he had offended the Duke of Ferrara by courting his sister Leonora, as Romantic legend proclaims, but rather because he had struck one of the duke's servants and had shown further signs of mental instability by writing letters to the Inquisition confessing his sins and also, perhaps, those of others in the Ferrarese court.[9] Although in some of his letters he claims, like Hamlet, that his madness is merely feigned, he certainly felt while writing the *Apologia* that his psychic and spiritual as well as his literary identities were endangered.[10] The *Apologia* testifies throughout to his sense of being besieged, like the inhabitants of Jerusalem in his epic, by forces at every gate. Attacked in the Cruscan pamphlet by critics whose names he did not know, Tasso associated his literary persecutors with his fears—largely unfounded—that he had offended his spiritual judges in the church.[11] The newly formed Accademia della Crusca, as Francesco de Sanctis observes, did bear a striking resemblance to the Council of Trent: "It too excommunicated writers and posited dogmas."[12] Tasso's attempts to defend himself against both secular and religious judges produce a text which is itself like a dark romance landscape in which an author-hero is repeatedly drawn into battles he does not fully understand. The genre of the *Apologia* might best be described with the phrase Tasso applies to Ariosto's poem: an "animal of uncertain nature." What makes the text so remarkable is that it combines a theoretical inquiry into the relation between romance and epic with fictions that belong, quite precisely, to that genre Freud called "family romance."

Freud's little essay entitled "Family Romances" (1909) discusses the "works of fiction" the child creates to liberate himself from the authority of his parents. "It is quite essential that that liberation should occur," Freud asserts, but he adds that "there is a class of neurotics whose condition is recognizably determined by their having failed in this task" (*SE* 9: 237). How large this class is Freud does not say; by the time he wrote *Civilization and Its Discontents* in 1930, it would theoretically include everyone. Even in his early essay, there is no clear distinction drawn between the "normal" and the "neurotic" family romance; the latter seems merely to involve that more "marked imaginative activity" which is characteristic of neurotics and "also of all comparatively highly gifted people" (*SE* 9: 238).

There are many plots in the genre of family romance; the basic one, which we have observed already in Du Bellay's *Deffence*, involves replacing the biological parents (particularly the father) with imaginary figures "who, as a rule, are of higher social standing" (*SE* 9: 239). Tasso, as we shall see, employs this plot repeatedly: replacing both his father and Ariosto with substitutes drawn from literary sources, he constructs a fictive genealogy that denies his debts both to Ariosto and to Bernardo. His family romance plots, paradoxically, show Tasso's effort to escape the influence of the chivalric romance tradition that Ariosto had so brilliantly exploited and also transformed into what his admirers praised as a genuine creation of the Renaissance period.[13] Such praise of Ariosto provoked Tasso to see him not only as a father, but also as an elder brother and rival for the inheritance of ancient and medieval ancestors. "A younger child," Freud remarks, "is very specially inclined to use imaginative stories . . . in order to rob those born before him of their prerogatives—in a way which reminds one of historical intrigues" (*SE* 9: 240). As we shall see, Tasso frequently treats Ariosto as the illegitimate son while presenting himself as the true son and heir of poets like Virgil and, in the vernacular tradition, Dante.

Dante is particularly important for Tasso's fictive genealogy because the *Commedia* provided a model of a post-classical poem which differed both in structure and in ethos from the medieval romances Ariosto drew on for the *Orlando*.[14] Moreover, the story Dante tells at the end of the *Purgatorio* about leaving his "sweetest father," Virgil, behind to journey with Beatrice to paradise profoundly influenced Tasso's conception of his own literary and personal autobiography. He interprets his life to be a journey away from earthly and pagan fathers toward the realm he calls "the heavenly Jerusalem"; in the revised version of his epic, he portrays that realm as a beautiful woman resembling Dante's Beatrice—and also the mother Tasso had lost as a child.[15] The mother plays a strange role in Tasso's family romance stories, as she does in his theory about the vexed relation between romance and epic. Freud quotes the old legal tag "pater semper incertus est, mater est certissima" to illustrate his view that the (boy) child old enough to understand sexual difference no longer uses fantasies to cast doubt on his maternal origin, "which is regarded as something inalterable" (*SE* 9: 239). For Tasso, however, memories of the maternal origin are a source of aesthetic and moral questions. The image of women like Virgil's Creusa and Dido, deserted or wounded by virtuous epic heroes, haunts his imagination and contributes enormously to his ambivalence about the ethos of romance poetry, which he associates not only with Ariosto and his father, but also with a siren-like female spirit that resists the ideas of order that the author or hero of a Christian epic is required to support.

The *Apologia* shows Tasso's attempts to defend and define his identity on a border between romance and epic, between a realm he associates with the claims of the flesh and the past and one he associates with spiritual duty and the future. If he remains trapped in this border territory, it is partly because he cannot create a theoretical fiction that can efface his memory of his earthly origin, of the biological parents who created him, and of the poet, Ariosto, who most influenced his imagination. Although at times Tasso strives to stand like Shakespeare's Coriolanus, "As if a man were author of himself / And knew no other kin," and though he also tries to stand as if he knew no father but God, he is in fact a striking example of a man haunted by memories of past authors, parental and literary. He is pursued by ghosts, or, to use his own term, by "phantasms."

The concept of the phantasm is one of the knots that prevent us from separating the autobiographical strands of discourse in the *Apologia* from the theoretical ones: a "phantasm," for Tasso, is both the ghostly voice of a dead or absent person and the term he uses in an astonishing variety of ways to designate the epistemological and spiritual errors of the romance imagination itself. These errors produce "simulacra" that are false, according to Plato's discussion of imitations in the *Sophist*, and sinful, according to Tasso's conception of the Christian poet's duty to imitate the workings of God's providence rather than to create "phantasms" through the workings of his own imagination. The problem Tasso probes repeatedly in his later writing concerns the difficulty of distinguishing between phantasmic and true imitations. His acute awareness of his own "frenetic" mental processes led him to suspect that even divine revelations might really be products of the human *fantasia*—a term which has the broad range of meanings in his discourse that "phantasy" does in Freud's, signifying, first of all, the works of fiction generated by desire.[16]

In a letter written in December 1585, he describes the imaginative picture of the Virgin with her son in her arms which came to him during the "terrors" and "griefs" of a fever:

> And although it may easily have been a fantasy because I was mad, and almost always disturbed by various phantasms, and full of infinite melancholy, nevertheless, by the grace of God, I may sometimes "refrain from consent" [i.e., from consenting to believe in these phantasms], which operation is that of a wise man. . . . Hence I should rather believe that this [image] was a miracle of the Virgin.

> E benchè potesse facilmente essere una fantasia, perch'io sono frenetico, e quasi sempre perturbato da vari fantasmi, e pieno di maninconia infinita; nondimeno, per la grazia d'Iddio, posso *cohibere assensum* alcuna volta; la qual operazione è del savio. . . . laonde più tosto devrei credere che quello fosse un miracolo de la Virgine.[17]

The epistemological doubts generated by Tasso's experience of "maninconia infinita" led him to approach, uneasily, the territory Freud explored in his discussions of religion as a phantastic cultural version of the family romance. "If the Emperor and Empress appear in dreams, those exalted personages stand for the dreamer's father and mother," Freud writes in "Family Romances" (*SE* 9: 241). In his later works he takes this point to its logical conclusion, arguing that God himself is "an enormously exalted father" and implying, somewhat more equivocally, that the "oceanic feeling" Romain Rolland considered the "true source of religious sentiments," prior to and independent from "every belief and every illusion," is really a phantastic memory of the infant's experience at its mother's breast, at a stage of consciousness where he does not "distinguish his ego from the external world as the source of the sensations flowing in upon him."[18] Tasso, I think, anticipates Freud's theory that the human consciousness never fully liberates itself from primal memories and that its journey forward in time is also a return to the past. In this double journey, the authorial psyche wages war with a host of phantasms which it both loves and hates, believes in and distrusts. Tasso represents an important battle of this war in the first part of the *Apologia*, to which I now turn.

Defenses and Detours: The Apologia, First Part

> *Remember thee?*
> *Ay, thou poor ghost, while memory holds a seat*
> *In this distracted globe.*   —Hamlet

Tasso devotes the first third of his treatise to a defense of his dead father.[19] He feels himself duty-bound to defend Bernardo's spirit, which "lives" in the poem that critics had attacked:

> Because my father, who is dead in his sepulchre, may be said to live in his poem, anyone who seeks to offend his poetry, attempts to give him death a second time.

> Perché mio padre, il quale è morto nel sepolchro, si può dir vivo nel poema, chi cerca d'offender la sua poesia, procura dargli morte un'altra volta. [p. 630]

Tasso attempts to avenge (or to prevent: the temporality of ghost-killing is complex) the critics' offense to his father's spirit. Like Hamlet, however, he finds it hard to perform his memorial filial duty, in part because he must contend with a Claudius figure: Ariosto. Moreover, there is a basic conflict between his obligation to obey what he calls "the natural laws that pertain to the sepulchre" (p. 630) and his obligation to other sets of laws, notably those which define the work of an epic poet in terms of Aristotelian formal principles and rigorous Counter-Reformation conceptions of thematic decorum.[20] Bernardo's poem did not obey such laws any more than Ariosto's did, and hence Tasso cannot unequivocally defend it without betraying his own poetic ideals; his defense of Bernardo's ghost is, therefore, also a defense against it—and against the guilt caused by the son's symbolic complicity in the critical act he defines as "giving death a second time."

By beginning with a defense of Bernardo rather than with a defense of his own epic, Tasso underscores his desire to behave according to a clear hierarchy of obligation, one in which temporal and evaluative series harmoniously coincide. History, however, as well as the critics, had provided a script in which the notion "first things first" was highly problematic. Ariosto had preceded Bernardo Tasso in the historical line of Italian poets, and Tasso can therefore hardly accept historical priority as a sign of poetic superiority; to do so would be to agree with the critics in the Accademia della Crusca who had ranked Ariosto above both Bernardo and Torquato Tasso. But he also cannot agree with his critical supporters, notably Camillo Pellegrino, who had begun the critical war with a dialogue called *Il Carrafa o vero della poesia epica*, in which Pellegrino argues for Tasso's superiority over Ariosto—but also over Bernardo.[21] To be promoted at his father's expense seemed to Tasso a violation of natural laws, which enjoin the son to honor and defend his father.[22] His critical friends, as well as his enemies, had put Tasso in an unbearable position, as he insists when he writes that, instead of being grateful to his "amici," he must "lament [the action] of those who, in raising me where I do not deserve to climb, did not look out for the precipice" ("più tosto dovrei lamentarmi di coloro che, inalzandomi dove non merito di salire, non hanno risguardo al precipizio" [p. 629)].

Tasso's first response to his dangerous position (and position, of course, is what is at stake) is to assert his father's absolute right to primacy: the criticisms of Bernardo's poem offend him more than those of his own poem, Tasso writes, "because I voluntarily cede to him in all types of composition, and I cannot bear that in any of these types anyone should be placed before him" ("perché io gli cedo volontieri in tutte le maniere di componimenti, né potrei sostenere che in alcune di esse alcuno gli fosse anteposto" [p. 630]). The vehemence of this final phrase points to a problem already implicit in the notion of a "voluntary" ceding: that which Tasso cedes to his father he may take back. Indeed, only a few sentences later he significantly qualifies his assertion of Bernardo's primacy. Instead of being unable to bear that anyone should be placed before his father, he is now offended by those who would rank Bernardo below "any other of the same sort." That person offends Bernardo, Tasso writes, "who would make him inferior to any other of the same sort, and particularly to the *Morgante* or to Boiardo" ("e ciascuno l'offende, che lo vuol fare inferiore ad alcun altro delle medesima sorte, e particolarmente al *Morgante* ed al Boiardo" [p. 630]). Here, evidently, Tasso is no longer ceding his place to Bernardo, but is rather ceding a major point to Bernardo's critics, among whom were Tasso's own admirers. For this formulation implies that Bernardo is the first among the second-rate poets, which is precisely the opinion that Pellegrino advances in his *Carrafa* dialogue. Pellegrino judges poetic performance in terms of how closely it conforms to an Aristotelian conception of unity: the best poem should "from one single action form one single body which, as Aristotle wishes, should be such as may be perceived in one single view."[23] According to Pellegrino, digressive romances such as Pulci's *Morgante* and Boiardo's *Orlando Innamorato* were the lowest kind of poety; Bernardo Tasso was indeed superior to these poets, since he, like Ariosto (indeed Pellegrino constantly treats the two as equals), achieved some part of epic perfection. Bernardo's failure to create a "unity of action" prevents him, however, from attaining the highest rank; among the moderns, according to Pellegrino, only the younger Tasso approaches perfection in the writing of epic.[24]

Tasso's best known theoretical work, the *Discorsi*, which he composed in two versions between 1564 and 1594, shows his fundamental agreement with Pellegrino's views about the superiority of poems possessing "unity of action."[25] When one reads the *Apologia* along with the *Discorsi*, one appreciates how difficult it was for Tasso to defend his father's poem without denying the principles upon which he had constructed his own epic. In the first part of the *Apologia* he makes what is, in effect, a dutiful detour from his own critical and poetic path in order to justify the *Amadigi*. His detour involves some remarkable acts of theoretical juggling. (My favorite is Tasso's argument that if one is to have multiple actions in a poem, it is better to have extreme multiplicity, as Bernardo did, than to have mediocre multiplicity, as Ariosto did.)[26] The detour is most interesting, however, if we see it as a psychological drama of rationalization. The drama begins with Tasso stating that he cannot bear that anyone should be placed before Bernardo and ends with Tasso tentatively asserting his belief that if Bernardo "wanted to be surpassed, he did not want to be surpassed by anyone other than by me" ("se egli voleva esser pur superato, non voleva esser superato da nissun altro che da me" [p. 643]).

The detour Tasso takes in the first part of the *Apologia* brings him back to the summit on which his supporters had originally placed him; but it does so by means of a circuitous rather than a direct path, one which avoids vertiginous views of the precipice. The precipice, Tasso's own metaphor for the dangers or punishments which threaten him, may also be used to describe his fear that he deserves punishment for committing a crime of impiety against his father's spirit. The crime seems to involve, for Tasso, both the writing of a poem that differs from Bernardo's and the belief that the difference is a sign of superiority. The purpose of his detour is, therefore, not just to reach a goal, but to reach it in a psychologically as well as theoretically justifiable way. His dilemma is similar to the one he depicts in the famous "bleeding tree" episode of *Gerusalemme Liberata* (canto 13), where the hero Tancredi is deflected from his Christian mission by his encounter with a ghost from the past. The phantasmic voice of Clorinda—the beloved pagan whom Tancredi had mistakenly killed in a duel—issues from a tree that Tancredi has slashed in the fulfillment of his duty to the Christian leader Goffredo, who needs wood to rebuild a siege tower. The ghostly voice accusing Tancredi of offending the souls of the dead is a creation of the pagan magician Ismeno, an artist figure who rivals Goffredo in the epic and who is intent on preserving the material realm of nature and romance against the Christian forces. Tancredi is like a son caught between a spiritual and a natural father; to fulfill his duty to the former, he must withstand the power of the latter—a difficult task because he is himself tied to Ismeno's romance ethos by bonds of love and guilt. Ismeno, I suggest, is an allegorical figure who threatens Tancredi in some of the same ways Bernardo and Ariosto threaten Tasso. We shall see, moreover, that Tasso's biography offers rich material for associating Clorinda with the beloved mother Tasso lost as a child, and whose loss he blamed, in part, on the "confusions" of his father's political career.[27]

There is a significant parallel between the conflict of duties Tasso represents for Tancredi in his epic and the conflict he attempts to resolve in the tortuous rhetoric of the *Apologia*. Tancredi is torn between his duty to heed Clorinda's accusing voice, which tells him he is a murderer if he continues to violate the woods, and his duty to Goffredo, to whom he is bound by his honor as a Christian knight. Tasso is torn between his duty to Bernardo and what he considers to be his Christian duty, which requires that he write a severely doctrinal kind of poetry. He exposes this dilemma most dramatically in the pages of the *Apologia* he devotes to criticizing Ariosto. In fact, he uses Ariosto's poem—a safer object of criticism than Bernardo's—as a kind of allegorical field in which he can examine his ambivalent attitude toward his father, toward romance poetry, and toward the ethical problem of duty in general.

Tasso begins his critical commentary on Ariosto's *Orlando Furioso* in order to show that it is inferior to Bernardo's *Amadigi*. As one reads Tasso's critique, however, it becomes clear that his real aim is not to highlight the relative merits of Bernardo's poem but rather to examine some problems of moral conduct which pertain both to his own life and to his father's. Focusing on the faulty moral choices made by Ariosto's hero, Ruggiero, Tasso makes Ruggiero into a surrogate on whom he projects feelings of hostility toward Bernardo and also, I think, toward himself. His aggressive criticisms of Ariosto's plot and hero, expressed in a strange, quasi-autobiographical mode of discourse, can help us understand his interesting habit of reading life histories as if they were serious fictions—and vice versa.

Ruggiero's prime offense, in Tasso's eyes, is that he repeatedly betrays his duty and fails to establish a hierarchy of obligation. Tasso first criticizes him for behaving indecorously as a lover; he not only acts improperly toward the heroine Bradamante by playing the role of pursued rather than of pursuer, but also acts as if he "despises her and holds her in low esteem" (p. 638).

Ruggiero's disloyalty to Bradamante is a sign of the general weakness that he exhibits by repeatedly placing a lower duty above a higher one and thereby reneging on his debts. "Being most obliged to Bradamante, through whom he was twice rescued from a shameful prison," Tasso writes, Ruggiero erred in placing his duty to his king before his duty to his lady (p. 638; Tasso is concerned here with events recounted in cantos 38–40 of *Orlando Furioso*). Since the king was Agramante, leader of the pagan forces, Ruggiero errs in his understanding of his duty as well as in his performance of it:

> He places his king before his lady, [even though to the king] he had no particular obligation; indeed the king was not his natural prince, since he [Ruggiero] was born of a Christian father, who had been killed by the father of Agramante.
>
> Prepone a la sua donna il suo re, al quale non aveva alcuno obligo particolare; né veramente era suo principe naturale, perché egli era nato di padre cristiano, uccisogli dal padre d'Agramante. [pp. 638–39]

As he recounts Ariosto's intricate plot, Tasso becomes increasingly aggressive toward Ruggiero, even as his paraphrase confirms the point Ariosto himself was making: Ruggiero's dilemma was not wholly of his own creation, for the dilemma's origins are in the dark backward and abysm of time—specifically, as the passage quoted above indicates, in the time of the fathers. Tasso begins to sound like a reader who is determined to take a tragedy of fate as a tragedy of character—and character conceived in terms of a strangely simplified theory of Christian voluntarism. Tasso writes here as if he takes Aristotle's notion of *hamartia*—generally translated by modern scholars as "error" or "ignorance"—to mean something like "willful sin."[28] This is significant, since both Ariosto and critics writing earlier in the century had been interested in freeing the hero from judgment according to a simple binary opposition between virtue and vice: Bartolomeo Maranta, for instance, in a treatise published in 1564, interprets *hamartia* as error but suggests—in a remarkable flight from Aristotle to the realm of sixteenth-century court life—that the error need not be the hero's; on the contrary, it may belong to those who control the hero's fate, those who "are great in esteem and authority."[29]

The paragraphs which describe and criticize Ruggiero's actions are repetitive and contradictory; Tasso is unable to avoid transposing into his own narrative precisely that formal and ethical confusion he attacks in Ariosto's poem: *Orlando Furioso* lacks unity and is full of "indecorous" representations.[30] Having condemned Ruggiero for preferring his king (the false pagan one) to his lady, Tasso himself lapses into inconsistency; in an almost comic illustration of the imitative fallacy at work, he goes on to fault Ruggiero for not remaining constant in his erroneously assumed duty:

> Having preferred [Agramante to Bradamante], he [Ruggiero] did not continue in his firm preference; rather, after he had agreed to be the champion of his king

against a knight of Charlemagne, and after he had sworn to abandon the king if he intervened in the contest, through weakness and inconstancy of spirit he showed himself to be so inferior to Rinaldo that the king of Africa and Agramante himself despaired of his [Ruggiero's] victory.

Avendogliele proposto, non continua nel suo fermo proponimento: anzi, dopo ch'egli ebbe accettato di esser campione del suo re contra un cavaliero di Carlo, e giurato d'abbandonarlo, s'egli disturbasse la contesa, per debolezza ed inconstanza d'animo si mostra tanto inferiore a Rinaldo che i re dell'Africa ed Agramante medesimo dispera della sua vittoria. [p. 639]

With heavy irony Tasso recounts how the "faithful Ruggiero" went from being a public champion to being almost a "public traitor." He reprimands Ruggiero for "preferring his love to his honor" and underscores the self-serving aspect of Ruggiero's decision to abide by his oath to stop fighting Rinaldo if Agramante should intervene in the contest:

Ruggiero reconfirmed the oath, perhaps because the confirmation would make [Agramante's] error grow and thereby take away any excuse of obedience [on Ruggiero's part].

E Ruggiero di nuovo conferma il giuramento, forse perché la confirmazione accrescesse l'errore e togliesse ogni scusa d'ubbidienza. [p. 639]

Tasso then embarks on a vehement attack on perjury as the greatest sin against faith, concluding with the sweeping statement that if "oaths are broken, the world is ruined" ("rompendosi il giuramento, si guasterebbe il mondo" [p. 640]). Ruggiero is no longer merely an erring character, but represents a threat to the stability of the whole world. What seems to offend Tasso most is that Ruggiero repeated his perjury, sinning not once but "di novo":

[Ruggiero], being with his first oath freed from his obligation to be faithful to his king [that is, conditionally freed: if Agramante intervenes in the battle, Ruggiero may desert him], and being, with his second oath in fact freed of all obligation [Agramante having intervened, Ruggiero's duty to him is canceled altogether], he then—not by any obligation of faith, but rather by a vain opinion of constancy—breaks first the one and then the other oath, and the one and the other faith which was owed to God. And *again* he places before his God not his king, but, before his *true* God, someone who was no longer his true king, since he [Agramante] had with his oath ceded all reasons why he might have supremacy over Ruggiero.

Essendosi co'l primo giuramento disobligato della fede che aveva al suo re, e co'l secondo cancellato l'obligo affatto, non per obligo alcuno di fede, ma par una vana opinione di constanza, rompe l'uno e l'altro giuramento, e l'una a l'altra fede, che era dovuta a Dio. E *di novo* prepone non il suo re al suo Dio, ma al suo vero Dio quello che non era più suo vero re, perché co'l giuramento aveva ceduto ogni ragione ch'egli potesse aver sopra Ruggiero. [pp. 640–41; my emphasis]

Tasso is like a serious fly caught in the sticky comedy Ariosto's text creates.

For the episode Tasso criticizes is, in fact, a stunning satire on the very notion of faith; this satire focuses on the bankruptcy, in both the religious and the political spheres, of the feudal concept of a faith which governs the relation between lord and vassal. Ruggiero and Rinaldo, who have both sworn oaths of allegiance to their respective lords, are now swearing an oath to break their prior oath if either lord should exercise his right—guaranteed in the original oath—to control his vassal's action in any way. Although the vassals are to fight only to serve their respective kings' interests (Ruggiero indeed against his will, since by fighting Rinaldo, who is Bradamante's brother, he offends his betrothed), their new oaths in effect cancel the first ones by guaranteeing the vassals their right to act independently. Ariosto's satire illuminates several of the issues Machiavelli discusses in *Il Principe*, notably in the famous eighteenth chapter, "How Princes Should Keep Faith" ("Quomodo fides a princibus sit servanda"). Like Machiavelli, Ariosto examines the gap between the ideal ("How praiseworthy it is for a prince to maintain his faith and live by honesty and not deceit, everyone knows") and the reality of sixteenth-century Italian politics ("Nevertheless we see, by what goes on in our own times, that those princes who have accomplished great things are the ones who have cared little for keeping faith, . . . in the end they won out over those who founded themselves on loyalty").[31]

Ariosto looks with particular shrewdness at the vexed relation between small Italian princes—represented, I think, by Ruggiero and Rinaldo—and the larger powers who claimed to control them. France and Spain, which vied throughout the sixteenth century for domination of Italian territory, stand in relation to principalities like Ferrara and Florence as Agramante and Charlemagne do to their vassals Ruggiero and Rinaldo. By stressing the vassals' potential to break free of their duty to their kings (a duty that in Ruggiero's case is clearly onerous), Ariosto points to the common Italian longing for independence from imperial domination. Ariosto does not, however, suggest that the political motives of the imperial rulers are either better or worse than those of their vassals; his satire does not appear to contain covert prescriptions for political action but rather exposes contradictions that characterized contemporary Italian politics. Mocking the empty ceremonials of sixteenth-century peace treaties, he also glances wryly at the gap between what is promised in the grandiose rhetoric of political oaths and what can be delivered by mortal men in a world where religious and secular aims are confusingly intertwined. At the end of canto 38 (stanzas 81–86), he shows Charlemagne and Agramante each swearing on his respective holy book an oath that conflicts, in a fundamental way, with the fealty these two servants of religious causes owe their Gods. The kings promise, in the event that their champions should lose the battle about to be fought, to pay tribute to the opposing sovereign and, moreover, to enter immediately into a "perpetual" truce. The word "perpetual," which is repeated, highlights the kings' unexamined belief that they have a God-like power to control the future.[32] Events rapidly prove them wrong, since the battle does not result in a clear victory for either side. Like the language of the oaths, which oscillates between sacred hyperbole and secular litotes (the amount of tribute "perpetually" promised is a paltry twenty measures of gold), the plot of Ariosto's poem calls into question the very notions of absolute faith and the unbreakable promise.

Tasso's attack on Ariosto's Ruggiero is an anxious effort to defend the feudal notion of loyalty that Ariosto considered an anachronistic though beautiful fiction. Tasso's own doubts about the ideal of absolute loyalty, in both the political and the personal realms, contribute to the vehemence with which he defends the ideal: "An oath," he asserts, "must be observed inviolably" (p. 640). He doth protest too much, one suspects; and the protest works as a rationalization or payment to conscience, at once revealing and assuaging Tasso's anxiety about the circumstances that prevent him from obeying such a rigid and simplistic moral imperative. His rhetorical procedure here follows the same pattern we observed earlier in the treatise when, after insisting that he could not bear that anyone should be placed before his father, he began to qualify that absolute position. Here, after insisting that oaths must be observed inviolably, he begins to comment on passages in Ariosto's poem that show why some kinds of oaths are perhaps honored better in the breach than in the observance. He focuses, as we might expect, on passages where Ariosto shows Ruggiero trapped—as Tasso himself is—in situations of rivalry where his self-interest conflicts with some abstract notion of moral duty. His focus is influenced by Cicero's *De officiis*, which discusses such situations of conflict from a perspective considerably more complicated than that implied by Tasso's initial statement about the inviolability of oaths.[33] As we look at Tasso's treatment of Ruggiero's moral dilemma, we should keep in mind Cicero's remark about Ennius's lines: "Núlla sancta sócietas / Néc fides regni ést" ("There is no fellowship inviolate, / No faith is kept, when kingship is concerned"). Cicero writes that "the truth of [Ennius's] words has an uncommonly wide application. For whenever a situation is of such a nature that not more than one can hold preeminence in it, competition for it usually becomes so keen that it is an extremely difficult matter to maintain a 'fellowship inviolate.'"[34] Ennius's lines and Cicero's gloss illuminate two aspects of Tasso's situation that made it hard for him to determine, much less perform, his ethical duty: his involvement in a literary struggle for kingship which pitted him against his father and Ariosto, and his continuing imaginative involvement in the primal competition that pits fathers against sons in the family romance.

The one passage from Ariosto's *Orlando Furioso* that Tasso actually quotes in the first part of the *Apologia* depicts a complex triangular relation between a son, his father, and a hero—Ruggiero—who is admired and feared both by the father and the son; the son, moreover, wants to marry the lady to whom Ruggiero is betrothed. The quotation occurs when Tasso has shifted his critical attention from Ruggiero's duel with Rinaldo to an episode in canto 45. There Ruggiero, having fled from all service in the war between pagans and Christians, and having been shipwrecked on an island where he is baptized a Christian by a hermit who then urges him to marry Bradamante, encounters the man who has in the meantime gained Bradamante's parents' consent to marry her. That man is Leone, a Greek prince, and Ruggiero intends to kill him. Instead, Leone rescues Ruggiero from a dungeon where he has been condemned to die by Leone's father. Ruggiero is now in a situation of having to choose between his duty to Bradamante and his new obligation to his savior Leone, who asks him to pay his debt by taking Leone's place in a battle to win Bradamante's hand. Ruggiero accedes to Leone's request, and thereby incurs Tasso's disapproval; Tasso feels that Ruggiero's obligations to Bradamante were not only qualitatively greater than but temporally prior to his obligations to Leone:

> And [his obligations to Bradamante] were not only greater, but prior; and the prior should take from the later almost all force; therefore, for the one and the other reason Ruggiero should have put love of Bradamante before friendship of Leone.

> E non solo erano maggiori, ma primi; e i primi sogliono togliere a gli ultimi quasi ogni forza: dunque, per l'una e per l'altra cagione l'amor di Bradamante doveva essere preposto da Ruggiero a l'amicizia di Leone. [p. 641]

When he has once again invoked those notions of "the greater" and "the prior" which are so important in defining his own relation to both Bernardo and Ariosto, Tasso quotes Ariosto's description of Leone's and his father's first view of Ruggiero, a description that shows their sentiments of admiration and friendship (they have just seen Ruggiero's prowess in battle) to be motivated by self-interest: the friendship of Leone, Tasso writes, was based on a "regard for utility and his own reputation, as may be gathered from the verses of the poet"; Tasso proceeds to cite these lines from *Orlando Furioso* (45. 14):

> Non ha minor cagion di rallegrarsi
> del padre il figlio, ch'oltre che si spera . . .
> disegna anco il guerriero amico farsi
> con benefici, e seco averlo in schiera;
> né Rinaldo né Orlando a Carlo Magno
> ha da invidiar, se gli è costui compagno.

The son had no less cause to rejoice than the father: besides hoping [to capture more lands through Ruggiero's help; Tasso omits this line], he also proposed to

win the warrior's friendship by kindness, and to enlist his support. With a
comrade such as this, he would have no cause to envy Charlemagne for Rinaldo
and Orlando.[35]

Tasso reads this passage, perhaps half-consciously, as a polyvalent allegory; it serves as a cracked mirror in which he can see aspects of his own
peculiar relation to both his father and Ariosto while at the same time
criticizing what he feels to be "base motives" in all three of Ariosto's
characters and—by implication—in himself, his father, and Ariosto as well.
Tasso's relation to Ariosto is tainted in the same way Leone's relation to
Ruggiero is. A weaker character seeks to use a stronger one for his own
selfish aims, which include the desire for more "territory" (mentioned in the
important line Tasso drops from the quotation), as well as for a lady. In
addition, there is a structural parallel between Bernardo and Leone's father,
if Ruggiero is taken as a figure for Ariosto. By focusing on a father's and son's
apparently friendly but really antagonistic relation to a hero, Tasso exposes
competitive motives which elsewhere he denies. A few pages before the
quotation, for example, he writes that he is reluctant to engage in the
rhetorical game of comparing Ariosto to his father, since he knows that
Bernardo was "a friend, while he lived, to Ariosto; and contests between
friends, if indeed they are allowed at all, should be very different from those
among enemies" ("E so che mio padre fu amico, mentre visse, a l'Ariosto; e
le contese fra gli amici, se pur sono mai lecite, debbono esser molto diverse
da quelle che si fanno tra' nimici" [p. 637]). Only through the screen of
Ariosto's fiction, it seems, can Tasso approach the demystified truth about
his and his father's "friendship" for Ariosto.

If Tasso finds a partial image for himself in Leone, he also sees himself in
the character of Ruggiero, who must choose among his various obligations,
and who is the legitimate dynastic hero of Ariosto's poem. Insofar as Tasso
views Ariosto as a usurper, a Claudius figure whose "nuova gloria" threatens
the Tasso family, Ariosto is like Leone, who threatens the Estense line of
princes which is to be founded by Ruggiero.[36] According to this reading—
which entails a specular reversal of the allegorical identifications suggested
above—Ruggiero would represent Tasso, or, perhaps, Bernardo. (As Shakespeare shows in Henry 4, Part 1, father and sons may forget their own rivalry
to act as one when confronted with an outside challenge to a shaky dynastic
claim.) What is most interesting about Tasso's choice of an allegorically overdetermined quotation from Ariosto's poem is that it illustrates a triangular
relation of rivalry in which replacement is not only a theme but a necessary
act of interpretation.

Ruggiero's positions as Tasso describes them—between Brandamante and
Agramante, between Agramante and Charlemagne, between Leone and
Leone's father, or between a duty to Leone and a duty to Bradamante—

superimpose so many dilemmas of choice on each other that Tasso's critical narrative comes to resemble Ariostean romance, with its capacity for "an almost infinite lateral extension of its narrative material." Andrew Fichter uses that phrase to describe a formal characteristic of Ariosto's poem which Tasso rightly saw as a sign of metaphysical relativism: because *Orlando Furioso* "lacks an internal logic of causality or a sense of finite shape," Fichter writes, "it obeys neither esthetic rules for beauty nor natural laws governing organic form. . . . It denies, then, the premise on which Tasso erects his own mimetic theory [and which he attempts to illustrate in the structure of his epic, one might add], the idea that art should reflect the order inherent in nature."[37] The *Apologia*, however, points to Tasso's doubts about that premise; indeed the text invites us to see Tasso's vehement criticisms of Ariosto's aleatory plot as a defense against his own experiences in what seemed like an all too aleatory universe.

Tasso counters the metaphysical relativism reflected in Ariosto's plot by invoking the idea of a vertical hierarchy of values, a Neoplatonic ladder which provides an escape from insoluble ethical dilemmas. Summing up his objections to Ariosto's portrait of Ruggiero, the hero who, in addition to all his other errors, puts his duty to his "seeming" friend Leone before his duty to his lady, Tasso writes:

> In this manner all debts [were] forgotten, and all duties were perturbed in the person of Ruggiero: for we are first obligated to God; then to the king; in the third place to the wife or to the beloved who loves chastely; in the fourth place, to the friend whose goal is utility and ambition. Nevertheless Ruggiero put the ambitious Greek [friend] before the faithful wife; and the wife, who was not yet a wife, before the king, who was his king; and the king, who was not his [true] king, before his God, who was the God of the first Ruggiero, the second Ruggiero and the third Ruggiero.

> In questa maniera tutti i debiti dimenticati, e tutti gli uffici furono perturbati nella persona di Ruggiero: perciò che prima siamo obligati a Dio; poi al re; nel terzo luogo a la moglie o a l'amante che ama di casto amore; nel quarto, a l'amico che ha per fine l'utilità e l'ambizion. Nondimeno Ruggiero prepone l'ambizioso greco a la moglie fidele; e la moglie, che non era ancor moglie, al re, che era suo re; e il re, che non era suo re, al suo Dio, che fu il Dio di Ruggier primo, di Ruggier secondo e di Ruggier terzo. [p. 642]

This is a remarkable piece of rhetoric. The abstract statement of a hierarchy of moral imperatives stands like a tower between two descriptions of Ruggiero's failure to perceive his moral duty. The second of these descriptions, however, is so powerful in its repetitive phrasing and its tracing of the "nonbeing" of each successive recipient of duty (the wife not yet a wife, the king not a true king) that we are left with a sense of the impossibility of behavior that accords with the ideal hierarchy. As if in recognition of the

threat that his very description of Ariosto's narrative series poses to his ideal
of a hierarchy, Tasso attempts, in his concluding clause, to combine the two
concepts—of hierarchy and narrative series—by invoking a God who is not
only at the top of the hierarchy but also the governor of a temporal progression ("di Ruggier primo, di Ruggier secondo e di Ruggier terzo"). One
nevertheless feels that the kind of temporal series Tasso here envisions, with
its God's eye view of human time, does not fully resolve the problem of
representing a hero behaving virtuously in a narrative situation of conflicting
duties. In his epic, as we shall see, Tasso thematizes this problem in the story
of Tancredi, a hero who fails, as Ruggiero does, to distinguish between
higher and lower claims on his loyalty. If we turn now to the biography of
Tasso's father, and then to Tasso's efforts to interpret it, we can see more
clearly why he was haunted by Ariosto's portrait of a hero in whom "all
duties" were "perturbed" not once but repeatedly.

The Journey to the Past: Bernardo Tasso and the Neapolitan Rebellion

*Every past is worth condemning; this is the rule in mortal affairs, which always
contain a large measure of human power and human weakness. It is not justice
that sits in judgment here, nor mercy that proclaims the verdict, but only life, the
dim driving force that insatiably desires—itself.*—Nietzsche, *The Use and
Abuse of History*

Bernardo Tasso came from a family whose only claim to fame was its role in
organizing a postal service for the empire of Charles V.[38] There is a symbolic
irony in this fact, since both Bernardo and his son were men of letters who
served also as courtiers—and literally as couriers—in a world where communication among princes was rarely straightforward and where neither the
elder nor the younger Tasso possessed the tact necessary to perform his
political duties successfully.[39] Bernardo's career was marked by repeated
shifts of political allegiance caused not only by the breakdown of the feudal
relation between servant and master in sixteenth-century Italian courts but
also by the fact that Bernardo's chief patron, the Prince of Salerno, himself
changed his political allegiance. Bernardo became secretary to Ferrante
Sanseverino, Prince of Salerno, in 1532, after several years in the service of
Princess Renée of France. Renée, a Protestant sympathizer, had married
Duke Ercole d'Este of Ferrara. When Bernardo left Renée for Sanseverino,
he shifted from the French to the imperial cause, since Sanseverino fought
for his relative Charles V in the war against François I.[40] Edward Williamson
remarks that there is no indication that the change of political allegiance
perturbed Bernardo; but there is no doubt that it contributed to Torquato's
obsession with "perturbations of duty."[41] So, as we shall see, did Bernardo's
treatment of his wife, Porzia de Rossi, whom he married in 1536.

Bernardo's marriage was shadowed from the start by an economic problem that affected Tasso's life enormously: Porzia's brothers would not release the 5,000 ducats they had promised as a dowry. Bernardo began a lawsuit to acquire the money, which he needed desperately to lessen his dependence on court patronage. The suit, like the one in Dickens's *Bleak House*, dragged on interminably; Torquato continued to pursue it after his father's death in 1569.[42] Like his father, indeed, Tasso hoped the suit would bring him the means "to live comfortably without being dependent on anyone."[43] His lifelong involvement in this legal proceeding, and the impetus it gave him for associating his memories of his mother with hopes for an extremely earthly kind of bliss, underlie his literary portraits of himself as an injured defendant and his fictions about heavenly visions of richly adorned ladies.

Tasso was born in 1544, soon after an elder brother, also named Torquato, had died.[44] This fact is important for his family romance stories, particularly for his view of Ariosto as an elder brother and for his figurative description of his revised epic as a "second-born" child, superior to the first; I will return to it later. Another fact that shaped his fictions was his father's absence from Naples during the first year of Tasso's life. We can only speculate on how Bernardo's return disrupted Tasso's repose in a place very like the "nest" described in *Gerusalemme Liberata* (canto 12, stanza 90)—a nest from which "i figli non pennuti" ("the unfeathered children") are cruelly stolen, leaving the mother bird to weep.[45] Tasso tells us explicitly, however, that Bernardo caused his wife and son grief a few years later. The events which led to Tasso's being literally taken from his mother's breast (the phrasing is his) began in 1547, when the emperor's viceroy, Don Pedro Toledo, attempted to establish the Spanish Inquisition in Naples.[46] This provoked a rebellion of both nobles and commoners, who resisted the viceroy's authority as they had once before, in 1510—and as they would again in the even more violent insurrection which took place in May 1585, a few months before Tasso published the *Apologia*.[47]

The Neapolitan rebellion colored Tasso's imaginative life and ideological formation in a way that critics have not begun to appreciate. Not only did Bernardo's role in the drama lead Tasso in later life to defend his father, albeit ambivalently, and to brood on the justice of the Neapolitan cause against the representatives of imperial authority. The plot of the "Neapolitan story" probably influenced Tasso's choice of his epic subject matter and certainly influenced his interpretation of that historical narrative, the eleventh-century crusade which Godfrey of Boulogne led to conquer Jerusalem.[48] Tasso's epic is about a fundamental conflict between a city inhabited largely by pagans and the Christian forces which aim to "liberate" that city from its spiritual error. There are obviously parallels between the defenders of Jerusalem in Tasso's poem, who resist Goffredo's attempt to impose his secular and religious authority on them, and the Neapolitans, who resisted the attempt of Charles V and his viceroy to procure uniformity of belief (and revenue) through establishing a Spanish Inquisition. The parallels between the Neapolitan story and the one told in *Gerusalemme Liberata* invite us to question the dominant critical view of Tasso as a spokesman for Counter-Reformation ideology. If, as Thomas Greene suggests, Tasso's poem makes us "feel the plight of the besieged much more acutely than the necessity of besieging them," may we not surmise that Tasso doubted whether sieges were, in fact, necessary?[49] By following the trial of imperial authority which Tasso implicitly conducts in his writings on the Neapolitan rebellion—a trial in which he plays the roles of both prosecutor and defense lawyer—we can come to a better understanding of the complex political issues addressed in his epic.

Gerusalemme Liberata is no less informed by its author's interpretation of recent Italian history than *Paradise Lost* is by Milton's interpretation of recent English history. And even though Tasso may look, at first, like a Catholic conservative in contrast to Milton, the Protestant revolutionary, the labels, like the contrast, prove to be crude on closer inspection.[50] In Tasso's prose and poetry, as in Milton's, there is a complex dialectical labor of political thought, shaped by the author's experience of contradictions in the material of history and by his reading of previous texts. The *Aeneid* in particular is important for Tasso, for in its depiction of the battle between Aeneas's forces and the native inhabitants of Italy he found a model not only for the conflict between the Neapolitans and Charles V, and that between the inhabitants of Jerusalem and Goffredo; he also found a model for an authorial perspective which is deeply sympathetic to the values of those characters in the poem who resist the hero and the officially sanctioned values he embodies.[51]

In the Neapolitan rebellion, Bernardo Tasso and his patron Sanseverino opposed the policies of Charles V and his viceroy in a way that forced Tasso later to explain and justify the father he could not help seeing as a son rebelling against the emperor's paternal authority. The Neapolitan nobles had traditionally resisted the establishment of an Inquisition that would decrease the power of the Italian pope and increase that of a foreign monarch; the nobles' class interests depended on a balance of power between the papacy and the crown.[52] In 1547, the nobles' interests happened to coincide with those of the commoners, who had been suffering since the 1520s from the increasing divergence between prices and real wages, and who hated the viceroy and the taxes he imposed.[53] But the nobles were almost as troubled by what one historian calls "the germs of an autonomous popular movement" as they were by the viceroy.[54] Nevertheless, when the commoners tore up an edict announcing the establishment of an Inquisitorial Office, the nobles, according to Luigi Amabile, "showed themselves united with the people, giving them their hands when they met in the street."[55] In the midst of this tense period—during which Spanish troops sporadically shelled the city from the fortress to which Don Pedro had retired—news came of Charles V's victory over the Elector of Saxony, which prompted the Neapolitans to hold a three-day celebration to show themselves *fedelissima* to the emperor; the news also prompted them to choose two ambassadors, one a noble, one a commoner, to go to Charles and protest the actions of his viceroy. Sanseverino, nominated for the noble ambassadorial post, was counseled by Bernardo Tasso to accept the call of patriotic duty. A Florentine named Vincenzo Martelli, the prince's majordomo, advised Sanseverino to refuse the post. The differing opinions of the two counselors are the subject of Tasso's dialogue *Il Gonzaga overo del piacere onesto*, which I shall discuss after concluding the story of the Neapolitan rebellion.

Sanseverino ultimately accepted Bernardo's advice. By taking the ambassadorial post, however, he became, in the emperor's eyes as well as the viceroy's, a leader of a seditious cause. Charles V showed his displeasure by refusing to grant Sanseverino an audience; the prince waited for months at the imperial court in Augsburg, where Bernardo joined him in September.[56] The following spring, Sanseverino managed not to accomplish his original mission but rather to gain a pardon (which cost 10,000 ducats) for the Neapolitan rebels. Soon after returning to his city, however, he was hit by a bullet and, with much justification, attributed the attack to the viceroy.[57] He left Naples, possibly intending, as Bernardo evidently believed, to return to Augsburg to make an appeal for redress to the emperor. In fact, however, he went to France, and in 1552 a rumor reached Naples that he was about to attack the city with French and Turkish aid.[58] The rumor was false, but it shows that Shakespeare did not need to look only to Plutarch's Italy to find models for the kind of political career he depicts in *Coriolanus*.

Upon hearing of Sanseverino's traitorous shift of allegiance, the viceroy confiscated his estates and sentenced him to death, along with "whoever had been an author and accomplice of his rebellion."[59] Bernardo was thus named a traitor and fled to France. C. P. Brand remarks on the ambiguity of his motives: Was he honorably performing his duty to follow his patron, as he and Tasso later insisted? Or did he go to Paris because "he believed that an imminent French invasion would more than compensate for his temporary losses?"[60] Among those losses were not only his house at Salerno but his wife and children, who were left in the hands of the brothers who had refused to pay Porzia's dowry. Torquato had ample reason, therefore, to see in Ariosto's Ruggiero an image of the father who erroneously placed his duty to a false prince above his duty to his wife.

After some time in Paris, during which he wrote poems encouraging the French to invade the Kingdom of Naples (they did not, Henri II then being busy defending his own frontiers against Spain), Bernardo returned to Italy—not to Naples, where his family was in dire straits, but to Rome. Unable to arrange for his wife to leave Naples without losing the claims to her dowry, Bernardo sent for Torquato. His wife and daughter went to a convent and Tasso, at nine, was separated—as it turned out, forever—from his mother; she died two years later, possibly poisoned by her brothers. Donald Sutherland speculates that Tasso's loss of his mother, and his suspicions that she was poisoned, provide a key to understanding the psychic malady which caused Tasso to be imprisoned in Sant'Anna, and which was certainly worsened by the experience of imprisonment itself; his paranoid tendencies (including fear of poison) grew in prison and his alternations between manic and depressive states became more extreme.[61] Sutherland's hypothesis is supported by a poem he does not discuss, an autobiographical canzone entitled "O del grand'Apennino." In that unfinished poem, written in Urbino nine years after Bernardo's death in 1569, Tasso represents the traumatic moment of separation from his mother; he also obliquely accuses his father of causing the separation, before anxiously addressing his father's ghost in the poem's strange final lines.

The canzone shows Tasso returning in memory to a moment of Oedipal crisis, and it illuminates the biographical matrix of his critical theories about the relation between romance and epic. He associates the genre of romance itself, it would seem, with a fantasized image of his mother's body, conflated with mythologized images of the Neapolitan landscape in which he spent his early years. The darkly maternal *genius loci* of Naples—legendary home of the Sirens—haunted Tasso as the memory of his mother did after he was taken by his father to Rome. His father, whom he compares appropriately but with deep ambivalence to Rome's founder Aeneas, caused him to enter a "bitter exile." Instead of interpreting that experience as a necessary although painful stage of an epic career—as Aeneas's exile from Troy and later from Dido's Carthage was—Tasso stresses only the waste of his life and powers during the time of exile. His poem is about a loss so great that nothing can compensate for it.

Tasso introduces the subject of loss by alluding to the Siren Parthenope, who was, according to legend, born near the Bay of Naples and who drowned herself there when she failed to capture Odysseus with her song:

> Sassel la gloriosa alma sirena,
> appresso il cui sepolcro ebbi la cuna.

> The glorious and propitious siren, near whose cradle I was born, knows [my sufferings].[62]

The siren is a mythological analogue for Tasso's mother, who also resembles Virgil's Creusa and Dido—and Tasso's Clorinda—in being a woman deserted, and indirectly killed, by a man on an epic quest. The epic hero, for Tasso, is always in some sense guilty of murdering Eros; in this poem Tasso returns, as Tancredi does in the bleeding tree episode of *Gerusalemme Liberata*, to the scene of the crime, the haunted romance landscape in which the cradle and the sepulchre lie side by side. After comparing his own unfortunate fate to Parthenope's, he laments the fact that he, unlike Parthenope, did not find a peaceful tomb in his native place after Fortune's first blow.[63] He then explains, however, how "impious fortune" prevented him from taking refuge in a tomb—or, we may fairly say, a womb:

Me dal sen de la madre empia fortuna
pargoletto divelse. Ah! di quei baci,
ch'ella bagnò di lagrime dolenti,
con sospir mi rimembra e de gli ardenti
preghi che se 'n portar l'aure fugaci:
ch'io non dovea giunger più volto a volto
fra quelle braccia accolto
con nodi così stretti e sì tenaci.
Lasso! e seguii con mal sicure piante
qual Ascanio o Camilla, il padre errante.
   In aspro esiglio e 'n dura
povertà crebbi in quei sì mesti errori.

                                        [Lines 31–42]

Impious fortune uprooted me, a child, from the breast of the mother. Ah, I remember with sighs those kisses which she bathed with grieving tears, and those ardent prayers, which the fleeting breezes carried from her; for I am no longer able to reach her face to face, held between those arms with knots so tight and secure. Alas! and I, like Camilla or Ascanius, followed the erring father with insecure steps. In bitter exile and in hard poverty I grew in those grievous wanderings.

   It is significant that Tasso compares himself both to Aeneas's son Ascanius and to Camilla, the warrior maiden who is the Virgilian prototype of Ariosto's Bradamante and of Tasso's own Clorinda. The obvious point of the comparison is that Camilla's father threw her across a stream tied to a spear as he was fleeing into exile; Camilla, like Ascanius and also like Tasso, underwent a violent separation from her mother and birthplace. Tasso's double comparison becomes more interesting, however, when we recall that Camilla's father was a hated tyrant driven from his realm and that Camilla herself fought valiantly to prevent Aeneas's Trojan forces from winning Italy.[64] In its darker implications, Tasso's comparison serves to underscore Tasso's ambivalence toward his father and his awareness of his symbolic position as his father's enemy or rival as well as his dutiful son. Tasso's poem offers us, indeed, an astonishing retrospective view of a child's ambivalent identification with both his mother and his father at a moment when external circumstances created an unusually literal version of the experience Freud says every boy undergoes:

> Along with the demolition of the Oedipus complex, the boy's object-cathexis of his mother must be given up. Its place may be filled by one of two things: either an identification with his mother or an intensification of his identification with his father. We are accustomed to regard the latter outcome as the more normal; it permits the affectionate relation to the mother to be in some measure retained. In this way the dissolution of the Oedipus complex would consolidate the masculinity in a boy's character. [*The Ego and the Id, SE* 19: 32]

Tasso's development seems to have taken the former course, which resulted in a continuing and conflicted identification with both the female and the male parent. For Tasso, in fact, there was no real "dissolution" of the Oedipal crisis, much less a "normal outcome" of it. In his writing he returns repeatedly to the knot of love, hate, and guilt which was tied in his early years and which was only tightened by his father's death. Indeed Tasso's amazing apostrophe to his father's ghost at the end of the poem suggests that the grown man's grief at the second loss of a parent was deeply tainted by guilt; we may fairly speculate that the guilt derived in part from Tasso's obscure knowledge that he had never unequivocally loved his "erring" father and had consequently performed his filial duty adequately neither during Bernardo's life nor after his death. The final lines of the poem contain an ominous suggestion that Bernardo's ghost—a composite of the earthly father and a heavenly, judging deity—is watching Tasso disapprovingly, as, according to Freud, the superego "observes, directs and threatens the ego".[65]

Padre, o buon padre, che dal ciel rimiri,
egro e morto ti piansi, e ben tu il sai,
e gemendo scaldai
la tomba e il letto: or che ne gli alti giri
tu godi, a te si deve onor, non lutto:
a me versato il mio dolor sia tutto . . .
                    [Non finita]

Father, oh good father, who gazes down from the sky,
I wept for you ill and dead, and well you know it,
And moaning [with tears] I warmed
the tomb and the deathbed: now that
you rejoice in the high circles [of heaven],
to you is owed honor, not grief:
Let it be enough for me to have poured out all my grief . . .
                    [Unfinished]

No wonder Tasso couldn't finish this poem. The effort to transform the raw material of memory and psychic ambivalence into art is reflected in the extraordinarily baroque conceits and the difficult syntax. The effort does not result in aesthetic closure but it does produce a powerful autobiographical gloss on the scene in *Gerusalemmme Liberata*, infused with sexual and sepulchral taboos, where Tancredi violates a "secreta sede." The act of violence Tancredi performs when he strikes the tree in canto 13 is, I think, a version of that transgression Tasso associates with all memorial returns to the "secret seat" of family history. Before striking the tree, Tancredi reads hieroglyphic words inscribed on its bark which warn the passerby not to disturb or make war on the dead ("non dee guerra co' morti aver chi vive").[66] Tancredi disregards the warning, and so, I think, did Tasso, not only when he raked up the embers of his past in the "Apennino" canzone, but also when he wrote a series of texts ostensibly devoted to defending Bernardo's honor ("to you is owed honor not grief") but which in fact record his own continuing battle with the father for whom he could not grieve enough. In the *Apologia*, as well as in other prose works written during the decade between the unauthorized publication of *Gerusalemme Liberata* (1581) and the publication of the greatly revised version of his epic, entitled *Gerusalemme Conquistata* (1591), Tasso obsessively returns to his family history; seeking, like Oedipus, to understand the mystery of his own origins, he in effect retraces the steps his father took on his journey away from Naples into the "bitter exile" he shared with his son. Tasso's own path leads back to the "secret seat" of Naples, that place where cradle and grave lie side by side. Insofar as the journey requires Tasso to adopt a critical perspective on his father, it generates guilt; but it also serves to mitigate guilt by assigning some portion of it to Bernardo himself.

Tasso counters the sense of sacrilege that attends his inquiry into Bernardo's "conduct of life" by using literature—or, more precisely, methods of reading and writing—to create defensive shields. The critical commentary on Ruggiero in the *Apologia* constitutes one such shield; we can now appreciate how strikingly Ruggiero's behavior, as Tasso disapprovingly describes it, resembles Bernardo's: Ruggiero deserts his lady to serve a false prince who is warring against Charlemagne, a true king and servant of God; Bernardo deserted his wife to follow Sanseverino, a prince condemned as a traitor by the Holy Roman Emperor Charles V. Tasso can openly reprimand Ariosto's hero for repeatedly displaying a confused sense of moral duty; he can reprimand Bernardo only indirectly. But the motives for criticism are obvious, and we shall see them in more detail when we turn shortly to examine the works in which Tasso analyzes his father's role in the Neapolitan rebellion. One example of a justification that reads like an accusation should suffice to give the flavor of Tasso's rhetoric of defense:

Thus my father did not lack prudence, but rather fortune, because, in following
the fortune of his patron [Sanseverino], he manifested his faith, with the loss of
all his property, with which he could have honorably nourished his children.

Dunque non mancò la prudenza a mio padre, ma la fortuna; perciocchè egli
seguendo quella del padrone, manifestò la sua fede, colla perdita di tutte le
sostanze, colle quali poteva onorevolmente nutrire i figliuoli.[67]

This quotation is from the reply (hereafter referred to as the *Risposta*)
which Tasso wrote in 1585 to a Cruscan attack on his dialogue *Il Gonzaga,
overo del piacere onesto*.[68] The *Risposta* is really a defense of a defense,
since the *Del piacere onesto* dialogue (first published in 1583) attempts to
justify Bernardo's political and personal conduct at the time of the Neapolitan rebellion. The *Risposta* introduces the second shield Tasso employs in
his journey to the past, a journey we may consider a kind of trial in both
senses of the word, an ordeal and an inquiry into questions of guilt and
innocence. If the first shield involves a technique of reading that allows
criticism to be expressed in displaced form, the second involves a technique
of writing: the dialogue form itself, which allows conflicting opinions to
emerge without the author's having to take direct responsibility for any of
them. This form is especially useful if one seeks to prosecute—or, as Tasso
says, to "calumniate"—someone without seeming to do so. Tasso's comments on the dialogue form in the *Risposta* (and also in his short treatise
L'Arte del dialogo) invite us to see dialogue itself as a defensive weapon in
the hands of an author who is attempting to interpret the past critically but
without giving offense to the living or the dead.[69] In the *Risposta* he explains
his purpose:

And I have tried to renew memory, and I have renewed it not as an historian, but
as a writer of dialogue, who cannot make calumnies because he does not profess
to narrate the truth in all things; but obliges himself rather to the verisimilar than
to verity.

Ed io ho cercato di rinnovare la memoria, e l'ho rinnovato non come storico, ma
come scrittore del Dialogo, il quale non può calunniare, perchè non fa professione di narrar in tutte le cose la verità; ma piuttosto s'obbliga al verisimile che al
vero. [*Opere colle controversie*, 10: 151]

Although the first part of the *Apologia* is not formally cast as a dialogue (as
we shall see, Tasso adopts a dialogic persona only at the moment when he
turns from defending his father to defending his own poem), Tasso alludes
to prior texts—the critical pamphlets by Pellegrino and the Cruscans as well
as Bernardo's and Ariosto's poems—in a way that anticipates his use of
multiple voices in the later part of the treatise. If, as V. N. Voloshinov argues
in his study of dialogic discourse, certain uses of "reported speech" serve to
call into question the author's "ownership" of his words, for Tasso there was

much to be gained by relinquishing proprietary rights to opinions expressed in his text.[70] Improper or indecorous views can be at once articulated and condemned—such as, for example, the negative judgments about Bernardo's originality which Tasso quotes at length from the Cruscan pamphlet. Tasso refutes the criticisms—but with arguments so weak that one cannot help feeling that his sympathies are largely with his father's detractors.[71]

Dialogic discourse plays an important role in Tasso's struggle to define his perspective on his father. In both the *Apologia* and the *Del piacere onesto* dialogue, he manipulates multiple voices in a way that illustrates the punning definition of dialogue offered in the second part of the *Apologia*, when the speaker who represents Tasso says to a friendly interlocutor that "between us there is highest concord, because both of us have wished that sentiment should *give place* to reason" ("fra noi è stata somma concordia, perché l'uno e l'altro ha voluto che l'affetto *dia luogo* a la ragione" [p. 710; my emphasis]). In Tasso's textual dialogues with—and about—his father, sentiment does eventually "give place" to reason, when reason is defined in terms of Tasso's judgment that Bernardo erred in his life and in his writing and may therefore be legitimately corrected, and superseded, by his son.[72]

The first part of the *Apologia* moves from a vehement assertion of the son's duty to the father, through a middle stage of oblique criticisms of the father's poem that are intimately linked with Tasso's mixed feelings about his father's performance as a politician and as a *pater familias*, to an extraordinary final passage in which Tasso takes his father's place as a poet—but not without assuring the reader that Bernardo's ghost approves of the son's rise to supremacy. I shall defer consideration of this usurpation scene, which deserves to be read as genuine, if temporary, synthesis in a dialectical process, until I have analyzed the *Del piacere onesto* dialogue, which illuminates the issues at stake in the *Apologia*. Tasso originally wrote this dialogue in 1580; he revised it, under the title *Il Nifo overo del piacere*, both in 1582 and in 1587.[73] In May of 1585, two months before the *Apologia* was published and in the very month of a new Neapolitan insurrection, Bastiano de Rossi, a member of the Accademia della Crusca, venomously attacked the first version of the dialogue, taking issue in particular with the contrast drawn therein between Bernardo and the Florentine Martelli, who had counseled Sanseverino not to become a spokesman for the Neapolitan nobles in 1547.[74] Had the Cruscan critic not been blinded by Florentine patriotism, however, he would have seen that Tasso does not really insult Martelli in his dialogue—or, at least, he insults Martelli no more than he insults his father.

One of the many ironies that surrounds Tasso's participation in this critical war is that he was constantly accused of holding views that were gross oversimplifications of his actual positions; but, of course, he invited misinterpretation by using defensive modes of rhetorical indirection. There was a perverse dynamic of sadomasochism underlying Tasso's relation to the Cruscans in the battles of 1585; Tasso himself seems to have felt that he was trapped in a situation governed by irrational rules of repetition. Every time he attempted to defend his father—an enterprise which itself involved a repetition of past events—he provoked offense. In the *Risposta* he portrays himself as someone forced against his will into an "immortal war" (*Opere colle controversie*, 10: 141). It was a *guerra immortale* not only because the critics continually revived it, taking offense where Tasso says he had intended none, but also because the issue of dispute was a speech given by a man long dead. That speech, the one Bernardo made to Sanseverino at the time of the Neapolitan rebellion, bore an uncanny resemblance to Tasso's later written defenses: Bernardo, like his son, defended an ideal of honor; moreover, though his speech was intended to promote peace (or so Tasso maintains, as he insists on his own peaceful intentions), in fact it gave offense and generated further strife.[75] Tasso thus had ample reason to feel that he and his dead father were both fatefully trapped in a cycle of repetition.

He also had a great desire to escape from the conflict which imprisoned him. The strategy of escape he adopts both in the *Apologia* and in the *Del piacere onesto* dialogue involves returning to the past not to repeat it (or not only to repeat it) but to re-create it. Tasso's act of writing might, indeed, be considered in the light of the distinction Edward Bibring draws, in a 1943 paper, between a "repetitive tendency," on the one hand, and a "restitutive tendency," on the other. Attempting to clarify some of the problems posed by Freud's theory of the repetition compulsion, Bibring suggests that the phrase "repetitive tendency" be reserved for those unconscious modes of repetition that "preserve the traumatic situation" in a way truly "beyond the pleasure principle." The phrase "restitutive tendency," in contrast, should describe those operations whereby the ego attempts to "reestablish the pretraumatic situation." Among those various operations, Bibring writes, are "working-off mechanisms" that dissolve tension "gradually by changing the internal conditions which give rise to it."[76] While Bibring's concept of the "restitutive tendency" depends on a rather naive and optimistic view of the ego's powers over the id, his discussion is useful in that it reminds us that a work of art like Tasso's dialogue may perform a labor very similar to that performed in a psychoanalysis. In both, forms of repetition that are at least partly controlled by the conscious ego are used as weapons against the effects of trauma and repression. The weapons may well prove ineffectual, as Freud never ceased to admit, especially when he considered the weapon of repetition unique to the analytic situation, the transference.[77] But the battle, he felt, must nonetheless be waged—and *is* indeed waged by all of us in the work of mourning, whether or not it occurs within the special frame for repetition provided by a formal analysis or by a work of art. What makes

Tasso's dialogue so interesting is that it dramatizes similarities between the psychoanalytic task as Freud defined it and the quintessential Renaissance labor of digging in the past to bring buried truth to light. Like the psychoanalyst, Tasso necessarily transforms the material he sets out to discover or recover. But unlike many psychoanalysts, he forces us to consider this transformative process as a phenomenon that is profoundly affected by the political and economic circumstances that shape the individual's return to his past. Let us turn, now, to the *Del piacere onesto* dialogue, which sheds light on both the matter and the method of Tasso's *Apologia*.

The Transformation of Memory: The Del piacere onesto Dialogue

> *Full fathom five thy father lies;*
> *Of his bones are coral made;*
> *Those are pearls that were his eyes;*
> *Nothing of him that doth fade*
> *But doth suffer a sea change*
> *Into something rich and strange.*   —Shakespeare, *The Tempest*

In *Del piacere onesto* two interlocutors, the old Neapolitan philosopher Agostino Nifo and the young nobleman Cesare Gonzaga, retire to a seaside garden to have a friendly dialogue about another, less friendly, dialogue, one which exists, for the modern set of speakers, only in the form of written records. The old speeches are those given by Bernardo Tasso and Vincenzo Martelli when Sanseverino was deciding whether or not to accept the position of ambassador from the Neapolitans to Charles V. Agostino and Cesare discuss the relative merits of each speech, and in so doing they become Tasso's agents in the search he defines in the *Risposta* as a "renew-[ing] of memory." Tasso's inquiry into the past is actually based on the records of his father's and Martelli's speeches which the two men left in letters.[78] Tasso, however, took the liberty of revising the letters, and thereby incurred blame from Bastiano de Rossi, who accused him of deliberately falsifying the recorded truth and acting as if Martelli's actual words were "buried in the dark sepulchre of forgetfulness" (*Opere colle controversie*, 10: 153). In his reply to Rossi, Tasso defends himself against the charge of counterfeiting the truth by comparing his practice to Plato's in the *Phaedrus*. Plato "inscribed" into his dialogue speeches given (orally) by Socrates and Lysias, leaving ambiguous the degree to which his inscription was a new creation (p. 153). "In dialogues as in poetry," Tasso insists, "one does not necessarily seek the truth, but rather verisimilitude and decorum" ("Ne' dialoghi, come nelle poesie, non si ricerca necessariamente la verità, ma la verisimilitudine, e la convenevolezza" [p. 153]).

In his dialogue and in his defense of it Tasso offers a version of an argument that many Renaissance writers developed to establish their right to depart from the letter of various kinds of texts—historical, philosophical, and even scriptural. One might think of Luther's letter on translation, in which the man commonly viewed as the advocate of literalism defends his right to translate what Saint Paul meant rather than what the Vulgate says he said; and one might also think of Vasari's argument that Michelangelo's counterfeit of an ancient statue had more value than the original did.[79] Tasso's dialogic creation—which he justifies, paradoxically, by an appeal to the ancient authority of Plato—subtly rebels against the authority of past documents. He not only replaces those documents with his own version of the past, but insists that his version is superior to the original one; indeed Tasso tells his Florentine critics that they should be grateful to him rather than angry, since he has improved their countryman Martelli's reputation by changing the words of his speech:

> Nor did I falsify his opinion, because the falsifier of money, by mixing copper with silver, and silver with gold, makes [the money] worse; but I have improved [Martelli's] political arguments, by mixing them with arguments of philosophy, which are like purest gold.

> Nè falsifico il suo parere, perchè il falsificator delle monete, mescolando il rame coll'argento, e l'argento coll'oro, le fa peggiori; ma io ho fatte migliori le ragioni di Stato, mescolandovi quelle della Filosofia, che sono come oro purissimo. [*Opere colle controversie*, 10: 152]

As this high-minded metallurgical justification acknowledges, Tasso has indeed tampered with the literal evidence, and in fact his fictionalizing of Bernardo's and Martelli's accounts of their speeches is only the first step in the transmutation of the past accomplished by his dialogue as a whole. For Tasso's modern interlocutors, Agostino Nifo and Cesare Gonzaga, do not for long remain mere explicators or even judges of their predecessors' debate. On the contrary, they gradually expose errors in both Bernardo's and Martelli's arguments; their critical activity thus leads them to counterfeit an image of the past "as it ought to have been" for the image of the past "as it was." When the fiction created by the moral imagination has replaced the faulty script of history, the interlocutors, as if to underscore their power of interpretive transformation, shift their attention from the text of history to two artistic representations of a mythical metamorphosis: a picture of Glaucus being transformed into a sea god, and Giovanni della Casa's sonnet on the same subject. Agostino then offers two radically different allegorical readings of the Glaucus story, illustrating the important link between the free act of interpretation and that "virtù imaginatrice" which Tasso associates with Glaucus.[80] The dialogue that begins as an inquiry into history ends as a meditation on the power of the imagination, a "re-creative" power in both senses of the word.

The passage from history to fiction is figured emblematically in the dialogue's opening scene. There Tasso describes the encounter of two historical personages who in real life could not have met for much of an intellectual discussion, since Cesare Gonzaga was eight years old when Agostino Nifo died. Moreover, Agostino died in 1538, nine years before the debate between Martelli and Bernardo took place. Tasso calls attention to his departure from the facts of history by having his interlocutors meet just as Cesare is beginning a journey from the court of Salerno to a seaside villa. This detail foreshadows the concluding discussion of the sea-god Glaucus; it also metaphorically defines the text itself as a journey from the court, which symbolizes the world of history, to a garden, which represents an ahistorical realm of speculative fiction.

The interlocutors must, however, journey back into history before they can escape it; the movement of the dialogue thus parallels that of More's *Utopia*, where a discussion about the thorny political problems of recent history precedes and partly motivates Hythlodaeus's account of his visit to an ideal country of the mind. Tasso's young interlocutor Cesare, who resembles Plato's Phaedrus leading Socrates out of Athens, initiates the journey away from the tedious ceremonies of the court; he says, however, that the text he has hidden beneath his cloak will in some sense impede the forward motion of the journey: "You thought to distance yourself from the court of Salerno," Cesare wryly remarks to Agostino; but "this composition will as it were take you back there, since these are two orations [which] Vincenzo Martelli and Bernardo Tasso delivered to the Prince of Salerno" ("Voi credete d'allontanarvi dalla corte di Salerno, e questo componimento quasi vi ci riporterà, perciocché queste sono due orazioni di Vincenzo Martelli e di Bernardo Tasso al principe di Salerno" [*Del piacere onesto*, p. 175]).

The "composition" Cesare brings out from under his cloak—in a charming, sartorial version of the central Renaissance metaphor of bringing something hidden or buried to light—is altogether too wrinkled and smudged for comfort. Indeed there is a dark irony in the metaphor Tasso uses to dramatize the discovery of his father's and Martelli's speeches, since his interlocutors immediately begin a process that might be described as a "recloaking" of an unseemly body. The dialogue records an experience many Renaissance artists must have had, an experience which is a tragicomic subplot—or counterplot—to the drama of the Renaissance as an age of inspiring discovery of the past. The experience might be compared to what happens when a person digs in the ground for a beautiful classical statue and finds, instead, a misshapen piece of pottery from his recent ancestors' kitchen. The person can work for a while to clean the piece of pottery, or he can try to persuade himself that it is "in its own way" quite fine. Tasso adopts both these tactics in his dialogue's comments on Bernardo's political views. Eventually, however, he tries to remodel his father's speech altogether; it clearly reflects too many shameful political as well as familial problems to be displayed for long in the light of day.

A close reading of the dialogue suggests, indeed, that Tasso was deeply embarrassed by his father's speech, and in particular by the fact that later events had proven Bernardo's political judgment wrong. A passage from the *Risposta* dramatizes the difficulty Tasso faced in justifying a theoretical opinion which had not only been proven wrong by history, but had caused him personal harm:

> But because Martello [sic] weighs the good of his opinion, not according to reason, but according to results, one cannot conclude that the opinion of my father was bad . . . . And however much his advice appeared unhappy in the end, it was nevertheless not unhappy for the country, but perhaps harmful to the Prince, and to my father, and to me, [the person] now writing.
>
> Ma perchè il Martello pesa la bontà del suo parere non dalla ragione, ma dall'evento, non conchiude che quel di mio padre fosse cattivo . . . . E quantunque il consiglio paresse al fine infelice, non fu nondimeno infelice alla patria, ma forse dannoso al Principe, e a mio padre, ed a me, che scrivo. [*Opere colle controversie*, 10: 146]

As this passage suggests, Tasso relies heavily on the concept of "la patria," the fatherland, for his defense of Bernardo's honor. Bernardo's opinions caused harm to individuals but not, Tasso insists, to the Neapolitan *patria* itself. But the word *patria* has multiple and conflicting connotations for Tasso: it may be conceived, first of all, as referring not only to a fatherland but to a motherland. It may, indeed, be replaced by another word which denotes the same geographical territory: *matria*. This term, which Tasso uses in a letter to a Neapolitan friend, highlights the paradox implicit in the grammatically feminine but semantically masculine word *patria*.[81] The paradox is important for understanding the psychological and ideological conflicts which surround the concept of patriotic loyalty in Tasso's prose and poetry. Patriotism involves, on the one hand, a sentimental attachment to the place of birth and to the mother herself; on the other hand, it involves a juridical notion of duty to the father and, by extension, to the polity and its rulers. The term "patria" thus serves, in Tasso's discourse, as a marker for the problematic intersection of political and familial issues. One might indeed say that the real subject of Tasso's dialogue is family politics, the family being viewed both as a natural and as an ideological entity.

In attempting to present his father as a loyal servant of *la patria*, Tasso must deal immediately with the fact that Bernardo's service to Naples involved participation in a rebellion against an imperial paternal authority. For Tasso, as for any Italian in the era when Italy was a territorial pawn in the wars between the developing absolutist monarchies of France and Spain, there was an obvious conflict between the notions of loyalty to the city-state and loyalty to a larger patria ruled by a foreign monarch—in this case Charles V—whose title of Holy Roman Emperor, given him by the Pope, proclaimed him a legitimate heir to Caesar Augustus and Charlemagne. Tasso's ambivalent respect for the emperor's authority appears in his references to Charles V as a "Caesar" and in his description of the Neapolitan rebellion as the worst of all species of sedition: that in which nobles and commoners unite in opposing a king.[82] In an amazing effort to gloss over the facts of the case, Tasso suggests that his father, by urging Sanseverino to accept the role of ambassador, was serving the cause of peace, not sedition: Sanseverino's aim as Bernardo understood it, Tasso says, was to reunite the Neapolitans with Charles V, as the "obedient" members of a healthy body should be united with their "head."[83] This argument, which is patently an effort to reconcile the notion of loyalty to one's native city with the notion of obedience to an imperial father, shows Tasso's desire to read contemporary history ahistorically, in light of both Roman (imperial, not republican) and feudal theories of political authority. He cannot fail to see, however, that Charles V differs in important ways from a Caesar or a Charlemagne. The dialogue shows Tasso's doubt about whether a feudal lord like Sanseverino really owed fealty to an emperor whose primary concern was clearly neither the material nor the spiritual well-being of his Italian subjects, but rather "the growth of the monarchy" ("l'accrescimento della monarchia" [*Del piacere onesto*, p. 239]).

Tasso's interlocutors openly describe the emperor's viceroy, Don Pedro, as an illegitimate ruler: Agostino generally refers to the emperor with honorific terms ("giustissimo," "buono") but he counters the flattery when he speaks of Don Pedro's "iniquità" and "tirannide" (p. 243); moreover, at one point he even ventures to suggest that the monarchy ruled by Charles V belongs to the type of government to which Aristotle gave the paradoxical name of "legitimate tyranny." This type of government, Agostino remarks, was frequently used among ancient barbarians, "but whether it may be in use today or not, I wish to please myself by passing over in silence" ("la quale [tirannide legitima] era assai in uso tra' barbari; ma s'or sia in uso o non sia, voglio che mi giovi sotto silenzio trapassare" [p. 228]). By his very phrasing Agostino indicates the need for self-censorship in discussing the policies of an emperor like Charles V or, by implication, his successor, Philip II, who ruled Naples when Tasso wrote his dialogue. No member of what Gramsci calls the "subaltern" class of "intellectual functionaries," the class to which both Tasso and his father belonged, could afford to criticize openly those in power.[84] The economic constraints of the patronage system as well as the threat of Inquisitorial persecution obviously inhibited intellectual probing.[85]

Nevertheless, it is important to appreciate how far Tasso goes, with the
defensive aid of the dialogue form, in questioning both the legitimacy of the
emperor and the behavior of Sanseverino, a member of the noble class
which opposed the growth of imperial power not so much for love of *la
patria* as for socio-economic reasons. The strand of subversive questioning
in the dialogue, which contrasts with the strand of ideological conservatism
(if such a term can be used to describe Tasso's complex mixture of nostalgia
for past incarnations of political authority and prudence toward present
ones), is most evident in the passages which define *la patria* not as a
"fatherland" but as a "mother country," ill-treated by both her sons and her
husband.

Tasso invokes the concept of Naples as a "venerated mother" soon after
Agostino has decided that Bernardo Tasso's opinion about Sanseverino's
decorous course of action was erroneous; Agostino agrees with Martelli's
view that Sanseverino should not have accepted the ambassadorship because his primary loyalty should have been to the emperor rather than to
Naples. Paradoxically, Tasso criticizes his own father's opinion precisely at
the moment when he asserts, in theoretical terms, the primacy of an authoritarian paternal principle, for Agostino explains his belief that a man should
serve his king rather than his patria by comparing that patria to a woman:

> I concede therefore to Martello [sic] that the subject should be more obliged to
> the good king than to his *patria*, since sometimes the *patria* may be silly, or mad,
> or too proud in denying obedience where it is owed; [in such cases] it is
> appropriate to do violence to her, or to constrain her to obey him who may
> reasonably command her.

> Concederò io dunque al Martello [sic] che 'l soggetto sia più obligato al buon re
> ch'alla sua patria, perché talvolta la patria può esser stolta e forsennata o superba
> troppo in negare ubbedienza a chi deve; ond'è convenevole che si faccia
> violenza, che si costringa ad ubbedire a colui che ragionevolmente può com-
> mandarle. [*Del piacere onesto*, pp. 228–29]

After voicing this highly conservative opinion, however, Agostino suddenly shifts his perspective, giving an alternative hypothetical model for the
relation between city-state and king. Now taking the woman's point of view,
as it were, Agostino reminds us that his previous opinion was predicated on
the existence of a good husband-father king. "But it may happen," he says,

> that a city correctly, and decorously, judges her own good and then one must
> not force her, and criminal is that son, who dares to put hand on his venerated
> mother; nor can he legitimately excuse himself by saying that he does this
> [violence] in obedience to his natural prince, since a true natural prince is he
> who commands according to natural justice; but natural justice requires that the
> king have as his object the good of the governed people.

Ma s'avviene che la città rettamente e convenevolmente giudichi del suo bene, allora non le dee esser fatta forza; e scellerato è quel figliuolo ch'osi di por le mani violente sovra la sua madre veneranda; né le vale per scusa ch' egli adduca che 'l fa per ubbedire al suo principe naturale, perciocchè principe naturale veramente è colui che commanda secondo la giustizia naturale; ma la giustizia naturale vuol che 'l re si proponga per oggetto il ben de' popoli governati. [pp. 229–30]

The peculiar moment of slippage in this passage occurs when Agostino uses the term "figliuolo" to describe the perpetrator of a crime against natural justice. The political point Agostino is making logically implies an accusation directed against the emperor, who metaphorically plays the role of husband, not son, in relation to Naples, and who is forcing the city to accept the Inquisition against its will. Agostino shies away from directly accusing the emperor, however, and focuses his attention instead on a "son." He thus presumably refers to the viceroy, the emperor's surrogate who is, at the same time, his inferior, the servant who violates the rights of the Neapolitans with the excuse of performing his duty to Charles V. But there is a logical elision in Agostino's rhetoric which suggests how highly charged and overdetermined the concept of a "criminal son" is for Tasso. If Agostino is referring to Don Pedro's violence against Naples, the familial metaphor doesn't quite work, since Don Pedro was not a native son of the city; his crime is of a bureaucratic rather than an unnatural order. Perhaps, however, Agostino is referring hypothetically not to Don Pedro but to Sanseverino, who is a son of Naples and who would have been criminal if he had colluded with Don Pedro in establishing the Inquisition. This reading assumes Agostino's agreement with Bernardo's view that Sanseverino's primary loyalty should have been (as it in fact turned out to be, for a while at least) to Naples rather than to the emperor. If, however, Agostino is theoretically justifying Bernardo's political judgment, he is at the same time obliquely attacking Bernardo's personal conduct—and Tasso's as well—for Bernardo and his son, too, however unwillingly, did commit an unnatural crime by deserting Naples and the wife-mother who lived there.

Agostino's rhetoric therefore seems to work at cross-purposes at different levels of discourse, political and personal. The effect of the passage is to suggest, obscurely, that every male figure associated with the Neapolitan affair, whether in the social set of master-servant roles or in the "natural" set of father-son roles, is somehow guilty of a criminal act against something female. Different individuals may occupy the male roles which Tasso defines with reference both to social and to familial categories; moreover, a single individual like Sanseverino may occupy different positions in more than one binary opposition: he is a servant-son to the emperor, a master-

father to Bernardo There is, however, a stable bottom-line to this structural-
ist's dream-allegory of shifting hierarchical relations. The constant is the fact
of female violation itself, which Tasso seems to conceive as both an active
and a passive phenomenon, a rape and a desertion at once. This imaginative
conflation, so important for his epic poetry, arises in part, I think, from a
temporal conflation of various moments in Bernardo's life: the moment
when he failed in his attempt to protect the city and had to flee as a traitor
along with Sanseverino; and the moment when he urged the French king to
attack Naples, thereby becoming a would-be violator of the city no less
culpable than the Spanish viceroy.

Looking back at the bizarre chains of cause and effect which so often
turned good intentions into crimes, unable fully to exonerate or blame any of
the characters involved in the Neapolitan affair, Tasso alternates between
accusing and justifying all of them, from the emperor through Bernardo.
Tasso does, however, fault his father quite unequivocally for the final act of
the drama, the flight to France with a prince who was by that point serving
neither his emperor nor his city. Loyalty to a natural prince, Agostino says,
does not provide a legitimate excuse for offenses against natural justice. And
Tasso does not finally excuse his father for choosing "service of the patron"
("servizio del padrone") instead of service to his family, especially when
that patron was not being a natural prince at all, but was rather deserting
"such a beautiful and noble state, and rebelling against a victorious Emperor, to go to serve a foreign king, in distant lands" ("lasciava così bello e
così nobile stato, e si ribellava da uno Imperadore vittorioso, per andare a
servire un Re straniero, in paesi lontani").[86]

* * *

It should be clear why Tasso wanted to revise the text of history, a text
replete with either-or dilemmas and all too like a forest of romance in which
any step one chooses to take leads only to further erring. Tasso tries to
enlighten the text of history through the dialectical movement of his dialogue, in particular through the voice of Agostino, an old man speaking to a
young one. According to one critic, Agostino represents Bernardo Tasso
whereas Cesare represents Martelli; the case is rather more complex, however.[87] Agostino may more accurately be seen as replacing Bernardo and as
speaking, therefore, for Tasso's own revisionary intellect at work on the
material of history. The procedure of the dialogue implies that Tasso has
adopted the fictional role of an elderly father who takes it upon himself to
correct the historical father who seems, in retrospect, to be a prodigal son
figure. Moreover, the dialogue's portrayal of the friendly relation between
an old man and a young one is itself an imaginative correction of the
troubled relation between Tasso and Bernardo. Indeed we shall see that
Agostino's powers as a mediator give him maternal as well as paternal

qualities and thereby invite us to consider the dialogue as a symbolic reconstitution of an idealized family. Agostino's arguments are certainly aimed at showing how historical problems might have been resolved in a happier way, as we can see by looking briefly at two examples of Agostino's mediating and synthesizing labor. The first is his attempt to answer the questions posed by the establishment of the Inquisition, questions that are important for understanding Tasso's attitude toward spiritual authorities in the *Apologia*. The second is his attempt to define a golden mean between Bernardo's and Martelli's opposing views of what constituted a decorous course of action for Sanseverino.

Without explicitly criticizing the emperor, Agostino nevertheless suggests that the establishment of a Spanish Inquisition in Naples was unnecessary and unjust. He dwells on the differences between Spain and Naples; in Spain, where the Moorish and Jewish influence was strong, he grants that "supreme severity" was required to preserve the purity of the Catholic faith. But, he goes on to say, the "vehement medicines" and the "assiduous and vigilant physicians" required to heal the "infirm body" of Spain were likely to be poisonous to Naples, a realm "composed of another complexion, and other humors" (*Del piacere onesto*, p. 235). In Naples, he suggests, the care of souls should have been left to the Italian Church; the papal seat of Rome was nearby, there were few heretics among the Neapolitans, and the city had already shown its willingness to obey the emperor's commands without the added whip of the Inquisition (which, as Cesare drily remarks, was an instrument not only for procuring the "health of souls" but also for preventing the "mutation of states" [p. 237]). The kingdom of Naples, Agostino insists,

> has always been most ready [to reply] to all the emperor's signals to aid him with money, and with arms and men, not only in native wars but in foreign ones.

> il regno è sempre stato prontissimo a tutti i cenni dell' imperatore, non solo nelle guerre proprie, ma nelle straniere, ad aiutarlo de denari e d'arme e di genti. [p. 239]

Agostino now quite boldly and accurately suggests that the emperor's need for money over and beyond normal tributes made him desire to "enrich the treasury with the goods of the victims of the Inquisition" ("volesse arrichire il fisco de' beni de gli inquisiti" [p. 239]). If this is the case, two conclusions may be drawn, Agostino says, rather desperately attempting to find a way for the emperor to have his cake without eating the Neapolitans' civil rights:

> on the one hand the city and the kingdom cannot and should not refuse to aid Charles, beyond the ordinary tributes, with some great sum of money, when he finds it necessary to ask it for the purposes of defense, or for enlarging the monarchy or the city; on the other hand the city must not subject its citizens to

the tortures and torments of the Inquisition, and to the shame and civil infamy
which is too rigorously threatening them.

(dall'un lato la città e 'l regno non può né dee negare a Carlo di soccorrerlo oltra
gli ordinari tributi con alcuna grossa somma de denari, quand'egli per difesa o
per accrescimento della monarchia o della città sia necessitato a chiederlo;
dall'altro non dee sottoporre i suoi cittadini a gli strazi e a' tormenti dell' inquisizione e alla vergogna ancora e all'infamia civile che troppo rigorosamente è lor
minacciata. [pp. 239–40]

Agostino's argument is aimed at mitigating the severity and greed of that
distant father, the emperor. Looking as realistically as possible at the emperor's political and economic motives for establishing the Inquisition,
Agostino nevertheless speaks for the rights of the citizens and for a principle
of relative religious tolerance. This is significant, since the historical Agostino
Nifo was an Avveroist in his youth and, like Tasso himself, renounced his
early interest in heretical philosophical ideas.[88] Agostino, or rather Tasso
speaking through him, is therefore being disingenuous when he insists that
his arguments for clemency stem only from sympathy for others rather than
from any consciousness of impiety on his own part: "Né io d'uomini e di
materie tali così clementemente ragiono perch'a me stesso d'alcun' empietà
. . . sia consapevole" (p. 241). Precisely because it is not disinterested,
Agostino's expression of sympathy for erring souls provides an interesting
gloss on those moments in *Gerusalemme Liberata* when the epic narrator
passes a distinctly less severe judgment on his erring heroes than a character
like Peter the Hermit does (Peter being, in this epic, a spokesman for
Counter-Reformation orthodoxy): "Knowing the imperfections of the human intellect," Agostino says, "it is reasonable that I sympathize with those
who are deceived by appearances of truth" ("conoscendo l'imperfezione
dell'umano intelletto, è ragionevole ch'io compatisca a coloro, che dall'ap-
parenza della verità sono ingannati" [*Del piacere onesto*, p. 241]).[89]

Underlying Agostino's arguments for more merciful religious institutions
is a nostalgia for pre-Reformation Catholicism. Tasso is quite explicit about
the nature of the nostalgia; it is for an "age of Dante," an age Agostino
portrays as a "springtime" and which contrasts with the hot and fever-ridden
summer of contemporary history (p. 261). The fever is a symptom of the
disease of Protestantism, which forces present-day Catholic rulers to exercise extreme severity in preventing "mutazioni delle religioni" (p. 257). By
thus describing the establishment of the Inquisition as politically necessary,
while at the same time protesting its methods (the patients are too often
killed rather than cured), Agostino's discourse reflects an intractable historical problem, a disease, one might say, which the dialogue attempts to
diagnose but cannot cure.

It is significant, however, that the dialogue makes a counter-statement to the text of history even as it broods, impotently, on historical problems. Cesare praises Agostino's plea for religious tolerance (a plea the dialogue defines as unrealistic) in words which echo a passage from Dante's *Commedia*, the poem Agostino later describes as the product of a lost historical season of spring. The echo is fascinating, since it implies a parallel between Agostino and a woman—Piccarda Donata—who enlightens Dante in *Paradiso* 3, but who is herself a sinner. Her sin, an "involuntary" breaking of vows of faith, is clearly of great concern to Tasso; so is the fact that Dante places her, despite her fault, in paradise. Piccarda, who is both the recipient and the donor of mercy, is an important shadowy presence in a dialogue which argues, pessimistically, for mercy in the Counter-Reformation church. The lines Tasso echoes are from the Pilgrim's response to Piccarda's discourse on divine charity; her discourse at once satisfies him and creates in him a desire for more knowledge of love.[90] Agostino's exposition of a doctrine of mercy creates a similar effect on Cesare, who says:

> You nourish me with your doctrine in a way which at the same time entices me and so makes me desirous of new food: so please continue, for I do not mean to depart; until I am fully satisfied by your banquet, I shall not depart.
>
> Voi in guisa mi pascete della vostra dottrina che nel medesimo tempo allettando mi rendete vago di nuovo cibo; sì che, di grazia, seguite: ch'io non intendo di partirmi, ch'a pieno sazio dal vostro convito non mi diparta. [*Del piacere onesto*, p. 231]

This passage, which alludes not only to Dante's *Paradiso* but also to Plato's *Symposium*, provides an important clue to Tasso's use of dialogue as a defensive weapon against the text of recent history.[91] By imaginatively creating an ideal dialogic scene, in which an older interlocutor who possesses qualities of both a comforting mother and a benevolent father gives a younger one instruction mixed with pleasure (of an oral erotic kind), it dramatizes the restitutive psychological function of Tasso's own dialogue. Dividing himself into two speakers, the author gives and receives satisfaction, creating for himself and his readers the image of a harmonious inter- (and intra-) personal relation. Tasso's theoretical aim in the dialogue, to find mediating solutions to political problems, cannot be appreciated apart from his psychological aim, which is, as I have suggested, to reconstitute a family—not as it existed historically, but as it existed in desire (which is to say, "historically" in another sense).

The theoretical and the psychological aims are both served by Agostino's attempt to formulate a mediating or diplomatic solution to the dispute concerning Sanseverino's duty. The solution consists of a carefully rationalized account of what Sanseverino should have done to satisfy both his native city and his emperor. The political conflict is figuratively presented as a familial dilemma in which a son is torn between his mother-city and his father-emperor. In resolving Sanseverino's dilemma, Agostino is also figuratively resolving a problem in Tasso's autobiography. It becomes clear that if Agostino, that strangely androgynous figment of Tasso's imagination, had been able to replace the historical Bernardo as Sanseverino's counselor, events would have turned out differently and Tasso would not have been forced against his will to follow his father into bitter, motherless exile.

Agostino argues that Martelli was right in thinking that Sanseverino should have refused the position of ambassador—though Martelli was right for the wrong reasons. Bernardo, in contrast, gave the wrong practical counsel but had the right ethical perspective on the matter; he is particularly commended for believing that one must place one's moral duty above self-interest. As we have seen, Agostino is quite ambivalent about whether Sanseverino's moral duty involves primary loyalty to the emperor or to Naples; Agostino lucidly insists, however, that Sanseverino could effectively serve neither king nor his patria by accepting the role of ambassador. Had Sanseverino refused the mission to the emperor for the reasons of utility and self-interest adduced by Martelli, he would have been a "bad citizen" ("reo cittadino"); but had he refused for other reasons, he would have acted "for the good of the country" ("per ben della patria" [Del piacere onesto, p.244]). Those other reasons, which Agostino proceeds to enumerate, are, first, that no representative of an armed rebellion can succeed in a mission designed to win grace from the ruler; the mission itself was ill-conceived, and instead of agreeing to represent the seditious Neapolitans, a truly patriotic nobleman should have urged his countrymen "to put down their arms, and obey and then supplicate" ("deponga l'arme, e ubbedisca, e poi supplichi" [p. 248]). The second reason Agostino adduces has to do with the nature of the ambassador rather than the nature of the mission itself: Sanseverino was not the appropriate person to mediate between Naples and Charles V, since he was personally hated by the viceroy and belonged, moreover, to a family known to have French (and, Agostino obliquely suggests, Protestant) sympathies.[92] In fact, Agostino argues, a worse ambassador than Sanseverino could hardly have been found:

> the city could not send an ambassador more odious to the viceroy or more suspected by the emperor.... These conditions were most apt to increase the intrinsic difficulties of the negotiation ... [and were] reason enough to take faith and authority away from anything the Prince might say against the iniquity and tyranny of Don Pedro.
>
> non può la città mandare ambasciatore o più odioso al viceré o più sospetto all'imperadore. . . . Le quali condizioni tutte sono attissime ad accrescer la difficoltà che porta il negozio in se stesso ... [e] sarebbe cagione bastante a torre fede e autorità a tutte quelle cose che potesse il principe dire contra l'iniquità e la tirannide di don Pietro. [pp. 242-43]

Having demonstrated why Sanseverino should for the good of the city have refused the ambassadorial mission, Agostino pulls out a rather surprising trump card: had Sanseverino refused, the Neapolitans could have chosen someone "more apt" for the post, namely Ferrante Gonzaga, the father of the youthful interlocutor Cesare and the grandfather of that Ferrante Gonzaga who had befriended Tasso in Sant'Anna and to whom both the *Apologia* and the revised version of the *Del piacere onesto* dialogue are dedicated.[93]

This detail sheds an ironic light on Tasso's imaginative attempt to solve the political problems his father and Sanseverino faced; the need to please and flatter a powerful patron shapes even what is done in the dialogue's garden of civilized discourse. However ingenious and politically shrewd we may find Tasso's analysis of the faults in his father's and in Martelli's arguments, we cannot help noting that the analysis points, finally, to faults in history that are beyond any individual's power to remedy, even were he the emperor himself. Like Castiglione, Tasso knew from personal experience that the role of counselor to the prince—or to the emperor—was a dangerous one. With the advantage of hindsight he can point to errors in his father's performance of the counselor's role; but his doubts about whether even wiser counsel—such as that which he himself provides through Agostino—could really have altered the unfortunate course of history, are evident in the fact that the dialogue now turns away altogether from revisionary interpretation of past events. In the text we have been reading, the discussion shifts, as I have said, to the subject of the Glaucus myth and two artistic representations of it. In the later version of the dialogue entitled *Il Nifo overo del piacere*, the section on Glaucus is replaced by an abstract philosophical debate about the nature of "honest pleasure."[94] Both versions of the dialogue thus end with a formal and thematic escape into a realm of myth, art, and philosophy which contrasts dramatically with the rocky realm of history through which the interlocutors and the readers have been journeying. In *Il Nifo*, the shift of focus (one might well say of *topos*) is explicitly presented as an escape from material that is not only difficult but dangerous. Agostino makes this point just after Cesare has requested that he continue his labor of providing substitute speeches; the speech Cesare now desires, however, is the one that Sanseverino would have made if he had accepted the counsel that Agostino has been offering throughout the text as a substitute for the counsel given by Bernardo Tasso and Martelli. To articulate this speech, Agostino would imaginatively have to assume the role not of a courtier but of a prince; and this, Tasso evidently feels, would be somehow indecorous. But there is a further (and related) reason why Agostino chooses at this point to refuse his interlocutor's request. The speech which Cesare asks him to imagine for Sanseverino would be the speech in which the prince had to tell the Neapolitans that he had decided not to accede to their request that he become their ambassador. In denying Cesare's request for an imaginative reconstruction of a speech of denial—the most dangerous kind of speech, as every orator and especially every courtier knows—Agostino dramatizes the political dangers inherent in the speaker-listener relationship; his inability to predict whether the Neapolitan audience would have responded favorably to his speech is crucial to his decision that further dealings with the particulars of history would be dangerous. "The prince," Agostino tells Cesare,

> would perhaps be no more able to please the Neapolitans with my words than I would please myself in using someone else's. It would seem to me that what has been said of the prince, of Naples, of the viceroy and the emperor—things very uncertain on account of the uncertainty of the subject discussed, and yet none the less dangerous—should be presented in universal terms. To consider them in this way will make the solution easier while giving no cause for offense to any individual.

> Né 'l prencipe [sic] con le mie parole piacerebbe forse a'Napolitani, né io con l'altrui a me medesimo; laonde a me parrebbe che queste cose chi si sono dette del principe e di Napoli e del viceré e de l'imperatore, assai incerte per l'incertitudine del soggetto del qual si ragiona, né meno periculose, devessero esser ridotte a gli universali, ne'quali considerandole, non solamente sarà più facil la determinazione, ma ancora senza offesa d'alcun particolare. [*Il Nifo*, p. 223]

I know of no other Renaissance text that gives such a straightforward cost-benefit analysis of the movement from particulars to universals, whether that movement is accomplished by philosophical or by poetic discourse. Aristotle's famous statement that poetry is a "more philosophical and serious thing" than history because it deals with universals rather than particulars acquires an ironic political meaning in Tasso's text. Extending Agostino's point, Cesare remarks that the rise to the certainty of universals is also a "withdrawal from danger" ("ritirata dal pericolo") for the particular author or speaker whose security depends on not giving offense (*Il Nifo*, p. 224). Impotence in the arena of historical events is at once a cause and a result of the turn to speculative fiction, which Tasso himself invites us to consider as a defense against painful realities.

The "virtù imaginatrice" that Tasso's interlocutors go on to praise in the final section of the earlier version of the dialogue is a power that compensates for impotence in the political, or even the sexual, sphere. And it is significant, especially in light of Tasso's efforts in the earlier parts of the dialogue to offer harmonious solutions to the conflicts of history, that he defines the imagination as a mediating faculty which offers a link not only between particulars and universals but also between the body, which is the animal part of man, and the mind, which is the angelic part. After interpreting two representations of Glaucus, a pictorial and a literary one, in two different ways—as an allegory of the mind's descent into sensuality and as an allegory for the mind's ascent from sensuality—Agostino suggests that both interpretations are plausible because Glaucus himself is a mysterious figure "composed of two forms":

> The action of the intellect accompanied by the imagination, which the Greeks termed *dianoia*, is signified by that part of Glaucus where the two natures merge; because the imaginative virtue is always full of various sorts of phantasms, it combines things human with things divine, and the sensible with the intellectual; wherefore it is reasonable that Glaucus is figured in this phantastic figure.

> L'azion dell'intelletto, con l'imaginazione accompagnata, che dianoea da' Greci è detta, ci significa quella parte di Glauco ove le due nature s'accompagnano: percioché la virtù imaginatrice è sempre piena di varie sorti di fantasmi, compone le cose divine con l'umane e le sensibili con l'intelligibili; onde ragionevolmente in questa fantastica figura Glauco è figurato. [*Del piacere onesto*, pp. 282–83]

Glaucus is a figure who represents the power to figure, to conjoin disparate things into a unity. That unity, however, is problematic, as Tasso insists by refusing to allow his interlocutors to decide between the alternative interpretations of the myth. Indeed, Tasso's Glaucus seems to represent not only the figurative or "esemplastic" power, but the extraordinary difficulty— perhaps the impossibility—of arriving at a definitive judgment about the nature and moral status of that power. It is no accident that Agostino's two interpretations of Glaucus's story dramatize the potential for disagreement between two authorities who are extremely important for Tasso: Plato and Dante. In Book 10 of the *Republic*, Socrates compares Glaucus transformed into a sea creature to the soul deformed by the "countless evils" of life in the material world (611d). In *Paradiso*, canto 1, in a famous passage which Tasso's Cesare quotes, Dante turns Plato's allegory downside up, as it were, by likening his own mysterious experience of transcendence to Glaucus's metamorphosis:

> Nel suo aspetto tal dentro mi fei,
>   qual si fè Glauco nel gustar de l'erba
>   che 'l fè consorte in mar de li altri Dei.
> Trasumanar significar *per verba*
>   non si porìa; però l'essemplo basti
>   a cui esperïenza grazia serba.   [Lines 67–72]

At her [Beatrice's] aspect I was changed within, as was Glaucus when he tasted of the herb that made him one among the other gods in the sea. The passing beyond humanity cannot be set forth in words; let the example suffice, therefore, for him to whom grace reserves the experience.

Which allegory to choose, Plato's or Dante's? Cesare suggests that the decision has serious religious consequences: "It saddens me," he tells Agostino, "that with so little regard for [Glaucus's] divinity, you have converted him to a beast; wherefore I now wish that if it pleased you to make him a beast, it may finally please you to deify him, as Dante did" ("Molto con voi mi doglio che con sì poco riguardo della sua divinità l'abbiate in bruto convertito: onde or vorrei che, se piaciuto v'è d'imbestiarlo, vi piacesse finalmente, come fe' Dante, deificarlo" [Del piacere onesto, p. 278]). This gently admonitory speech from the young man to the old philosopher reminds the reader that what is at stake, in this textual game of allegorizing, is nothing less than the fate of the Christian poet's soul—and also the souls of his readers, who may be persuaded by his words to become brutes rather than angels. We may, indeed, regard the entire meditation on Glaucus as an allegorical trial of the poet who is glancing apprehensively throughout the apparently playful dialogic exchange at the scene of Last Judgment which awaits him ("You warn me well," Agostino says, after Cesare quotes Dante to him). If we see this section of the dialogue as a trial of the poet, we can better appreciate why Tasso's definition of the "virtù imaginatrice" alludes not only to Dante's Paradiso, but also to his Inferno. In the passage I quoted earlier, where Agostino explains what is "signified" by "that part of Glaucus where the two natures merge," the figure of Glaucus himself is verbally joined to Dante's description of a creature consigned to hell, the Centaur Chiron. In Inferno 12, which depicts the first circle of the violently sinful, Virgil approaches that part of Chiron's body "where the two natures are joined" ("dove le due nature son consorti" [l. 84]). Teacher of the wrathful Achilles, Chiron is an apt symbol for the poet who seeks—but ultimately fails—to teach his audience to restrain their passions. By linking Chiron with Glaucus, Tasso complicates his inquiry into the poet's moral nature: salvation may depend not only on the poet's own virtue, but on his success in engendering virtue in others.[95]

Pedagogical failure, or, more generally, rhetorical impotence, is a central theme in the tradition of interpreting Glaucus. In Plato's Republic, Glaucus has the status of a negative exemplum: his transformation illustrates, among other things, what happens to the soul when a poet inflames its "lower" passions. In this book where the philosopher banishes the poets and proclaims the philosopher's right to teach virtue, Glaucus serves both as a figure of the poet and as a figure for the audience which is not persuaded to follow the philosopher's high path to truth. In Ovid's Metamorphoses, Glaucus is also linked with the theme of rhetorical failure, though such failure is defined in a way the Platonic philosopher would consider perverse. Ovid's Glaucus narrates his own tale in Book 13, and he does so for a specific purpose: to seduce Scylla. He finds, however, that the magic herb which made him a god, and which he describes as "potent" (*vires*, l. 942), gives him neither the physical nor the verbal charm to win the lady's affections. After listening to his tale she flees, leaving him in a "mad rage" (*inritatus*, l. 967). Dante might well have put Ovid's Glaucus in the circle of the violent. Instead, he chose to pursue his own pedagogical aims by metamorphosing Glaucus from a bestial to an angelic figure. In so doing, he argues obliquely for the superiority of Christianity over paganism; he also demonstrates his own power to transform an Ovidian text, recalling to our minds his boast, in *Inferno* 25, that he can silence Ovid in the competitive game of representing metamorphoses. Here, he does not so much silence Ovid as sublimate the pagan poet's naturalistic view of rhetorical impotence. When Dante insists on his inability to represent his experience of transcendence in language ("Trasumanar significar per verba/non si porìa. . . ."), we are meant to see that such impotence is merely relative, and certainly no cause for grief or rage; on the contrary, as the blessed servant of an all-powerful God, Dante can be humbly proud of his inability to describe fully the experience which God's grace vouchsafed him. In the harmoniously paradoxical universe of the *Paradiso*, an awareness of verbal impotence goes hand in hand with the exercise of that powerful faculty Dante calls his "alta fantasia."[96]

Unlike Dante, Tasso is fundamentally uncertain about whether his "fantasia" is high or low; Glaucus represents that uncertainty in Tasso's dialogue. As a boundary figure whose two natures signal the two possible fates which await the poet, salvation or damnation, Glaucus is an emblem both for the poet's power and for its limits. Although the movement of the dialogue seems to suggest that Glaucus represents a contemplative man's escape into a "green world" that is far from the harsh realm of history, the actual debate on Glaucus, as we have seen, reveals a skull in Tasso's Arcadia. The poetic imagination as Tasso exercises it in this dialogue does succeed in partially re-creating the text of history, in the hypothetical mode praised by Shakespeare's Touchstone ("Your If is the only peacemaker; much virtue in If"); but the imagination "annihilates" the actual world only to find thoughts of death in its "green shade." The conclusion of the dialogue therefore at once displays and ironizes the mind's desire to withdraw from the world where displeased audiences or offended fathers censor free imaginative play. When Cesare chides Agostino for taking too much pleasure in interpreting Glaucus as a bestial figure, Agostino checks his speculations, acknowledging his fears of offending some deity ("io dubito nell'offesa di Glauco aver fatta offesa ad alcuna deità" [*Del piacere onesto*, p. 278]). This seaside garden, we see, is considerably darker than the world famously described in the "golden age" chorus of Tasso's *Aminta*. The chorus speaks of a time and a place where people are free from the "hard laws" of honor. In the garden of the pastoral imagination (which is not by any means identical with the scene of the *Aminta* itself), the soul escapes the duties imposed by rigid fathers, and lives instead according to the laws of a seemingly androgynous and paradoxically artful Nature, the "golden and happy laws / that Nature sculpted: 'If it pleases, it is permitted'" ("legge aurea e felice / che natura scolpì: 'S'ei piace, ei lice'"). [97]

The Ordeal of Rebirth: The Apologia Yet Once More

What is essentially new in my theory is the thesis that memory is present not once but several times over, that it is registered in various species of signs.— Freud, letter to Fliess

We are ready now to return to the *Apologia*, where very little that pleases seems to be permitted, and where we are most definitely not in a garden but in a court. Having seen the way in which Tasso's *Del piacere onesto* dialogue puts Bernardo Tasso's performance as a courtier on trial, we can better appreciate the complexity of Tasso's judgment, in the *Apologia*, of Bernardo's performance as a poet. In a fascinating early digression Tasso does not so much defend his father as excuse him, by attributing his failure as an epic poet to the fact that he was inhibited by his duties as a courtier. Bernardo's profession, Tasso says, "was that of a courtier, not a poet; and his proper praises were those that he merited in court" ("egli fece professione di cortegiano, non di poeta; e le sue proprie lodi furoni quelle che egli meritava in corte" [*Apologia*, p. 631]). Knowing Tasso's mixed opinion of those merits, we can remark the curious chiasmatic relation between his judgment of Bernardo in the *Del piacere onesto* dialogue and his judgment in the *Apologia*: in the former text Bernardo's failure as a courtier is linked to his inability to display the kind of imaginative power Agostino possesses; in the latter, Bernardo's failure as a poet is linked to his inability to escape his duty as a courtier. The anecdote Tasso tells to illustrate his father's dilemma is this: when he was in the Spanish court "through service to the Prince of Salerno his patron," Bernardo was asked to write a poem on the Amadis story. "Like one who best understood the art of poetry, and particularly that which Aristotle taught, he decided to make a poem of one single action" ("sì come colui che ottimamente intendeva l'arte poetica, e quella particolarmente insegnataci da Aristotele, deliberò di far poema d'una sola azione" [p. 632]). Tasso proceeds to describe his father's plan for a unified plot; after asserting that no master of art could have made a more beautiful design, he admits, however, that "finally, in order not to lose the name of good courtier, he [Bernardo] did not take care to retain forcefully that of best poet" ("finalmente, per non perder il nome di buon cortigiano, non si curò di ritener a forza quello d'ottimo poeta" [p. 632]). What happened, Tasso relates, was that Bernardo read some parts of this Aristotelian epic to his patron in a room full of "gentlemen listeners" who, by the time he finished reading, had all disappeared. From this embarrassing occurrence Bernardo inferred that "the unity of action lacked delightfulness by its nature, not by defect of art on his part: because he had treated [the material] in a way that the art could not be reprimanded; and concerning this belief he did not deceive himself at all" ("egli prese argumento che l'unità dell'azione fosse poco dilettevole per sua natura, non per difetto d'arte che egli avesse: perciò che egli l'aveva trattata in modo che l'arte non poteva riprendersi; e di questo non s'ingannava punto" [p. 632]).

This passage is a fine example of a case where reported speech is ambiguously permeated by what Bakhtin calls "authorial context"; Tasso is reporting a self-justifying story his father had evidently often told him, but he reports the story without granting it full credence.[98] "Of this he did not deceive himself at all" ("di questo non s'ingannava punto"), Tasso writes, commenting on Bernardo's belief that he could not be "reprimanded" for his artistry; the phrasing, however, invites us to wonder whether Bernardo did deceive himself about other things. If we reread the passage, we note that Tasso in fact withholds comment on Bernardo's inference about the meaning of his listeners' disappearance. The passages in the *Discorsi* where Tasso explicitly refutes the view that poems written according to Aristotelian structural rules are inherently less delightful than digressive romances only confirm the impression that Tasso here defends his father's judgment in a lukewarm way.[99] Significantly, however, he grows warmer toward his father when he mentions Ariosto at the end of this anecdote about Bernardo's fate as a courtly poet.

Tasso invokes Ariosto, I suspect, partly in order to compensate for his inability to make common cause with Bernardo when the two are, as it were, alone on stage. In this passage, the external threat of Ariosto is suggestively linked to the problem posed by the tastes of a courtly audience. Remarking that Bernardo's poem might not have been so badly received "if the prince had not added his commandment to the common persuasion" (the commandment being, presumably, that Bernardo should stop reading—and writing—a boring poem), Tasso asserts that his father nevertheless did not "despair" of retaining the name of "a great and good poet"; nor was he "frightened by the new glory of Ariosto, nor by the grace that he [Ariosto] had among princes, among cavaliers and ladies; which [grace] (as someone said) could hide all his defects, if he had any" (p. 633).

There is much irony, some of it rather nasty, in these words, which echo the opening lines of Ariosto's *Orlando* ("Le donne, i cavallier . . . io canto") and imply that Ariosto's aesthetic grace is really a function of his ability to obtain the grace of patrons through flattery. The passage shows how much Tasso's ambivalence toward his father is linked to his ambivalence both toward Ariosto and, more generally, toward that audience which confers favor on one poet while commanding another to change his style or be silent.

* * *

At the end of his defense of his father Tasso achieves an impressive, if temporary, resolution to his dilemma. This resolution occurs in the passage that I referred to earlier as a usurpation scene and suggested we approach through a reading of the *Del piacere onesto* dialogue, the text in which Tasso renews memory by transforming it through his "virtù imaginatrice." The first section of the *Apologia* ends, as the dialogue does, with an exercise of imaginative power; in both works Tasso uses that power to free himself from the burden of the past:

> And here I invoke memory, as the poets do, and him who gave me [memory] along with intellect, when he sent [me] to live in this body almost like a *peregrino*:[100] because in the last years of his life, when we were both in the rooms given him by the Duke of Mantua, he said to me that the love that he had for me had made him forget that which he had had for his poem: wherefore he could not love any earthly glory, and perpetuity of fame, as much as he loved my life, and he could delight in nothing more than my reputation. These words were in conformity with some that he wrote in my childhood to signor Americo Sanseverino; and if the testimony is alive, the memory [of it] should not be lost.

> E qui invoco la memoria, come fanno i poeti, e colui che me la diede insieme con l'intelletto, quando il mandò ad abitare in questo corpo quasi peregrino: che negli ultimi anni della sua vita, essendo ambedue nelle stanze dategli dal duca di Mantova, mi disse che l'amor che mi portava l'aveva fatto dimenticar di quel che aveva già portato al suo poema: laonde niuna gloria del mondo, niuna perpetuità di fama poteva tanto amare quanto la mia vita, e di niuna cosa più rallegrarsi che della mia riputazione. Le quali parole furono conformi ad alcune che scrisse nella mia fanciullezza al signor Americo Sanseverino; e se 'l testimonio è vivo, non deve esserne perduta la memoria. [*Apologia*, pp. 643–44]

In this extraordinary passage Tasso invokes a Muse who responds to his call by bringing him what is, at first, an ambiguously unpleasant memory of his father. The guise in which Bernardo initially appears—so similar to God himself that here, as in the "O del grand'Apennino" canzone, we may mistake the earthly for the heavenly father until we come to the mention of his death—is clearly not the kind of vision a poet aspiring to originality wants from his Muse. There is a note of slightly querulous accusation in the phrase defining the father as "him who sent me to live in this body almost like a *peregrino*." Throughout the rest of the passage Tasso labors to banish the ghost which blights his life and stands between him and his achievement of poetic maturity. One could not ask for a more interesting defensive weapon against an inhibiting memory than the one Tasso uses here: a counter-memory of a liberating forgetfulness. By remembering his father's declaration that his love for his son made him forget (*dimenticar*) his love for his own poem, Tasso clears the path for original creation, for the writing of an epic that will not offend his father however much it differs from the *Amadigi*. Remembering what happened in the Duke of Mantua's *stanze* (there is perhaps a pun on *stanze* as rooms and stanzas of a poem), Tasso in effect attributes to his dead father the sentiment Ben Jonson expressed in his poem "On my First Son," although in Jonson's case the father is living and the son is dead:

Rest in soft peace, and, ask'd, say here doth lye
Ben. Jonson his best piece of poetrie.

The son himself is the poet-father's best piece of work, Tasso tells us; thus, after all his tortuous meditations on hierarchies of loyalty, Tasso at last conjures up a memory that must have satisfied his real sense of natural justice: the father who had so often in life placed his loyalties to others and his own desire for poetic and political honor above his duty to his family now makes a just restitution by saying that he values his natural creation more than his artistic creation.[101] Tasso makes his father relinquish the traditional trope of the poem as the child; or rather, Tasso points, as Jonson does, to the inadequacy of the simple equation poem = child, insisting, on the contrary, that in the final analysis the child is worth more than any poem. By asserting the child's superior claim to life, Tasso implicitly deprives his father of the immortality traditionally associated with being a poet. The treatment of the theme of memory in the passage dramatizes the way in which Tasso is killing his father *as a poet* in order to re-create him as a natural man. The poem is traditionally seen as the monument that preserves our memory of the poet's existence, but here Tasso attributes an afterlife not to Bernardo's poem but rather to his spoken words—the ones that show love for his son. There is a fine poetic justice in the fact that the loving words resemble those contained in a letter to Americo Sanseverino, a poor relative of the patron who caused the Tasso family so much woe. In the phrase referring to this letter, "e se 'l testimonio è vivo, non deve esserne perduta la memoria," Tasso defends himself, perhaps, not only against a potentially skeptical reader, but also against the ghost of Bernardo, who might have forgotten this important spoken dialogue. The Muse has finally, with a little help from her son, brought forth a memory which gives nourishment to the poet. When Tasso initially invoked the Muse's aid, he did so as a writer not yet in full possession of poetic identity, being only *like* a poet ("come fanno i poeti"); by the end of the passage, however, he has created a room of his own. Were Bernardo to speak in his own voice he might well say at this point something like what Shakespeare's Henry IV says to Prince Hal: "Thy wish was father to that thought." If, however, Bernardo's ghost had thus accused his son of untimely usurpation, Tasso might well have replied, "You will live better through my writing than through your own." Anyone who has compared the *Amadigi* with the *Gerusalemme Liberata* will testify that this is the truth.

*   *   *

The invocation of the Muse of Memory functions in the *Apologia* as it does ideally in epic poems: it creates a link to the past that serves rather than works against the poet's vision of his future. Tasso signals what he has accomplished in his tortuous journey to a place where he can acknowledge his right to supersede his father when he offers, just before and just after the invocation passage, sentences that echo the one I took as the symbolic starting point of his defense. That sentence was Tasso's assertion that he "voluntarily ceded" to Bernardo in all manners of composition and that he "could not bear that in any of these [manners] anyone should be placed before him" (p. 630). Just before he invokes memory, Tasso revises his earlier view thus: "I am pretty certain that, if he wanted indeed to be superseded, he wanted to be superseded by no one other than me" ("sono assai certo che, se egli voleva pur esser superato, non voleva esser superato da nissun altro che da me" [p. 643]). Immediately after the invocation passage he concludes the revisionary echo: "I could not bear that the judgment of my father should be reproved in my compositions" ("Non dovrei dunque sostener che 'l giudizio di mio padre fosse riprovato nelle mie composizioni" [p. 644]). But the "giudizio" to which Tasso now refers is the one opinion of Bernardo's which he can bear to support, namely that the son's life and poem are more valuable than the father's.

The Court of Christian Conscience: Apology versus Defense

My conscience hath a thousand several tongues
And every tongue brings in a several tale,
And every tale condemns me for a villain.   —Shakespeare, *Richard III*

Suppose ye that I am come to give peace on earth? I tell you, Nay; but rather division. . . . The father shall be divided against the son, and the son against the father.—Luke 12: 51, 53

Tasso's invocation of the Muse of Memory, a threshold moment in the text which figures a death of the father and a birth, or rebirth, of the poetic son, is an appropriate prelude to the second and longer part of the treatise in which Tasso undertakes a defense of his own epic poetry. Like Keats's Hyperion struggling to "die into life" at the feet of Mnemosyne, however, Tasso cannot complete the passage into poetic identity: in the second part of the *Apologia*, as in the first, his path toward what he conceives as the Christian poet's goal is blocked by ghosts—chief among them the critics who are, like

Tasso's father and Ariosto, "not present" except in textual traces.[102] Moreover, the critics also keep Tasso bound to the past, not only because the terms of their accusations force him into a competitive comparison game with Ariosto, but also because he has to defend a poem he himself was coming to see as the unreformed work of his old self. In 1585 Tasso was in fact at a threshold moment in his career: midway through the decade between the unauthorized publication of the *Gerusalemme Liberata* and the completion of his revised epic, the *Gerusalemme Conquistata*, Tasso was already planning the new work he hoped would be "more reverent and venerable" than the *Liberata*.[103] The critics who require him to defend a poem about which he is already doubtful are therefore hindering his spiritual as well as his aesthetic development. He refers, in the *Apologia*, to his "nova invenzione" and to his hope that it will offer "things that are miraculous and in conformity with the teaching of Scripture" ("cose mirabili e conformi a la dottrina delle sacre lettere" [p. 672]). The implication is that the *Liberata* was not wholly justifiable from a Christian perspective. Having not yet written his new poem, however, Tasso's position is in some ways comparable to that of Aeneas in the underworld: encountering his father, seeing the shades of his yet unborn progeny, Aeneas pauses on a threshold between his past and his future with his own identity in a state of suspension.

* * *

The second part of Tasso's treatise consists of a strange and difficult conversation between Il Forestiero, a persona who represents Tasso and is modeled in part on the Stranger of Plato's late dialogues; a Catholic priest named Vincenzo Fantini; Fantini's secretary; and the absent prosecutor-critics, whose words Tasso quotes at masochistic length—though there is retaliatory sadism, which probably hurts the modern reader more than it hurt Renaissance critics, in Tasso's practice of quoting out of context from his predecessors' pamphlets. One can hardly follow Tasso's argument without having read those pamphlets, which are themselves full of contradictions and of little literary interest, except insofar as they dramatize the close connection between scholarly polemic and sexual insult. The charges against Tasso's poem range from lists of specific "improper" words and figures, through moral attacks on certain "impious" episodes in the epic, to cruel remarks about the "sterility" and "dryness" of Tasso's inventive faculty, which is contrasted to Ariosto's richly potent genius.[104] Without discussing in detail these charges or Tasso's responses to them, I want to comment on an aspect of the dialogue that is of general interest: Tasso's oscillation between self-justificatory and apologetic stances toward his epic and also toward the rhetorical activity of defense itself. A discussion of the dialogue from this perspective will prepare us for understanding the strategy Tasso employs to escape the imprisoning courtroom figured in the *Apologia*. He appears in that courtroom as a son being prosecuted and judged by numerous father figures, literary and spiritual; to escape this role, he must come to conceive of himself as a father and a judge.

*   *   *

Tasso's ambivalent attitude toward his epic can be described in terms of the distinction between excuse and justification that we discussed in Chapter One, apropos of Austin's "A Plea for Excuses." A justification, Austin says, occurs when we accept responsibility for something we have been accused of doing but argue that what we did was "a good thing, or the right and sensible thing, or a permissible thing to do, either in general or at least in the special circumstances of the occasion."[105] An excuse occurs, in contrast, when we admit to our accusers that we did something bad but we don't accept full, or even any, responsibility for it. Austin illustrates this distinction with a hypothetical case of a man charged with murder: if the man argues that the killing was done in battle, he is justifying his act; if he argues that the killing was only accidental, albeit reckless, he is excusing it.[106] Although no good defense lawyer would confuse the jury by shifting from one line of argument to the other, that is precisely what Tasso does. He justifies his poetic procedure in the *Gerusalemme Liberata*, for instance, when he insists that his representation of wicked characters and actions is not a fault, since the nature of artistic imitation requires the poet to show good and evil operating in the universe of the poem as it does in the real universe (*Apologia*, p. 677). He excuses his epic, however, when he says that he did not authorize its publication and was prevented by circumstances beyond his control from revising it (pp. 694, 689). The shifts from justification to excuse are particularly interesting because we can relate these different rhetorical stances to a distinction the text itself draws between defense, as an aggressive activity associated with the ethos and style of Greek Sophists; and apology, as a mode of discourse associated with the Platonic and Christian ideal of a person who loves truth more than himself.

If one thinks of the etymology of apology, from *apo* ("away") and *logoi* ("words"), one can see why it is a term that can be allied not only with Austin's concept of excuse (which involves admission of culpability) but also with the Christian concepts of confession and conversion, particularly as Augustine defined them in the work in which he confessed his sins and turned away from his own prior words toward God and a new self. When Tasso excuses his epic, he almost always does so in the mode of Christian apology, with a gesture of turning away from a past self toward a future one. Neither the *Gerusalemme Liberata* nor his other works, he says, for example, "were ever revised or recorrected or published by me: may it please God that I will be allowed to do it!" ("né questa opera mia né l'altre sono mai state né riviste né ricorrette né publicate da me: piaccia a Dio che mi sia conceduto di farlo!" [p. 694]). The problem, as this quotation suggests, is that the human will alone cannot accomplish the turn of conversion; divine grace, or at least the help of God's priestly representatives, is necessary. Tasso's fear that such help will not be vouchsafed him arises, I think, from his sense that both his past performance as a poet and his present status as a writer of a self-justifying treatise place him in a territory of outer darkness inhabited by phantasms.

Plato's distinction in the *Sophist* (236a–d) between "eikastic" (true) and "phantastic" (false) imitations plays a crucial role in Tasso's definition of a realm in which both the rhetorician and the poet may hide from the light of truth. Tasso sees his critical opponents and their hero Ariosto as denizens of this realm of phantasms, which is characterized by "non-being" and is therefore "hidden and covered in darkness and mist."

> There the sophist is wont to flee, and to surround himself with many barriers and screens, so that it is hard to extract him; and there the fantastic poet, who is the same as the sophist, is wont to seek [the images of 'non-being']; but in seeking them, there is great danger that he will lose himself.

> In quanto elle non sono, stanno ascose e ricoperte nelle tenebre e nella caligine di quel che non è: lì dove suol rifuggire il sofista, e circondarsi di molti argini e di molti ripari, perché sia malagevole il cavarnelo; e quivi suol ricercarle il poeta fantastico, il quale è l'istesso che 'l sofistico; ma ricercandone, è gran pericolo che perda se stesso. [pp. 651–52]

Tasso's fear that he may be in danger of losing himself in the realm of phantasms is evident throughout the dialogue, particularly in his convoluted discussion of the two types of the "marvelous": the first type is engendered by the "fantastic" part of the mind, which seems to mean, for Tasso, the faculty of autonomous human imagination; the second type is somehow divinely sanctioned, in that it represents the truth of God's providential scheme.[107]

The problem, for Tasso and his readers, is that these two types of "marvelous" representations cannot be distinguished by aesthetic or epistemological criteria; the distinction, if it exists at all, lies in the hidden realm of authorial intention. And Tasso clearly lacks the inner conviction that his poetry is sanctioned, much less directly inspired, by God. Unlike Milton, whose Protestant sense of himself as a chosen vessel allowed him to confront the temptation to Satanic autonomy inherent in the poetic vocation and to make that temptation an infinitely rich poetic theme, Tasso is intellectually and emotionally weakened by his glimpses of the theoretical difficulties surrounding the issue of divine imitations. The weakness is evident in his tendency to vacillate between defending his "marvels" in *Gerusalemme*

Liberata and apologizing for them, according to the pattern we have previously remarked: immediately after proclaiming that episodes such as the apparition of the angel (to Goffredo in canto 11 of the *Liberata*) may be "decorously accepted from a Christian poet," he acknowledges that he may "remove" some of the marvels in his revision, "in order that the marvelous of the simulated kind should not perhaps be excessive" (pp. 672–73).

Let us return to Tasso's discussion of the Sophists' realm, deferring for a while the questions raised by his promise to "remove" parts of his poem in an act of self-chastisement equivalent to a symbolic wounding or castration. He defends himself against the fear of being tainted by—or trapped in—sophistry by invoking the example of Dante as a contrast to Ariosto. Dante, who plays such an important role in Tasso's drama of good and bad fathers, and who occupies a privileged place midway between the ancient and modern sets of ancestors in Tasso's fictive genealogy, is described as a "divine poet" capable of imitating truth rather than falsehood. Tasso advises all those who are in danger of losing themselves in the dark realm of "non-being" to seek poetic material "in the light and splendor of that which is truly, as Dante did" (p. 652). Tasso goes on to name Dante as the source for some of his own "celestial" imitations, in a clear example of a defense-by-identification; at this point, however, the defense fails to dispel anxiety, and Tasso lapses again into apology:

> I treated some celestial things in imitation of [Dante] but not so exquisitely as I once thought, and as I shall if ever I am allowed to.
>
> Ad imitazione del quale [Dante] trattai alcune delle cose celesti; ma non così esquisitamente come aveva pensato, e come farò se mai mi sarà conceduto. [p. 652]

In this passage Tasso symbolically portrays himself in the very act of turning away from the Sophists and Ariosto toward a Christian mode of poetry which he had already attempted—though imperfectly—in *Gerusalemme Liberata*. The turn is at once a return, a repetition of an aesthetic and ethical choice already made, and an effort to go beyond his own past to a better future. The temporal and existential complexity of his situation, as he defines it in this passage and throughout the *Apologia*, is best described by comparing it not only to Aeneas's situation in the underworld but also to that of Dante's Pilgrim in the opening lines of the *Inferno*: there Dante figures a return that is also a new beginning, a paradoxical moment in the "middle of our life's journey," where the self "refinds" itself and is at the same time aware that it is lost:

> Nel mezzo del cammin di nostra vita
>   mi ritrovai per una selva oscura
>   chi la diritta vie era smarrita.

The crucial difference is that Dante, as an author, is looking back at this moment, whereas Tasso, like some modern novelist, not only is *in medias res* but is recording the experience, as it were, in the present tense. He is fully aware that the moment of refinding himself cannot be the prelude to a journey so long as he must battle sophistic critics who have, he says, so "confused" the words of his epic that "I no longer recognize them as mine; nor do I wish to seek them in a poem I have not read for ten years, and in which I would have changed many things . . . if I had given it the ultimate perfection" (p. 689).

* * *

It is clear why the activity of rhetorical defense is itself, for Tasso, an entrapment in the dark realm of the Sophist and the fantastic poet; it is also clear why he attempts, from the beginning of the dialogic section of the treatise, to dissociate his aims and methods of argument from those of his critical prosecutors. Although his desire to conduct a self-defense that is uncontaminated with self-interest seems paradoxical ("I will speak not for myself but . . . for the truth," Il Forestiero promises at the outset [p. 645]), it makes sense in light of Tasso's anxiety about being tainted by the ontologically and morally questionable influence of the Sophist who is "the same" as the fantastic poet. Tasso defends himself against this anxiety by having the priestly interlocutor, Fantini, give him permission to argue against the critics; but his doubts about the legitimacy of self-defensive rhetoric remain.[108] They are strikingly evident in the following exchange between Il Forestiero and Fantini, which I shall quote at length because it not only defines the conflict between a sophistic mode of defense and a "virtuous" but pragmatically ineffective course of verbal action; it also points to a possible way of resolving the conflict through an appeal to Virgil's authority. Aeneas is, for Tasso, an exemplary figure of a hero who used amoral "Greek" arms to preserve his life but who nevertheless succeeded in virtuously accomplishing his destined mission:

> *Il Forestiero*: When I am offended with my own judgment manifested to many, if I want to repel the blow that comes to wound me, it is necessary that I reprove myself. What then must I do, friends and lords? Wait for the blow and receive the iron in my throat, as the Roman senators did when Rome was taken by the French? or indeed, is any defense permissible against adversaries, however false or true that defense may be?
> *Fantini*: "Dolus an virtus quis in hoste requirat?" [Whether deceit or valor, who would ask in warfare?] Clothe yourself in the arms of the Greeks, as Aeneas did in the burning of Troy, and, mixing yourself among the enemy, demonstrate your valor, or rather your doctrine: for the arms of literary men are the sciences, and you are accustomed to use the Greek sciences, as well as ours.

Il Forestiero: Quando io sono offeso co'l mio giudizio medesimo manifestato a molti, se voglio ribatter il colpo che viene a ferirmi, conviene che riprovi me stesso. Che dunque debbo fare, amici e signori miei? aspettar la percossa e ricever il ferro nella gola, come fecero i senatori romani quando Roma fu presa da' Francesi; o pur ogni difesa è lecita con gli avversari, vera o falsa ch'ella sia?

Fantini: "Dolus an virtus quis in hoste requirat?" Vestitevi dell'arme de' Greci, come fece Enea nell'incendio di Troia, e, mescolandovi fra' nemici, dimostrate il vostro valore o la vostra dottrina più tosto: perché l'arme dei letterati sono le scienze, e voi solete le greche, non che le nostre, adoperare. [p. 695][109]

The figure of Aeneas appears, in this passage, as a saving mediator between two extremes: the sophistic theory that "any defense is permissible" and the opposing view, which has Platonic, Stoic, and Christian sources, that no merely strategic defense is allowed to the virtuous man.[110] Although Fantini's final sentence implies that the problem of harmonizing past ("Greek") and present ("our") cultures is not fully resolved, his approval of Aeneas as an ethical model represents an important victory in Tasso's struggle to define a viable authorial identity. Fantini, who functions along with Plato as a kind of moral censor or superego in the *Apologia*, is shown releasing Tasso from a strict construction of his duty to virtue, a duty presented as requiring a passive martyrdom and, symbolically, a death of the poetic power (if the defendant receives the "iron in his throat," he will be virtuous but permanently silent).

By means of the quotation from *Aeneid* 2. 390, Tasso literally blends Virgil's voice with Fantini's; this rhetorical ploy argues for a metaphysical conjunction between Virgil's ethical perspective and an official Christian one. Dante had also meditated on that conjunction—though he insisted, as well, on the ultimate distance between the Christian pilgrim and his ancient guide. Nevertheless, it seems clear that Tasso is for his own purposes mining the rich vein of medieval and Renaissance admiration for Virgil as a "proto-Christian," the poet whose Fourth Eclogue was widely read as a prophecy of Christ's birth and whose epic depicted a hero whose piety was compatible with much Christian doctrine. Tasso praises the *Aeneid* earlier in his treatise as an epic "less subject" to Plato's strictures against poetry than Homer's epics were (p. 655); he invokes Aeneas now as a major proof in his argument for a legitimate use of defensive rhetoric.

Here again we see a defense-by-identification at work; indeed Tasso's repeated efforts to associate his poetic and rhetorical practice with that of "good" literary fathers like Virgil and Dante are crucial to his general attempt to win a favorable judgment not only from critics of poetry, such as Plato and the priests of the Catholic Church, but also from the even more severe judges seated in his "court of conscience." That phrase, which I take from Kenneth Burke, seems particularly apt for Tasso: more than any other major Renaissance poet, he suffers from the "inferiority complex," as Burke defines it in *A Rhetoric of Motives*:

> An "inferiority complex" is a sense that one's *kind of* being is inferior to another *kind* of being (or is endangered by that other *kind*). It is not merely an implied comparison between the self and another; it is a comparison between what I think I stand for and what I think the other stands for, in the terms of some *social* judgment. No individual could give another individual an "inferiority complex." Without the notion of an audience, an outside observer, to judge of the relation, the most one would feel would be the awareness of a literal inferiority. But there is a wide discrepancy between inferiority and an "inferiority complex." The first is merely a "fact" (a fact about everybody, by one test or another); the second is an accusation, in which one passes a social judgment upon oneself, condemning oneself from the standpoint of some real or imagined court of conscience.[111]

Tasso's court of conscience is more imagined than real: none of the many priests of the Inquisition to whom he submitted his work for criticism and confessed his errors considered him as guilty as he considered himself.[112] His personal situation at the time he wrote the *Apologia*—imprisoned by the Duke of Ferrara and also, metaphorically but no less woundingly, by the critics—undoubtedly exacerbated his guilt; as Freud remarks in *Civilization and Its Discontents*, "ill luck—that is, external frustration— . . . greatly enhances the power of the conscience in the super-ego. As long as things go well with a man, his conscience is lenient and lets the ego do all sorts of things; but when misfortune befalls him, he searches his soul, acknowledges his sinfulness, heightens the demands of his conscience, imposes abstinences on himself and punishes himself with penances" (*SE* 18: 126).

Although Tasso's conscience was hardly lenient even before his imprisonment, it is worth noting that he virtually stopped writing poetry during the time he was in Sant'Anna. The silencing of his poetic muse seems to have been one of the penances he imposed on himself. In his letters he laments the drying of his "vein" of inspirational genius; the blood-letting battles with the critics surely contributed to the loss of poetic power.[113] What is important for our present purposes is that Tasso did manage to placate his internal and external censoring judges enough to accomplish his own goal of revising his epic—an act which he regarded as the invention of a new poem, though we can see that it was as much a critical as a creative act. Indeed the new epic seems all too aptly titled, since it shows a poetic talent no longer liberated but almost conquered by the power of moral censorship[114] Nevertheless, the writing of the *Conquistata* represented a major achievement in Tasso's own eyes, and it constitutes the final act of the drama of defense we have been observing. The conclusion of the *Apologia* provides a clue to the psychic defense which enabled Tasso to regain enough confidence in his poetic authority to create the *Conquistata* and—what is equally important—

find it an admirable rather than imperfect "child of his intellect." Let us turn, then, to the end of the *Apologia*, where Tasso metaphorically transforms his dialogic persona from a defendant to a paternal judge. This transformation reveals the workings of a complex psychic defense which requires analysis from both an economic and a dynamic point of view.

The Economy of Judgment: Revision, Repression, and *the* Gerusalemme Conquistata

I think it most decorous that in these my ripe years I should know myself better than anyone else . . . and the man who knows himself, and understands what he writes, may judge his own work.—Tasso, *Giudizio sovra la "Gerusalemme Conquistata"*

Inevitably, in such [cases of revision], . . . I could but dream the whole thing over as I went—as I read; and, bathing it, so to speak, in that medium, hope that, some newer and shrewder critic's intelligence subtly operating, I shouldn't have breathed upon the old catastrophes and accidents, the old wounds and mutilations and disfigurements, wholly in vain.—Henry James, Preface to *The Golden Bowl*

To write *Gerusalemme Conquistata*, Tasso had to escape the court of conscience as the *Apologia* defines it; he had to cross the threshold from defending an old poem to writing a new one, or at least one he felt was qualitatively different. He accomplished this crossing by identifying with a figure of paternal authority he had himself created: Goffredo, the hero who leads the epic crusade on Jerusalem. Tasso's identification with Goffredo at the end of the *Apologia* is a complex rhetorical gesture which must be subjected to a cost-benefit analysis similar to that which Freud performs in *Civilization and Its Discontents*; there, in brilliant speculative prose, he gives his version of a story that Virgil and Tasso (but not Dante or Ariosto) had told before him, a story that elaborates the following tragic formula: "the price we pay for our advance in civilization is a loss of happiness through the heightening of the sense of guilt" (*SE* 21: 134).

Let me first consider what Tasso gains by presenting Goffredo as the final proof of his ability to write "pious" poetry. His tone takes on a new accent of authority as he praises a character in his old poem whose actions could be faulted neither by a philosopher like Plato nor by a priest like Fantini: Goffredo is a character of exemplary virtue, the one hero in the *Liberata* who is never tempted, much less defeated, in the magic forest of romance that lies outside Jerusalem. He is also, as Thomas Greene notes, the only character in Tasso's epic "who could not conceivably have appeared in the *Orlando Furioso*."[115] The treatise that began with an ambivalent defense of a father who never knew clearly where his artistic or moral duty lay concludes with unequivocal praise for a surrogate father who always knows that his duty is to God and God alone—and who is, moreover, not only an elected and sanctified political leader but a figure of the Christian poet. The image of Goffredo upon which Tasso rests his case is, significantly, that of a king in the role of an orator giving his audience the fruits of his wisdom, his *sentenza*, which also means "sentence" or "judgment" in a legal sense. In a striking sign of his identification with Goffredo in this role of orator-judge, Tasso refers to Goffredo's audience as "readers," *lettori*. Asking his own readers to observe Goffredo's wisdom, Tasso concludes the treatise by recalling scenes from *Gerusalemme Liberata* where Goffredo addresses audiences of princes and diplomats (courtiers):

> From his first oration made to Christian princes, and from his response to the Egyptian ambassadors, [Goffredo] begins to demonstrate, loosen, increase and diminish and prepare the souls of readers, using some universal propositions concerning that which one must pursue or avoid in actions; from whence without doubt I venture to affirm that the wisdom of that captain is the upright judgment of a good prince, and full of all excellences and all perfections.

> Sin da la prima orazione fatta a' principi cristiani, e da la risposta data a gli ambasciatori d'Egitto, [Goffredo] comincia a dimostrare, a sciogliere, ad accrescere e diminuire e a preparar gli animi de' lettori, usando alcuna proposizione universale intorno a quello che si dee seguire o schifar nell'azioni: laonde senza dubbio ardisco d'affermare che la sentenza di quel capitano sia il diritto giudizio del buon principe, e pieno di tutte le eccelenze e di tutte le perfezioni.
> [*Apologia*, pp. 719–20]

The apologetic note which has sounded so often in the treatise is notably absent from this peroration; "narcissistic supplies," to borrow Bruno Bettelheim's phrase, are clearly flowing into Tasso's rhetoric here. They should, for the praise of Goffredo represents a remarkable compromise solution to several of the problems defined in the *Apologia*. Goffredo serves, above all, to counter the critical views about the immorality of poetry in general which Tasso associates with the cultural authority of Plato and Fantini. As we have seen, Tasso previously attempted to counter such criticisms by invoking the examples of poets like Virgil and Dante, with whose moral perspectives he sought to identify his own. Now, however, by invoking the example of a hero he himself created, Tasso more forcefully claims a place in the family of ethically acceptable poets. He also succeeds in more firmly dissociating himself from the realm of romance inhabited by "fantastic" poets like Ariosto and Bernardo.

At the same time, moreover, Tasso implicitly counters the attacks on his powers of invention made by Ariosto's supporters. "Virtù," in the sense of strength, was at least as important to Tasso as ethical virtue, and the critics' derogatory remarks about the "sterility," "dryness," and even "smallness" of his poem, in comparison to Ariosto's, are such thinly veiled sexual insults that they provoke Tasso to frenzied, and slightly ludicrous, arguments of self-defense: even if his poem is "picciolo," he writes, it is nevertheless equal in length to Virgil's and even bigger than Dante's (p. 668). The praise of Goffredo is a more dignified version of such arguments: it serves—in an autotherapeutic way—as an assertion of poetic virility as well as of pious intention. This is quite a feat, a synthetic response, we might say, to the demands both of the psyche and of the society which shapes it. Tasso clearly perceived that when the critics used sexual metaphors to describe Ariosto's greatness, they were talking about a crucial fact of Italian Renaissance culture, which is that poems were judged (and poets rewarded) according to their power to delight audiences; hence the metaphors of erotic potency testified to Ariosto's actual success with his audience.[116] Tasso had to convince himself that there could be a "great" poetry that did not depend solely on the power to delight as Ariosto so amply possessed it, for that power—as I think Tasso knew from his own experience of reading Ariosto's lush and skeptical poem—generated anarchic desires in the minds of readers.

How does the praise of Goffredo serve, for Tasso, as a proof of poetic virility? The answer to this question has to do with a substitution we all know from daily life, and which Freud brooded about in many discussions of the aggressive or destructive instinct. Whether that instinct is defined as a primary or secondary phenomenon (only in his later works and with great reluctance did Freud posit a primary aggressive instinct separate from libidinal instincts), it frequently manifests itself as a substitute for that erotic satisfaction which the ego is denied either by the biological father or by cultural authorities. In the famous discussion of his grandson's "fort-da" game (*Beyond the Pleasure Principle*), Freud refers to an aggressive "instinct for mastery" which operates at once as the child's defense against the absence of his mother and (possibly) as an independent source of gratification.[117] Tasso's praise of Goffredo shows, I suggest, that the idea of aggressively mastering an audience serves to counter his fear that he lacks Ariosto's power to delight.

Tasso necessarily conceives of such power to delight in social (hence political) terms. His praise of Goffredo becomes even more interesting when one remembers his anecdote about Bernardo's failure to please an audience with a poem constructed according to Aristotelian principles of unity. For Goffredo represents a political principle of "single rule" which is clearly linked to Tasso's theories about the aesthetic superiority of well-governed narratives with a single major plot. In canto 1 of the *Gerusalemme* (both the original and the revised version), Goffredo is elected supreme commander of the Christian forces. This divinely decreed election, as Thomas Greene remarks, is "at variance with history, and Tasso knew it. During the actual crusade, Goffredo was only one of several generals who acknowledged no supreme commander."[118] Peter the Hermit rationalizes the election in a speech that is significant because it links praise of an authoritarian political system with a bitter critique of the injustices perpetrated in countries governed by "diverse" lords. Italy was, of course, such a country. However ambivalent Tasso was about the imperial claims of men like Charles V and Philip II, he had suffered too much in the courts of petty princes to avoid idealizing (as Dante also did) the concept of a supreme and just ruler. He had developed a strong sense of "injur'd merit," and one may speculate that it was exacerbated by Ariosto's popularity in a country where nobles preferred multiple plots to unified ones in both the aesthetic and the political spheres.[119] In Peter's words we can hear traces of Tasso's lifelong involvement in trials where his cause was, he felt, unfairly judged:

Ove un sol non impera, onde i giudìci
pendano poi de' premi e de le pene,
onde sian compartite opre ed uffici
ivi errante il governo esser conviene.   [*Gerusalemme Liberata*, 1.31]

Where divers Lords divided empire hold,
Where causes be by gifts, not justice, tried,
Where offices be falsely bought and sold,
Needs must the lordship there from virtue slide.

By presenting an image of Goffredo as an orator-judge in a position of mastery over his audience, Tasso creates proof of authorial virtue and power which is, in his opinion, satisfactory enough to bring the textual trial to a close. Although the trial is really interminable (in the psychoanalytic sense), the ending of the *Apologia* nevertheless marks a significant change: in the critical works written after 1585, Tasso characteristically adopts the role of paternal judge rather than that of filial defendant. This shift may be observed in the treatise from which I took one of the epigraphs for this section, a work left unfinished at Tasso's death (1595) and subsequently published with the title *Del Giudizio sovra la Gerusalemme di Torquato Tasso da lui medesimo riformata*. In this treatise Tasso assumes the role of judge and insists that he has earned the right to it by "reforming" his work and himself.[120] The conclusion of the *Apologia* not only anticipates Tasso's later critical stance of self-judging, self-reforming author; it also accomplishes a provisional resolution of an identity crisis, a resolution similar to the one he achieves at the end of his defense of Bernardo. There, through the invocation to the Muse of Memory which we have analyzed, he conjures up an image of the past which aids his vision of his future and enables him to turn from defending his father to defending his own epic. Now, having labored so long in the task of justifying a poem that he claims not to have read for ten years—a poem that therefore belongs to the past as much as Bernardo's does—he is once again figuratively poised|on a threshold; and again he remembers something from the past which can help him journey forward in his career.

The memory of the admirable hero he created in *Gerusalemme Liberata*, which replaces his more anxious memories of the epic, effects a change in the scene of the trial itself. By identifying with a hero who bestows wisdom, as an author ideally does, instead of asking for approval from others, Tasso regains some of the authority he had relinquished at the beginning of the dialogic trial when he hid beneath the name Il Forestiero and humbly begged Fantini to perform the role of judge.[121] The praise of Goffredo is indeed a piece of verbal action that transforms the power relations within the text and also, by implication, in that larger courtroom constituted by an author's relation to his readers. Goffredo comes, as it were, to occupy Fantini's place; by means of this substitution, which is a veiled usurpation, Tasso asserts his right to judge as well as be judged by critics.

He also fulfills a wish expressed a few paragraphs before the conclusion, a wish for an end to the debate among multiple voices: "But no more of this," Il Forestiero says after a particularly tedious exchange about the relative merits of Tasso's and Ariosto's choice of poetic diction; "let us be silent . . . about all the comparisons, and all the praises, and all the dispraises of me" ("Ma non più di questo; e tacciamo . . . di tutte le comparazioni, e di tutte le laudi, e di tutti i miei biasimi" [p. 718]). Tasso effectively displaces those various critical voices which have infiltrated his text by giving the last word to Il Forestiero, who describes Goffredo speaking to an attentively silent audience. Tasso thus figuratively silences not only his actual and potential prosecutors, among whom are the readers of the *Apologia* as well as the critics who had judged his epic harshly; he also silences (temporarily at least) that masochistic voice which confessed so often to a need for criticism. "I have always believed little in my judgment," he wrote in one of his many letters to critical authorities;[122] at the end of the *Apologia*, he figures a moment when he does believe in his judgment, and he thus portrays himself as a victor in the trial.

*   *   *

The victory, however, is Pyrrhic; and the trial, as I have said, does not end with the conclusion of the *Apologia*. The final scenes occur in the pages of the *Gerusalemme Conquistata* itself, and in Tasso's statements about the relation between his two epics. Consider first this brief and fascinating one from a letter written in 1593 to a Catholic bishop:

> I am most affectionate to the new poem, or the newly reformed one, as to a new birth of my intellect; from the first poem I am alienated as fathers are to rebellious sons, whom they suspect to have been born from adultery. This [second] poem is born from my mind, as Minerva was born from Jove's.

Sono affezionatissimo al nuovo poema, o novamente riformato, come a nuovo parto del mio intelletto: dal primo sono alieno, come i padri da' figliuoli ribelli, e sospetti d'esser nati d'adulterio. Questo è nato da la mia mente, come nacque Minerva da quella di Giove.[123]

This passage suggests that the price Tasso paid for conceiving of himself as a father was a rejection of his first-born son, the epic which was too permeated with the phantasms of romance to be worthy of the Christian poet. By metaphorically disinheriting his first epic, on the grounds that it is bad not only in its plot (like a rebellious son) but also in its origin (born, he suspects, of adultery, and hence not really his son at all), Tasso forcefully, if somewhat confusingly, denies the existence of continuity between his present and his past authorial identities. The reader's confusion arises from Tasso's figurative definition of his first poem as a rebellious son who may also be the son of someone else. The passage thus conjures up the image of not one but two possible sexual rivals to the author presently writing. However bizarre it may seem at first glance, the idea that both the *Liberata* and its author are Tasso's sexual rivals makes perfect sense once we note that Tasso comes to associate both his first epic and his "youthful" self with the poems and authorial identities of two men: Ariosto and Bernardo, Tasso's competitors for the favor of the Italian Muse and the biological mother respectively. If my own exposition seems to be leading into a nightmare world of romance doublings, that is appropriate, for what Tasso cannot bear in his first poem —what he fears may nauseate his readers, as he says in a letter—is the romance ethos it shares with the poems of fantastic writers like Ariosto and Bernardo.[124] In the *Giudizio sovra la "Gerusalemme,"* he criticizes the errors of his first epic in a way that dramatizes the hostility he feels toward its romance elements:

The narration of that first canto was indeed imperfect, and obscure, and similar to those opaque and shadowy places, in which passages are hard and the road uncertain, unless they are illuminated by new light.

La narrazione di quel primo canto era quasi imperfetta, e oscura, e simile a' luoghi opaci, e tenebrosi, ne' quali i passi sono malagevoli, e incerto il cammino, finchè da nuova luce non sono illuminati.[125]

This description, which echoes the first lines of Dante's *Commedia*, also recalls the passage in the *Apologia* where Tasso condemns Ariosto and the whole company of sophistic poets for hiding in the obscurity of "non-being" rather than seeking the light of truth as Dante did. Having now written *Gerusalemme Conquistata*, Tasso is at last in a position where he, like Dante, can look back on his past erring and can legitimately liken himself to the poet who turned palinodically from his early work—the love poetry and the "vain" philosophical speculation of the *Convivio*—to the higher labor of the

Commedia. Morever, by conceiving of his life as an imitation of Dante's, Tasso can further justify his journey away from Ariosto and from the father he compared to Aeneas in the "O del grand'Apennino" canzone. There he portrayed himself as following his father unhappily into exile; now, in a remarkable shift of perspective, he sees himself as resembling not Ascanius but Dante, the poet who began his journey homeward by following Virgil, but who left the paternal guide behind when he met a beloved woman at the top of Purgatory.

To understand what is really at stake in Tasso's attitude toward his two poems and in his act of revision itself, we must see that the *Conquistata*, that "new birth" of his intellect, is associated in Tasso's mind not only with his assumption of a new paternal authority, but also with a triumph over the realm of the flesh which allows him to imagine a spiritual reunion with his mother. In a strange example of (psychic) life imitating art (or using art as a vehicle for expressing inchoate fantasies), Tasso finds in Dante's account of his reunion with Beatrice a model for the contrast between his old and new poems. A passage from the *Giudizio*, which offers a rich gloss on his letter about his affection for the *Conquistata*, compares the new poem to Beatrice as Dante first sees her in the *Purgatorio*, "conquering" her "antique self" as Tasso felt he had conquered his past self (the "old Adam" of the flesh) by writing the *Conquistata*. The passage introduces the theme of competition between old and new by explicitly putting the *Liberata* in the place the critics had previously assigned to Ariosto's *Orlando*; having thus once again equated a poem which is chronologically older with a negative idea of youthful rebellion, Tasso reiterates his affection for his second-born epic, personifying it, once again, as a woman:

> I shall not, then, compare myself to Ariosto, or my Gerusalemme to his Furioso, as my enemies and friends have almost equally; but rather I shall compare myself already old, and close to death, to myself still young and in an immature period . . . and I will make a comparison between my almost earthly Jerusalem, and that which, if I do not deceive myself, is much more similar to the idea of the heavenly Jerusalem. And in this comparison, I will be allowed without arrogance, to prefer my mature poems to the unripe ones, and the labors of this age to the games of the younger age, and without blushing I shall assert, apropos of my Gerusalemme, the same thing that Dante said of Beatrice when she had already been made blessed and glorious: "She seemed here to triumph over her ancient self."

> Non paragonerò dunque me all'Ariosto, o la mia Gerusalemme al suo Furioso, come han fatto gl'inimici, e gli amici miei quasi egualmente; ma me già invecchiato, e vicino alla morte, a me giovane ancora, e d'età immatura . . . e farò comparazione ancora fra la mia Gerusalemme quasi terrena, e questa che, s'io non m'inganno, è assai più simile all'idea della celeste Gerusalemme. Ed in questo paragone mi sarà conceduto, senza arroganza, il preporre i miei poemi

maturi agli acerbi, e le fatiche di questa età agli scherzi della più giovanile, e potrò affermare della mia Gerusalemme senza rossore quel, che disse Dante di Beatrice, già fatta gloriosa e beata: "Vincer pareva qui se stessa antica."[126]

Here we see that the epic entitled *Gerusalemma Conquistata* stands, for Tasso, as a testimony or proof that he has conquered his "antique self." The very passage in *Purgatorio* to which he alludes, however—canto 31. 83–85— dramatizes a major reason why Tasso could not truly conquer his earthly self, in the sense of transcending his all too human concern with worldly success. Indeed Dante's passage may well have interested Tasso because it associates a surpassing of a former self with a surpassing of earthly rivals; the full sentence from *Purgatorio* reads:

> Sotto 'l suo velo e oltre la rivera
> vincer pariemi più sè stessa antica,
> vincer che l'altre qui, quand'ella c'era.

Beneath her veil and beyond the stream she seemed to me to surpass her former self more than she surpassed the others here when she was with us.

If, as I suspect, Tasso's persistent concern with poetic competition underlies his choice—and interpretation—of the lines from Dante, we can use the allusion as a starting point for exploring the important differences between his conception of conversion and Dante's.[127] The allusion to *Purgatorio* 31 directs our attention to a poetic scene of trial (in both senses of the word) which illuminates Tasso's literary autobiography by a series of parallels and contrasts. Dante's text may help us understand, above all, why Tasso could not write his life story as a "commedia"; he gives us instead a problem play which purports to end happily (with a Christian conversion) but which in fact has tragic implications.

The line Tasso quotes occurs after Beatrice has accused Dante of betraying her memory, of committing adultery, as it were, with the famous *pargoletta*, that ambiguous sexual or intellectual object Dante pursued after Beatrice's death.[128] In her role of stern accuser, Beatrice is at once a father figure and a harsh mother-wife calling an erring man to task for his sins. Dante stresses the conflation of sexual roles in a way that has obvious significance for Tasso's imaginative autobiography and which clarifies his mention of adultery in the letter about his two epics. On first seeing Beatrice in *Purgatorio* 30, Dante echoes the words Dido speaks when she is about to betray her first husband's memory through passion for a second man who will then betray her: "conosco i segni dell'antica fiamma." Dante speaks these words to Virgil, but Virgil, who has just been compared to a comforting mother, is gone, at once honored by the echo and dismissed by the advent of Beatrice, the woman who will be both a better surrogate father to Dante (leading him to God) and a better surrogate mother.[129] At first, however, she seems herself very like Dido accusing Aeneas of betraying her. But Dante insists that both Beatrice and the Pilgrim know a love which allows them to transcend sexual difference. If Beatrice is at once like Dido and Aeneas, the grieving woman and the "pious" hero who harshly subordinates eros to duty, she is at the same time radically different from Virgil's characters, as is Dante; he also resembles both Dido and Aeneas but comes, during the course of this trial, to see that the battle between the sexes, like the battle between flesh and spirit, can be resolved on a higher plane.

Such a dialectical resolution is precisely what Tasso cannot achieve, although he strives for it: his two descriptions of his two poems can certainly be read as attempts to imagine a family composed of a father-son united in one unfleshly person and worthy, therefore, to be joined in some mysterious way with a woman who seems to be both a mother and a daughter. The metaphor in his letter of an author who "gives birth," as Zeus does, to a beloved female child, suggests Tasso's desire not only to resemble the divine creator but also to conceive of that creator as an androgynous Being. This desire may contain a fantasy either of becoming one with the mother or of escaping the need for her by assuming her creative powers; the distinction between erotic and envious sentiments in Tasso is never very clear. One might also speculate that when Tasso came to write and justify his second epic, he was at the same time creating family romance stories which reflect not only the child's fantasies about his parents, but also a parent's fantasies about his child (or children). Freud did not explicitly discuss a genre of family romances written, as it were, from the parent's point of view; but such a genre seems particularly important for authors who brood, as Tasso does, not only about their poetic offspring, but about the sibling rivalries and sexual differences among them.[130] By personifying the *Conquistata* as female and comparing it to Beatrice, Tasso takes us into an imaginative country where the boundaries between texts and people are shadowy indeed.

The Dantesque allusion also suggests how far Tasso was from being able to conceive of a happy family reunion among either texts or people. The line he quotes, from a scene so richly concerned with betrayal, loss, surrogate loved ones, and exchanges of sexual identities, occurs after Dante has confessed his past errors to Beatrice but before he has received absolution for them; the absolution is a necessary prelude to the experience of rebirth which enables him to cross the threshold from Purgatory to Paradise. Tasso could not have chosen a more brilliant way of indicating his own characteristic position between confession and absolution; nor could he have evoked a better symbol for the barrier between him and bliss than the river of Lethe, which Dante mentions in the line preceding the one Tasso quotes. At this moment in canto 31, Lethe separates Dante from Beatrice; he must cross it to be spiritually reborn. Lethe is Dante's symbol for man's need to be freed from guilt; by crossing it and tasting of its waters, Dante is psychologically as well as theologically prepared to obey the Pauline command which is a major subtext of the *Commedia* as a whole: "Put off the old man with his deeds; and . . . put on the new man, which is renewed in knowledge after the image of him that created him" (Colossians 3:10-11). But Dante does not only cross Lethe, the river "which takes from men the memory of sin" (*Purgatorio* 28. 128); he also crosses a second river which springs from the same divine fountain as Lethe, but which gives memories back rather than taking them away. This is Eunoe, "well-mindedness," which "restores [the memory] of every good deed" (l. 129). The myth of Eunoe—indeed the name itself—is Dante's original creation; it is a remarkable supplement to the Pauline and Augustinian theory of conversion as a radical break between the old and the new selves.[131] Dante insists that conversion includes a double experience of discontinuity and redemptive continuity; without the latter, which he presents as a restoration of memory and a testimony to the ultimate link between Eros and Agape, earthly passion and heavenly *caritas*, the psyche would be permanently wounded. He diagnoses this wounded state—from which, I believe, Tasso never escaped—as one of remorse; the pilgrim's heart is so bitten by self-recognition (*riconoscenza*; cf. the Middle English phrase "agenbite of inwit") that he hates both himself and Beatrice. The burden of such guilt is too great, and he falls in a deathly faint.[132] Without the intervention of that grace represented by Beatrice's love, and without the mysterious double restoration symbolized by the crossing of the memory-healing rivers, the Christian would, Dante implies, lose his mind. Reading Dante's poem, Tasso would have found a frightening portrait of himself in the lines immediately following the one he quotes to assert his triumph over his "antique self." The man who wrote the *Conquistata* and called it a "new" poem, but who nevertheless retained many episodes virtually unchanged, must have known on some level that he remained where Beatrice describes Dante at the beginning of canto 31: on the far side of the river which prevents madness by effacing memories of sin.

* * *

Freud's earliest work was with patients who suffered "mainly from reminiscences."[133] His explorations of the territory on the far side of Lethe and Eunoe can help us understand the meaning of Tasso's act of revising his epic; but Tasso can at the same time illuminate an aspect of Freud's own career which has not often been discussed in relation to his theoretical concern with processes of repetition, revision, and distortion. Like Tasso, Freud constantly revised his own works; also like Tasso, he leads us to consider the dark parallels between the act of revising one's own work and the act of revising ("reseeing," as Henry James calls it) a work produced by another mind. "In its implications, the distortion of a text resembles a murder,"

Freud wrote in *Moses and Monotheism*; "the difficulty is not in perpetrating the deed, but in getting rid of the traces." (*SE* 23: 43). He is discussing the scribal revisions of the biblical text here, but his comment applies equally well to *Moses and Monotheism* itself, a work which "has been written twice," he tells us, and which tormented him "like an unlaid ghost" when he determined to give it up (p. 103). The revisor, whether an ancient scribe, Tasso, or Freud himself, practices an art of "distortion" (*Entstellung*). Explaining the term, Freud writes:

> We might well lend the word "Entstellung" the double meaning to which it has a claim. . . . It should mean not only "to change the appearance of something" but also "to put something in another place, to displace." Accordingly, in many instances of textual distortion, we may nevertheless count upon finding what has been suppressed and disavowed hidden away somewhere else. [p. 43]

This comment casts an ironic light on the apology Freud makes for the text of *Moses* itself. Its "method of exposition," he writes, "is no less inexpedient than it is inartistic. Why have I not avoided it? The answer to that is not hard for me to find, but it is not easy to confess. I found myself unable to wipe out the traces of the history of the work's origin" (p. 103). By his phrasing here, Freud places his own activity of revision firmly within the sphere of criminality he defined by likening rewriting to murder. Moreover, he calls attention to the existence of suppressed meaning in his text, although he does not (and cannot) say what it is. He cannot because a text, as he suggests not only in *Moses* but throughout his work, functions as an extension of the psyche, and a person can "know" his writing only in the partial way he can know himself. He can, however, attempt to analyze the earlier products of his psyche, and this, I think, is what Freud and Tasso both do when they engage in the process of revision and meditate, in quasi-autobiographical, theoretical discourse, on the vexed relation of the old and the new.[134] Freud's discussions of psychic defenses are particularly useful for an analysis of Tasso's revisions because Freud's own discourse, like Tasso's, repeatedly blurs the boundaries between interpsychic, interpersonal, and intertextual conflicts.

* * *

To understand what is at stake in Tasso's act of revision we must return to the tortuous familial metaphors he uses to describe the relation between his two poems. Through those triangular figurations he asserts his alienation from his original text; but he also invites us to see that text as a phantasmic object—part corpse, part ghost—to which he is still emotionally bound. A father may disown his first-born son but he does not therefore cease loving him; nor does a lover altogether forget his dead lady's body when he is granted a vision of her spiritual beauty. Most importantly, however, an author cannot lose his narcissistic attachment to a "child of his intellect" even if he is, like Tasso, engaged in harshly molding that child into a new shape, changing something in almost every stanza, cutting out major erotic episodes and adding scenes which elaborate the religious allegory so as to bring the poem more into "conformity with sacred doctrine."[135]

As anyone who has ever revised his or her own writing knows, the process involves sado-masochistic feelings. In Tasso's case, however, those feelings appear to have been extraordinarily violent and only slightly mediated by the conscious ego. He so graphically describes his first epic as a bodily object tainted by the sins of the flesh that one's own flesh crawls (or mine does) when one sees that the text of *Gerusalemme Liberata* came to signify, for Tasso, the rebellious part of his own body, the part which he had to cut off in order to satisfy the demands of his conscience. He seems also to have unconsciously identified the text of his epic with the bodies of his parents, whose fleshly union had produced him and from whom he also felt a powerful need to sever himself, perhaps taking revenge not only on his parents but on death itself, the Grim Reaper whose scythe had already cut down members of Tasso's family. In an absolutely uncanny way, Tasso's act of revision dramatizes his resemblance to a violent Roman who bore the name Torquatus.

In Book 6 of the *Aeneid*, Virgil refers to this man as "Torquatus of the savage axe."[136] There is no possibility that Torquato Tasso did not know the story of his ancestor in name, for the man of the savage axe is mentioned not only in the book telling of Aeneas's encounter with his father in the underworld, but also, at greater length, in Cicero's *De officiis*, the series of letters from a father to his son which so influenced Tasso's views on moral duty. Manlius Torquatus gained his surname by killing a gigantic Gaul in single combat and taking from him his golden neck chain (*torquis*). He gained his greatest fame, however, by severing his own son's head from his body with the "savage axe" to which Virgil refers. His son had disobeyed his command not to engage in single combat against the Latin enemies of Rome. There are several paradoxes in the story of Manlius Torquatus. The one most important for our present purposes is that his strictness toward his son is specifically linked, by Cicero, to his "thoughtfulness" toward his father, who had banished him when he was a youth. Torquatus's father, a dictator of Rome, was accused by a tribune of the people of committing various crimes—among them, banishing his son inhumanely. Torquatus came to his father's defense, but his act of filial loyalty, like everything else he did, was marked by violence. Entering the room of the prosecuting tribune, he "immediately drew out his sword," Cicero writes, and "swore that he would kill the tribune on the spot, if he did not swear an oath to withdraw the suit against his father."[137] Cicero's mildly ironic comment about the inconsistency of Torquatus's behavior—"he was one who, while more than generous to his father, would yet be bitterly severe toward his son"—invites us to see the dangerous tendency toward excess in a man whose savagery toward his son seems clearly a displaced expression of violence toward his father. This labile aggressiveness is what makes the Roman story so eerily relevant to the one we have been tracing, in which a later Torquatus attacks his "first-born" poem as if it were his father's body and a part of his own at once.

Tasso's writing often reveals a deep resentment of the body itself as a mortal object. Recall the passage in the *Apologia* where he implicitly reproaches his father for having sent him "to live in this body almost like a *peregrino*." In that passage, where the mother is also figuratively invoked as the Muse of Memory, Tasso voices an oblique protest against earthly life itself and against anyone, man, woman or God, who is responsible for creating it. Like Hamlet, brooding on "sullied flesh" and "the thousand shocks that flesh is heir to," Tasso seems to suffer from a nameless disease whose symptoms include an aggressivity that may be directed toward the self (suicide) as easily as toward others (murder). Tasso's hero Tancredi, as we shall see, suffers from this same disease.

If the text of the *Liberata* is, for Tasso, an object which reminds him of his own sullied flesh and the parental bodies from which it issued, we may view his revision as both a symbol for and a product of that complex psychic defense Freud called "identification."[138] He discusses one aspect of that defense in *Civilization and Its Discontents*, in a passage about the "familiar mechanism of identification" which enables the (boy) child to escape the "economically difficult situation" of the Oedipus complex only to find that there is also a "great economic disadvantage in the erection of a super-ego," with its accompanying sense of guilt (*SE* 21: 127). The passage is particularly relevant to Tasso's case because it describes a process which occurs, according to Freud, at a specific stage of a child's development but which may, nonetheless, be repeated in adult life, as the superego's power is "reinforced" by suppressions of instinct that structurally resemble those which occurred in childhood:[139]

A considerable amount of aggressiveness must be developed in the child against the authority which prevents him from having his first, but none the less his most important, satisfactions, whatever the kind of instinctual deprivation that is demanded of him may be; but he is obliged to renounce the satisfaction of this revengeful aggressiveness. He finds his way out of this economically difficult situation with the help of familiar mechanisms. By means of identification he takes the unattackable authority into himself. The authority now turns into his super-ego and enters into possession of all the aggressiveness which a child would have liked to exercise against it. *The child's ego has to content itself with the unhappy role of the authority—the father—who has thus been degraded.* Here, as so often, the [real] situation is reversed: "If I were the father and you were the child, I should treat you badly." The relationship between the super-ego and the ego is a return, distorted by a wish, of the real relationships between the ego, as yet undivided, and an external object. That is typical too. But the essential difference is that the original severity of the super-ego does not—or does not so much—represent the severity which one has experienced from it [the object], or which one attributes to it; it represents rather one's own aggressiveness towards it. If this is correct, we may assert truly that in the beginning conscience arises through the suppression of an aggressive impulse, and that it is subsequently reinforced by fresh suppressions of the same kind. [*SE* 21: 129–30; my emphasis]

This complex formulation fully supports Freud's claim in the *New Intro-ductory Lectures* that his "hypothesis of the super-ego really describes a structural relation and is not merely a personification of some such abstraction as that of conscience" (*SE* 22: 64). The structural model that the passage sketches, which is also a dynamic model, provides a useful way of understanding Tasso's identification with Goffredo at the end of the *Apologia*. That identification signals an internalization of paternal authority which I take to be crucial for Tasso's writing of the *Conquistata*. The writing of the *Conquistata* involves an aggressive turning against a "degraded" product of the poet's ego, the *Liberata*, and against the two father figures he associates with that poem, Bernardo and Ariosto.

Freud's account of an introjection of paternal authority suggests that Tasso's aggressiveness toward the ethos of romance may also be viewed as a displacement of the violence he would have liked to exercise against the figures of social and religious authority who deprived him of "instinctual satisfaction," chief among them the duke who had imprisoned him in Sant'Anna. Aggressiveness turned against one or another father figure, however, is not the only factor at work in Tasso's revision of his epic. If the text of the *Liberata* becomes a complex surrogate object in Tasso's imaginary depiction of a war between severe fathers and rebellious sons, it is also, as I have suggested, an object which Tasso associates with his mother and the siren song of Romance. To illustrate this point let me consider a passage in which Freud deals with the psyche's defense against the loss of a beloved object.

Such loss occurs for the boy during the Oedipal crisis when he is forced to renounce his erotic fixation on his mother; at that time, he resorts to a type of defensive identification that may also occur, Freud says, at any stage in life.[140] The defense consists of identifying with an object that has been renounced or lost in a way that allows that object to be introjected into the ego, thus creating an internal substitute. Freud sees this process as characteristically occurring in the cases of male homosexuality, where the boy's strong identification with his mother causes his ego to be "remolded" on the model of the lost but introjected object.[141] Freud also suggests that this kind of identification produces the symptoms characteristic of melancholia. In *Group Psychology and the Analysis of the Ego* (1921) he writes:

> A leading characteristic of these cases [of melancholia] is a cruel self-depreciation of the ego combined with relentless self-criticism and bitter self-reproaches. Analyses have shown that this disparagement and these reproaches apply at bottom to the object and represent the ego's revenge upon it. The shadow of the object has fallen on the ego. . . .
>
> But these melancholias also show us . . . the ego divided, fallen into two pieces, one of which rages against the second. This second piece is the one which has been altered by introjection and which contains the lost object. But the piece which behaves so cruelly is not unknown to us either. It comprises the conscience, a critical agency within the ego, which even in normal times takes up a critical attitude towards the ego, though never so relentlessly and so unjustifiably. [*SE* 18: 109]

I have deliberately chosen passages in which Freud presents the defense of identification in terms of a battle between the sexes which rages within the psyche. An introjected father, the superego, directs its cruelty against an ego that has been "altered" by its introjection of a (maternal) object. This is an oversimplification of Freud's theory, but it provides an important paradigm for Tasso, and also for Freud himself; it haunted him even when he modified it by describing the superego, for instance, as a product of the child's identification with both parents, or by describing a "negative" form of the Oedipus complex in which the boy-child desires his father and hates his mother.[142] The simplified version of Freud's primal story is complex enough for our purposes, however, because it not only corresponds to the basic plot of Tasso's psychic biography, so far as we can infer it, but also to the ur-plot of both his epics and to the story of the relation between them. The narrative weirdly repeated in all these registers tells of a battle among a father, a son, and a mother who is at once a pretext for the battle and a participant in it. The son identifies with both parents but insists that the father achieves victory in the end; this victory is, however, not only costly, but morally and epistemologically doubtful.

The most abstract version of this story concerns the relation between the two epics. I have suggested that Tasso identifies with Goffredo in order to write the *Conquistata*, and indeed one way to understand the revised epic is to think of it as if it were largely written by Goffredo himself, acting as a severe superego governing Tasso's decisions about what to suppress and what to add in order to "reform" his epic. The very body of the second text serves as a kind of bizarre economic emblem for what is gained and lost when Tasso tries to write as if he were Goffredo: the *Conquistata* is considerably longer than the *Liberata*, but many of the first poem's erotic episodes are cut from the second version.[143] It is as if Tasso has earned the right to paternal size (recall his anxieties about the relative length of his poem and

Ariosto's) by relinquishing his attachment to erotic episodes in his first poem.[144]

And there is another symbolic reward for the renunciation of carnal pleasures, or the pleasures of representing them. In one of the new episodes of the *Conquistata*, Goffredo has a vision of the Heavenly Jerusalem which parallels Tasso's vision, in the *Giudizio*, of the poem itself as a heavenly lady like Dante's Beatrice. The "città nuova" appears to Goffredo in a dream after a series of Old Testament scenes showing men committing sins of lust and idolatry; God, Tasso writes, turned away from these men with "paternal scorn" (*Gerusalemme Conquistata* 20. 15). Goffredo exhibits the same quality of "paterno sdegno" in turning his eyes away from the visions of sin toward the vision God grants him of a joy promised by the New Testament—specifically, by Revelation 21:2, where John sees the new Jerusalem "coming down from God from heaven, prepared as a bride adorned for her husband." Goffredo also sees a city like a bride:

> Come sposa real che in gioia e'n festa
> le prezïose pompe altrui dispieghi;
> e 'l suo candido seno e l'aurea testa
> di rare gemme e d'òr circondi e leghi
> ....
> così parea quella cittade adorna,
> che di luce immortal mai sempre aggiorna.
>
> [*Gerusalemme Conquistata* 20. 27]

> As a royal bride who in joy and festivity
> displays the precious pomp to others,
> and her white breast is encircled with
> rare gems, and her golden head is bound with gold
> ....
> so that city seemed adorned,
> which always and forever
> dawns with eternal light.

By patterning his hero's vision on John's, Tasso implicitly defines his own new "vision"—the *Conquistata* itself—as a divinely inspired text. Moreover, he invites us to see that his own turn from an old earthly poem to a new heavenly one parallels Goffredo's turn from scenes of sin to visions of beatitude: the poet's career thus becomes an allegorical version of salvation history, one which serves the same exemplary purpose Tasso attributes to Goffredo's dream itself in the *Giudizio*; there he compares the dream to an allegorical structure built on the foundation of history: "that structure, like the words of a most serious father, may serve not only as an exposition to theologians, but also as a lesson to poets and in particular to those who do not wish to write vainly" ("sovra i fondamenti dell'istoria conviene fabricar coll' allegoria una fabbrica intellettuale . . . la qual, quasi sentenza del gravissimo padre, può servir non solamente per esposizione ai teologi, ma per ammaestramento a' poeti, ed a quelli particolarmente, che non vanamente vogliono poetare").[145]

If the image of the poem as a beautiful and richly adorned bride shows Tasso's desire to conceive of himself in the authoritative role of "gravissimo padre," like Goffredo, John, and God himself, it also shows his interest in that ideal of a pure heroic love which Christian Neoplatonists such as Ficino adumbrated with reference to the supposed etymological link (mentioned in Plato's *Cratylus*) between *eros* and *heros*.[146] But even in the *Conquistata* there are signs that this ideal of sublime love cannot silence the voice in Tasso which anticipates Freud by telling us that sublimation, as a defense, is theoretically indistinct from repression. And that which is repressed returns.

In the *Conquistata*, it returns in virtually the same way it does in the *Liberata*: in the story of a hero who is at once Goffredo's figurative son and his dark double. Tancredi too has a dream vision of a beautiful heavenly woman. In canto 12 of the *Liberata* and canto 15 of the *Conquistata*, Clorinda's spirit appears in a dream to pardon him for having killed her and to promise him a seat in heaven if he refrains from the sin of despair.[147] Alive, Clorinda had wounded Goffredo and had prevented him from breaching Jerusalem's walls with his huge wooden tower on wheels.[148] Tancredi is clearly serving the cause of Goffredo and the Christian father when he fights and mortally wounds the pagan woman he loves but does not recognize during the night battle. For Tancredi, however, the reward of seeing his beloved in the spirit does not compensate for the grief caused by the loss of her body. Nor does the pardon she gives him absolve his guilt. Indeed the epistemological and moral status of his dream vision is radically called into question by his experience in the following canto, where Clorinda's phantasmic voice issuing from the bleeding tree makes him forget her heavenly voice and his own Christian mission. The vision of the beatified lady is retrospectively defined by the bleeding tree episode as a text which must compete for authority with the one jointly created by the pagan magician and by the hero's own guilty memories and desires.

In *Beyond the Pleasure Principle* Freud cites Tasso's bleeding tree episode, in which the hero "wounds his beloved once again," as "the most moving poetic picture" of a fate governed by the "compulsion to repeat" (*SE* 18: 22). But Freud does not mention the aspect of the picture which makes it most relevant to his own autobiography and Tasso's: the hero turns his aggression against a phantasm, a fiction or "simulacrum," which he wounds but cannot kill or silence.[149] Moreover, the phantasm wounds his consciousness in return, using accusing words like a sword to remind the hero that in attempting to serve (and imitate) Goffredo he has committed an excessive crime against love and the flesh:

>   —Ahi! troppo—disse
> —m'hai tu, Tancredi, offeso: or tanto basti.

Tu dal corpo che meco e per me visse,
felice albergo, già mi discacciasti.

Ah! Too much—it said—have you offended me, Tancredi. Now so much
suffices. You already drove me away from that body, happy home, which lived
with and by me.[150]

That these same words appear in both versions of the epic dramatizes the
parallel between Tasso's fate and Tancredi's, a parallel I would now like to
examine: neither succeeds in putting off the "old man with his deeds"
because neither escapes the family romance.[151]

The bleeding tree episode shows how powerfully that romance is shaped,
for Tasso, by literary as well as familial memories; indeed the episode is a
profound allegorical meditation on the relation between the writer, who is
also a reader, and his precursors. Tasso not only imitates the stories told by
Virgil, Dante, and Ariosto of a hero's encounter with a bleeding tree;[152] he
also implicitly draws an analogy between his authorial act of imitation and
the hero's act of wounding a tree. Tancredi strikes the tree after reading a
mysterious ancient inscription warning him not to wage war with the dead
by disturbing "this sacred seat."[153] His wounding of the tree challenges the
inscription's authority; it is therefore a symbolic version of the act which
Tasso describes, in the *Apologia*, as a "killing for the second time." He
applies that phrase, as we have seen, to the critical attacks on his father's
poem. His own poem suggests, however, that such acts of textual violence
are inevitable: he who does not engage in the erotic and aggressive activity
of wounding past texts by imitating and changing them—that is, by violating
their authority as sacred and integral objects—would himself be dead as an
author, for he would no longer be sparked with the desire to "spy, again, the
hidden causes."[154]

The phrase is Tasso's; or rather it is his revised version of a line Aeneas
speaks when describing his action of tearing a second shoot from a bleeding
bush:

rursus et alterius lentum convellere vimen
insequor et causas penitus temptare latentis.

Once more, from a second also I go on to pluck
a tough shoot and probe deep the hidden cause.
[*Aeneid* 3. 31–32; Loeb ed. pp. 350-51]

Tasso's echo marks a crucial difference between his hero and Virgil's. Like
Aeneas, Tancredi wounds a tree not once but repeatedly; the voice Tancredi
hears, however, unlike the one Aeneas hears, brings him knowledge that the
epic narrator defines as false. Indeed Tancredi's major difference from all his
epic predecessors is that his encounter with a voice from the past impedes
rather than furthers his mission and his understanding of it. None of Tasso's

precursors raise epistemological questions about the tree-voice, though all
brood on the ontological mystery of a bleeding, speaking creature in the
border realm between the human and the nonhuman, and between life and
death. Tasso alone makes the ontological mystery into an epistemological
and moral danger, calling the voice a "simulacrum" which lies to the hero
ambiguously about its—and his—identity.

The contrast with Virgil's episode is easiest to see, since it involves a
dramatic spatial reversal. From his encounter with Polydorus, the dead
Trojan buried beneath the bleeding bush, Aeneas learns that he must go
forward on his epic quest, leaving the tainted soil of Thrace where Polydorus was betrayed and killed by a king greedy for gold. Tancredi, in contrast,
is persuaded by the phantasmic voice of Clorinda to halt his journey and
turn back, empty-handed and shamed, to Jerusalem and Goffredo. Tancredi
symbolically loses his heroic male identity when he drops his sword in fear
of Ismeno's creation (*GL* 13. 45; *GC* 16. 49). He picks up his sword at the end
of the episode, but he does not use it as the epic narrator implies he should: to
wound the tree yet once more and thus discover the falsity of the phantasm.
Aeneas wounds the bush three times; Tancredi wounds the tree only twice.
Had he taken the final violent step, Tasso implies, he could have gone
forward rather than backward. Tasso echoes Virgil's line about the "hidden
cause" at the moment when Tancredi turns away from the tree, underscoring his hero's failure not only to wrest knowledge from the dead, but to leave
them behind, as Aeneas does, after a ceremony of pious reburial:

> Pur non tornò, né ritentando ardio
> spiar di novo le cagioni ascose.   [*GL* 13. 47; *GC* 16. 51]

> Then he did not return, nor did he dare, by trying again, to spy once more the
> hidden causes.

Tasso's narrator judges the hero's error, however, without simply condemning it. Unlike Peter the Hermit, who accuses Tancredi of straying
"wittingly and willingly" from his Christian path,[155] the epic narrator adopts
the role of a physician analyzing a patient who is only partly responsible for
his behavior. The narrator here resembles Freud in *Beyond the Pleasure
Principle*, seeking the "hidden causes" of an illness for which the cure also
remains unknown. Even some "normal" people, Freud writes, give an
impression "of being pursued by a malignant fate or possessed by some
'daemonic' power; but psychoanalysis has always taken the view that their
fate is for the most part arranged by themselves and determined by early
infantile influences" (*SE* 18: 21). In the stanza following the bleeding tree's
accusation (a stanza Freud fails to mention), Tasso explores just this paradoxical notion of a fate at once "arranged" by the individual and imposed on
him by external influences. But Tasso insists on a point Freud was not eager

to acknowledge with respect to his own fate as a writer: the "influences" come from literary as well as familial sources:[156]

Qual l'infermo talor ch'in sogno scorge
drago o cinta di fiamme alta Chimera,
se ben sospetta o in parte anco s'accorge
che 'l simulacro sia non forma vera,
pur desia di fuggir, tanto gli porge
spavento la sembianza orrida e fera:
tal il timido amante a pien non crede
a i falsi inganni, e pur ne teme e cede.   [*GL* 13. 44; *GC* 16. 48]

As the sick man that in his sleep doth see
   Some ugly dragon or some chimera new,
Though he suspect or half persuaded be
   It is an idle dream, no monster new,
Yet still he fears, he quakes, and strives to flee,
   So fearful is the wond'rous form to view:
So fear'd the knight, yet he both knew and thought
All were illusions false by witchcraft wrought.

Analyzing both the symptoms and the causes of a malady he clearly shares with his hero, Tasso returns, once again, to the question that preoccupied him throughout his life: How does one know the difference between a "simulacrum" and a "true form"? Tasso's obsession with this epistemological question and his inability to resolve it suggest that it should be regarded as an intellectual screen for the psychic struggle between his libidinal fantasies and the demands of his superego. His conscious ego, one might say, translates the superego's demand for renunciation of satisfaction into a demand that fantasies be recognized as such and rejected. At the same time, however, his ego refuses to deny altogether the "truth of fictions." The poetic ego might thus be compared to a judge in a trial, not an Inquisitorial judge, but rather one who is asked to mediate in a bitter dispute between labor and management. In his later career, Tasso was less and less able to represent both sides of any question, but even in the *Conquistata*—in the bleeding tree episode for instance—he creates scenes of trial in which the poet exercises his powers of judgment by refusing to hand down a definitive sentence. Tasso's epic narrator attempts, at such times, to define a trial where justice consists of deferring or suspending decisions. The man who doubted whether a vision of the Virgin Mary with her Son in her arms was "true" or a product of his own *fantasia* (hence true in a different sense), gives us in his greatest poetry an argument against black and white judgments that parallels Rabelais's defense of the apparently foolish delaying tactics used by a judge named Bridlegoose (*Bridoye*) in *Le Tiers Livre*. Bridoye, who is clearly a figure for the author himself, postpones hermeneutic decisions as long as possible because "he doubted his own knowledge and capacity, knew the inconsistencies and contradictions of the laws, edicts, customs, and ordinances, and was aware of the deceptions of the eternal Calumniator, who often disguises himself as a messenger of light . . . [and] turns black into white."[157]

*   *   *

In representing the undecidable trial of Tancredi's divided consciousness, Tasso could not avoid confronting the author whom his Christian conscience judged most harshly but whom he nevertheless loved as he loved a part of himself. Ariosto is the most powerful and overdetermining influence on Tasso's bleeding tree episode. Not only does Tancredi resemble Ariosto's Ruggiero, who encounters Astolfo's metamorphosed spirit in a tree; Tancredi also resembles Orlando, the hero who goes mad when he discovers that he has lost his beloved Angelica to a pagan knight named Medoro. In a fit of furious aggression and frustrated desire, Orlando uproots a whole forest of trees (*Orlando Furioso* 23. 95–136). His lady's name and her lover's are inscribed on the bark of those trees; one of the inscriptions, written in Arabic, is indeed what brings Orlando the knowledge of betrayal that his consciousness cannot sustain. Fragmentary echoes of Ariosto's central episode appear throughout Tasso's story of Tancredi in the forest; this is significant, since both poets are thematically concerned with the relations between fragmented texts, fragmented objects like lances and trees, and fragmented human beings whose spirits are sundered from their bodies or whose rational faculties are divorced from their passions.[158] Tasso and Ariosto both portray heroes who go mad not only because their erotic desires are frustrated, but also because they are confronted with texts which they have not authored. Tasso, however, differs from Ariosto in a crucial way: Tancredi "goes outside of himself" ("va fuor di sé" [*GL* 13. 45]) because he half-wittingly believes texts which Tasso defines, ambiguously, as false: the ancient inscription and the phantasmic voice of Clorinda.[159] Orlando, in contrast, loses his reason because he comes to believe, against his will, in texts which Ariosto defines as true: the inscriptions by Angelica and Medoro telling of their love (*Orlando Furioso* 23. 106–11).

The difference between Tasso's and Ariosto's judgments about the epistemological status of powerfully influential texts dramatizes the contrast which Tasso attempts to establish between his theological views and Ariosto's. His attempt, as we shall see, is not wholly successful. When Tancredi goes "outside himself," he sees his lady weeping and sighing as if she were present to his eyes:

> Va fuor di sé: presente aver gli è aviso
> l'offesa donna sua che plori e gema.[160]

He goes outside himself: his offended lady, who weeps and sighs, seems present
to him as if face to face.

This imaginative vision, so strikingly similar to Tasso's vision of his mother in
the "O del grand'Apennino" canzone, is described in the following stanza as
a "falsa imago."[161] The epic narrator thus insists that the product of Tancredi's imagination, like the "simulacrum" of Clorinda created by Ismeno's
magic, is a delusion the Christian should resist. How? Presumably by remembering the "true" dream vision of Clorinda that appeared to him in the
previous canto, where he saw his lady "beautiful and happy" in heaven, and
where instead of accusing him and weeping, she called him "fedel mio caro"
and absolved him of guilt (GL 12. 91; GC 15.101). The difficulty is that to
remember this true vision, Tancredi (and the reader) must forget the act of
murder which occurred in the past, or must accept Peter the Hermit's view
that the murder was a necessary part of the "scourging" God designed to
bring Tancredi back to his "straight path" (GL 12. 86; GC 15. 99). Moreover,
to remember and believe in the "true" vision of Clorinda, Tancredi must
relinquish not only his other memories and guilt, but his imaginative powers
themselves, which substitute human visions for divinely authored (or authorized) ones. Tasso shows such renunciation to be virtually impossible, since
the forces which militate against it come not only from the hero's psyche, but
also from the powerful influence of the magician's phantasm. In fact, Tasso
presents his hero as an artist who is creatively inspired by the very influence
which works his moral downfall. The phantasm sparks Tancredi's imagination, leading him to give visionary shape and the semblance of "presence" to
what had previously existed only in disembodied words. And when Tasso
shows his hero at once contaminated and inspired by a previous artist's
creation, he gives us an important clue to his own inability, as a poet, to resist
the influence of earthly sources of inspiration. Ariosto is the most important
of these, I think, because, like Tasso's Ismeno, Ariosto openly challenges the
authority of Christian doctrine and undermines the distinction Tasso wants
to draw between true and false images.

Ariosto's attack on the authority of Christian scripture and on the ethical
system that defines human errors as punishable sins takes a particularly
vigorous form in the episodes relating the adventures of Astolfo. This is
significant for our purposes because Astolfo, the spirit who speaks from the
bleeding tree, plays in Ariosto's episode the same structural role that Ismeno's phantasm plays in Tasso's. But the two poets give their tree-spirits
apparently antithetical powers, since Tasso's phantasm endangers Tancredi's spiritual well-being, whereas Ariosto's spirit, who is not dead but temporarily metamorphosed, later in the poem assumes the Christ-like role of
liberating savior and healer. It is, indeed, Astolfo's resemblance to the hero
of the New Testament, as well as to the hero of Dante's poem, which makes

him such a threat to Tasso—and such a tempting inspiration to unorthodox ideas. Astolfo embodies Ariosto's vision of a human savior. Although he uses magic—a metaphor for artistic power—he is full of human foibles; and he is Ariosto's spokesman for a "cure" to madness which rests on no theory of revealed, absolute truth and holds out no promises for perfect happiness in this world or any other. Indeed Astolfo cures Orlando only after a voyage to the moon which gently mocks traditional Christian views of heaven and somewhat less gently mocks the truth-claims of sacred texts.

Astolfo is guided to the moon by Saint John, identified as the author of the "mysterious apocalypse" and also of the Fourth Gospel.[162] John is presented as a kindly guide, but by the time Astolfo returns to earth, the saint's authority has been radically called into question. Immediately after commenting on the ways in which writers traditionally gild the truth to flatter their patrons and thus gain rewards, John remarks to Astolfo that "in your world I was a writer too" ("al vostro mondo fui scrittore anch'io" [*Orlando Furioso* 35. 28]); he goes on to blur the distinction between authors of sacred and secular texts by referring to Christ as his "patron" and mentioning the rewards he gained by praising that patron (stanza 29). Characteristically, Ariosto does not suggest that there is no truth in John's writings, only that they should be read, like all products of the fallible human brain, with some skepticism.

Ariosto questions not only the authority of scripture but also the binary system of virtues and vices, rewards and punishments, which underlies Christian ethics.[163] In particular, he invites us to take John's moral view of Orlando's madness with a large grain of salt. Orlando is mad, John tells Astolfo, because God is punishing him for taking "the standards committed to him away from the straight path" ("'l vostro Orlando, perché torse / dal camin dritto le commesse insegne, è punito da Dio" [34. 62]). This is one way of viewing the matter, and clearly a sobering one for an author like Tasso who feared punishment for deviating from the path of orthodoxy.[164] But Ariosto shows both by precept and by example that there is another, less moralistic, way of understanding punishment in general and madness in particular. Moreover, he suggests that there is a modest therapy for madness provided not by Christ or Catholic priests, but by time and the human artist.

As Ariosto diagnoses it, Orlando's madness is an extreme version of a disease which infects us all: the disease of unfulfilled desire. Desire, which Ariosto, like Cervantes, links to our unlimited capacity for fiction-making, is inevitably disappointed by the realities of our condition as mortals in a world of social and material limits. Ariosto does not purport to cure this illness of desire (the epic narrator insists he suffers from it, too).[165] The poem does, however, provide a defense against the direst onslaughts of the disease, a defense which works rather like an antibody. Epistemological skepticism, combined with a wry moral stoicism, may protect the psyche from the grief of massive disillusionment suffered by a character like Orlando. Skepticism in small doses, coated with humor and expressed in the course of narratives which ask us to suspend belief as well as disbelief, is what Ariosto offers his readers.[166]

* * *

Tasso read Ariosto's poem very closely, but he could not hear Ariosto's therapeutic voice, any more than Romeo could hear Mercutio's or Dora could hear Freud's. The resistance was too great, the historical circumstances too unpropitious, and the personality structure too rigid for Ariosto's modest yet demanding "cure of the ground" to work on Tasso. Astolfo restores Orlando's wits by throwing him, quite literally, on the ground and making him breathe the "vapors" of his own brain.[167] This is not a cure Tasso could accept; his hatred of the earth and his longing for pure and superhuman sources of inspiration were too great. Nevertheless it is too simple to say that Ariosto's therapy, or rather his poetic vision of what it entailed, had no effect on Tasso. It seems to have worked on him for a time, at least, as an incentive to resist the pressures of Christian orthodoxy and the ideology which defined fiction-making as either sinful or useless. Ariosto's poem inspires Tasso to create "false" images as Ismeno's phantasm inspires Tancredi to imagine his lady as she was on earth rather than as she will be in heaven. Such creation, which makes the dead live in the form which the poet rather than God bestows on them, is essential for secular immortality. In a revealing passage of the *Discorsi*, Tasso broods on Ariosto's fame and links it to his willingness to deviate from precedents and rules which other poets, like Trissino, observed "religiously." Ariosto is "read and reread by all the ages," Tasso observes, despite the fact that he left "the footsteps of the ancient writers and the rules of Aristotle" (and, one might add, the rules of the church). The obedient Trissino, in contrast, is now "mentioned by few, read by even fewer, silent in the theatre of the world and dead to the light."[168] The light Tasso is concerned with here is not heavenly.

The irony is that in his later career Tasso sought more and more to obey rules which severely limited autonomous imaginative activity.[169] And in his attempts to obey, Tasso came more and more to resemble Ariosto's Orlando, the unruly hero who turns his energies to destruction rather than creation. In his efforts to reject as false the stories of earthly romance, Tasso attacked the text of *Gerusalemme Liberata* as Orlando attacks the trees inscribed with the signs of an adulterous passion. Moreover, Tasso's aggressive and erotically charged assault on the *Liberata* resembles not only Orlando's (and Tancredi's) assaults on symbol-bearing trees; it also resembles Goffredo's culturally sanctioned act of aggression against Jerusalem, a city inhabited by women and men who resist the authority of the Christian father. Tasso's literary career thus acts out a version of the drama represented in his epic, a drama which writers from Virgil through Shakespeare to Freud have seen as occurring within the individual as well as on the stage of history. A metaphor Freud uses to describe both the individual superego and the repressive force of civilization seems a particularly apt gloss on Tasso's epic plot and career: "The institution of the superego which takes over the dangerous aggressive impulses [of the id], introduces a garrison, as it were, into regions that are inclined to rebellion" (*New Introductory Lectures, SE* 22: 110). In *Civilization and Its Discontents*, he varies the figure in a way that illuminates the title of Tasso's revised epic: "Civilization . . . obtains mastery over the individual's dangerous desire for aggression by weakening and disarming it and by setting up an agency within him to watch over it, like a garrison in a conquered city" (*SE* 21: 123–24).

Like Tasso and Virgil, Freud brooded on the costs of establishing such garrisons, and he saw that the force which sets up the defense may be theoretically and practically indistinguishable from the "rebellious" forces it is supposed to subdue. All too often, he observes, particularly in cases where there is a strong "unconscious sense of guilt," the superego "displays its independence of the conscious ego and its intimate relations with the unconscious id" (*The Ego and the Id, SE* 19: 52). In attacking his epic as Goffredo attacks Jerusalem, and as Orlando and Tancredi attack the forests of romance, Tasso provides a confirmation of the "intimate connection" between the forces of the id and those of the superego. He also makes us see the equally intimate relation between the acts of aggression a culture defines as legitimate and sane, and those it defines as illegitimate and seeks to suppress or punish.

The problematic nature of the distinction between legitimate and illegitimate expressions of aggression is highlighted by Tasso's major poetic symbol for the political and religious values of the Counter-Reformation, the huge wooden tower on wheels that Goffredo uses to besiege Jerusalem. This tower, filled like a prison with soldiers whose violence is being trained on enemies rather than on the leader against whose authority they elsewhere rebel, recalls the wooden horse which Homer's Greek soldiers used to penetrate Troy.[170] Goffredo loses his siege tower in the middle of Tasso's epic as Orlando symbolically loses his head in the middle of *Orlando Furioso*. In canto 12 of the *Liberata* (canto 15 of the *Conquistata*), Clorinda and a pagan man burn the tower which represents Goffredo's power. The leader and "head" of the Christian forces is thus undone, for a time, just as Orlando is when he discovers he has been betrayed by the pagan couple Angelica and Medoro. The phallus and the head, symbols of potency and reason respectively, are linked (and wounded) at critical moments in both

Ariosto's and Tasso's epics. And in Tasso's poem this linking makes it impossible to distinguish between sexually motivated acts of aggression and acts that are motivated by the religious zeal that Tasso's culture defined as an exercise of reason. When Goffredo sends his figurative son and surrogate, Tancredi, into the forest to cut trees for the new siege tower, Tancredi is serving the Christian cause and also avenging both the literal wound Clorinda gave to Goffredo in canto 11 and the symbolic wound she gave to all the Christian men by burning their siege tower. Tasso's poem should therefore be read in light of Freud's argument that the "ideologies of the superego" derive much of their coercive force from the fact that the superego is not merely the "successor" of the parental agency, "but actually the legitimate heir of its body."[171] In Tasso's poetic universe, the body is always a major and barely disguised issue in religious battles; and the body cannot be disowned, no matter how severely the upper parts of it struggle to be free of the lower ones (and vice versa).

* * *

If Tasso himself, as well as his heroes Goffredo and Tancredi, resembles Ariosto's wounded and wounding Orlando, there is a deeply ironic point to be drawn from a speech of Goffredo's which appears in the "reformed" text of the *Conquistata* but not in the *Liberata*. Defending a desire his advisors see as unreasonable and unworthy of the man entrusted with duties of leadership—a desire to fight as a humble foot soldier in the siege of Jerusalem—Goffredo says:

> Al magno Carlo
> già vecchio Augusto, disegual son io:
> ma s'Orlando vedesti, a seguitarlo,
> lecito fosse, è il mio sommo desio.

> I—an already old emperor—am too unequal to Charlemagne: But if you saw Orlando, my highest desire, if it were allowed, is to follow him.[172]

A pious reader concerned with historical accuracy would no doubt say that Goffredo here must be referring to the "original" Orlando, the hero of the *Chanson de Roland* who died without fulfilling his earthly ambition to conquer Saracen Saragossa. Even according to this reading, the passage has ironic force, since it suggests that Goffredo's "highest desire" is for death rather than for military triumph. But there is another interpretation which competes with the first. The Orlando best known to Tasso and his readers, though not to the historical character Goffredo, is the hero of Boiardo's and Ariosto's huge romance.[173] If the highest desire of Tasso's Goffredo is to follow that Orlando—*innamorato* and *furioso*—the desire is paradoxically fulfilled. For Goffredo, like his author, follows Orlando in defensively at-

tacking the forests of romance. The ghosts which inhabit that forest, however, can be wounded but not killed. One sign of this is Tasso's inability to
cut the bleeding tree episode from the *Conquistata* and thus silence the
accusing and powerful voice of Clorinda, which is also the voice that speaks
for the poet's ties to his familial and literary past. Another sign, from a
different but related order of evidence, is the fact that Tasso's readers have
granted an afterlife to the *Liberata* while placing the *Conquistata* in the
sepulchre only scholars explore.

There are some fine ironies in this verdict from Tasso's secular judges.
First, as we have seen, Tasso himself draws a contrast between Ariosto's
poem and Trissino's which seems an uncanny prediction of the fate of his
own epics. The epic by Ariosto which disobeyed rules, like Tasso's rebellious first poem, is "read and reread by all ages," whereas Trissino's epic, like
Tasso's religiously obedient second poem, is "dead to the light [and] buried . . . in libraries."[174] Moreover, the verdict from a jury of readers which
includes so many great writers, among them Rousseau, Leopardi, Byron, Shelley, Browning, Goethe, and Freud, paradoxically shows that Memory, that
cord to the past which Tasso so often tries to cut, plays as fateful a role in his
literary afterlife as it did when he was on earth.[175] Consider this comment by
one of Tasso's modern readers, C. P. Brand, and think of the bleeding tree
episode where Tasso shows his hero's "new life" as a Christian to be fatefully
endangered by a voice from the past:

> If we did not have the *Liberata* we should I think consider the *Conquistata* a
> great poem. . . . It deserves to stand on its own as a work of art. It is, however,
> difficult to read it independently of the *Liberata* which is unquestionably supe-
> rior: our memories of the earlier poem impede us and magnify the pomp and
> the didacticism of the later work, which seems unbalanced with the love stories
> so castrated. Thus the *Conquistata* has really been denied a fair hearing from the
> start.[176]

This passage points to an ideal of justice which would allow both poems
and people to be judged "for themselves alone." But Tasso's case illustrates
the impossibility of realizing this ideal in the realm of literary judgment,
where both writers and readers always assess works in relation to previous
ones, and where judgment is therefore always biased by memory. Is this
bias an impediment to justice? Brand implies that it is, and so does Tasso in
the episode where he shows how a "false" image of the past usurps the
authority of a "true" image of the future. But Tasso also suggests that the
poet and his readers are in a courtroom where there is considerable disagreement about what constitutes justice: a "fair hearing" for some (or for
some parts of the psyche) may involve denying others their right to speak.
So Tasso defines a trial where the standards of justice are continually
subjected to intense scrutiny, and where the claims of romance and the past
are countered but never settled in the court of conscience.

IV

Sir Philip Sidney: Pleas for Power

*It is remarkable that we find it so hard to impute our own best sense to a
dead author.*
> —Emerson, *Journals and Miscellaneous Notebooks*

In 1586, a year after Tasso wrote his *Apologia*, Sir Philip Sidney died of a
wound he received while fighting for the Protestant cause in the Nether-
lands. He left unfinished the revision of his *Arcadia*, a prose romance which
concludes, in its original version, with a dramatic scene of trial. Like many of
his readers, Sidney was evidently unsatisfied with the resolution of that trial:
a father condemns his son and nephew to death for their crimes of passion,
but the sentence is miraculously suspended when a supposedly dead king
revives and pardons the princes. The work thus ends happily, but the ethical
and political questions raised by the trial of the young princes are left
unanswered.[1]

Sidney addressed many of these same questions in the work studied in this
chapter: the famous *An Apologie for Poetrie*, also known as *The Defence of
Poesie*. The titles were devised by the two different publishers who printed
it in 1595, in what were, perforce, unauthorized versions.[2] We shall never
know which title Sidney himself would have preferred, just as we shall never
know how—or if—he would have revised the trial that concludes the *Old
Arcadia*. The literary testimony he left, however, suggests that he would
have relished the ambiguity created by his text's two titles, and would have
seen that both are relevant to the problems he explores not only in his critical
essay but also in works of poetry and fiction like *The Lady of May*, *Astrophil
and Stella*, and the *Old* and *New Arcadia*. In all of these works, Sidney
portrays young male heroes who seek to justify their desires for amorous or
political action of a type not allowed by social conventions. At the same
time, however, these heroes explicitly or implicitly acknowledge a "fault" in
their rebellious desires; their rhetoric therefore oscillates between apology
in the "Greek" sense of self-justification and apology in the modern sense of a
plea for pardon or indulgence.[3] To read the *Defence* in the light of Sidney's
lifelong concern with trials in which young men who resemble their creator

find themselves accused of crime by social authorities or by the "voice of reason" in their own minds, is to see the text not only as an important work of literary theory, but also as a work of quasi-autobiographical allegory. Allegory, which Sidney's contemporary Puttenham called "the courtly figure," was an important weapon of defense for an Elizabethan aristocrat. Indeed Sidney used allegory to anatomize the "brazen world" of the court itself, which he often saw as a place very like the fallen England Blake later described in *Jerusalem*: "the Visions of Eternity, by reason of narrowed perceptions,/Are become weak Visions of Time and Space, fix'd into furrows of death;/Till deep dissimulation is the only defense an honest man has left."[4] Sidney was a master of "deep dissimulation"; unfortunately, he dissimulated so well that many of his later readers have failed to notice the political and autobiographical issues at stake in his *Defence of Poesie*.

Intellectual condescension appears so often in modern critical judgments of Sidney's *Defence* that one suspects the judges of being defensive. The most interesting responses to Sidney's text are not those which simply condescend ("Sidney does not understand Aristotle although he thinks he does"; the relation between "form and content" is a question "Sidney's thought was hardly sophisticated enough to reach"), but, rather, those which offer a mixed verdict on his critical performance—a verdict that raises questions precisely about the relation between "form and content": the *Defence* "wins support for its theory of poetry by means of sophisticated exercises in audience psychology rather than by intellectually cogent argumentation"; "the strong grace of the *Defence* and its eclectic representative value for sixteenth-century literary theory compensate for its lack of profundity or of original thinking."[5]

These quotations, offered as preliminary evidence for my argument that Sidney's text deserves a new trial, illustrate Hugh Kenner's point in *The Counterfeiters*: "A blunder, no less than an imposture, requires that we postulate the man who committed it."[6] In this chapter I argue that if we grant Sidney the intelligence to be a counterfeiter rather than a blunderer, his case for poetry becomes at once more cogent as a theoretical statement and more interesting as a literary performance. I also suggest that in reading his *Defence* we should remember that it was originally addressed to a court in which the Queen played the role of chief judge.

The Egoistic Project

Self-love, my liege, is not so vile a sin/As self-neglecting.—Shakespeare, *Henry V*

A defense, whether a legal, military, or psychical phenomenon, always responds to preexisting charges, attacks, or threats. J. L. Austin underscores the peculiar secondary of the language of defense (or justification, or excuse) when he remarks that "the average excuse gets us only out of the fire into the frying pan."[7] This secondarity is similar to what Sidney himself describes, in a letter to his brother Robert, as the "predicament of relation": certain things can be known, he writes, only in their relation to other things. His example is military strength: "You cannot tell what the Queen of England is able to do offensively or defensively, but through knowing what they are able to do with whom she is to be matched."[8] Because Sidney's poetic theory and rhetorical practice in the *Defence* are products of a social and intertextual "predicament of relation," it will be useful to approach his text by way of an analogy to the defensive project which Freud describes in the chapter of *The Ego and the Id* devoted to the ego's "dependent relations." The ego, Freud says, is "menaced by three dangers: from the external world, from the libido of the id, and from the severity of the super-ego" (*SE* 19:56). Sidney's defensive strategies respond to three analogous threats: from the world of factual truth, represented by the historian; from poetry's own capacity for "abuse," which lies, for Sidney, chiefly in its power to inflame the passions ("not only love, but lust, but vanity, but . . . scurrility possesseth many leaves of the poets' books"); and from severe moralism, represented by the philosopher and the Puritan (like Stephen Gosson) who would banish poetry from the state or have it "scourged out of the Church of God."[9]

The analogy between Sidney's project and that which Freud describes for the personified ego is particularly apt because Sidney himself stresses the narcissistic dimension of his defense. "Self-love," he remarks in the opening paragraph, is "better than any gilding to make that seem gorgeous wherein ourselves are parties." Like Erasmus's Folly, and unlike modern defenders of poetry such as I. A. Richards, Sidney calls attention to the bond of love that links him to the subject of his theoretical discourse.[10] Indeed he plays with the classical roles of forensic and epideictic orator in ways that deliberately blur the distinction between the authorial subject and the theoretical subject, poetry.[11]

As a poet intent on protecting his "title," Sidney has obvious reasons for identifying his own cause with that of "poor poetry." But there is another facet of his identification which arises from what he calls the "affinity" between poetry and oratory as modes of discourse.[12] "Persuasion," as Neil Rudenstine remarks, "lies at the heart of Sidney's entire theory of poetry."[13] Sidney is perfectly aware that as an effort of persuasion his treatise is in crucial respects a double of the poetry it defines and defends. He is, moreover, aware that the affinity between his own rhetoric and the "moving" force of poetry raises questions about the use and abuse of power. When he echoes Aristotle's defense of rhetoric to formulate a definition of poetry as a morally ambiguous power, he invites us to see that, in this trial, the lawyer is as guilty or innocent as his client.[14] Modern scholars of Renaissance literature who chide Sidney and his peers for their "erroneous" transgression of the

Kantian boundary between aesthetic and practical discourse lead one to surmise that the modern anxiety about the abuse of verbal power has blinded critics to the subtlety with which Sidney handles his own anxiety about power.[15] It is an irony of literary history that those who rely on Kantian, Aristotelian, or other theories of aesthetic formalism to fence off a sphere for innocent art (and innocent criticism) simply repeat a defensive strategy which Sidney himself employs in a dialectical and self-reflexive way. When, toward the end of the *Defence*, he presciently expresses his fear that he will be "pounded" for "straying from poetry to oratory" (p. 119), he is engaged, as he is throughout the treatise, in both establishing and transgressing the boundary between a language of play and a language of power.

The relation between poetry and oratory is one part of the general predicament of relation which shapes the defensive enterprise itself. The apologue of Menenius Agrippa, which Sidney borrows from Plutarch to illustrate "the strange effects of . . . poetical invention," dramatizes the link between rhetoric, poetry, and a project of defense which is conceived as a mediation between conflicting but interrelated forces. Menenius Agrippa uses his fable of the body to mediate between the hungry plebians and the patricians who store Rome's corn supplies. Like the ego Freud alternately describes as a "constitutional monarch" and as a "poor servant"—and which Paul Ricoeur compares to a courtier—Menenius Agrippa exists in a complex matrix of master-servant relations.[16] In his attempt to defend the unity of the body politic he not only mediates between masters and servants but in the process plays the role of both master and servant. He serves the ruling class by rhetorically mastering the plebians' desire to rebel against authority, but he also serves the plebians by appealing to their self-interest and, as we learn from Plutarch, by promising to mitigate the harshness of the Senate's laws.[17] Menenius effects a "perfect reconcilement," Sidney says, "upon reasonable conditions." Moreover, Menenius effects this reconciliation only by symbolically humbling himself: he appears before his audience in the guise of a "homely and familiar poet." Sidney adds this detail to Plutarch's account because he is using the story as an extended allegorical allusion to the defense of poetry as a beneficent power, a power which masters only in order to serve the general good. His curious remark that Menenius was not the kind of orator who used "figurative speeches or cunning insinuations" makes sense only if we read it as a symbolic constraint on the orator's will to power—a constraint which appears in the orator's willingness to behave like a "homely and familiar poet."

> He telleth them a tale, that there was a time when all the parts of the body made a mutinous conspiracy against the belly, which they thought devoured the fruits of each other's labour; they concluded they would let so unprofitable a spender starve. In the end, to be short (for the tale is notorious, and as notorious that it

was a tale), with punishing the belly they plagued themselves. This applied by him wrought such effect in the people, as I never read that only words brought forth but then so sudden and so good an alteration; for upon reasonable conditions a perfect reconcilement ensued. [p. 93]

The "notorious" tale told by a figure who is at once orator and poet, master and servant, is, as one would expect, an emblem not only for Sidney's theory of poetry but for his rhetorical project of defending poetry. The double focus occurs because the theory and the practice are both based on the concept of mediation. Let us look first at the belly as an emblem of Sidney's theory of poetry. In Plutarch, the belly is a metaphor for the patricians; in Sidney's account, it alludes to what he earlier calls "the senate of poets" (p. 82). The poets, like the belly, are threatened by a "mutinous conspiracy" which includes the charge, common from Plato to Gosson, that poetry is an "unprofitable spender" of public goods.[18] Sidney has argued, however, that poetry benefits both the individual and the body politic; poetry mediates between reason and passion and thereby promotes virtue in those whose nature consists of an "erected wit" and an "infected will" (p. 79). Between head and loins, the belly is metonymically linked to the poetic power Sidney has likened to a "cluster of grapes," a "medicine of cherries," and a "food for the tenderest stomachs" (pp. 92, 93, 87).

The project of defending the belly is like the project of defending poetry not only because the defender identifies with the object of defense but because Menenius, like Sidney, is trying to prevent civil war. Defenses occur, as Austin notes, when there has been "some abnormality or failure" in the status quo.[19] At the beginning of his oration Sidney implies that his "defence of poor poetry" is an effort to remedy the effects of a fall, a disruption of order. Since poetry has fallen from "almost the highest estimation of learning . . . to be the laughing-stock of children," there has been "great danger of civil war among the Muses" (p. 74). As the body politic is threatened by internal conflict, so the body of culture is threatened, Sidney suggests, by the conflict among the Muses. When we see the parallel between Sidney's project and Menenius Agrippa's, we can read the long section of the treatise devoted to defending poetry's "works" against the philosopher and the historian as an effort to reestablish a balance of power in the body of culture. Sidney's effort, however, is not so simple as Menenius Agrippa's; it involves a staging of conflict which exposes the ambiguities of the mediator's own relations to power. The ambition inherent in the mediator's role is dramatized by Sidney's adaptation of a conventional pastoral *topos*: the singing match. Sidney implicitly structures his *confirmatio*—the section of the oration devoted to the defense of poetry's "works"—as a competition in which the poet initially plays the role of the pastoral moderator or judge; in this unconventional singing match, however, the moderator eventually steals the prize from the original contenders. The revision of the singing match convention is therefore designed to enhance the poet's position by tactics adapted not only from poetic models but from rhetorical manuals: Sidney puts into practice Aristotle's advice to the epideictic orator whose object of praise is weak: "If you cannot find enough to say of a man himself, you may pit him against others."[20]

The Defense against Philosophy and History

Come, shadow, come, and take this shadow up,/For 'tis thy rival.
— Shakespeare, *Two Gentlemen of Verona*

By the trope of *prosopopeia* ("counterfeit in personation") Sidney makes poetry's rivals each voice its own claim to be the best guide to wisdom, "which stands . . . in the knowledge of a man's self, in the ethic and politic consideration, with the end of well-doing and not of well-knowing only" (*Defence*, p. 83).[21] The "counterfeit in personation" is a clever device, since it allows each competitor to act not only as a weapon against the other but also as an unwitting self-destroyer. Moreover, the "speaking pictures" of the philosopher and the historian link the idea of epistemological inadequacy— presented as a lack of self-knowledge—with the representation of stylistic weakness. The singing match thus sets the stage for Sidney's covert argument that the best teacher of virtue must acknowledge the existence of desire, with its potential for vice, both in himself and in those he would teach. The philosopher's "thorny" style ignores the need to entice people to learn; the historian's garrulous style ignores the need to regulate people's passions by presenting them with edited images of virtue and vice. One might say that Sidney uses both the positive and the negative aspects of the libido against the philosopher and the historian.

The "moral philosophers" are vividly sketched in their "sullen gravity" and are caricatured as Puritans ignorant of their moral hypocrisy: "rudely clothed for to witness outwardly their contempt of outward things, with books in their hands against glory, whereto they set their names, sophistically speaking against subtlety . . ." (p. 83). Signs of moral delusion slide into signs of stylistic delusion. The Ramistical and Puritan demand for a "plain setting down" of things is slyly mocked as Sidney gives his amalgam of scholastic and preacher a style that is nothing if not tortuous; indeed he underscores the point by giving the philosophers only an indirect discourse:

> These men casting largess as they go, of definitions, divisions, and distinctions, with a scornful interrogative do soberly ask whether it be possible to find any path so ready to lead a man to virtue as that which teacheth what virtue is; and teach it not only by delivering forth his very being, his causes and effects, but also by making known his enemy, vice, which must be destroyed, and his cumbersome servant, passion, which must be mastered. [p. 83]

The philosopher's inability to hold a listener's attention is exposed by the fact that the historian interrupts him; "scarcely [giving] leisure to the moralist to say so much," the historian appears "laden with old mouse-eaten records." Lack of self-knowledge ("better acquainted with a thousand years ago than with the present age, and yet better knowing how this world goeth than how his own wit runneth") is again equated with stylistic unattractiveness ("a tyrant in table talk") (p. 84). The historian's speech, peppered with Latin tags (inaccurately quoted from Cicero) and names of battles, undermines the philosopher without establishing the historian's own claim to teach an "active" rather than a merely "disputative" virtue. Sidney rescues us from what would be, he implies, an interminable speech ("innumerable examples, confirming story by stories") and fills the obvious gap left by the historian's assertion that if the philosopher "make the songbook, I put the learner's hand to the lute." What is missing is the singer himself; the resolution of this uncivil dispute is provided by the poet-moderator, who possesses both the philosopher's "precept" and the historian's "example" and therefore deserves "to carry the title from them both" (p. 84).

Having devalued both precept and example by ridiculing their proponents, however, Sidney would appear to have won a Pyrrhic victory for the poet. The synthesis of two weaknesses is not necessarily strength. But the flexing of rhetorical muscle which has performatively established the poets' claim to be "princes over all the rest" is merely the prelude to a second round of the singing match. This time Sidney treats poetry's rivals with more respect, and poetry emerges as a correspondingly more complex synthesis of philosophy and history.

The complexity stems from Sidney's concessions to the philosopher and the historian, concessions which introduce a double standard of value and define poetry's nature in terms of weakness as well as strength. Sidney admits, first, that the historian has a legitimate claim to superiority in his use of "images of true matters, such as indeed were done, and not such as fantastically or falsely may be suggested to have been done" (p. 87). He grants, moreover, that "if the question were whether it were better to have a particular act truly or falsely set down, there is no doubt which is to be chosen, no more than whether you had rather have Vespasian's picture right as he was, or at the painter's pleasure, nothing resembling." He offsets this concession, significantly, by turning to the authority of a philosopher—and to a philosopher's doctrine that "poetry is *philosophoteron* and *spoudaioteron*, that is to say, it is more philosophical and more studiously serious than history" (pp. 87–88). Aristotle's theory is less important, here, than his authority, for with it Sidney goes on to portray history as a slave to the world of fact and to fortune's unjust tendency to reward vice and punish virtue: "History, being captived to the truth of a foolish world, is many times a terror from well-doing, and an encouragement to unbridled wickedness" (p.

90). Despite the appeal to Aristotle and the corollary argument that the poet is a "master" teacher by virtue of his freedom from "the truth of a foolish world," the discussion of history exposes a problem. If there are two truths—that of "moral use" and that of faithfulness to fact—the poet has only one of these. Moreover, Sidney's illustration of the argument that "a feigned example hath as much force to teach as a true example" (p. 89) raises the ante in the dialectical game by putting both the poet's moral teaching and the historian's faithfulness to fact in contact with the complex world of practical politics. Sidney compares the "true" story of Zopirus with the "feigned" story of Abradates; both were "faithful" servants engaged in spying missions, and both needed to "counterfeit" themselves in disgrace with their kings in order to win "credit" with the enemy. Zopirus, in order to "verify" his counterfeit disguise, cut his nose off. Abradates "did not counterfeit so far." "Now would I fain know," Sidney punningly concludes, "if occasion be presented unto you to serve your prince by such an honest dissimulation, why you do not as well learn it of Xenophon's fiction as of the other's [Herodotus's] verity; and truly so much the better, as you shall save your nose by the bargain" (p. 89). Paul Alpers finds this "a trivial argument, couched in a tasteless joke."[22] But clearly a courtly reader would have found this passage *serio ludere* in its meditation on the virtue of "honest dissimulation" required of royal servants. The passage casts an ironic light on the distinctions between true and feigned, moral and immoral, and it raises an oblique question about the degree to which poets (and their readers) are less "captivated to the truth of a foolish world" than are historians.

Sidney's concession to the philosopher also implies a double standard of value and leads to a questioning as well as an assertion of the poet's claim to superiority. "For suppose it be granted," Sidney says, "that the philosopher, in respect of his methodical proceeding, doth teach more perfectly than the poet, yet do I think that no man is so much *Philophilosophos* as to compare the philosopher in moving with the poet" (p. 91). This is a curious sentence, since the "methodical proceeding" would seem, in light of Sidney's earlier complaints about the philosopher's "thorny" and "hard" style, to be precisely what makes the philosopher imperfect as a teacher. "Method," however, is a Ramistical term which Sidney employs to refer to the content of moral instruction.[23] The drift of his argument was hinted earlier when he said that the poet gives a "perfect picture" of "whatsoever the philosopher saith should be done" (p. 85). In this account, the poet simply provides the enticing ("moving") form, while the philosopher provides the substance of teaching. The poet is not so much the philosopher's superior as he is the philosopher's translator and servant. But the servant from one perspective is the master from another: "moving is of a higher degree than teaching," Sidney says, because "it is well nigh both the cause and effect of teaching."

He goes on to give a radical Protestant twist to this point, citing the "learned men" who believe that moving the will is the only function of teaching, since "once reason hath so much overmastered passion as that the mind hath a free desire to do well, the inward light each mind hath in itself is as good as a philosopher's book" (p. 91).

The second round of the competition results in a more ambiguous victory for the poet because the establishing of poetry's claim to power (to be "monarch" of all sciences) is counterpointed by a questioning of that claim. By granting specific virtues to the historian and the philosopher ("true images" and "methodical proceeding"), Sidney shows that the poetic "synthesis" involves a cancellation as well as a preservation of merits. The philosopher's and the historian's virtues, however, are also questioned. All three competitors are presented in terms of strength and weakness, mastery and servitude. Sidney's imagination, Hazlitt complained in his comments on the *Arcadia*, "always interferes to perplex and neutralise."[24] But the perplexing and neutralizing is precisely what allows Sidney to achieve his defensive aim in the *confirmatio* if we see that aim as an effort to show poetry's role in the system of "dependent relations" which constitutes the body of culture.

To gain recognition for poetry, Sidney shows it rising from a position of low esteem to a monarchy based on its "moving" power. In the course of this rhetorical ascent, poetry metaphorically usurps the places of the philosopher and the historian; the poet is titled "the right popular philosopher," and the historian is said to be the poet's "subject" because the poet can literally (and freely) take over the historian's subject matter: "whatsoever action, or faction . . . the historian is bound to recite, that may the poet (if he list) with his imitation make his own" (p. 89).[25] Sidney's own procedure, moreover, illustrates the power he is ascribing to the poet: as Geoffrey Shepherd notes, "Sidney turns arguments which he had found applied to another discipline [e.g., Sir Thomas Elyot's arguments for history] into arguments for poetry."[26] The undersong of this theory and practice of power, however, is the admission that poetry's teaching may be "questionable"—an admission obliquely dramatized in the example of the "feigning" that teaches "honest dissimulation."

Poetry's power is questionable because it may be "abused" as well as "rightly used." At the beginning of the *confirmatio*, Sidney promises the "title of princes over all the rest" to those teachers whose "skills most *serve*" to bring forth "virtuous action" (p. 83; my emphasis). Having at the end of this section proclaimed the poet to be the "most princely" mover, Sidney's task is to prevent the prince from becoming a tyrant who forgets his duty to serve others. In the *refutatio* and *digressio*, roughly the second half of the oration, he defends poetry against its own potential to abuse the reader. In so doing, he offers yet another perspective on the body of culture as a system of dependent relations. In this defense, the philosopher and historian reappear not only as challengers and critics (the former charges that poetry promotes "wanton sinfulness," the latter charges that poetry lies), but as allies in the effort to protect the health of a body, which is now clearly revealed to be a metaphor for the individual as well as for society.

The Defense against "Abuse" of Power

Meseemes I hear, when I do hear sweet music,
The dreadful cries of murd'red men in forests.
                    —Sidney, "Ye Goatherd Gods," *Old Arcadia*

In the economy of this defense, weakness on one front is strength on another. In the first half of the oration, Sidney uses the link between poetry and passion to counter rival claims to power; in the second half, he uses the philosopher and the historian to counter the dangers of that same link between poetry and passion. He uses them, however, not as representatives for kinds of writing but as symbolic aspects of an act of reading, one which can withstand the "abuse" of poetry's "sweet charming force." The philosopher and the historian become allies in the defensive project because they are metamorphosed from deluded writers into astute readers.

To see how the defense of poetry becomes a defense of the reader we must look at the "principal" charge against poetry: that it "abuseth men's wit," "training" people to vice rather than virtue. Sidney, like Plato in Book 10 of the *Republic*, sees the threat that poetry poses as an erotic one. Socrates, after offering poetry a chance to defend herself against his attacks, says that if her defense fails, we must act like those "who have once fallen in love with someone, and don't believe the love is beneficial"; such persons "keep away from the beloved, even if they have to do violence to themselves."[27] Sidney's argument starts, as it were, from this famous moment. Acknowledging the charge that "Cupid hath ambitiously climbed" over all modes of poetry, he writes:

Alas, Love, I would thou couldst as well defend thyself as thou canst offend others. I would those on whom thou dost attend could either put thee away, or yield good reason why they keep thee. [*Defence*, pp. 103–04]

The defense of poetry necessarily involves a defense of Eros; Sidney's strategy is to show that one can no more banish poetry than one can banish love. Both powers have the potential for good and evil. As Sidney says, "my masters the philosophers spent a good deal of their lamp-oil in setting forth the excellency of [love]," but they also spent time abusing it: "read *Phaedrus* or *Symposium* in Plato, or the discourse of love in Plutarch, and see whether any poet do authorize abominable filthiness, as they do" (pp. 104, 107).

Sidney's strategy is as ingenious as it is simple: "Judge not, that ye be not judged.... And why beholdest thou the mote that is in thy brother's eye, but considerest not the beam that is in thine own eye?" (Matthew 7:1–3). This is a strategy of encircling the enemy: poetry may have an intimate liaison with passion, but so does philosophy, so does history. All the members of the "body of culture" are together with the poet in the "fellowship" with desire that Sidney ruefully laments in *Astrophil and Stella*, sonnet 72; that poem's conclusion, indeed, epitomizes Sidney's reply not only to Plato and the Puritans who would banish poetry, but to all those who think their own discourse is innocent: "but thou, Desire, because thou wouldst have all,/ Now banisht art, but yet alas how shall?"[28] By linking the problem posed by poetry's double nature to the universal problem posed by the double nature of love, Sidney establishes a Christian metaphysical frame for turning around the moralist's charge against poetry: the accusers, he says, "will find their sentence may with good manners put the last words foremost, and not say that poetry abuseth man's wit, but that man's wit abuseth poetry" (*Defence*, p. 104).

This reversal signals a shift in Sidney's definition of poetic power which corresponds to the universalizing of the problem of "abuse." Sidney's treatment of the issue much debated in Italian critical treatises—whether poetry is "eikastic" or "phantastic"—shows that poetic power is now viewed as a circuit of energy which goes from author to work to reader. Unlike Tasso, whose discussion of these terms follows Plato's *Sophist* by focusing on the essential nature of poetic imitation, Sidney presents the issue with the following relative formulation:

> For I will not deny but that man's wit may make poesy, which should be *eikastike* (which some learned have defined: figuring forth good things), to be *phantastike* (which doth, contrariwise, infect the fancy with unworthy objects). [p. 104]

Poetry's moral value, which Sidney had previously defined in terms of its representational content ("the right describing note to know a poet by" is that "feigning notable images of virtues, vices, or what else" [p. 81]), is now viewed as a function not only of "content" but of authorial intention and the interpreter's response. The "abuse" caused by "man's wit" is first located in intention, through the comparison of the poet to a painter who pleases "an ill-pleased eye with wanton shows of better hidden matters." But Sidney goes on to compare the abuse of poetry to the abuse of "God's word," which makes the interpreter's wit the culprit. In the argument about morally ambiguous powers which Sidney adapts from Aristotle, Plutarch, Ovid, and others, the concept of abuse appears as a problem that must be confronted by the body politic as a whole:

> But what, shall the abuse of a thing make the right use odious? Nay truly, though
> I yield that poesy may not only be abused, but that being abused, by the reason
> of his sweet charming force, it can do more hurt than any other army of words:
> yet shall it be so far from concluding that the abuse should give reproach to the
> abused, that, contrariwise, it is a good reason that whatsoever, being abused,
> doth most harm, being rightly used (and upon the right use each thing conceiv-
> eth his title), doth most good. Do we not see the skill of physic, the best rampire
> to our often-assaulted bodies, being abused, teach poison, the most violent
> destroyer? Doth not knowledge of law, whose end is to even and right all things,
> being abused, grow the crooked fosterer of horrible injuries? Doth not (to go to
> the highest) God's word abused breed heresy, and His name abused become
> blasphemy? . . . with a sword thou mayst kill thy father, and with a sword thou
> mayst defend thy prince and country. [pp. 104–05]

The ultimate source for this "double-edged sword" argument, as Plutarch
explains in his essay "How the Young Man Should Study Poetry," is the
Odyssey's description (4. 230) of the Egyptian drug Helen put in Menelaus's
wine—the aesthetic drug par excellence, whose power prevented Menelaus
from grieving at the retelling of the Trojan tale. Plutarch compares poetry to
the "mixed" power of such drugs and says that there are two solutions to the
threat they represent: either one can avoid them altogether, in which case
one loses their potential for good; or one can use them with the safeguard of
an antidote.[29] Like everyone from Aristotle through Derrida, Plutarch uses
Plato against Plato when questions of verbal drugs arise. It seems likely that
Plutarch is alluding to Plato's banishment of the poets from the Republic
when he refers to Lycurgus, the Thracian king who responded "without
sense" to Bacchus's presence in his land: "When many became drunk and
violent, he went about uprooting the grapevines instead of bringing the
springs of water nearer, and thus chastening the 'frenzied god,' as Plato says
[*Laws*, 773d], 'through correction by another, a sober god'" ("Young Man,"
pp. 79, 81).

Sidney follows Plutarch not only by sophistically using Plato against Plato
(the *Ion's* praise of poets shows that Plato did not mean to banish poets but
only their "abuses" [*Defence*, p. 108]), but also by adopting the notion of an
antidotal defense against poetry's power. Near the end of the *refutatio*
Sidney points to his source: "Plutarch," he says, "teacheth the use to be
gathered of [poets]; and how, if they should not be read?" (p. 109). The
question is slyly phrased, since what Plutarch teaches, in addition to the fact
that we cannot "root up or destroy the Muses' vine," is precisely how to read
poetry in a morally useful way. Plutarch advises the young man to be a
strong reader who can resist the Sirens of poetry by relying on the ethical
precepts of philosophy.[30] Sidney adopts Plutarch's notion of a strong reader
but rejects his faith in the moral authority of philosophy. What Sidney does,
in effect, is borrow from Plutarch two methods of defending readers against

all kinds of writing—including philosophy—that contain potential for abuse. Sidney thus uses Plutarch's text for his own ends, which include transforming the historian and moral philosopher from rivals in writing to allies in defining a method of reading.

The first method of defense that Sidney adopts from Plutarch might be called the "aesthetic shield." The reader who is armed with the knowledge that poets always lie, Plutarch says, will never obey a text by believing it uncritically.[31] This argument is the basis of Sidney's "paradoxical but true" assertion that "of all writers under the sun the poet is the least liar, and, though he would, as a poet can scarcely be a liar" (p. 102). The phrase "though he would" is significant, for it makes the inability to lie a function not of the poet's intention but of the reader's expectations about poetry—the reader's awareness that fiction is fiction. It is at this point, however, that Sidney subverts Plutarch by suggesting that all kinds of discourse are as false as poetry and deceive, unlike poetry, precisely because they lead the reader to expect truth from them. The astronomer, the geometrician, the physician, Sidney says, all lie, and so do others who "take upon them to affirm." The poet, however, "nothing affirms, and therefore never lieth. For, as I take it, to lie is to affirm that to be true which is false. So as the other artists, and especially the historian, affirming many things, can, in the cloudy knowledge of mankind, hardly escape from many lies" (p. 102). Sidney singles out the historian here because the charge that poetry lies by departing from empirical truth is a historian's charge—it is, indeed, one that Jacques Amiot mentions in the preface to his translation of Plutarch's *Lives*. History, Amiot says, is the best discipline because it uses "the playne truth, whereas Poetry doth commonly inrich things by commending them above the starres."[32] What Sidney is doing, textually and by intertextual allusion, is to denigrate the historian's authority as a writer while rehabilitating him as a function of critical reading: the reader who "knows" that a representation is not the thing itself has the ideal historian's ability to distinguish between fact and not-fact. Readers of history are generally deceived because they are not good enough historians to realize that signs are never identical to things: "And therefore, as in history, looking for truth, they may go away full fraught with falsehood, so in poesy, looking but for fiction, they shall use the narration but as an imaginative ground-plot of a profitable invention" (p. 103). The reader who uses poetry simply as the "ground-plot" for his own inventive act is hardly likely to be morally abused by the poet.

The second defensive strategy Sidney adapts from Plutarch also protects the reader from abuse by imposing a theoretical constraint on the poet's power and by emphasizing the reader's critical faculties. The reader, Plutarch says, should bind himself to "some upright standard of reason," as Odysseus bound himself to the mast when passing the Sirens ("Young Man," p. 79). We can observe Sidney's version of this strategy in the penultimate section of the treatise, the *digressio* on English literature. Here Sidney himself plays the role of reader-critic and asks those who "delight in poetry" to "look [at] themselves in an unflattering glass of reason" (*Defence*, p. 111). He is, of course, directing his remarks to poets—including himself, for he is "sick among the rest"—but his critical practice illustrates a method of reading which cures abuse by submitting poetry to the authority of Plato's "sober god." Significantly, however, the philosopher, like the historian in the defense against lying, is allowed authority only as a model reader, not as a privileged kind of writer. In the digression, indeed, Sidney is asking all writers to become critical readers of themselves and thus to exercise the faculty of judgment in both roles. His argument differs from Plutarch's precisely because the reader whom Sidney is protecting is identified with the writer who generates abuse. The section begins by praising a series of "patrons" who are simultaneously poets and readers; the list concludes with Michel de l'Hôpital, the French poet and patron of poets whom Sidney holds up as a model of "accomplished judgment . . . firmly builded upon virtue" and whom he admires for his ability "not only to read others' poesies, but to poetize for others' reading" (p. 110). De l'Hôpital, one could say, represents a symbolic fulfillment of the wish Sidney expressed at the end of the *refutatio*, that Plato "shall be our patron and not our adversary." The digression continues the encircling strategy of defense: "we have met the enemy and he is us."

If we see this section as Sidney's attempt to enlist the philosopher's authority in the defense against "abuse," we can accept O. B. Hardison, Jr.'s observation that Sidney's tone and theoretical stance change here, without accepting his view that the change is caused by vicissitudes of compositional history.[33] The "censuring" which Hardison finds in the digression's curious attack on poetry does indeed contrast with the freedom emphasized earlier in the *Defence*, most notably in the famous description of the "golden world" which the poet creates by "freely ranging only within the zodiac of his own wit." That free ranging is now checked, brought down to the very earth: "Yet confess I always that as the fertilest ground must be manured, so must the highest-flying wit have a Daedalus to guide him"—and Daedalus's wings are made of "art, imitation, and exercise" (pp. 111–12). The "invention" earlier praised for its power to make "things either better than nature bringeth forth, or, quite anew, forms such as never were in nature, as the Heroes, Demigods, Cyclops, Chimeras, Furies, and such like" (p. 78), is now subjected to a rule of verisimilitude. *Gorboduc*, for instance, is censured because "it is faulty both in place and time"; it sins against "Aristotle's precept and common reason" (p. 113). It does seem, as Hardison suggests, that Sidney has moved from a neo-Platonic to a neo-Aristotelian theory of poetry. The shift cannot be adequately explained by the fact that he is now considering the special problems of dramatic representation:

earlier in the oration he had praised the "coupling" of dramatic genres that produces the "tragi-comical"; now he attacks the "mongrel tragi-comedy" for its lack of "decency" and "discretion." Eros, the poet's ally in the defense of poetry's "works and parts," has had his wings cut in the defense against poetry's abuse.

Hardison thinks that Sidney inadvertently undermined his case for poetry by adding, several years after finishing the rest of the *Defence*, this splenetic critique of English letters. But we need not explain textual disunity by putting it onto an extratextual time line.[34] The "voice of freedom" and the "voice of censuring" Hardison hears are produced by the diplomatic defensive project whose aim is necessarily double: to establish poetry's power (the *confirmatio's* "monarchy") and to protect that power from its potential for abuse (the checks of the *refutatio* and the *digressio*). This double defensive aim provides the logic for the double theory of poetry as both a rhetorical power (that which "holdeth children from play" [p. 92]) and an "aesthetic" and harmless phenomenon (the "play" no child "doth believe" [p. 103]).

The concept of a diplomatic or "mediatory" defense has, I hope, shed some light on the way Sidney's theory of poetry emerges as a response to conflicting threats which exist both in the "body of culture" and in the individual. The diplomatic project, however, is aimed not only at defending poetry but at defending the "Sidnaiean show'res of sweet discourse," which are the *doppelgänger* of poetry's "sweet charming force." I want to turn, now, to an examination of Sidney's defense of the *Defence*, which both repeats and complicates the strategies employed in the defense of poetry. The complications arise from the fact that Sidney's defense of his own rhetoric explicitly makes the reader a part of the "predicament of relation" in which the author finds himself. Freud can continue to be our metaphorical guide only if we take seriously his remark that "the ego behaves like a physician during analysis"[35]—and Sidney's physician is analyzing not only the "other" of his own discourse but the "other" of the reader. Sidney's "I" repeatedly stages a dialogue between a self which speaks and a self which responds critically to that speech; it also attempts both to master and to serve a reader by means of an always incomplete dialogue. "There is," Lacan says, "no Word without a reply, even if it meets no more than silence, provided that it has an auditor."[36] The problem, for Sidney, is that the oratorical notion of the auditor is threatened by the fact that a written medium implies a reader who perhaps cannot (or will not) understand his words at all.

The Dialogic Defense: Irony

Si j'écris deux textes à la fois, vous ne pourrez pas me châtrer. Si je délinéarise, j'érige. Mais en même temps, je divise mon acte et mon désir. Je—marque la division et vous échappent toujours. . . . Je me châtre moi-même. . . .
—Jacques Derrida, *Glas*

In the world culture of the past, there is much more irony, a form of reduced laughter, than our ears can catch.—Mikhail Bakhtin, *Rabelais and His World*

The *Defence* begins with Sidney playing the role of an audience listening to an oration which prefigures his own. John Pietro Pugliano's encomium of horsemanship and horses is an exquisite miniature (but not quite a parody) of the praise of poetry and poets that we are about to read. Like Sidney, Pugliano has a vocational interest in the "object" of his praise, and his argument, as critics have noted, is patterned like Sidney's.[37] What critics have not noted is that the horseman who praises an image of himself is presented as a socially and ethically ambiguous creature who effects a rhetorical *coup d'état* as peculiar as the one Sidney effects in the *confirmatio*'s establishment of the poet as a monarch. Pugliano first describes horsemen as the "noblest" of the noble estate of soldiers; then he calls them "masters of war," "triumphers both in camps and courts," and finally he identifies them with the ruler himself: "no earthly thing bred such wonder to a prince as to be a good horseman" (*Defence*, p. 73). There is, however, a counterpoint to this progress up the social scale, a counterpoint first hinted in the phrase that could apply to the horse as well as to the rider ("speedy goers and strong abiders") and continued when Pugliano slides from praising horsemen to praising horses. The riding master engaged in an exercise of self-promotion (an "exercise" of his "contemplations," as Sidney says) obliquely undermines his case when he praises the horse as "the only serviceable courtier without flattery." The "peerless" horse suddenly emerges as superior to the horseman in one respect—its lack of speech makes it a better servant than its master, the emperor's servant who excels in self-flattery.

Sidney's response to Pugliano's speech continues the play on the ambiguities of the master-servant relation: "If I had not been a piece of a logician before I came to him, I think he would have persuaded me to have wished myself a horse." Sidney, Pugliano's "pupil" in horsemanship, becomes a masterly listener, one who is not persuaded. But his assertion of mastery derives from a quality of mind that he says he possessed "before" he became Pugliano's pupil, and the temporal complexity of the implied analogy between speaker-master, listener-servant is underscored by the fact that Pugliano's entire speech is in indirect discourse, an example of the dialogic style V. N. Voloshinov terms "pictorial" and finds characteristic of Renaissance literature: an "author's context . . . permeates the reported speech with its own intonation—humor, irony, love or hate," and thereby tends to "break down the self-contained compactness of the reported speech, to resolve it, to obliterate its boundaries."[38]

What we have observed so far in the opening paragraph is a dialogue between speaker and auditor which "pre-presents" the two major defensive movements of the oration as a whole. Pugliano's praise of horsemen is not only analogous to Sidney's praise of poets in the *confirmatio* but is also a "performance" of the poetic imagination as Sidney defines it in the first part of the *Defence*: Pugliano too is a "maker" who imitates the divine maker and, "lifted up with the vigour of his own invention, doth grow in effect [into] another nature . . ." (p. 78).[39] He exercises that power which Sidney, like Shakespeare and Bacon, knows to be morally ambiguous in its ability to "raise and erect the Minde, by submitting the shewes of things to the desires of the Minde"; the imagination, Sidney says, "may make the too much loved earth more lovely."[40] As in the *confirmatio*, Sidney's voice "perplexes and neutralises" the poet-rhetorician's rise to power; his irony prepares for his assumption of the role defined in the second half of the treatise—the role of critical reader who, as logician and historian, resists being swayed by an image of desire.

In this dialogue between poet-rhetorician and poet-critic, the latter's voice seems considerably more authoritative than the former's. But the dialogue is, in fact, a genuine match of strength, and those who find Pugliano merely the victim of Sidney's irony misjudge the complexity of the master-servant relation sketched and resketched in the *exordium*. For Sidney does not simply master Pugliano's rhetoric by resisting it; the speech moves him to reflection, though not in the way the speaker intended: "But thus much at least with his no few words he drave into me, that self-love is better than any gilding to make that seem gorgeous wherein ourselves be parties" (p. 73). This sentence, which exposes the self-love that motivates not only Pugliano but the orator who insists that he "followeth the steps of his master," is, from one perspective, the ultimate narcissistic defense of author against reader. The defense consists of an irony which denies us the pleasure of deconstructing the text because it has already been deconstructed. Critics have not given sufficient credit to the epistemological problem Sidney creates by impugning his text's credibility. Swift, however—or someone counterfeiting him—recognized that Sidney's "drie mock" of himself prevents the reader from mastering intention. "Sidney wrote *as if* he really believed himself," says the author of the ironic "Letter of Advice to a Young Poet" (my emphasis).[41]

The ambiguity of this "as if" frames Sidney's discourse and puts the status of all his claims for poetry into radical question. In the *peroratio* he circles back to his beginning, with a Cheshire Cat smile. He sums up his defense of the "ever-praiseworthy Poesy" by "conjuring" his readers—"you all that have had the evil luck to read this ink-wasting toy of mine"—to leave off laughing at poets "as though they were next inheritors to fools," and to replace scorn with belief: "to believe, with Aristotle, that they were the ancient treasurers of the Grecians' divinity; to believe, with Scaliger, that no philosopher's precepts can sooner make you an honest man than the reading

of Virgil" (p. 121). The list of authorities continues, with Sidney himself
slipping in between Hesiod and Landino. The hyperbolic claims for poetry
not only recall Pugliano's enthusiastic claims for horsemen but echo (sometimes contradictorily) the arguments made in the body of the oration. That
"body," indeed, is now exposed as a multiple entity; the *Defence* has the
tenuous (and comic) unity of a community project.[42] The ironic repetition of
the verb "believe" advises the reader that he should believe in the authority
of this text no more than Sidney believed in the authority of his "master,"
Pugliano. When the conjuring concludes with the command that we believe
the poets themselves "when they tell you they will make you immortal by
their verses," the analogy between Sidney's response to Pugliano and the
audience's response to the *Defence* could not be clearer: if we believe, we
shall show our narcissistic identification with the object of praise. The
conjuration which begins by claiming that poets are not the "next inheritors
to fools" ends by suggesting, as does Erasmus's Folly herself, that Philautia
and Kolakia, self-love and flattery, are intimate companions of both poets
and their readers.[43]

If, however, we take the hint and do not believe in the authorities' claims
for poetry, we shall necessarily believe the claim made by Sidney himself in
his comic role of authority: "Believe, with me, that there are many mysteries
contained in poetry, which of purpose were written darkly, lest by profane
wits it should be abused" (p. 121). This assertion, syntactically similar to the
others and seemingly similar in its import (*mysteries* has a positive connota-
tion), is in fact subtly different: it makes no specific claim for poetry's value,
only for its ability to hide potentially valuable meaning. The assertion traps
us in the paradox of the Cretan liar: if we do not believe that Sidney's
discourse "says what it means," then we do believe it when it says that it does
not say what it means. Moreover, we see that in this complex act of conjuring
Sidney is at once confirming and undermining his previous definitions of
both the poet and the orator: the poet "never maketh any circles around your
imagination, to conjure you to believe for true what he writes" (p. 102); and
the orator is someone who "[pretends] not to know art" in order to "win
credit of popular ears (which credit is the nearest step to persuasion, which
persuasion is the chief mark of oratory)" (p. 118).

From an epistemological point of view, there is no exit from the circle of
irony Sidney draws around his "I" and his oration. The text undermines that
"assumption of intelligibility" which, according to Paul de Man, makes "the
mastering of the tropological displacement the very burden of understanding."[44] How can we master an irony which allows us to be certain of no
intention but the intention to hide intention: "to believe, with me, that there
are many mysteries . . . which of purpose were written darkly, lest by
profane wits it should be abused"?

The Dialogic Defense: Allegory

Speculation turns not to itself
Till it hath travell'd and is mirror'd there
Where it may see itself.   —Shakespeare, *Troilus and Cressida*

Tell all the truth but tell it slant
Success in circuit lies
Too bright for our infirm delight. . . .   —Emily Dickinson

The epistemological barrier Sidney erects between his intention (desire) and his discourse is not an impenetrable barrier because it is located in the circle of Narcissus—a circle in which lack of cognitive certainty need not entail lack of moral awareness. In the *exordium* and the *peroratio*, the text offers the reader a choice not between error and truth but between error and recognition of the inevitability of error in the self. If we counterfeit an allegorical intention for Sidney, we shall be doing what he does for Pugliano when he finds in Pugliano's self-loving rhetoric an image for the potential falseness of his own discourse. Sidney does not imply that the recognition of self-love leads to a transcendence of it: on the contrary, by portraying himself as "following" Pugliano's example, he sketches a circular movement whereby the pupil who "masters" his master's rhetoric in a moment of "gnosis" becomes again, in his own rhetorical "praxis," a pupil asserting his desire for mastery over the audience of the *Defence*. If we resist Sidney's claims on our belief as Sidney resists Pugliano's, we will, moreover, simply be replacing a naive form of self-love with a sophisticated one. Instead of identifying with the object of praise (wishing oneself a horse or wishing to be immortal like the poet) we shall be identifying with the interpreter who substitutes his own reading for the "surface" meaning of the text. Sidney suggests that the act of interpretation is no less motivated by self-love than is the oratorical performance: the reader who seeks the "mysteries" of a text is, of course, flattering himself that he is not a "profane wit." But self-love, for Sidney, is not simply the moral sin that *amor sui* is for Augustine. It is the ground for sin, but also the ground for the possibility of being educated in virtue. Sidney plays on the ambiguity of the concept of self-love when he argues that the reader makes a poem the "imaginative groundplot for a *profitable* invention." His entire theory of poetry's "moving" power also stresses the educational role of self-love: we cannot be moved to virtue without being delighted, and "delight we scarcely do but in things that have a conveniency to ourselves or to the general nature"—nature here being that double human nature that consists of an "infected will" and an "erected wit."

"The possibility of interpretation," Emerson wrote, "lies in the identity of the observer with the observed."[45] The possibility of reading the *Defence* as an allegory lies in readers' willingness to find themselves figured in Sidney's images of a self-reader whose intentions are good although they cannot be proved to be so. To read allegorically, one must accept, on faith, the claim Sidney makes for the ideal poet and, implicitly, for himself: "pretending no more, [he] doth intend the winning of the mind from wickedness to virtue" (*Defence*, 92). Sidney himself suggests that such an allegorical intention does not truly exist until it is confirmed by the reader, who becomes, indeed, a kind of co-creator. The poet's "delivering forth" of his "*idea* or fore-conceit" is made "substantial," Sidney suggests, only insofar as the poet's word, like God's, becomes flesh: the imagination "so far substantially . . . worketh, not only to make a Cyrus, which had been but a particular excellency as nature might have done, but to bestow a Cyrus upon the world to make many Cyruses, if they will learn aright why and how that maker made him" (p. 79).

Although Sidney may wish that the human maker, like the divine, had the power to guarantee "substantial" confirmation of his intention, he is neither so naive nor so sinful as Andrew Weiner suggests when he argues that Sidney's "right poet" "denies the reader the choice" of being moved to evil rather than to good.[46] Sidney's own illustration of "how much [poetry] can move" shows beautifully how much poetry *cannot* move an unwilling reader. The "abominable tyrant Alexander Phereus," murderer of many, watched a tragic representation of murder, Sidney says, and was moved to tears—but not to virtue: "And if it wrought no further good in him, it was that he, in despite of himself, withdrew himself from hearkening to that which might mollify his hardened heart" (pp. 96–97). It is no accident that the audience which responds to a representation aesthetically but not morally is figured as a tyrant. The allegorist who intends to promote virtue is a slave to the very phenomenon which gives the ironist power: the divorce between intention and discourse. To read Sidney's text as allegory, we must at least begin to make that divorce a marriage by entering the game Sidney defines in terms of the Christian's (and, more problematically, the courtier's) para-doxical duty to be master and servant at once.

"The irony of irony," Friedrich Schlegel wrote, "is the fact that one becomes weary of it if one is offered it everywhere and all the time."[47] A remarkable passage in the *Defence*, where Sidney once again reflects on his own mode of discourse, suggests that the weariness of irony is the weariness of language itself, of its endless "turning." In this passage, the concept of allegory appears as an escape from the realm in which "playing wits" can turn any word into its opposite. The passage I have in mind is Sidney's reply to the *mysomousoi*, or "poet-haters"; the reply is not to a "substantial" charge against poetry but merely to the objectionable form in which some objections are made—the form of rhetorical mockery which is used, Sidney says, by "that kind of people who seek a praise by dispraising others" (p. 99). "That kind of people" obviously includes the author who has praised the poet by dispraising the philosopher and the historian. "We have ears as well as tongues," says Sidney, introducing the *mysomousoi's* objections; what he offers is another instance of the rhetorician listening critically to a "speaking picture" of himself. Commenting on the "playing wit" which can turn bad into good by praising "the jolly commodity of being sick of the plague," Sidney gives a complex example of the process of "turning" upon which he is reflecting:

> So of the contrary side, if we will turn Ovid's verse *Ut lateat virtus proximitate mali*, that good lie hid in nearness of the evil, Agrippa will be as merry in showing the vanity of science as Erasmus was in the commending of folly. [p. 100]

The first thing to note is that the logical expectations of progress engendered by the phrase "So of the contrary side" are turned to nothing. We expect an alternative, epistemological or moral, to the "playing wit"; instead we get (after a hypothetical clause to which we shall return) not one but two further examples of the same phenomenon. The use of the conditional mood in the phrase "Agrippa will be as merry as Erasmus was" suggests, moreover, that the adducing of examples here itself involves a willful act of interpretation: not every sixteenth-century reader took Cornelius Agrippa's *De incertitudine et vanitate scientiarum et artium* as a playful text.[48] By naming Agrippa as a playing wit, Sidney calls attention to the fact that an ironist can always find doubleness in another text. The *Defence*, indeed, makes extensive double use of Agrippa by borrowing his arguments against philosophy and history for the *confirmatio's* praise of poetry, and by borrowing his arguments against poetry for the *refutatio's* formulation of objections. In the realm of epideictic oratory, which Aristotle defines as the "ceremonial oratory of display," dispraises can be transformed into praises as praises can be transformed into dispraises; here signifiers truly float.[49]

In the hypothetical middle of this "turning" sentence Sidney locates the rhetorician's duplicity in the duplicity of language itself: "if we will turn Ovid's verse," Sidney says, and he then performs a "turn" by misquoting Ovid's line, which is, in the original, "Et lateat vitium proximitate boni" ("And let a fault's nearness to virtue conceal it"). One editor notes that "Sidney adapts the verse to his purpose by replacing *vitium* by *virtus*, and *boni* by *mali*."[50] But what is Sidney's "purpose"? Ovid's line (*Ars amatoria* 2. 662) occurs in a passage about the lover's intention to win his lady by deceiving her: "With names you can soften shortcomings" ("Nominibus mollire licet mala"), Ovid says, and proceeds to give examples of replacing a bad signifier with a good one ("if short, call her trim").[51] Sidney's "imitation"

of Ovid's theory and practice of concealing truth with words opens up an
intertextual vista of suspicion about the very concept of authorial purpose.
The *Ars* was condemned by Augustus because he thought its intention was
to teach immoral behavior; Ovid, banished from Rome, defended himself
in the *Tristia*, arguing that he had not intended to teach immorality, that
poetry is a double-edged sword, and that the responsibility for abuse is the
reader's, not the author's.[52]

Sidney's hypothetical clause, in which a falsified original is doubled by a
translation, is a space of "as if," a space in which the play of same and
different replaces the work of ascertaining truth and falsehood. The whole
sentence is, one might say, a performance of the paradox that "good lie hid
in nearness of the evil." The turnings of language merely reflect the inevitable errings of man's will. "Neither shall any man or matter escape some
touch of these smiling railers," Sidney adds, underscoring the universality of
this problem as he had underscored the universality of poetry's and love's
"abuse." His next sentence, however, offers an escape—the Christian escape:
"But for Erasmus and Agrippa, they had another foundation than the superficial part would promise." This other foundation is located neither in the
individual author's intention nor in the text: it is the Word whose true
promise the reader must find beneath the false promises of human words.

Unlike modern hermeneutic theorists such as E. D. Hirsch, who defines
textual Meaning (what Frege called the unchanging *Sinn*) as "whatever
someone has willed to convey by a particular sequence of linguistic signs,"[53]
Renaissance authors pay little attention to protecting the intentionality of
individuals or texts from the dangers of subjective interpretation. The
reader is not only allowed but encouraged to master any secular (literary)
authority in order to serve his true "self-interest," which for Sidney, as for
Erasmus and Agrippa, is the state of his soul. "You therefore O ye asses,"
writes Agrippa in the conclusion of his work, "if ye desire to attain to this
divine and true wisdom, not of the tree of knowledge of good and evil, but
of the tree of life, set aside the Traditions of Men . . . conversing now not
with the Schools of Philosophers and Sophisters, but with your own
selves."[54]

If we consider the parallels Sidney appears to announce between his own
rhetorical project and those of authors like Agrippa and Erasmus, we may
be tempted to read the *Defence* as a "self-consuming artifact" of the kind
Stanley Fish describes. A work "consumes" itself, he argues, by undermining its own rhetorical authority, as Donne does in his *Sermons*: "by emptying
his art of its (claims to) power, he acknowledges his own powerlessness,
becoming like us and the shell of his sermon a vessel filled by and wholly
dependent on the lord."[55] Following Fish, we could interpret the "other
foundation" of Sidney's egoistic project as an attack on the ego and all its

works. Not only Christianity, but also Platonism, requires such an attack from the writer whose aim is to serve rather than conceal the truth. In the *Gorgias*, for instance, Socrates attacks the Sophist's view of rhetoric as an amoral phenomenon. For the philosopher who serves truth rather than expediency, rhetoric is "of no use at all," Socrates says, if it is used "for pleading in defense of injustice, whether it is oneself or one's parents or friends, or children or country that has done the wrong"; Socrates goes on, however, to suggest a different conception of rhetoric. It may be used legitimately, he suggests to his interlocutor Polus, if "one were to suppose, perchance . . . that a man ought to accuse himself first of all, and in the second place his relations or anyone else of his friends who may from time to time be guilty of wrong; and instead of concealing the iniquity, to bring it to light in order that he may pay the penalty and be made healthy" (480b–c; Loeb ed., p. 375).

I think that Sidney's text does have this Christian and Platonic "other foundation." By dramatizing the philosopher's and the historian's lack of self-knowledge, by offering examples of an act of critical self-observation, the *Defence* becomes, like the poetry it paradoxically praises, an "exercise of the mind" aimed at turning the reader "inward for thorough self-examination."[56] But there is, inevitably, an egoistical dimension to this altruism, another "other foundation" which exposes the error of thinking that self-love can be transcended or that rhetoric can "empty" itself of its claims to power. Aristotle's pragmatic reply to Plato's argument that rhetoric should be used to accuse rather than to excuse the self is appropriate here. Aristotle introduces his justification of rhetoric as a double-edged sword by associating the power of speech with the natural human activity of self-defense. He simply avoids the question of whether the self is just or unjust and focuses, instead, on the fact that "all men" defend themselves with their *logos* as well as with their limbs.[57] "Aristotle defends rhetoric," W. K. Wimsatt remarks, "on approximately the same grounds as those on which Plato condemns it."[58] Sidney's *Defence* recreates the irresolvable debate between the idealist and the pragmatist in an interesting way. The irony of Sidney's allegory is that the desire to promote virtue in others is also the desire to promote the self in the eyes of others.

The interweaving of these two desires is evident in the passage that offers proof of the power of fiction. There are two proofs: the first is the story of Menenius Agrippa which we examined at the beginning of this chapter; the second is the story of Nathan the prophet, whose parable of the rich man who "ungratefully" stole the poor man's lamb made the adulterous David "as in a glass see his own filthiness" (*Defence*, p. 94).[59] Both stories illustrate a use of allegory as a mirror in which the audience sees an image of its present condition of error; by recognizing itself, the audience recalls what it should be, which is exactly what it was before erring. These are profoundly conservative stories, both epistemologically and socially. Knowledge consists of remembering one's proper role, which for both plebians and king involves submitting to the higher authority, the Senate in the first case, God in the second. The audiences which have rebelled against authority are corrected by being made to submit to verbal authority—authority which resides, significantly, not in the tales but in the tellers. The fables themselves, unlike the poetry Sidney later defines as "pictures [of] what should be" (p. 103), merely translate a condition of error into the simple terms of a nominative substitution; it is the orator's application of his fable that produces moral change. The orator has usurped the role of interpreter, leaving the audience no room (or time) to misunderstand: in the biblical story, King David remains in ignorance of the parable's meaning for him until Nathan says, "Thou art the man" (2 Samuel 12:7); in Plutarch's account, Menenius concludes his fable by explaining, "such, then, is the relation of the senate, my fellow citizens, to you."

Taken together, these stories of stories offer a complex image of Sidney's own "golden world." Classical orator and biblical prophet, the twin ideals of English humanism, represent eloquence in service to one's country and one's God, rhetorical power sanctioned by authority (Menenius is the senate's chosen diplomat, Nathan is God's instrument). George K. Hunter has shown how the humanist ideal of "pious eloquence" was tarnished by the realities of Elizabeth's court; and historians like Lawrence Stone have shown the economic and social constraints which that court placed on its potentially "over-mighty subjects."[60] Sidney, born to "great expectation" in a family tainted by treason, was deeply frustrated by Elizabeth's refusal to grant him scope for "virtuous action": "The unnoble constitution of our time doth keep us from fit employments," he wrote in 1580, summing up his particularly intense experience of "the crisis of the aristocracy."[61]

During the period when Sidney wrote the *Defence*, he would naturally have associated the ideal of rhetorical power with his personal desires for action in the service of God and England—desires foiled, as Sidney tells Hubert Languet, by Leicester's and Walsingham's failure to "persuade" Elizabeth to take "a more active course" in the Protestant wars in Belgium. "Unless God powerfully counteract it, I seem to myself to see our cause withering away," he wrote in 1578.[62] The next year the Queen even more seriously threatened the cause by her plan to marry the French Catholic d'Alencon. With a boldness his tact could not hide, Sidney assumed the role of orator-teacher in his "Letter to the Queen Touching Her Marriage with Monsieur." The *Defence* appears to have been written soon after the letter: both texts develop Menenius's metaphor of the endangered "body politic," and both contain an erratic quotation from Seneca's description of tyranny's self-destructiveness.[63]

The defense of "poor Poetry," fallen on evil days, in many respects resembles the letter in which Sidney courted (and won) disfavor by telling a monarch, in "simple and direct terms," that "your own eyes cannot see yourself."[64] Some moments in the *Defence* are dangerously simple and direct: Elizabeth is figured in poetry's "ungrateful" enemies (especially in Plato, the banisher of poets, whom Sidney desires to make "our patron and not our adversary"), in the "tyrant" Alexander Phereus, who "hardened his heart" against a poet's images of virtue, and, with hardly any disguise, in the *digressio's* inquiry into "why England, the mother of excellent minds, should be grown so hard a stepmother to poets" (especially to a poet whose own "idleness" is clearly caused by England's "overfaint quietness").[65] "Heretofore," Sidney writes, poets "have in England also flourished, and, which is to be noted, even in those times when the trumpet of Mars did sound loudest" (*Defence*, p. 110).

Neither the courtier nor the author of a written text, however, can make an audience "note" his words, and Sidney's ambivalent recognition of this fact makes his discourse oscillate between two modes of allegory—an "old" one associated with classical oratory (with its emphasis on "clarity"), and a new one closer to what Puttenham recommended to those who would safely address the Queen: "Allegoria," the "courtly figure," to "speake one thing and thinke another."[66] Indeed the passage about Menenius and Nathan is an "allegory of allegory" in which both modes dialogically confront one another: it is a complex mirror that refracts not only Sidney's desires for a golden world but his awareness of a brazen one. "My only service is speech, and that is stopped," he wrote in 1580.[67] In the *Defence*, his efforts to serve both himself and the Queen take many shapes of "false semblant."

The relation between orator and audience figured in the stories of Menenius and Nathan is the allegorical "other" of the relation between Sidney and his reader. Addressing an audience he can neither see nor control, he offers not one but two fables whose meaning must be construed by an active rather than a passive mental process. The fables are "so often remembered that I think all men know them," Sidney begins: but "knowing" does not consist, for us, in remembering only, since Sidney's intention must be deduced in part from the ways he changes his sources (by adding the phrase "so unprofitable a spender" to Plutarch, for instance, and by adding the word "ungratefully" to the Bible's account of an "unholy alliance").[68] Meaning is a function of difference as well as resemblance, of textual and intertextual labor. Sidney's own "proofs" of the power of fiction are, therefore, the epistemological opposite of the certain (and narcissistically gratifying) confirmation of power he imagines for Menenius and Nathan. These figures point to "another nature" beyond writing: a world where intention passes without distortion through words and is made substantial in an audience's immediate and favorable response. Unlike Menenius and Nathan, the author of the

Defence is trapped in a temporal "predicament of relation" in which he can never know his own strength until he knows the strength against which he is to be matched.

Menenius Agrippa, the ideal orator-mediator, effects a "perfect reconcilement" between his own desires and his audience's, between masters and servants, and between authority and the desire to rebel against it. Sidney's text cannot offer such a "perfect reconcilement"; instead it offers a model of that relation between text and reader which consists of a constant turning of master into servant and servant into master. In this turning, at once an exercise of ambition and a contemplation of it, the boundaries between oratory and poetry, play and persuasion, invention and interpretation, are repeatedly drawn and transgressed. The text establishes and undermines rhetorical authority, its own and others', as it explores the paradox that poetry "must be gently led, or rather it must lead" (p. 111). It thereby provides an unsettling model for the activity of the reader who is also a writer. The power of this model is obliquely confirmed by W. K. Wimsatt, a critic whose arguments against the intentional and affective fallacies erect a defense of poetry and criticism which seems antithetical to Sidney's. "*The Defence of Poesy*," writes Wimsatt in *Literary Criticism*, "is a kind of formal beginning of literary criticism by the English man of letters, and a brilliant enough one—written in the high, enthusiastic, occasionally a-syntactic style of the gifted amateur champion, headlong to outdazzle the lowness and myopia of professional moral grumblers."[69] The sentence registers a complex resistance to Sidney's style—a resistance informed, I suspect, by the professional American critic's distrust of English men of letters, amateur champions, and rhetoric itself. The irony is that Wimsatt sounds very much like Sidney listening with "logical" detachment to the enthusiastic "high-style" of John Pietro Pugliano. And Wimsatt, like Sidney, offers a brilliant imitation of the very "headlong" and power-seeking style he distrusts, showing that Sidney was indeed "brilliant enough" to turn those who would master him into servants of his always double image.

Conclusion: *Amicus Curiae* Briefs

Alas love, I would thou couldst as well
defend thyself as thou canst offend others.
                                    —Sidney, *Defence of Poetry*

The prospect of ending a piece of work, like the prospect of beginning one, so frequently generates defensive discourse that one is led to speculate, a bit nostalgically, about the medieval convention of the retraction. As a version of the Augustinian confession, with its drama of a conversion from secular words to sacred ones, the retraction served psychological and aesthetic, as well as religious, aims by providing a formal channel for the apologetic impulse that perennially besets authors preparing to take leave of their books.[1] Although the retraction may seem a dead convention today, its ghost lives on in the uneasy rhetoric of conclusions, postscripts, and afterwords, including this one. If, however, one is so foolish as to acknowledge the ghost's presence in one's own pages, one should at least engage it in battle, using, to begin with, a weapon employed by Folly herself. "I see you are expecting a peroration," she says to her audience near the end of the *Encomium Moriae*. "But you are just too foolish if you suppose that after I have poured out a hodgepodge of words like this I can recall anything I have said."[2]

I cannot claim such perfect forgetfulness, but what I *do* remember from my preceding chapters—particularly the material illustrating the intimate link between Memory and Apology—strengthens my desire to imitate Folly. Instead of offering either a peroration or a retraction—exercises in recapitulation which create guilt in the writer and boredom in the reader—I shall set off, as Folly so often does, on a seemingly new path. It will not by any means lead us out of the territory of defensive discourse, but it will at least give us some new sights, notably passages in defenses by Boccaccio and Shelley, and also some new perspectives on familiar material. Above all, it will allow questions about ends—both as aims and as terminations—to be rephrased in the light of a long-deferred comparison between Freud's rhetorical practice of defense, on the one hand, and the practices of poet-critics, on the other.

*   *   *

Freud begins one of his *New Introductory Lectures on Psychoanalysis* (1933 [1932]) by addressing a problem that has, he says, "very little theoretical interest" but that nonetheless concerns his audience closely, insofar as its members are "friendlily disposed toward psychoanalysis" (*SE* 22: 136). The problem, which has considerable theoretical interest for the student of defensive discourse, has to do with the existence of people *unfriendly* to psychoanalysis, people whose prejudice toward it resembles the traditional prejudice of Christians toward Jews. Brooding on the nature of this prejudice, which he sees as an "after-effect" of a negative judgment "by the representatives of official science" (p. 137), Freud defines his position in a cultural court which strikingly resembles those in which poets have often pled their cases (and not only in periods when powerful social institutions censored literary production). The rules of such cultural courts are hardly just, for they tend to presume defendants guilty until proven innocent: moreover, they generally allow defendants to state their cases only after they have been sentenced. If poets from ancient times to modern ones have been irritated by the way in which Socrates challenges "poetry and her friends" to speak only after the philosopher has handed down the sentence of banishment from the Republic, Freud is equally irritated by the way in which "official" scientists (many of them members of the Nazi party) allow him to speak only from a position outside the walls of the university.[3] "You must not," he dourly tells his audience, "expect to hear . . . that the struggle about analysis is over and has ended in its recognition as a science and its admission as a subject for instruction at universities" (p. 138).

The concept of "recognition" (*Anerkennung*) is what links this passage most clearly to defenses of poetry. Before showing why this is so, however, I should note again that Freud is concerned, in this lecture, not only with the results of an "official" judgment against psychoanalysis, but also with prejudice as an ideological phenomenon which manifests itself in such apparently "polite" forms as remarks in casual conversations or in novels—texts which purport to reflect social reality but which do not, in Freud's view, treat psychoanalysis with the respect it deserves. If you take up "a German, English or American novel," he observes, you will often find "facetious" remarks about psychoanalysis, remarks "intended by the author to display his wide reading and intellectual superiority" (p. 136). As offended by the assumption of superiority as he is by the content of the remarks, Freud compares novelistic statements about psychoanalysis to those made in social gatherings: "You will hear the greatest variety of people passing their judgment on [psychoanalysis], mostly in voices of unwavering certainty. It is quite usual for the judgment to be contemptuous or often slanderous or at the least, once again, facetious" (p. 136). Freud proceeds to liken such modern trials-by-opinion to those ordeals which occurred in the Middle Ages "when an evil-doer, or even a mere political opponent, was put in the pillory and given over to maltreatment by the mob" (p. 137). The historical analogy is then extended to include a not-so-distant past, that time when Freud himself was "more or less alone" as the founder of psychoanalysis; and he now considers the tactics that a victim of prejudice should *not* employ. "There was no future in polemics," he asserts; and "it was equally senseless to lament and to invoke the help of kindlier spirits, for there were not courts to which such appeals could be made" (pp. 137–38).

Freud dismisses polemics and appeals for aid as ineffective means of defense, but we shall see that he uses subtle versions of both tactics. In so doing, he practices an art of defense very like that which we have observed in Du Bellay's, Tasso's, and Sidney's treatises. This art, which involves a complex double movement of attack and courtship, is aimed not so much at winning a verdict of innocent as at making prosecutors and judges see that they in some sense share the defendant's guilt. To make others see their resemblance to you is a major aim of the defensive writer, who seeks to gain recognition. When I use that term in this chapter, I mean not only the act of "knowing again," but also the act of acknowledging someone or something to be "true, valid, or entitled to consideration."[4]

Like a defender of poetry, Freud seeks recognition from an audience that includes persons who possess (or claim to possess) political power and cultural authority. Representatives of rival intellectual disciplines play a particularly prominent role in Freud's conception of a prosecutory audience: the novelist is for Freud what the historian or philosopher is for Sidney—a competitor whose claims to superiority must be challenged. In addressing an audience which he not only perceives but half creates, the defendant characteristically engages in a complex process of projection and introjection. Somewhere in the textual court sits an imagined version of the censoring and judging agency Freud called the superego.

With the notion of a composite prosecutory audience in mind, let us return to Freud's description of his experience in a "court of no appeal." Deciding that polemics offered no escape from that court, he tells us that he chose to take "another road": "I made a first application of psychoanalysis by explaining to myself that this behavior of the crowd was a manifestation of the same resistance which I had to struggle against in individual patients" (*SE* 22: 138). Freud here universalizes the phenomenon of offensive prejudice by viewing it as a defense employed by all psyches. His own move is at once an offense and a defense: it masters the opposition's views not by refuting them but by explaining their origin; and that act of "explaining *to [him]self*" protects Freud by suggesting that nothing specific in his character, or in his science, has merited censure. The "cause" of attack is not in the defendant, but in the offenders' psyches.

Freud's own phrasing suggests that psychoanalytic theory here serves a defensive function. In his book *The Ordeal of Civility*, J. M. Cuddihy has argued, indeed, that Freud's entire metapsychology should be seen as an elaborate defense against the problems that Jews faced in bourgeois Christian society. "Freud transformed various social offenses against the *goyim* into various psychological defenses against the id," Cuddihy writes.[5] His argument is interesting but crude, not only because it assumes that a theory which can be used defensively is merely a defense, with no conceptual validity independent of its immediate sociological context, but also because it is reductive even as an account of what Freud does in a passage like the one discussed above. There Freud views his opponents' social offenses as psychological defenses, doing for the Christians the same thing Cuddihy sees him doing for the Jews. He does, to be sure, ascribe to the enemies of psychoanalysis precisely the qualities often ascribed to psychoanalysis in particular and to Jews in general: earlier in the passage, he remarks that "there was no violation of propriety and good taste, to which the scientific opponents of psychoanalysis did not give way" (*SE* 22: 137). But this is a tactic defenders of poetry also employ, and in their texts too it often appears in conjunction with "universalizing" theories, theories which, while they lack the systematic scope of Freud's, serve as his does to shift attention from the alleged sins of the defendant to the character and motives of the prosecution. These are the *tu quoque* arguments that appear frequently in Renaissance defenses: in Du Bellay's argument that the Romans stole literary riches from the Greeks as the modern poet steals from his precursors, for instance, or in Sidney's argument that philosophers and historians lie no less (albeit less self-consciously) than poets do.

The very presence of such arguments in defenses of poetry invites us to see Freud's practice of textual defense from a broader historical and theoretical perspective than Cuddihy provides. Consider, for a moment, a comparison between Freud's description of his dilemma, in the days when he felt himself to be "virtually alone" as the creator of a socially offensive discipline, and Boccaccio's description of the poet's dilemma in the penultimate book of the *Genealogia deorum gentilium*, a monumental work of humanist scholarship which collects and comments on the myths of pagan antiquity. The Preface and final two books of the *Genealogia* are important because they constitute not only a defense of poetry but also—and more explicitly than the later Renaissance texts studied in this book—a defense of interpretation.[6] In the following passage from Book 14, Boccaccio recapitulates a series of arguments traditionally made against poets, but he mentions, in addition, an accusation that has particular relevance to his own work as an interpreter of myth who may choose, as Freud so often does, to read an inherited story sacrilegiously:

They say poetry is absolutely of no account, and the making of poetry a useless and absurd craft; that poets are tale-mongers, or, in lower terms, liars; that they live in the country among the woods and mountains because they lack manners and polish. They say, besides, that their poems are false, obscure, lewd, and replete with absurd and silly tales of pagan gods, and that they make Jove, who was, in point of fact, an obscene and adulterous man, now the father of gods, now king of heaven, now fire, or air, or man, or bull, or eagle, or similar irrelevant things; in like manner poets exalt to fame Juno and infinite others under various names. Again and again they cry out that poets are seducers of the mind, prompters of crime, and, to make their foul charge, fouler, if possible, they say they are philosophers' apes, that it is a heinous crime to read or possess the books of poets; and then, without making any distinction, they prop them-selves up, as they say, with Plato's authority, to the effect that poets ought to be turned out-of-doors—nay, out of town. [pp. 35–36]

This passage presents the poet's relation to society as a vicious circle: the poet offends society by threatening conventional codes of manners or mor-als; society defends itself against the poet by threatening to expel him; and this defense paradoxically undermines the code of civility it purportedly protects. As Boccaccio implies, there is an illogical link between the poet's offense of "living in the country" and "lacking manners," and society's unmannerly decision to turn the poet "out-of-doors—nay, out of town." The poet's dilemma resembles that which Cuddihy describes for late nineteenth-century Jews, the "'pariah people' closed out from . . . respectable society " because they were "deemed wanting in respectability in the first place." [7]

The very resemblance between the poet's dilemma and the Jew's suggests that Cuddihy overlooks something important when he explains Freud's theory simply as a response to a particular historical situation. If Freud's science offended the "manners and morals" of his society, it constituted a threat similar to the one that many kinds of literature have constituted for various social orders; there seems to be something in both literature and psychoanalysis which causes, as well as reflects, social tensions.[8] Boccaccio shows that the poet's marginal position is created not only by the social group's hostility toward one of its members but by the poet's own activity, which requires detachment from the group, and, implicitly, from its norms of behavior and value. Poets, as Boccaccio explains, "seek their habitation in solitudes because contemplation . . . is utterly impossible in places like the greedy and mercenary market" (*Genealogia*, p. 55).[9] The psychoanalyst also practices an art of contemplation which requires detachment from the social group and which therefore may be perceived as threatening by those who feel themselves to be (critically) observed. Freud and defenders of poetry acknowledge, moreover, that their practices involve an unmasking or expo-sure of things that both ordinary and powerful members of society may wish to keep hidden. "Your own eyes cannot see yourself," Sidney wrote to

Queen Elizabeth; his defense of poetry testifies to his awareness that the poet courts danger when he attempts to open a person's eyes to the "sack of his own faults . . . hidden behind his back."[10] Defenders of poetry and Freud admit that their arts constitute a threat; at the same time, they protest against society's hostile perception of them. The rhetoric of defense characteristically manifests the author's ambivalent desire to be both outside and inside the social group.

If you believe yourself to be in some sense guilty, the best strategy of defense is to make others see that they share your guilt. Defenders of poetry, as I have said, frequently resort to *tu quoque* arguments; "Judge not, lest ye be judged," is the formula, both plea and command, which underlies these arguments. Boccaccio offers a relatively simple version of the "judge not" motif when he insists that poetry's opponents should "look to their own speciousness before they try to dim the splendor of others. . . . When they have made themselves clean, let them purify the tales of others, mindful of Christ's commandment to the accusers of the woman taken in adultery, that he who was without sin should cast the first stone" (*Genealogia*, p. 51). Boccaccio directs this argument explicitly to the philosophers ("If these disparagers still insist in spite of everything that poets are liars, I accuse the philosophers, Aristotle, Plato, and Socrates, of sharing their guilt" [p. 67]); he is more subtle when he addresses poets' most powerful enemies, the theologians. Those who condemn fiction, he writes, should realize that they thereby condemn "the form [of parable] which our Saviour Jesus Christ . . . often used when He was in the flesh" (p. 49). In such arguments Boccaccio does precisely what he says poetry's enemies do when they are threatened by one who differs from them: "It is a trait of abandoned characters to wish above all that others should be like them . . . in self-defense" (p. 57).

Whether or not Boccaccio intended such a comment to apply to his own rhetorical practice of self-defense, we can apply it heuristically to the "universalizing" arguments which occur so often in later defenses of poetry, and which underpin Freud's metapsychological theory as well. Without reductively saying that arguments about the universality of self-love (Sidney) or of unconscious drives (Freud) are *merely* defenses against powerful ideologies and political practices that stress qualitative differences among people of different races, classes, or professions, we must nonetheless remark that a certain tendency to reductive theorizing appears to be a hallmark of defensive discourse. To reduce differences among persons and stress their common ground (and common weaknesses) is, it would seem, a desire Freud shares with defenders of poetry.

* * *

A theoretical focus on likenesses among persons is, of course, related to the defendant's characteristic desire to be recognized by others. The texts by Du Bellay, Tasso, and Sidney analyzed in the earlier chapters of this book all contain apologues designed to persuade an audience to see the author as he wishes to be seen. Du Bellay invites the cardinal to recognize his young kinsman as a David ready to conquer Goliath or as a "Hercule Gallique" capable of drawing his audience behind him by a chain linking his tongue with their ears. Tasso invites his readers to see him as the heroic Goffredo, addressing an admiring audience of nobles. Sidney asks his countrymen, and in particular his Queen, to see him as a powerful but peaceloving orator like Menenius Agrippa, who creates a "perfect reconcilement" among struggling social classes. And Freud, too, offers us a fable manifesting a wishful desire for recognition, a fable which portrays the defendant in the very act of converting a skeptical interlocutor into a person who admires and believes in a heretofore unrecognized authority. The weapon of defense which Freud employs is a fiction that resembles the parables used by Christ and later preachers to lead an audience to a truth that cannot be empirically demonstrated, a truth "which eye cannot hear and ear cannot see," as Bottom, parodying Saint Paul, puts it in *A Midsummer Night's Dream*. And it is appropriate that both Freud and defenders of poetry should resort to such parabolic fictions to defend their disciplines, since both disciplines, like Christianity itself, base their claims to truth on the authority of words and of word-wielders who may look, to those in positions of political power, like dangerous magicians or frauds who threaten the social order. It is no accident that literature and psychoanalysis have both been seen, by their critics, as threats to established religions. Literature and psychoanalysis make claims which are fundamentally religious in nature, and which imply a contract characteristic of religious systems: believe in me and my words, and I will repay you with an increase in knowledge and/or happiness.

Freud's fable of recognition—or of conversion—occurs in the same lecture from which I quoted earlier; the story is indeed a kind of coda to the passage about the psychoanalyst's situation in a "court of no appeal." In the story, Freud uses a subtle version of the very tactic he had previously dismissed as useless: an "invocation of kindlier spirits," which is tantamount to a plea for a more enlightened audience of judges. Here, however, Freud is not simply "invoking" a kindlier spirit; he is creating one. In so doing, moreover, he is actively seeking to transform his actual audience, providing them with a model of a person persuaded by Freud to relinquish a skeptical attitude toward psychoanalysis. The subject of the story is a "world-famous critic"; Freud tells us that he succeeded in effecting a "rapid conversion" in this critic during the course of a conversation. Whetting our curiosity by not revealing the critic's identity, Freud writes:

> You will easily guess whom I mean. Nor was it I who introduced the subject of psycho-analysis. It was he who did so, by comparing himself with me in the

most modest fashion. 'I am only a literary man,' he said, 'but you are a natural scientist and discoverer. However, there is one thing I must say to you: I have never had sexual feelings towards my mother.' 'But there is no need at all for you to have known them,' was my reply; 'to grown-up people those are unconscious feelings.' 'Oh! so *that's* what you think!' he said with relief, and pressed my hand. We went on talking together on the best of terms for another few hours. I heard later that in the few remaining years of his life he often spoke of analysis in a friendly way and was pleased at being able to use a word that was new to him—'repression.' [*SE* 22: 139]

To appreciate the allegorical significance of this story, we should note that Freud initially presents the critic to illustrate a theory about a "buffer-layer" that "has formed in scientific society between analysis and its opponents." The "buffer-layer," which includes "some distinguished men," consists of persons whom Freud describes as "half- or quarter-adherents" to the new discipline. Dante would have called such persons the "lukewarm," and the religious analogy is worth keeping in mind as one reads Freud's description of those who maintain a critical, even a scientific, attitude toward his science:

This [buffer-layer] consists of people who allow the validity of some portions of analysis and admit as much, subject to the most entertaining qualifications, but who on the other hand reject other portions of it, a fact which they cannot proclaim too loudly. It is not easy to divine what determines their choice in this. It seems to depend on personal sympathies. One person will take objection to sexuality, another to the unconscious; what seems particularly unpopular is the fact of symbolism. [p. 138]

Freud does not explain how or why the "fact of symbolism" makes psychoanalysis an unpopular (*unbeliebte*) discipline, but the passage calls attention to a problem that underlies Freud's own discourse and is at the heart of his defensive attempts to prove that psychoanalysis is a science in its own right, with its own proper methods and objects of study. The problem has to do with what Freud himself, at the end of *Beyond the Pleasure Principle*, calls "the scientific terms, that is to say . . . the figurative language, peculiar to psychology (or, more precisely, to depth psychology)."[11] What is the epistemological status of the language Freud acknowledges to be "figurative"? He insists, to be sure, that the problem would not be solved if one could "replace the psychological terms by physiological or chemical ones," since these latter "too are only part of a figurative language" (*SE* 18: 60). But it is clear that psychoanalysis, a newcomer which poaches on territories occupied by other, more familiar languages, is in need of constant defense because it consists of an "artificial structure of hypotheses" that may, at any moment, be blown away by rival disciplines. "The uncertainty of our speculation," Freud remarks, "has been greatly increased by the necessity for borrowing from the science of biology" (p. 60). The defense of psycho-

analysis, which is inextricably linked to a defense of its figurative or symbolic language, is an especially difficult enterprise because that language is
so obviously "borrowed"—or stolen—from others, and hence is never truly
"peculiar" to psychology in the sense of being its property.

How is this problem highlighted by the description of the "buffer-layer" in
the *New Introductory Lectures*? Because the metaphor of the "buffer-layer"
so strikingly resembles that of the "protective shield" in Chapter 4 of *Beyond
the Pleasure Principle*. The people who constitute the "buffer-layer" play the
same structural role in a cultural drama that the protective shield plays in a
psychobiological one: the people admit only portions of psychoanalysis as
the protective shield of the psyche's perceptual apparatus admits only
selected "stimuli" from the "external world." The parallel between the two
passages erects a kind of figurative bridge between the study of the individual psyche and the study of social relationships, including the one between
the analyst and the analysand. The notion of the transference (*Übertragung*)
that Freud developed with specific reference to the analytic situation may,
however, be understood in a more general theoretical context when we
recall that Freud's concern with figurative language and the vicissitudes of
"passages" or "transfers" from one realm to another includes a concern with
the relation between psychoanalysis and rival cultural disciplines. In addressing the problem of the boundary between his science and other fields,
Freud employs metaphors which highlight the difficulty of distinguishing
what is "inside" from what is "outside" a particular discursive territory. And
in so doing, he invites us to remember the connection between the German
term *Übertragung* and the Greek *metapherein*, "to carry across."

In the *New Introductory Lectures*, Freud describes psychoanalysis itself
as something which occupies the place both of an outsider and an insider.
The passage about the "buffer-layer" quoted above presents psychoanalysis
as a phenomenon which certain people are intent on warding off; they
perceive it as a dangerous force that must be kept outside the university and
individual minds. Psychoanalysis as described here is analogous to "the
external world charged with the most powerful energies" in the passage
from *Beyond the Pleasure Principle*. But the conversion story which occurs a
few pages later in the lecture gives a different perspective on the nature and
metaphorical "place" of psychoanalysis. The critic who represents the
"buffer-layer" between psychoanalysis and its crude enemies is now assigned the part previously played by psychoanalysis: the critic is the outsider
"carried across" into the sacred space where the master teaches his disciples.
Psychoanalysis has become the "inside" now, and it is Freud himself who
serves (figuratively) as the "protective shield" for his discipline. He admits
the critic into the circle of secret knowledge constituted by psychoanalysis,
but he does so by making the critic relinquish a threatening part of himself—

his claim to mastery, his stance of superiority. Implicitly protecting and increasing his authority as the founder of a new field, Freud uses his story to illustrate the point that even those who have admirably mastered their own fields should "suspend their judgement" when they encounter psychoanalysis. The story appears to be a plea for tolerance, but in fact it is a subtly aggressive verbal performance: it not only converts a "partial" enemy into a friend, but partly divests him of his power of judgment. The critic, as Freud portrays him, is not only modest (" 'I am only a literary man,' he said"), but also a slightly comic object of condescension. Like the plebians instructed by Menenius Agrippa in Sidney's *Defence*, the critic in Freud's story comes, symbolically, to play a child's part, though Freud begins by remarking that the critic was over eighty years old and "still enchanting in his talk." When the critic insists that he "never had sexual feelings towards [his] mother," however, he is corrected in a tone one would use in speaking to a boy: "But there is no need at all for you to have known them," Freud replies; "to grown-up people those are unconscious feelings."

In constructing this quasi-autobiographical fiction in which he is relatively stronger than his audience, and in which his authority engenders in others feelings of affection, not anger, Freud follows previous literary defendants in using words to transform a brazen world of social reality into a golden world of fulfilled desire. And his miniature allegory, like Sidney's tale of Menenius Agrippa, supports Angus Fletcher's argument that "virtue, the positive ideal of moral allegory, needs to be given its original sense of 'power,' and moral fables need then to be reinterpreted as having to do chiefly with polarities of strength and weakness, confidence and fear, certainty and doubt."[12]

Authors of literary defenses—including Freud—are characteristically uncertain about their claims to possess virtue either as an ethical quality or as a rhetorical power. This uncertainty is, I think, a major reason why literary defendants so often depict allegorical scenes in which a speaker masters an audience. Unlike the writer, the speaker can experience the narcissistic pleasure of seeing his audience acknowledge his authority. Even if the audience fails to understand the speaker's intellectual point, as the critic in Freud's story evidently failed to grasp the full meaning of the term "repression" ("Oh so *that's* what you think," says the interlocutor, and Freud's tone implies that the critic may have learned a new word but not its real meaning), the affective event of a contact is what gratifies the speaker and constitutes proof of recognition. The moment when the critic presses Freud's hand is indeed the symbolic center of the story. We can see why it is so important when we note that Freud is concerned, in this lecture, not only with persons from other disciplines who accept only "portions" of psychoanalytic theory, but also with men from within Freud's own circle who have branched off from the paternal trunk. Psychoanalysis, Freud asserts early in the lecture, is "a unity from which elements cannot be broken off" (p. 138). Pupils like Jung and Adler, however, had not only broken off from Freud but had taken "elements" of his science as the bases for theories which challenged his authority.[13] The story of the critic who willingly accepts the subordinate role of pupil, and who is rewarded by having his doubts about his own unconscious desires allayed, serves in this text to allay Freud's own anxiety about the meaning of his pupils' "secessions." Explaining those secessions later in the lecture, Freud remarks on the "strong emotional factors that make it hard for many people to fit themselves in with others or to subordinate themselves" (p. 143). He insists, however, that actions motivated by such "emotional factors" do not constitute evidence that can legitimately "be used either for or against the validity of psycho-analytic theories" (p. 143). One would be more persuaded by this argument if Freud had presented his theories, in this lecture, as a set of scientific hypotheses that could be tested. Having described psychoanalysis as "a unity from which elements cannot be broken off," however, Freud forces us to wonder whether the defections of rebellious or skeptical pupils do not, in truth, constitute damaging evidence against Freud's own claims to quasi-religious authority.

Viewed in the light of Freud's continuing concern with secessions from the fold, his story of the critic's "rapid conversion" may be interpreted as a defensive fiction which wards off (as well as signals) the grief and self-doubt that was caused, we may surmise, by his estrangement from pupils like Adler and Jung, the latter a Christian in whom Freud had once invested his hopes for making psychoanalysis a less purely "Jewish science."[14] But the conversion story serves not only as a defense against the emotions engendered by his troubled relations to his disciples; it serves also as a defense against the medium of the written word, a medium traditionally associated with a certain kind of estrangement between the author and his audience. Not only is the writer unable to see his audience or see them respond to his words; he is also, as writers from Plato onward have lamented, unable to control the effect of his words. He is neither the master nor the sole possessor of his text. Stories like Freud's account of a moving conversation, or Sidney's of the successful orator Menenius Agrippa, allow the author temporarily to forget his actual situation of isolation and the fears of verbal impotence which arise from his inability to control his readers' interpretations of his words. Stories in which writers are figured as speakers and readers as persons present at a scene of effective oratory may thus be read as defenses against the medium of the written or printed word.

It is time now to mention the fact that Freud never delivered his *New Introductory Lectures*. In the preface to the 1933 German edition, he remarks that this set of lectures, unlike his earlier *Introductory Lectures*, was not presented to an audience. "My age," Freud explains, "had . . . absolved me from the obligation of giving expression to my membership of the University (which was in any case a peripheral one) . . . and a surgical operation had made speaking in public impossible for me. If therefore I once again take my place in the lecture room during the remarks that follow, it is only by an artifice of the imagination; it may help me not to forget to bear the reader in mind as I enter more deeply into my subject" (*SE* 22: 5). This "artifice of the imagination" (*Vorspiegelung der Phantasie*) is, one might say, doubly at work in the passage where Freud offers his metaphorical listeners a model dialogue between himself and a "literary man." "You will easily guess whom I mean," he begins, and he creates, with this sentence, an illusion of intimacy, inviting the listener-reader into the charmed circle of his conversation. But the reader, unless he is truly an intimate of Freud's, will not be able to guess the secret. A note in the *Standard Edition* (though not in the *Gesammelte Werke*), provides the omitted name and refers the curious reader to other texts—a letter to Fliess, a letter to Freud's niece Margit, and Ernest Jones's biography. "It was Georg Brandes, the celebrated Danish scholar (1842–1927), for whom Freud had always had an admiration," the editor tells us (*SE* 18: 139, n.1), and when we trace the clues we learn, among other things, that in March of 1900 Freud heard Brandes give a lecture "on reading." "The subject," Freud tells Fliess, "was nothing out of the way, the lecture difficult, the voice harsh . . . but the man was refreshing" and spoke "raw home truths" which "must have seemed pretty outlandish to the worthy Viennese."[15] Impressed by the lecturer, Freud sent a copy of the *Interpretation of Dreams* to him. "So far there has been no response— perhaps he actually took it home to read."[16] It seems unlikely that there ever was any response other than the one portrayed in the *New Introductory Lectures* twenty-one years later—a belated response, not to Freud's book, but to his conversation and person. In a letter to his niece, written after Brandes's death in 1927, Freud gives a slightly different account of the meeting; addressing an intimate audience, he emphasizes his humility to-ward a man who was not only a literary critic, but an eminent Jew:

> Probably it wasn't even a question of changing his mind, rather that psychology had always been very alien to him and that . . . disarmed by my guilelessness, he was ready to relinquish a prejudice where he was unable to form an opinion. He could not fail to realize how highly I respected him. When he modestly tried to take second place behind the 'scientist,' I pointed out to him his position among the descendants of our prophets.[17]

My purpose in quoting these supplementary texts is not to analyze Freud's story in light of them, but to reflect on their implications for the interpreta-tion of defensive writing. Freud's story clearly does not give its readers the "whole" truth; we must approach that truth asymptotically, by going to other texts and to other places in the lecture itself. This process of detective labor is of course necessary for reading any literary text, but some works—of the type Mikhail Bakhtin describes as "monologic"—employ formal and rhetorical devices in a way that masks rather than calls attention to the phenomenon of intertextuality.[18] Works which call themselves defenses, in contrast, are not only dialogic in their mode of discourse, but insistently so; they announce by their titles and by numerous formal and rhetorical devices that they constitute moments in an ongoing cultural debate and must be interpreted in relation to other texts. The defense characteristically quotes or paraphrases or parodies the voices of prosecutors in a way that prevents us from even using the metaphor of the text as a "well-wrought urn." The prosecution is at once outside and inside the textual space of defense, and defenses, whether they occur in the form of an entire text like Sidney's or in the form of prefaces, postscripts, or simply moments in literary or theoretical works, characteristically call attention to the problem of defining a textual unit. Freud's writing, I would suggest, also and repeatedly challenges readers to question their assumptions about what constitutes a textual unit. The way in which Freud alludes to other works, his own as well as those by ancient and contemporary writers in various disciplines, seems designed to undermine interpreters' confidence in their detective abilities, if that confidence reposes, as it so often does, in the belief that meaning can be simply located and uncovered. Freud reminds us insistently, by his style as well as his theoretical arguments, that meaning is not something to be uncovered but is rather something that must be generated by an uneasy alliance between author, text, and reader. This alliance may at any moment become a battle or a competition. Freud also meditates, as defenders of poetry characteristically do, on the problem posed by the nature of writing itself, as a temporal sequence of signs which prevents the author's intention from ever being recognized except in the mode of the synecdoche—the part, often the distorted part, for the whole. And because Freud insists that a maker of signs—an author or analysand—is also an interpreter—a reader or an analyst—he highlights the problem that preoccupies the Renaissance authors studied in this book: the author's inability to recognize himself, in the mirror of his own text, as a "whole" subject. What one sees, when one looks into the cracked glass of one's quasi-autobiographical allegorical defense, is at best a partial reflection of one's original intention. Even if the idea of an "original intention" is subjected to the scalpel of deconstruction—Marxist, Lacanian, or Derridian—the phenomenon that Sidney called the "idea or fore-conceit" may be said to exist, for all writers, as an "effect" of desire. And it is the idea *of* the foreconceit, or the desire *for* it, that concerns me here and leads me to invoke the name of Percy Bysshe Shelley.

In the *Defense of Poetry*, which pays homage to Sidney in its very title, Shelley broods on the phenomenon he calls "inspiration"—the "power" that "arises," he says, "from within," but that fades "as soon as composition begins."[19] Shelley's *Defense* forms a crucial link in the speculative chain I am drawing from Renaissance defenses to Freud's work because Shelley brilliantly connects the problem of self-recognition with the process of writing itself, the "composition" that mars the "inspiration." Moreover, he connects both of these problems with that of gaining recognition from others, from that audience of jurors which includes not only those contemporary "reasoners and mechanists" who deny the poet's right to the "civic crown," but also those previous writers and future readers through whose eyes the poet must measure himself. "The jury which sits in judgment upon a poet, belonging as he does to all time, must be composed of his peers," Shelley asserts (p. 38); his text shows, however, that he confronts a jury that is threatening precisely because it is not composed of persons with whom the writer can confidently assume equality and from whom he can expect a fair judgment.

Late in Shelley's *Defense* there is a dialogue scene that dramatizes the problem of recognition which underlies the defendant's uneasy relation to his contemporary audience, to prior texts, and to his own medium of expression. The interlocutors here, represented by pronoun "shifters," raise the same questions about authorial identity and authorial "ownership" of discourse that Tasso's interlocutors raise in the *Apologia*.[20] Like Tasso's Il Forestiero, Shelley's textual persona is created, here, through an allusion to a character created by another author, a character who may or may not represent his author's "real" opinions. Moreover, the authors in question—Plato in Tasso's case, Milton in Shelley's—may belong to the prosecutor's party rather than to the defendant's. The Shelleyan passage reads:

> Let us for a moment stoop to the arbitration of popular breath, and usurping and uniting in our own persons the incompatible characters of accuser, witness, judge, and executioner, let us decide without trial, testimony, or form, that certain motives of those who are "there sitting where we dare not soar," are reprehensible. Let us assume that Homer was a drunkard, that Virgil was a flatterer, that Horace was a coward, that Tasso was a madman, that Lord Bacon was a peculator, that Raphael was a libertine, that Spenser was a poet laureate. It is inconsistent with this division of our subject to cite living poets, but Posterity has done ample justice to the great names now referred to. Their errors have been weighed and found to have been dust in the balance; if their sins were as scarlet, they are now white as snow: they have been washed in the blood of the mediator and redeemer, Time. Observe in what ludicrous chaos the imputations of real or fictitious crimes have been confused in the contemporary calumnies against poetry and poets; consider how little is, as it appears—or appears, as it is; look to your own motives, and judge not, lest ye be judged. [pp. 75–76]

With the phrase "Let us stoop"—a subjunctive locution that creates a fiction of unity between author and reader—the passage begins its protest against judgment. The metaphor of stooping implicitly defines one party as higher than the other; the fictional persona initially represented by the pronoun "us" belongs, evidently, to the same place in a spatial hierarchy as the poets who are "there sitting where we dare not soar." By the time the passage arrives at this quoted fragment, however, "we" have been incorporated into the body of "incompatible characters" which prosecutes the poets, so that the perspective represented by the pronoun "we" changes from one that looks down on the "popular breath" to one that looks up at the poets.

The oscillation of perspectives figured in this passage can be seen, first, as a response to a text that used imagery of height and depth to define a hierarchy of cultural value. Thomas Love Peacock's little pamphlet entitled *The Four Ages of Poetry* (1820) argued that in an age of scientific progress,

> the poetical audience will not only continually diminish in the proportion of its number to that of the rest of the reading public, but will sink lower and lower in the comparison of intellectual acquirement. . . . The poet must still please his audience, and must therefore continue to sink to their level, while the rest of the community is rising above it: we may easily conceive that the day is not distant, when the degraded state of every species of poetry will be as generally recognized as that of dramatic poetry has long been.[21]

Peacock goes on to picture "mathematicians, astronomers, chemists, moralists, metaphysicians, historians, politicians and political economists," as occupying a "pyramid" in the "upper air of intelligence" from which they look down at the "modern Parnassus" and smile "at the little ambition and the circumscribed perceptions with which the little drivellers and mountebanks upon it are contending for the poetical palm and the critical chair" (p. 21).

Although Peacock attacked poetry as a "mental rattle" with his tongue in cheek, facetiousness, for Shelley as for Freud, was offensive. "Your anathemas against poetry itself," Shelley wrote Peacock, "excited me to a sacred rage . . . of vindicating the insulted Muses."[22] Shelley promises to "break a lance" with Peacock, and he does so when he reverses Peacock's spatial hierarchy by portraying poets as "stooping" to popular judgment. This is clearly a stooping to conquer, but it paradoxically confirms Peacock's point that the poet is bound to his audience, to whose level he must "sink." Shelley insists, however, that if his text adopts, for a moment, his opponents' perspective, the gesture is not one of simple subservience; the "uniting" is also a "usurping."

Usurpation, indeed, is both a technique and a theme of Shelley's passage, which literally takes over the opposition's voice by quoting a fragment of poetry, "there sitting where we dare not soar." This extraordinary ventriloquistic moment forces on poetry's enemies a quotation—or rather, a misquotation—of words spoken by Milton's Satan to the "good angels" who discover him in the act of trying to corrupt Eve in Eden. Elsewhere in the *Defense* Shelley praises Milton's Devil as a "moral being . . . far superior to his God" (p. 60). Shelley's effort to subvert both Peacock and poetry's general rivals should be seen in light of his complex revisionary reading of *Paradise Lost*, a reading which insists that Milton "refuted" rather than justified the "popular creed" of Christianity, with its crude moral system of "rewards and punishments" (pp. 59–60). Shelley's effort to make Milton of the Devil's party clearly informs the ironic denunciation of "moral" attacks on poetry. Shelley's well-known view of Satan as a figure of imaginative liberty is, however, complicated in this passage, which alludes to a moment when Satan is epistemologically as well as dramatically trapped by others' views of him:

> Know ye not then, said Satan, filled with scorn,
> Know ye not me? Ye knew me once no mate
> For you, there sitting where ye durst not soar.
> Not to know me argues yourselves unknown,
> The lowest of your throng. . . .   [*Paradise Lost* 4:827–31]

"Know ye not me?" is the question that links Shelley's text emblematically to the allegorical pleas for recognition we have observed in Renaissance defenses and also in Freud's lecture.[23] And Shelley, like his fellow defendants, shows us why the question must be posed again and again, and why the answers to it are never satisfactory. In the very act of asking for recognition the author hides himself in the tropes of language.[24] Those readers who already know poetry can, of course, decode the allusion and see the analogy between the poet's situation and Satan's: both experience crises of identity when confronted with an audience which knows them not. Shelley's and Milton's passages present a subject whose self-knowledge, which has heretofore derived from a sense of possessing superior qualities and power, is radically threatened in the moment when he sees himself through others' eyes, and therefore sees that his knowledge of himself and his power is not only relative knowledge, but is perhaps altogether false. But Shelley's passage deepens the crisis by making the poet now "speaking" a part of the very audience that is looking at, but not recognizing, those "there sitting where *we* dare not soar." By substituting "we" for Milton's pronoun "ye," Shelley's text dramatizes the loss of identity that occurs not only when the defendant identifies with the perspective of a hostile audience, but also when he identifies his narrative voice with that of a character in another poet's text.

Such an identification necessarily involves a rupture in the fragile shell of poetic "selfhood," for by making his voice double, as it were—by propping it on Milton's—Shelley reveals the close kinship between "inspiration" and "influence." Like the sleeping Eve in Milton's poem, Shelley has Satan "close at his ear," penetrating his mind and partly controlling his fancy. But

Shelley's own meditations on "inspiration" in the *Defense* focus precisely on the ambiguous nature of a "power" that at once belongs and does not belong to the autonomous, conscious ego. Inspirational power "arises from within," Shelley asserts, but he also compares the "mind in creation" to a "fading coal, which some invisible influence, like an inconstant wind, awakens to transitory brightness" (p. 71). "The conscious portions of our natures," he adds, "are unprophetic either of its approach or its departure." Our conscious selves do, however, recognize, and lament, the absence of the mysterious power, as Shelley shows in *Adonais*, his elegy for the dead Keats and also for the departed imaginative power which Keats symbolizes. In stanza 38 of *Adonais*, Shelley alludes to the same line from *Paradise Lost* that he misquoted in the *Defense*; and once again, although differently this time, he changes Milton's line to create an ambiguity of pronomial reference:

> Nor let us weep that our delight is fled
> Far from these carrion kites that scream below;
> He wakes or sleeps with the enduring dead;
> *Thou canst not soar where he is sitting now.*
> Dust to the dust! but the pure spirit shall flow
> Back to the burning fountain whence it came,
> A portion of the eternal, which must glow
> Through time and change, unquenchably the same,
> Whilst thy cold embers choke the sordid hearth of shame.[25]   [my emphasis]

The pronoun "thou" seems, at first, to refer to the critics who spilled their "venom" on Keats while he lived. "Live thou, whose infamy is not thy fame!" Shelley writes in the preceding stanza, addressing a hostile audience, as he does in the *Defense*, with bitter irony, spilling his own "venom" on the enemies of poetry. "But be thyself and know thyself to be," he tells them, parodying Polonius's advice to Laertes. By employing against his enemies the same verbal weapons they employ against him, however, Shelley inevitably becomes implicated in the crime of being "untrue" to himself, or rather, to the ideal of poetic ethics which he articulates in the *Defense*: "The great secret of morals is love," he writes, "or a going out of our own nature, and an identification of ourselves with the beautiful which exists in thought, action, or person, not our own" (p. 40). The defensive poet is therefore "immoral" according to Shelley's own standards, for he identifies not with what is beautiful but with what is ugly in others. He thus taints his "pure spirit" and the "burning fountain" from which that spirit comes. Shelley obliquely acknowledges the problem of his own complicity in battles of tainted words when he employs the ambiguous pronoun "thou" in stanza 38 of *Adonais*. It is not only the poet's enemies but Shelley himself who is potentially addressed in the line: "Thou canst not soar where he is sitting now." Splitting his poetic self into a criminal and a pure part, identifying syntactically both with the "infamous" ones who suffer everlasting "shame" and with the "pure spirits" of dead poets who have realized their creative potential and are rewarded by eternal life, Shelley gives us a portrait of the writer who is trapped, until death, in a court where he cannot know himself fully because he cannot know the verdict that will ultimately be handed down on his works by that jury of readers "impanelled by Time" (*Defense*, p. 38).

*   *   *

A couplet spoken by the German Satan, Goethe's Mephistopheles, can link Shelley's analysis of the defendant's dilemma with a passage in which Freud reflects on textual defense.

> Das Beste, was du wissen kanst
> Darfst du den Buben doch nicht sagen.
>
> The best of what you know may not, after all, be told to boys.

These lines appear in the chapter "Distortion in Dreams" in *The Interpretation of Dreams*.[26] The couplet, which was one of Freud's favorites, seems a neat formula for expressing an author's sense of superiority toward his readers. Taken in context, however, the quotation suggests that Freud's superiority is ambiguously related to an actual or perceived inferiority—in the realm of power, if not of knowledge. Freud quotes Goethe during the course of explaining the phenomenon of "unrecognizable" wish-fulfillment in dreams:

> In cases where the wish-fulfillment is unrecognizable, where it has been disguised, there must have existed some inclination to put up a defence against the wish; and owing to this defence, the wish was unable to express itself except in a distorted shape. I will try to seek a social parallel to this internal event in the mind. Where can we find a similar distortion of a psychical act in social life? Only where two persons are concerned, one of whom possesses a certain degree of power which the second is obliged to take into account. In such a case the second person will distort his psychical acts or, as we might put it, will dissimulate [*sie verstellt sich*]. The politeness which I practise every day is to a large extent dissimulation of this kind; and when I interpret my dreams for my readers I am obliged [*genötigt*] to adopt similar distortions. The poet complains of the need for these distortions in the words:
>
> > Das Beste, was du wissen kannst,
> > Darfst du den Buben doch nicht sagen.   [*SE* 4: 141–42]

It is not hard to see in Freud's "social analogy" the traces of the Jew's experience in bourgeois Christian culture. But Freud's extension of the analogy ought to give us pause: "And when I interpret my dreams for my readers I am obliged to adopt similar distortions." This sentence and the quotation that follows it define the relation between author and reader in a paradoxical way. The reader is first likened to a socially powerful person who "obliges" a weaker one to dissimulate; but then the analogy is apparently turned upside down, as the reader is likened to "boys" who are denied access to secret knowledge. Which is the master here, and which the servant? The passage works like an elaborate Jewish joke, whose turns of wit flatter the reader, insult him, and then flatter him again. After all, Freud *is* telling us a secret when he advises us that the text we are presently reading is not the "whole" truth, only a part of it.

This moment of metacommentary, with its shifty revelation of the fact of concealment, works, I think, to undermine both of the static "superiority-inferiority" models implied by the passage. According to the first model, the reader would be Freud's superior in power, capable of "obliging" Freud to dissimulate politeness. According to the second model, the reader would be Freud's inferior in knowledge, incapable of hearing the master's secrets. Neither of these models can account for the moment when Freud tells the reader that his text dissimulates.

This moment is, I think, emblematic of a mode of defense which occurs in a realm on the border between the psychic and the social—a realm in which interpersonal relations are mediated by writing. The kind of dissimulation that Freud at once reveals and conceals when he reflects on his textual practice can be compared to the dissimulation Sidney points to when he warns his reader that "self-love is better than any gilding to make that seem gorgeous wherein ourselves are parties." This kind of dissimulation is different from the other two kinds mentioned in Freud's passage. The first, the dream distortion, is an unconscious process that occurs in an individual's psyche; the second is a conscious process that occurs when a socially weak person successfully hides his feelings in an actual encounter with another person. The third kind of dissimulation, if one tries to define it in terms of the distinctions between the unconscious and conscious or intrapsychic and interpersonal, would fall somewhere in the middle of the spectrum.

It is, I suggest, a "middle" or "boundary" mode of defense, which is characteristic of acts of writing that are also readings or interpretations. Freud is, after all, describing a dissimulation that comes into being when he communicates to his readers what he himself has read from those prior texts that are his dreams. And his chapter indicates that the analyst's "sense organ" of consciousness is engaged in a theoretically interminable struggle against the "power" of the censoring agency, a power which prevents the self-interpreter from perceiving the whole meaning of the "data that arise elsewhere."[27]

I want to conclude by suggesting that the defenses examined in this book at once perform and reflect on the crime of interpretive distortion. In addition to responding to cultural threats and manifesting desires for power and love, defensive writing at once reveals and wards off the various forms of guilt engendered by the tropological nature of writing itself. The "middle" mode of defense is, from this perspective, a defense against defense, when the latter phenomenon is seen as involving a distortion of meaning. Let me illustrate this hypothesis with examples from Boccaccio and Freud.

As I suggested earlier, Boccaccio's defense of poetry in the *Genealogia* is also a defense of interpretation, specifically, of his own act of interpreting the sacred myths of an ancient culture. Because these myths were defined not only as profane but as highly dangerous to Christian faith by the religious authorities of Boccaccio's own society, his project of collecting and glossing pagan myths is, he senses, potentially sacrilegious on not one but two counts: he may offend Christian authorities by dealing with pagan stories, and he may also offend the spirits that lurk in the ancient texts themselves. Like Du Bellay, Boccaccio expresses the quintessential humanistic fear that his attempt to gather the "fragments" of ancient texts may somehow offend the ghosts buried in those ruins. He conflates that fear, which derives in part from the very perception of a problematic distance between present and past cultures, with another: that his future interpreters will violate his intentions as he has inevitably violated those of ancient authors. In the Preface to the *Genealogia*, he gloomily predicts his inability to receive a "fair judgment" from his readers. Many of them, he imagines, "will rise up against my work, and wherever they find it weak, they will seize it with their impious jaws and tear it to pieces" (p. 17). This striking image of the text as a torn body should be read in light of another passage in the Preface, where Boccaccio apologizes for the "maimed" condition of his text and defines interpretation itself as an act of "tearing." "I would warn you now," he tells his readers,

> not to expect that a work of this sort will have a body of perfect proportion. It will, alas, be maimed—not, I hope, in too many members—and . . . shrunken, and warped. Furthermore . . . to arrange the members in any order, I must proceed to tear the hidden significations from their tough sheathing, and I promise to do so, though not to the last detail of the authors' original intentions. [p. 11]

The humanist scholar who elsewhere in the Preface compares himself to Aesculapius, who gathered the torn limbs of Hippolytus and restored them to life, here broods on the ways in which an effort to "remember" the past is necessarily, and simultaneously, a "dismembering";[28] in attempting to give ancient texts a rebirth, the modern author also performs an act of killing. Boccaccio defends himself against the guilt engendered by this symbolic murder, I think, by calling attention to the "maimed" nature of his own text. The acknowledgment is at once a kind of expiatory gesture of self-chastisement and a defense against those future readers who may judge him harshly. By naming his own text as a maimed object, Boccaccio steals his future readers' swords, as it were, wounding his own textual body in a symbolic act of apology that is both masochistically expiatory and aggressively preemptive.

Boccaccio's dangerous project in the *Genealogia deorum gentilium* invites comparison with Freud's in *Moses and Monotheism*, the late work (1939) in which he undertook the reinterpretation of the sacred texts of Judaism. Freud's project, like Boccaccio's, involves both a remembering and a dismembering; he too seeks to "tear the hidden significations from their tough sheathing." He acknowledges the guilt engendered by this tearing in a passage that applies both to the biblical text and to his own. I have already quoted this passage, in Chapter Three, but it bears repeating:

> In its implications the distortion of a text resembles a murder: the difficulty is not in perpetrating the deed, but in getting rid of the traces. We might well lend the word "Entstellung" [distortion] the double meaning to which it has a claim but of which today it makes no use. It should mean not only "to change the appearance of something" but also "to put something in another place, to displace." Accordingly, in many instances of textual distortion, we may nevertheless count on finding what has been suppressed and disavowed hidden away somewhere else, though changed and torn from its context. Only it will not always be easy to recognize it. [*SE* 23: 43]

Freud's interpretation of the Bible, which centers on the shockingly unorthodox argument that Moses was an Egyptian "father-figure" murdered by his Jewish followers, does commit a kind of murder of his peoples' sacred text—and does so, as Freud was well aware, at a historical moment when the Jews were being violently persecuted.[29] Freud defends himself against his guilt, however, by exposing, rather than hiding, the "traces" of his crime. Apologizing to his readers in the Preface to Part 2 (one of the three strange "Prefaces" to this text), Freud writes that his method of exposition "is no less inexpedient than inartistic. I myself deplore it unreservedly. Why have I not avoided it? The answer to that is not hard for me to find, but it is not easy to confess. I found myself unable to wipe out the traces of the history of the work's origin" (*SE* 23: 103). By not wiping out the traces of his textual repetition of the story told both in *Totem and Taboo* and, with specific reference to Jewish culture, in *Moses and Monotheism*—the story of a primal murder of a father by his sons and followers—Freud at once expiates his guilt and defends himself against his own followers and future readers. The defense consists of a challenge: "Kill me if you can," Freud seems to say; "violate the authority and integrity of my text by offering new interpretations of it. I, however, will have the last word, for I have predicted that you will attempt to do this. Moreover, I will have preceded you, as the poets preceded me, by announcing that my discourse (*Darstellung*) is also a distortion (*Entstellung*) whose claim to truth is protected by the age-old weapon of the Cretan liar." This weapon, which is also a mode of seduction, involves using one's verbal power to name oneself "truly" as a liar, thereby preventing others from claiming to master one's discourse because they can expose its falsehoods. This is the paradoxical weapon Touchstone employs in Shakespeare's *As You Like It*, in a miniature defense of poetry that can serve, here, as a concluding touchstone for this study of defensive writing. In a dialogue with the woman he hopes both to master and to marry, Touchstone punningly dramatizes the bond between fiction-making ("feigning") and desire ("faining"):

> *Audrey:* I do not know what "poetical" is. Is it honest in deed and word? Is it a
> true thing?
> *Touchstone:* No, truly, for the truest poetry is the most feigning, and lovers are
> given to poetry; and what they swear in poetry may be said as lovers they do
> feign.   [*As You Like It* 3. 3. 17–22]

Touchstone's speech, like Sidney's "paradoxical but true" argument that the poet is the "least liar" because he at least acknowledges his capacity for lying,[30] does not establish the poet's innocence. But Shakespeare's fool, like Sidney's Astrophil, does insist that poets are not the only guilty parties in that universal "fellowship" which is created by desire.

Appendix: Freud's Concept of "Defence"

Freud first used the term *Abwehr* ("defense") in 1894, when he coined the phrase "defence hysteria" for cases showing hysterical amnesia.[1] He claimed "defence hysteria" as his personal discovery and treated it, as Laplanche and Pontalis remark, "as the prototype of the neuro-psychoses of defence."[2] After he wrote *Studies on Hysteria* with Josef Breuer in 1895, he dropped the term "defence hysteria." "It is almost as though it was only introduced in order to establish the primacy of the idea of defence over the idea of the hypnoid state," write Laplanche and Pontalis, referring to Freud's rejection of Breuer's theory of the "hypnoid state" as the constitutive phenomenon of hysteria (*Language of Psychoanalysis*, p. 108). If, as I suspect, Freud associates the metaphor of defense with his sense of making "personal discoveries" about the psyche—discoveries which led to departures from the theories of men like Janet and, eventually, Breuer—this would partly answer the question Harold Bloom raises when he wonders why Freud chose the term *Abwehr* to refer to the process that puts an idea out of the range of consciousness. This choice, Bloom observes, "was in some respects a misleading one. Freud's *Abwehr* is set against *change*; it is in the first place, then, a stabilizing mechanism. Defense, in war or in sport, seeks more than stability; it seeks victory or the annihilation of change."[3] Bloom suggests that Freud may have selected the word *Abwehr* "because he intuited even then, back in 1894, that the ego's pleasure in defense is both active and passive, and so ambiguous a concept of ego required a more ambiguous process than mere stabilization in its operations against internal excitations" (Bloom, "Defense and Poetic Will," p. 5). This seems to me a plausible hypothesis; it may be supplemented, however, by another: Freud may have selected the word *Abwehr* because he also intuited that his own ego was actively, even aggressively, staking out a conceptual territory for the new science he was to call "depth psychology." Although Freud used the term "repression" (*Verdrängung*) almost as often as the term "defence" in his early work—and to refer to the same process of putting ideas out of

185

consciousness—in later years, as we shall see, he wrote as if the notion of *Abwehr* had been the key element in his early theory.[4]

"The emphasis on defense is really the beginning of psychoanalysis," writes Richard Wollheim; he adds that Freud's linking of the ideas of defense and resistance is crucial for the development of psychoanalysis as a "dynamic theory of the mind."[5] The metaphor of *Abwehr*, I would suggest, plays a central role in Freud's conception of the dynamic development of his own theory. In an addendum to *Inhibitions, Symptoms and Anxiety* (1926), he gives a slightly "misleading" explanation of his past and present use of the term "defence."[6] He attempts, in particular, to clarify the "uncertain" relation between defense and repression. "In the course of discussing the problem of anxiety," he writes in his addendum, "I have revived a concept, or, to put it more modestly, a term, of which I made exclusive use thirty years ago when I first began to study the subject but which I later abandoned. I refer to the term 'defensive process' [*Abwehrvorganges*]. I later replaced it by the word 'repression,' but the relation between the two remained uncertain. It will be an undoubted advantage, I think, to revert to the old concept of 'defence,' provided we employ it explicitly as a general designation for all the techniques which the ego makes use of in conflicts which may lead to neurosis, while we retain the word 'repression' for the special method of defence which the line of approach taken by our investigations made us better acquainted with in the first instance" (*SE* 20: 163).

This explanatory justification of his terminological usage is odd for two reasons.[7] First, it provides a somewhat inaccurate account of the past, since Freud did not altogether "abandon" the term "defence" after his early work on the psychoneuroses. The term appears (as his English translators note in the appendix which they felt obliged to add to Freud's addendum) in the *Psychopathology of Everyday Life* (1901), in the book on jokes (1905), and again in the metapsychological papers of 1915, where "the 'vicissitudes' of the instincts, only one of which is 'repression,' were regarded as 'modes of defence' against them."[8] But the term also appears in two passages where Freud is reflecting on this historical development of his views, and in both of these passages, he stresses the idea that the concept of defense was replaced by that of repression. Discussing the period immediately after his collaboration with Breuer, he writes, in 1914, "I looked upon psychical splitting itself as an effect of a process of repelling which at that time I called 'defence,' and later, 'repression' " (*On the History of the Psychoanalytic Movement, SE* 14: 16).

An earlier passage, from the 1906 paper entitled "My Views on the Part Played by Sexuality in the Aetiology of the Neuroses," suggests that Freud saw his terminological shift as an essential part, or signal, of the change that gave sexuality an increasingly large role in the psychoanalytic theory of neurosis. Commenting again on the early period of his career, Freud writes:

At that time, and even before sexuality had been given its rightful place as an aetiological factor, I had maintained that no experience could have a pathogenic effect unless it appeared intolerable to the subject's ego and gave rise to efforts at defence. . . . Accidental factors receded still further into the background as compared with 'repression' (as I now began to say instead of 'defence'). . . . Accidental influences have been replaced by constitutional factors and 'defence' in the purely psychological sense has been replaced by organic 'sexual repression.' [*SE* 7: 276, 278]

When one reads these passages in relation to the 1926 addendum, one begins to see that the term "defence" refers, in Freud's works, not only to psychic processes but to a problematic aspect of the historical drama which might be entitled "The Origin and Development of Freud's Science." Only if we consider this dimension of the term's meaning will we begin to understand a second peculiarity of the 1926 addendum, namely that it gives a slightly inaccurate account not only of Freud's past use of the terms "defence" and "repression," but also of his use of them in *Inhibitions, Symptoms and Anxiety* itself.

In that work, as Peter Madison notes, Freud continues to use "repression" as a general term for various defensive processes, as he had earlier in his career. "In speaking of the two clinically related defenses of isolation and undoing," for instance, "Freud refers to them as 'variations of repression'" ([*SE* 20: 119]; Madison, *Repression and Defense*, p. 24). Madison cites several other passages which show that Freud evidently forgot to clarify his terminological usage in the very work in which he explains "his decision to adopt a consistent usage for 'repression'—meaning amnesic forgetting (as in hysteria)—and 'defense'—the [general] term, including repression as one of ten or so defenses" (pp. 22–23). Did Freud really forget to revise the text of *Inhibitions* in accordance with the terminological clarification set forth in the addendum? If this is a "Freudian slip," it is a very interesting one— especially when we note that even after 1926 Freud continued to use both "repression" and "defence" as general category terms. Madison answers this question by suggesting that the two concepts were too closely linked theoretically to "allow separation through a simple agreement on terminology" (p. 27). But this does not explain why Freud chose at certain moments in his career to call attention to this terminological problem. Nor does it explain why he stated his intention, in 1926, to resolve the problem by "reintroducing the old concept of defence" and "subsuming repression under it as a special case" (*SE* 20: 164).

We cannot explain terminological problems in Freud's works by saying they are merely terminological problems, as if the theory somehow existed independently of the words. Nor should we consider theory as somehow separate from the history of verbal usage. Freud in fact provides us with not one but two ways of understanding the complex history of the term "defence" in his own work. The first involves studying his descriptions of his verbal usage—descriptions that employ a highly affective autobiographical vocabulary that includes terms like "revive," "abandon," and "exclusive use." The second involves looking at Freud's actual uses of the word in his metapsychological and technical writings. But this second approach is complicated by the fact that if we take Freud at his word, we must study the uses of the term "repression" in order to understand that concept of defense which was—ambiguously and for a time—"replaced" by the evolving concept of "repression." Instead of a history of the concept of defense, then, we have two complex historical series, each of which illuminates the other and poses problems for the reader who seeks to interpret the odd discrepancies between Freud's explicit statements about his verbal usage and his actual textual praxis.

If we read *Inhibitions, Symptoms and Anxiety*—both text and addendum—in the light of a later passage where Freud returns to discuss the relation between defense and repression, we may see how central this relation itself is to Freud's understanding of his own history as a writer. The later passage is from *Analysis Terminable and Interminable* (1937; SE 23: 216–53); it at once continues and retrospectively illuminates the meditation on history which Freud sketches in his 1926 text. That meditation should be taken to include both his actual use of the terms "repression" and "defence" as if they were synonymous—for instance, in the question, "Is it absolutely certain that fear of castration is the only motive force behind repression (or defence)?" (*SE* 20: 123)—and his description of a nonlinear terminological history in the addendum. There he presents us with a miniature and graphic model of history in which an old term ("defence") returns—after having apparently been "abandoned"—to take the place of a later term ("repression"). The later term does not disappear, but it is relegated to a subordinate status. In *Analysis Terminable and Interminable*, Freud returns, as I have said, to the problematic relation between his two central terms; now, however, he manages to have his cake and eat it too: he underscores the special importance of the concept of repression (*primus inter pares* among the mechanisms of defense) while at the same time reaffirming his earlier point that "defence" is the general category term. He illustrates this complex resolution to the terminological problem posed by his own textual practice by giving us, appropriately enough, an elaborate analogy between a psyche and a text. Meditating, as he has so often done before, on the history of his own theory, he writes that "the ego makes use of various procedures for fulfilling its task, which, to put it in general terms, is to avoid danger, anxiety and unpleasure. We call these procedures *mechanisms of defence*. . . . It was from one of those mechanisms, repression, that the study of neurotic processes took its whole start. There was never any doubt that repression was not the only procedure which the ego could employ for its purposes.

Nevertheless, repression is something quite peculiar and is more sharply differentiated from the other mechanisms than they are from one another. I should like to make this relation to the other mechanisms clear by an analogy, though I know that in these matters analogies never carry us very far" (*SE* 23: 235–36).

There is a good deal of revisionary wit in this statement, for in it Freud not only alters earlier accounts which suggest that defense, not repression, was the starting point for the study of neurosis; he also retroactively changes the relation between defense and repression, which he described in 1926 as "uncertain," to a matter about which "there was never any doubt." There is, however, a striking difference between Freud's methods of revision and those employed by the persons he goes on to criticize: the "official censors" who play the major role in the analogy he draws in the passage following the one quoted above. This analogy, introduced in a wryly deprecatory way ("analogies never carry us very far"), compares the varieties of psychic defense to the methods employed by censors to render a book "innocuous." Although at "the present day," the "only defensive mechanism to which the official censorship could resort would be to confiscate and destroy every copy of the whole edition," in eras before the age of print, Freud says, there were numerous methods available to deal with offensive manuscripts. These methods included scoring through passages so that they become illegible or—when the aim was to "conceal any indication that the text has been mutilated"—replacing words with new ones, interpolating whole sentences, and erasing the passage completely, to replace it by "one which said exactly the opposite" (p. 236). Freud concludes this analogy with the following statement: "We may say that repression has the same relation to the other methods of defence as omission has to distortion of the text, and we may discover in the different forms of this falsification parallels to the variety of ways in which the ego is altered" (pp. 236–37).

This passage illuminates the specifically autobiographical connotations which the notions of defense and repression have for Freud the writer, the man concerned with the fate of books produced by his own ego. He dramatizes this concern by introducing his analogy with an example of a writer whose works, like Freud's own, offended political and religious authorities. The books of Flavius Josephus, Freud says, "must have contained passages which were offensive to later Christendom." Josephus (d. ca. 100 A.D.) was a Jewish historian who took a leading part in the Jewish war of 66 A.D. After being taken prisoner, however, he won Vespasian's favor by prophesying that he would become emperor; during the siege of Jerusalem, Josephus earned the hostility of the Jews by serving as interpreter to Titus. His two major works are the *Jewish War* and the *Antiquities of the Jews*; scholars believe that his reference to Christ in the latter text (18. 3. 3) is probably an early Christian interpolation.[9]

Freud's analogy between a psyche and a text, with its allusion to a Jewish author involved in complex relations with the Roman authorities of his day, illuminates his own decision, in his textual practice, not to choose definitively between the terms "defence" and "repression." To omit one word in favor of the other, Freud's analogy suggests, might involve an act of censorship or suppression. The "full story" of psychoanalysis, as a historical phenomenon invented by a Jew with shocking ideas about the history of both the individual and civilization, requires a complex interplay between two metaphors that both have strong political connotations. One (defense) suggests direct action of the sort Josephus engaged in when he fought the Roman authorities who sought to suppress the Jews; the other metaphor (repression) connotes a hidden psychic process that social authorities may set in motion when they require the individual to suppress ideas or libidinal desires. If, as I suspect, Freud identified both with the Josephus who openly rebelled against the Romans and with the man who somehow accommodated himself to the oppressors, serving as their "interpreter" and suffering, eventually, a censorship of his writing at the hands of Christian authorities, this hypothesis helps explain why Freud needed the concepts both of defense and of repression to define his own ambiguous attitude toward the vexing problem of the individual's relation to society.

Although there is much in Freud's theory which can be—and has been—read as expressing a highly conservative view of the individual's need to "adapt" to "reality" (conceived as a set of social norms), there is a more radical political statement, I believe, in Freud's textual practice. He fights against "official censorship"—which operates in modern times, as he well knew, in more insidious and invisible ways than it did in the days when specific individuals held most of the power to suppress ideas, libidinal desires, or entire races of people—by refusing to censor his own historical development in a way that would bring the past into clear conformity with the present. His revisions modify his views, to be sure, but unlike the revisions of an official censor, Freud's do not erase the evidence that he once held different views. His use of the terms "defence" and "repression" serves, I think, as an emblem of this powerful albeit oblique statement about the value of not repressing ambiguities. By giving us both "repression" and "defence," and by implying in his 1926 addendum that the terms are interlocked in a historical process of competition, Freud asks us to see them not as synonyms, but rather as signs that exist in dialectical relation to each other and which point, it seems, to different moments in the history of Freud's own theoretical development.

There is, I would argue, a subtle but important difference in the meaning of the two terms, a difference which can be appreciated if we think about the figure of Flavius Josephus in relation to Freud's clues about the changing prominence of the two terms at different stages of his own career. His retrospective accounts of his usage of the terms, however "misleading" in relation to details of his actual practice, suggest that he emphasizes defense at times when he is particularly concerned with theoretical or personal problems about the individual's relation with the "outside world." He emphasizes repression, in contrast, during the period when he is chiefly concerned with elaborating the conflicts that occur "within" the psyche, and which have to do specifically with the role of sexuality in generating neuroses. Support for my hypothesis that Freud associates the metaphor of defense with theoretical questions about the psyche's relation to the "outside world" appears in a passage from his late *An Outline of Psychoanalysis* (written in 1938, published in 1940). This passage suggests, indeed, that the relation between the concepts of external and internal danger is no less dialectical than that between defense and repression, and that a larger dialectic governs all four concepts:

> Driven by the combined operation of these two influences, the contemporary real danger and the remembered one with its phylogenetic basis, the child embarks on his attempts at defence—repressions—which are effective for the moment but nevertheless turn out to be psychologically inadequate when the later re-animation of sexual life brings a reinforcement to the instinctual demands which have been repudiated in the past. [*SE* 23: 200]

> Durch das Zusammenwirken beider Einflüsse, der aktuellen realen Gefahr und der erinnerten phylogenetisch begründeten, bezwungen, nimmt das Kind seine Abwehrversuche—Verdrängungen—vor, die für den Augenblick zweckmässig, sich psychologisch doch als unzulänglich erweisen, wenn di spätere Neubelebung des Sexuallebens die damals abgewiesenen Triebansprüche verstärkt. [*Gesammelte Werke* 17: 131]

The parallel constructions in this sentence hint that the term "defence" may be conceptually aligned with the notion of an "immediate real danger," while the term repression may be linked with the notion of a "remembered" danger. I would not press this idea very far, were it not for the fact that Freud chose to "revive" his old concept of defense in a work which is explicitly concerned with the problematic relation between external and internal sources of danger. Moreover, in that work he uses the term "defence" in a way that conflicts with the widely held psychoanalytic view that the theory of defense refers exclusively to conflicts between the ego and the instincts. "The two poles of the conflict," Laplanche and Pontalis assert, "are invariably the ego and the instinct; it is against an internal threat that the ego defends itself." In Chapter 2 of *Inhibitions, Symptoms and Anxiety*, however, Freud not only uses the term *Abwehr* to refer to the psyche's response to an "external stimulus," but suggests that this type of defense has logical priority over defenses directed against internal threats: "a defence against an unwelcome internal stimulus," he writes, "will be *modelled upon* the defence adopted against an external stimulus" (*SE* 20: 92; my emphasis).[10] Later in this same work, he offers a theoretical statement about phobias that revises his earlier view about the ultimate "source" of danger, which he now locates not in the instincts but in the "external world":

> On a previous occasion I have stated that phobias have the character of a projection in that they replace an internal, instinctual danger by an external, perceptual one. The advantage of this is that the subject can protect himself against an external danger by fleeing from it and avoiding the perception of it, whereas it is useless to flee from the dangers that arise from within. This statement of mine was not incorrect, but it did not go below the surface of things. For an instinctual demand is, after all, not dangerous in itself; it only becomes so inasmuch as it entails a real external danger. . . . [p. 126]

This position is new, as Laplanche and Pontalis remark, because it involves treating "neurotic anxiety, or anxiety in the fact of the instinct, as purely derivative."[11] Freud by no means maintains this position consistently, even in *Inhibitions*; but his articulation of it is, I believe, important to an understanding of his dialectical theory of defense and repression. The notion of defense is emphasized, both in the text and in the Addendum of *Inhibitions, Symptoms and Anxiety*, in part because Freud is here focusing his attention on what he calls "realistic anxiety" (*Realangst*) and thereby continuing the inquiry into "traumatic neuroses" that sparked the revisionary theories of *Beyond the Pleasure Principle* (1920), with their still-controversial hypothesis of a "death instinct."

If, as Laplanche and Pontalis insist, Freud always maintained the distinction "between external excitations on the one hand, from which flight is possible or against which a damming mechanism is set up for the purpose of filtering them . . . and, on the other hand, internal excitations which it is impossible to evade," there is no reason to conclude, as they do, that Freud's theory of defense deals only with the psyche's reactions to "aggression from the inside."[12] *Abwehr*, after all, means not only defense, but also resistance, repulse, guard, parrying, and warding off. I argue in this book that Freud's "theory of defense" includes his meditations on "blocking" mechanisms that do not necessarily involve repression in its technical sense: "an operation whereby the subject attempts to repel, or to confine, to the unconscious, representations (thoughts, images, memories) which are bound to an instinct." In particular, I argue that Freud, like the other writers studied in this book, was deeply concerned with modes of defense that arise from an individual's difficult relations with cultural rivals and with authorities who may threaten censorship, forcing an author to adopt his own defensive methods of self-censorship. The metaphor of the "protective shield" which I discuss both in my introductory and concluding chapters provides an important gloss on the relation between defense and censorship. In his comments on the "protective shield," Freud figuratively defines a process whereby signals are "filtered" across a border or barrier that exists both "within" the psyche and between it and the threatening external world. Defense, according to this model, is at once an interpsychic and a social phenomenon.

Notes

Chapter I

1. The aphorism is attributed to Benjamin Jowett by A. L. Smith, who was a tutor at Balliol and later became Master. See his "Reminiscences of Jowett" in the Oxford undergraduate journal *The Bluebook*, 7, no. 3 (London, n.d.), 201.

2. See M. H. Abrams, "Belief and the Suspension of Disbelief," in *Literature and Belief*, p. 3.

3. Abrams, p. 2.

4. Jowett's predilection for a laconic style of "plain speaking" is mentioned in Lionel A. Tollemache's memoir of him; see *Benjamin Jowett*, p. 21, where Tollemache reports Jowett's opinion that Browning's style was "needlessly cumbrous and distorted." See also p. 117 for Tollemache's comments on another, somewhat less elegant version of the aphorism attributed to Jowett: "Never retract. Never explain. Get it done and let them howl."

5. The distaste for apologetic explanation appears to have been widespread in Victorian England. "I do loathe explanation," writes J. M. Barrie in *My Lady Nicotine* (1890); "I never apologize," says a character in Shaw's *Arms and the Man*. Disraeli, according to J. Morley in his *Life of Gladstone*, was fond of saying "Never complain and never explain." An ideology of the "inside group" informs such statements, as may be seen even more clearly from a final example: "Never explain: your friends will understand and your enemies will not believe you anyhow" (Elbert Hubbard, *Orphic Sayings*, 1900; cited, as are all of the previous examples, from *The Oxford Dictionary of Quotations*). Anyone interested in the ideology of discursive modes should consider statements which belong to the family of Jowett's rule in the light of Frank Kermode's discussion of New Testament parables in *The Genesis of Secrecy*. See especially his comments on the ways in which parables serve to draw "a particularly sharp distinction . . . between those who are outside and those who are inside" (p. 23). Apologetic discourse, as we shall see, characteristically seeks to blur precisely this distinction.

6. See the *OED's* list of examples for the first meaning of "apology," as a speech of defense without any explicit or implicit acknowledgment of error. The earliest example given, from 1533, is *The Apologie of Thomas More Knyght*, a text that clearly alludes to Socrates' situation in the Athenian court that sentenced him to death. Although the *OED* does not mention this, Renaissance uses of "apology" or "apologia" as a title term meaning "a speech in defense" also frequently allude to the Christian tradition of polemical writing represented by Tertullian's *Apologeticon* (ca. A.D. 198). More's *Apologie*, and also Montaigne's *Apologie de Raymond Sebon* (*Essais* 2: 12, published 1580), suggest that the notion of apology was closely linked to the idea of religious dispute in general and the defense of Christianity in particular. Socrates had been accused of impiety, and Montaigne alludes to this when he undertakes a defense of a Christian theologian whose views he subtly questions throughout the *Apologie*. Sebon's *Theo-*

logia naturalis (1489), which Montaigne translated at the request of his father in 1569, praises man's capacity for faith based on natural reason; Montaigne's severely skeptical essay attacks rather than defends this view of human nature.

7. The second meaning the *OED* gives for "apology"—"justification, explanation, or excuse, of an incident or course of action"—points to a shady semantic area between the older idea of apology as self-righteous justification and the modern idea of apology as "an explanation offered to a person affected by one's action that no offense was intended, coupled with the expression of regret for any that may have been given" (*OED*, third meaning). Excuse, it would seem, occupies an ambiguous intermediate position between a speech act that says "I am in the right for the following reasons" and one that says "I am sorry for offending you." The Renaissance texts studied in this book cross and recross the area between the poles of justification and the plea for pardon. As Donald Cheney remarked to me in a letter, the Renaissance examples given by the *OED* for the modern sense of apology are, in fact, quite ambiguous; both examples occur in dramatic contexts which point to the older meaning of apologia while at the same time ironically implying the ethical need for a genuine plea for pardon. The first example is a line Buckingham speaks to Richard during the notorious scene in which both characters are mounting a "show" of religious zeal: "My Lord, there needs no such apologie" (*Rich. III* 3. 7. 104). The second example is from *Paradise Lost* 9. 853–54: "in her face excuse/came Prologue, and apologie to prompt." Neither Shakespeare nor Milton gives any clear sign that such apologies imply acknowledgement of a fault or regret for it.

8. I owe this formulation to Donald Cheney, of the University of Massachusetts.

9. The *OED* defines "apologue" as "an allegorical story intended to convey a useful lesson; a moral fable"; the first use cited is from a 1552 sermon by Bishop Latimer: "To teach the people in apologies, bringing in how one beast talketh to another." I strongly suspect that Sidney had this sense of "apologie" in mind when he included the famous "fable of the belly" in his *Apologie for Poetrie*. Menenius Agrippa's fable was a common example of the apologue in the Renaissance, as Battaglia's *Grande Dizionario* indicates when it cites this sentence from Bartolomeo Cavalcanti's *La Retorica* (1569) to illustrate the meaning of *apologo*: "Tale è la favola della congiura dei membri contra il ventre . . . e queste cosi fatte favole sono nominate apologi."

10. Here and elsewhere in this book I quote from Allan Bloom's excellent annotated translation of the *Republic*; the passage cited is from p. 290.

11. See Bloom's note (p. 455) on the first use of *apologia* in the *Republic* (4. 420b): "The facts that Socrates was a man who finally really was accused, who presented an *apology* in a court, and who was put to death play an important role in this drama. All uses of the word *apology* in the *Republic* refer to this event and cast light on it." On the historical facts known about Meletus, Socrates' chief accuser, see the introduction to the *Apology* by Harold North Fowler in the Loeb Classical Library edition, p. 63. Socrates himself says that Meletus was "angered on account of the poets" in *Apology* 23d.

12. See Bloom's note on the punning connection between *apologos* and *apologia* which Plato implies in *Republic* 10. 614b, when Socrates says he will not tell "a story of Alcinous" (*Alkinou . . . apologon*) but, rather, one about a "strong man," Er. There are puns here not only on *apologos* and *apologia*, but also on the name "Alcinous" and the word for "strong" (*alkimou*), which differs, as Bloom says, "only by the measure of an *m* instead of an *n* from the genitive form of the king's name used here" (p. 471, n. 13.) On the wordplay in this sentence, see Arthur Platt, "Plato's *Republic* 614b," *Classical Review* (1911), 13–14. Since the phrase "apologue of Alcinous" proverbially meant "a long-winded tale," Plato makes a double verbal thrust at Homer's authority in this passage where he substitutes his own tale of a "strong man" for the one told by that powerful speaker, Homer's Odysseus.

13. See the opening paragraph of "A Plea for Excuses," in *Philosophical Papers*, pp. 175–204.

14. Austin, "Plea for Excuses," p. 175. One of the distinctions Austin makes in his preliminary effort to "hound down the minutiae" is the important (albeit logically and rhetorically problematic) one between "justification" and "excuse." His definition of "justification" as a type of defensive speech act which occurs "when we accept responsibility" for something "but deny that it was bad," bears an obvious resemblance to the definitions of *apologia* in its Greek sense. His definition of "excuse," in contrast, points to the same ambiguous semantic territory occupied by the word *apology* in the examples from Shakespeare and Milton cited above (note 7): an excuse, Austin writes, occurs "when we admit something was bad but don't accept full, or even any, responsibility" (p. 176). Austin acknowledges that the two types of argument "can be combined or overlap or run into each other"; indeed, his own essay provides a performative example of such an overlapping, for his essay includes, as he explicitly says, an attempt "to justify" that method of doing philosophy known as "ordinary language philosophy" (pp. 181–82). The aim of justifying his method of study prompts the initial effort to separate excuses as "objects" of inquiry from justifications, which he says he is "not so anxious to talk about . . . because they have enjoyed more than their fair share of philosophical attention" (p. 176). But even if one accepts his statement that "by and large, justifications can be kept separate from excuses," it seems evident, when one reads the essay closely, that the separation is problematic both in terms of Austin's own theory (which involves looking at the minute exceptions to "large" classificatory schemes), and in terms of his discursive practice.

15. See Paul Ricoeur, *Freud and Philosophy*, pp. 32 ff., and also his discussion of Marx, Nietzsche, and Freud in *The Conflict of Interpretations*, pp. 148–50.

16. Ludwig Wittgenstein, *Philosophical Investigations*, section 129, p. 50^e.

17. The metaphor of the *Grenzwesen*, the "frontier" or "boundary" creature, appears in the *Ego and the Id* (1923), *SE* 19: 56.

18. On Sidney's imitation of the forensic oration, see Kenneth Myrick, *Sir Philip Sidney as a Literary Craftsman*, pp. 46–83. See also chap. 4, n. 11, below.

19. *Apology* 17c–d, quoted from the Loeb Classical Library edition, trans. Harold North Fowler, pp. 70–71. All quotations from the *Apology* and the *Phaedrus* are taken from this volume.

20. For a useful discussion of Plato's attempt in the *Apology* to distinguish Socrates from the Sophists with whom he was associated by his accuser Anytus (an enemy of all Sophists, according to the author of the *Apologia* of Socrates attributed to Xenophon), see James A. Coulter, "The Relation of the *Apology of Socrates* to Gorgias' *Defense of Palamedes* and Plato's Critique of Gorgianic Rhetoric," *Harvard Studies in Classical Philology* 68 (1964): 269–303.

21. See Derrida's "La Pharmacie de Platon," originally published in *Tel Quel* (1968) and reprinted in *La Dissémination* (Paris, 1972), pp. 70–196. In a passage central to Derrida's argument—*Phaedrus* 276a—Plato refers to writing as a "bastard" brother of speech.

22. See Eric Havelock's *A Preface to Plato*, especially chapter 2, "Poetry as Preserved Communication."

23. See *Preface to Plato*, pp. 40–42, on "the silent revolution" that made the cultivated Greek public into "a community of readers"; and pp. 226–27, on Plato's attempt to "focus on the permanence of the abstract whether as a formula or a concept" and his definition of "abstracted objects of knowledge" in statements that are "timeless" because their "syntax excludes tenses of the verb 'to be.' "

24. See *Preface to Plato*, p. 244, and also p. 47, where Havelock explains his thesis that "the history of Greek poetry"—from Homer through Hesiod and the tragedians to the Sophists—"is also the history of the early Greek *paideia*." The Sophists, in Havelock's view, belonged to the "semi-oral" tradition which Plato wanted to supplant with his own method of education, aimed at "scientific rationalism" (pp. 46–47). I am oversimplifying Havelock's subtly nuanced exposition; still, one must wonder why he gives such short shrift to Plato's explicit association of the Sophists' verbal art with writing rather than speech in the *Phaedrus*. Havelock mentions that

dialogue only in notes; see especially p. 56, n. 17, where he says that Plato's "preference for oral methods as expressed in *Phaedrus* 274 was not only conservative but illogical, since the Platonic *episteme* which was to supplant *doxa* . . . was being nursed to birth by the literate revolution."

25. See W. K. Wimsatt's account of Aristotle's movement in the *Rhetoric* from an apparent agreement with Plato's view of the Sophist ("What makes the Sophist is not skill in argument but defect of moral purpose," *Rhetoric* 1. 1), toward an "empirical and anti-Platonic procedure of justifying rhetoric as it is in fact found to be" (W. K. Wimsatt and Cleanth Brooks, *Literary Criticism*, p. 68).

26. See Richard Lanham, "*Astrophil and Stella*: Pure and Impure Persuasion," *ELR* 2, no. 1 (1972): 100–15.

27. See Kenneth Burke, *A Rhetoric of Motives*, p. 268.

28. Ibid., p. 269.

29. In *Tristia* 2. 207, Ovid says that his downfall was caused by "two crimes, a poem and a blunder": "perdiderint cum me duo crimina, carmen et error." Quoted from the Loeb Classical Library edition of the *Tristia*, trans. A. L. Wheeler, p. 70; Wheeler argues in his introduction that Augustus had been offended not so much by the erotic content of the *Ars* as by its explicitly didactic form (p. xx). He also gives a good summary of the various hypotheses critics have offered to explain Ovid's mysterious "error."

30. Quoted from the unnamed translator's introduction to *The Works of Apuleius* (London, 1889), p. vi. See also Philip Ward, *Apuleius on Trial at Sabratha*.

31. Gorgias's text is traditionally titled *Helenes Encomion*, but as Mario Untersteiner says, it is actually "not an encomium but an apologia, as had already been noted by Isocrates"; quoted from Untersteiner's *The Sophists*, trans. Kathleen Freeman, p. 99, n. 53. See pp. 101–31 for Untersteiner's discussion of the *Helen*, which uses a scheme of proof "derived not from juridical practice but from philosophic logic." See also Laszlo Versény's comments on the *Helen* in *Socratic Humanism*, pp. 43–47. As he observes, Gorgias himself referred to this work as a *paignion*, "a playful exhibition or game"; but beneath the play (the vindication of Helen) there is a serious argument about the nature and power of the Sophists' *logos*—an argument which Plato is at pains to refute both in the *Gorgias* and in the *Phaedrus*. The Greek text of the *Helen* is available in H. Diels and W. Kranz, *Fragmente der Vorsokratiker*, 6th ed. (Berlin, 1952), 288–94. Kathleen Freeman provides a summary, though not a complete translation, of the *Helen* in *Ancilla to the Pre-Socratic Philosophers*, pp. 131–38.

32. Quoted from *Moll Flanders*, ed. James Sutherland, p. 5.

33. For Flaubert's mock-trial, see *Madame Bovary*, part 2, chap. 14. By having a pharmacist take up the "defence of letters" against a priest, Flaubert wittily alludes to the ancient metaphor of poetry or rhetoric as a drug (*pharmakon*) which may harm the body rather than help it. For an analysis of this metaphor—famously used by Gorgias in the *Defense of Helen*—see Derrida, "La Pharmacie de Platon," especially pp. 132–33. There is a particularly nice historical irony in Flaubert's representation of a "trial of fiction," since *Madame Bovary* was itself the object of a civil trial in 1857. Both the defense and the prosecution in that trial unwittingly elaborate arguments made by the pharmacist and the priest in the novel. A transcript of this trial is available in Flaubert's *Oeuvres complètes* (Paris, 1885), 1: 481–556.

34. As Colie rightly observes, the Renaissance genre of the mock-encomium derives from works like Gorgias's *Helen* and Isocrates' *Thersites*, rhetorical exercises which blur the distinction between forensic and epideictic oratory; see *Paradoxia Epidemica*, pp. 3 ff.; see also the comments on ancient examples of the *paignia* ("playful exercises") in George S. Kennedy, *The Art of Persuasion in Greece*, p. 152.

35. For useful discussions of the genre of the *paragone* in the Renaissance, see Erwin Panofsky, *Galileo as a Critic of the Arts*, pp. 1–4; Beatrice Mendelsohn-Martone, "Benedetto Varchi's 'Due Lezione'"; and M. Pepe, "Il 'paragone' tra pittura e scultura nella letteratura artistica rinascimentale," *Cultura e scuola* 8 (1969): 120–31. For information on the *paragone* I am indebted to Andrée Hayum of Fordham University and my colleague at Yale Judith Colton.

36. See George Puttenham, *The Arte of English Poesie*, bk. 3, chap. 7; quoted from the edition of Edward Arber (1906), reprint edition 1970 with an introduction by Baxter Hathaway, p. 166.

37. See Ong's "The Province of Rhetoric and Poetic," in Joseph Schwartz, ed., *The Province of Rhetoric*, p. 52.

38. O. B. Hardison, Jr., "The Orator and the Poet," *Journal of Medieval and Renaissance Studies* 1, no. 1 (1971): 44.

39. Northrop Frye, *Anatomy of Criticism*, pp. 7–8, 4–5. For a searching philosophical critique of the Kantian notion of "disinterested" theory, see Jürgen Habermas, *Knowledge and Human Interests*, pp. 301–17.

40. Quoted from *Miscellaneous Prose of Sir Philip Sidney*, p. 73.

41. *Anatomy of Criticism*, pp. 11–12. For a shrewd analysis of the theoretical implications of Frye's attempt to equate literary texts with "silent" works of visual art, see Geoffrey Hartman, "The Sweet Science of Northrop Frye," in *Beyond Formalism*, pp. 24–41.

42. For a fine discussion of the problems pertaining to the status of psychoanalytic explanation and interpretation, see Meredith Anne Skura, *The Literary Use of the Psychoanalytic Process*, pp. 21–24. See also Edward Glover, "The Therapeutic Effect of Inexact Interpretation," *International Journal of Psychoanalysis* 12 (1931): 397–411; R. M. Loewenstein, "Some Thoughts on Interpretation in the Theory and Practice of Psychoanalysis," *The Psychoanalytic Study of the Child* 12 (1957): 127–50; and Stan Leavy, "Psychoanalytic Interpretation," *The Psychoanalytic Study of the Child* 28 (1973): 305–30.

43. I am using the term "metapsychological" here in the sense given it by J. Laplanche and J. B. Pontalis in *The Language of Psychoanalysis*, p. 249; s.v. "metapsychology": "Term invented by Freud to refer to the psychology of which he was the founder when it is viewed in its most theoretical dimension. Metapsychology constructs an ensemble of conceptual models which are more or less far-removed from empirical reality." For a recent American attempt to limit the term's meaning to what Freud supposedly intended the word to mean—"the psychology of the unconscious," without any connotations of "highly speculative" theorizing—see Charles Brenner, "Metapsychology and Psychoanalytic Theory," *Psychoanalytic Quarterly* 39 (1980): 189–214.

44. Laplanche and Pontalis note two major problems in the psychoanalytic theory of defense and defense mechanisms. First, the term "defence" itself, "especially when used in its absolute sense, is full of ambiguity and necessitates the introduction of notional distinctions. It connotes both the action of *defending*—in the sense of fighting to protect something—and that of *defending oneself*." They suggest it would be helpful to distinguish between different "parameters" of defense, "even if these coincide with one another to some extent, *viz.*, the *stake of defence* . . . the *agent of defence* . . . the *aim of defence* . . . the *motives of defence* . . . and the *mechanisms of defence*" (*Language of Psychoanalysis*, p. 107). Second, they wonder if the concept of defense is "really an operational one" when it is used to refer to processes as diverse as "rationalization, which brings complex intellectual mechanisms into play, and turning against the self, which is a 'vicissitude' of the instinctual aim" (p. 110). For another recent effort to clarify the terminological and conceptual problems in the psychoanalytic theory of defense, see Roy Schafer, "The Mechanisms of Defence," *International Journal of Psychoanalysis* 49 (1968): 4–62 (see especially pp. 52–53, on the problems raised by the concept of "mechanism"). Two important articles by Jean Laplanche and Daniel Lagache deal, respectively, with the relation between "defense" and "prohibition," and between "normal" and "pathological" modes of psychic defense: see Laplanche's "La Defense et l'interdit," *La Nef* 31 (1967): 43–55, and Lagache's "La Psychanalyse et la structure de la personnalité," *La Psychanalyse* 6 (1961): 5–68.

45. *Language of Psychoanalysis*, p. 105. Showing the influence of Jacques Lacan, Laplanche and Pontalis warn against the danger of seeing the defense *of the ego* as a phenomenon which opposes "a supposedly pure instinctual demand which, by definition, is devoid of any

dialectic of its own" (pp. 110–11). To illustrate this danger they quote from Anna Freud's classic *The Ego and the Mechanisms of Defense* (1936).

46. Otto Fenichel, *The Psychoanalytic Theory of Neurosis*, p. 130.

47. Freud himself distinguished between "internal" and "external" threats on the grounds that one can respond to the latter by "attempts at flight" whereas it is impossible to evade the former. But when he writes that "repression is an equivalent of this attempt at flight" (*Inhibitions, Symptoms and Anxiety, SE* 20: 92), then the epistemological status of this distinction begins to seem questionable—especially when one considers the implication of his phrase "*attempts at flight*" (*Fluchtversuch*). If in a situation of "real danger" the individual *fails* to flee, may we not surmise that he then employs "defence mechanisms" that do not necessarily involve repression of unconscious ideas? (For a fuller discussion of this question, see the Appendix.)

48. For a brief explanation of the revisionary concept of anxiety set forth in *Inhibitions, Symptoms and Anxiety* (1926), see the translators' introduction, *SE* 20: 78–86. See the Appendix for my speculations on why Freud added a discussion of his use of the terms "defence" and "repression" to this particular work.

49. *De oratore* 3. 31. 124: "In hoc igitur tanto tam immensoque campo cum liceat oratori vagari libere atque ubicumque constiterit consistere in suo. . . ." Quoted from the Loeb Classical Library edition, trans. H. Rackham, 2: 98–99.

50. "Theses on the Semiotic Study of Culture," by B. A. Uspenskij and other members of the "Tartu Group," in *Structure of Texts and Semiotics of Culture*, p. 1.

51. Ibid., p. 7. See also the collection of essays by the Czech semiotician Jan Mukařovský, *Structure, Sign and Function*, trans. and ed. John Burbank and Peter Steiner; as Steiner notes, Mukařovský was specifically concerned with the ways in which cultural "codes" or "languages" become "interlocked in an ongoing struggle for domination, at the same time influencing each other and being influenced" (p. xviii).

52. Abrams, "Belief and the Suspension of Disbelief," p. 2.

53. Abrams makes his *ad hominem* attack on Plato with considerable wit, but one should not therefore overlook the ideological significance of his gesture: an American intellectual committed to the notion of "critical pluralism," Abrams points to an important element of post-war American ideology when he focuses on an individual to explain the "cause" of a social problem. One should also consider the relation between Abrams's belief in the value of pluralism and his failure even to mention the fact that not only poets but philosophers and scientists have been forced, in various historical eras, to defend their ideas. Socrates, whom Abrams portrays only in his role of unjust prosecutor of poetry, was of course a defendant in a real trial, and he refused to accommodate his views to those held by his fellow citizens. Socrates the uncompromising apologist, I would suggest, poses a greater challenge to the American critic's ideal of "separate but equal" fields of knowledge than does Socrates the prosecutor of poetry.

54. Quoted from *John Milton: Complete Poems and Major Prose*, p. 728. Blake revised this Miltonic statement into his famous aphorism, "Without contraries is no progression."

Chapter II

1. The *Deffence* is generally considered to be Du Bellay's first work, but in fact it was published simultaneously with the *Olive*, a collection of Petrarchan love sonnets; licensed together in Paris in March, 1549, the *Deffence* and the *Olive* were frequently reprinted in a single edition. See Henri Chamard, *Joachim du Bellay*, pp. 96–97, for a full discussion of the early publishing history of the *Deffence*. Bakhtin's discussion of the struggle among languages is in *Rabelais and His World*, pp. 465 ff.

2. Du Bellay mentions the Tower of Babel in the first paragraph of the *Deffence*; he links it

with the idea of an exile or fall from Nature. For a fuller discussion of the Babel *topos*, see below, p. 29.

3. For the charge of incoherence see, e.g., Henri Chamard's discussion of *La Deffence* as a hasty reply to Thomas Sebillet's *L'Art Poétique Françoys* (1548), in *Histoire de la Pléiade*, 1: 163-65; see also Chamard's comments on *La Deffence* as a "marqueterie . . . faite de morceaux de toute provenance, assemblés souvent au hasard," in the introduction to his edition of *La Deffence*, p. vi. All citations to the *Deffence* refer to this edition.

4. For the shift from "Brigade" to "Pléiade"—the name Ronsard gave his group of six friends in an elegy addressed to Jean Bastier de la Peruse in 1553 (*Oeuvres complètes*, 2: 315-16)—see Chamard, *Joachim du Bellay*, pp. 48-49. For a discussion of who belonged to the "Brigade" and who to the "Pléiade," see Arthur Tilley, "Dorat and the Pléiade," *Studies in the French Renaissance*, pp. 228-32.

5. For a discussion of Du Bellay's scornful attitude toward French poets of the preceding generations (e.g., Marot, Heroët, the "Grands rhétoriquers"), see Michel Dassonville, "De l'unité de *La Deffence et illustration de la langue françoyse*," *BHR* 27 (1965): 100-02.

6. The title of a futurist manifesto printed in 1912 by a group of Moscow writers, including Mayakovsky and Khlebnikov. See Renato Poggioli, *The Poets of Russia, 1890-1930*, pp. 242-43.

7. See Poggioli's *The Theory of the Avant-Garde*, p. 4. Poggioli denies that a group like the Pléiade can properly be called "avant-garde," since this term, in his view, belongs only to the Romantic and post-Romantic eras. For Poggioli, all pre-nineteenth-century literary and artistic groups constitute "schools," whereas the avant-garde is a "movement" (p. 20). In contrast to the movement, which is "essentially dynamic," the school, Poggioli writes, is "preeminently static and classical." Alas, Poggioli's distinction is too static to account adequately for a group like the Pléiade, which fits his definition of a modernist movement better than it fits his definition of a school as a phenomenon which "presupposes a master and a method" and which "does not take account of history, only of time" (p. 20). It is not clear whether the "master" of the Pléiade was Dorat or Ronsard or the ancient authors themselves; and it is certain that the members of the Pléiade took account of history.

8. With the exception of Etienne Jodelle, who came from a bourgeois family of lawyers and notaries, all the members of the Pléiade belonged, or claimed to belong, to the nobility. See Henri Weber's *La Création poétique au XVIe siècle en France*, pp. 71-73.

9. For the role of bourgeois professors like Dorat in shaping values that differed from those traditionally held by members of the aristocracy, see ibid., pp. 74-76. In Weber's view, the humanist emphasis on "spiritual values and personal merit" opposed the feudal ideals of "military valor and pride of race." One should remark, however, that Dorat's worship of ancient texts fostered in his pupils an *odi profanum vulgus, et arceo* attitude that existed in some tension with humanist notions of "individual merit." On the *odi profanum* theme, see Robert Clements, *Critical Theory and Practice of the Pléiade*, pp. 44-77. On Dorat's ideal of an "aristocracy of the mind," see Grahame Castor, *Pléiade Poetics*, pp. 25-26. For a good discussion of Dorat's pedagogical program at Coqueret, see Tilley's chapter "Dorat and the Pléiade," *Studies in the French Renaissance*, pp. 219-32.

10. For an example of Du Bellay's attitude toward native precursors, see the *Deffence* bk. 2, chap. 11, where he expresses a desire to make French "healthy" by cutting out "this ulcer and corrupted flesh of bad poetry" (p. 179). The violence of this metaphor provides counterevidence, in my view, to Dassonville's argument that Du Bellay did not have truly hostile feelings toward native precursors and popular poetic genres ("De l'unité," p. 101).

11. At a time when the so-called *noblesse de robe* was growing rapidly and threatening the class identity of the traditional *noblesse d'epée*, aristocrats like Du Bellay were particularly eager to embrace theories about humanist poets as members of a highly select company,

addressing a "fit audience though few." "Aussi est le nombre petit, et peu cognu, de ces parfaits studieux," writes Pontus de Thyard in his *Solitaire première* (cited in Castor, *Pléiade Poetics*, p. 26), expressing a common Pléiade notion. For a useful discussion of the blurring of traditional class distinctions in sixteenth-century France (and for a persuasive argument that the concept of "class" should be applied to a Renaissance society legally divided into "estates"), see Robert Mandrou, *Introduction to Modern France, 1500-1640*, especially pp. 100-18.

12. "Trop dedaigneuse est ceste exhortation de laisser les vieilles poësies aux [Jeux] Floraux de Tholose," exclaims Aneau apropos of Du Bellay's remarks on native poetry and provincial academies in bk. 2, chap. 4; see *Deffence*, pp. 108-09, and, for Aneau's response, p. 109, n. 1. Aneau's entire pamphlet is reprinted in the notes to Henri Chamard's edition of *La Deffence*. All citations to Aneau's pamphlet refer to that edition; translations are my own. On Aneau's literary and pedagogical career, see Henri Chamard, "La date et l'auteur du *Quintil Horatian*," *Revue d'histoire littéraire de la France* 5 (1898): 54-71.

13. See Dassonville, "De l'unité," p. 98, for a discussion of the humanists who expressed "marked disdain" for the vernacular. For a detailed survey of the opposition to the vernacular among educators and Catholic theologians, see Ferdinand Brunot's chapter "Les Obstacles," in *Histoire de la langue française des origines à nos jours*, 2: 6-26. Of particular relevance to Du Bellay are arguments such as those set forth by a priest named Rotier, who published in 1548 a treatise against translating the scriptures into the "vulgar tongue" on the grounds that French was unstable, poor, and wanting in "majesty" (ibid., pp. 23-24).

14. See *Deffence*, p. xi: A "Hercules factitius," Aneau writes, is someone "qui se forge luy mesme des monstres faits tout à propos, tels qu'il les puisse aisément defaire: combien qu'ils ne soient, & n'ayent esté jamais."

15. The description of the nobility is from Perry Anderson, *Lineages of the Absolutist State*, p. 31. For a discussion of the financial problems besetting the nobility and driving many noble-class younger sons into clerkly labor, see Mandrou, *France*, pp. 104-09.

16. Quoted from *Joachim du Bellay, Oeuvres poétiques*, ed. Henri Chamard, 1: 11-12. All citations to Du Bellay's French poetic works, other than *Les Antiquitez de Rome* and *Les Regrets*, refer to this edition, which will henceforth be abbreviated as *OP*. For a useful discussion of the traditional aristocratic prejudice against writers, see Weber, *Création*, pp. 73-76.

17. After the death of François I in 1547, Jean du Bellay's career suffered a temporary eclipse; Henri II had hated François and was not inclined to favor his father's servants. Although Henri sent the cardinal to Rome soon after the coronation, the mission represented a "disguised disgrace," according to Chamard (*Joachim du Bellay*, p. 275). Joachim's fulsome praises of the cardinal's diplomatic skills should, I think, be read not only as flattery of the cardinal, but also as an oblique effort to help raise him in the King's opinion. For Henri II's hostile attitude toward his father's associates, see Donald Stone, *France in the Sixteenth Century*, pp. 68-69.

18. Aneau writes: "Car quelle semblance est d'un Cardinal à un Rost [Roscius] jongleur, d'une ambassade ou legation royale à une comedie, d'un affaire serieux à un jeu?" (pp. 3-4, n. 2).

19. For the Reform influence on the *Deffence*, see, e.g., pp. 31, 80, 137-38; see also Chamard's discussion of the role of the Reform in the defense of the vernacular in *Histoire de la Pleiade*, 1: 173-74.

20. The home in Anjou, so important for Du Bellay's later poetry, is not explicitly evoked in the *Deffence*, but its imaginative presence may be traced in several passages praising an ideal of stable country life; see, for example, the mention of a "siege & demeure certaine" in bk. 2, chap. 12 (p. 188). For an important discussion of Rome as a seat of patriarchal authority (of the sort which Du Bellay seems to associate, specifically, with the figure of Augustus), see Hannah Arendt, "What is Authority?" in *Between Past and Future*.

21. For a discussion of the blurring of distinctions between nobles and wealthy bourgeois in humanist circles such as the Collège de Coqueret, see Weber, *Création*, pp. 73-75. On the

general issue of the threat posed to the traditional nobility (*d'epée* or *de race*) by bourgeois men obtaining places in the so-called *noblesse de robe* through their own industry, see J. H. M. Salmon, "Sword and Gown," in *Society in Crisis*, pp. 92–113.

22. *Replique aux furieuses defenses de Louis Meigret*, quoted in Castor, *Pléiade Poetics*, p. 115. For a general discussion of sixteenth-century attacks on Du Bellay's treatise, see Joseph Vianey, *"Les Regrets" de Joachim du Bellay*, pp. 33–34.

23. For the relation between the concept of imitation and the psychoanalytic notion of identification, see J. Laplanche and J. B. Pontalis, *The Language of Psychoanalysis*, pp. 205–07. Laplanche and Pontalis remark that Freud uses the term "identification" (*identifizierung*) in a variety of senses, the most important of which is "identification of oneself *with*"; this sense "overlaps a whole group of psychological concepts—e.g., imitation, Einfühlung (empathy), sympathy, mental contagion, projection, etc." (p. 206). For a discussion of identification as a major psychic defense, see Anna Freud, *The Ego and the Mechanisms of Defense*, especially chap. 9, "Identification With the Aggressor," where she describes how a person masters his anxiety about a powerful rival by imitating him.

24. For a survey of Du Bellay's imitations of works such as Bembo's *Prose della lingua volgare*, Gelli's *Ragionamenti*, and above all, Speroni's *Dialogo delle lingue*, see Pierre Villey, *Les Sources italiennes de la "Deffense et illustration de la langue françoise."* One recent critic who *has* considered some of the theoretical implications of Du Bellay's imitative practice is Terence Cave, in his important book *The Cornucopian Text*. Cave does not consider the specifically political implications of Du Bellay's use of Italian authors, but he does comment usefully on the paradox inherent in Du Bellay's textual practice: "The voice of the author as he pleads for the distinctive and authentic character of his language and for his own right to authorship is caught repeating the words of other men" (p. 75).

25. On the aristocratic belief that "war was the solution to material difficulties" and that plunder of foreign territories was "an easy remedy for financial embarrassment," see Mandrou, *France*, p. 106.

26. See the address "Au Lecteur" at the end of the *Deffence*, where Du Bellay describes his "petit ouvraige" as a "desseing & protraict de quelque grand & laborieux edifice" (p. 201). See also pp. 87–89, where he uses the verb "ebaucher" and elaborates the architectural metaphor by comparing the poet and the orator to the two pillars that support "l'edifice de chacune Langue." Since Etienne Dolet had already formed the orator in his *L'Orateur françoys*, Du Bellay will devote himself to forming the poet. (It is an irony of literary history that Dolet's treatise was apparently "rough-hewed" but not finished—a fact which Du Bellay either didn't know or chose not to mention. See p. 86, n. 2.)

27. For an interesting discussion of the distinction between Latin, defined as a *sermo patrius*, and the European vernaculars, defined as "mother tongues," see Leo Spitzer, "Muttersprache und Muttererziehung," *Essays in Historical Semantics*, pp. 15–65.

28. On the importance of the notion of historical differences among cultures in Renaissance literary theory (particularly in debates about the issue of Ciceronianism), see Cave, *Cornucopian Text*, especially pp. 41ff. See also the excellent discussion of contextual practices in Renaissance historiography—a discussion which is highly relevant to Du Bellay's meditations on history both in *La Deffence* and in *Les Antiquitez de Rome*—in Lawrence Manley, *Convention: 1500–1750*, pp. 231–40 and passim.

29. See Du Bellay's claim to have been "le premier des Francoys" to introduce, "quasi comme une nouvelle poësie," the Petrarchan love sonnet, in his *Olive* (*Deffence*, p. 90); see also *Les Antiquitez de Rome*, sonnet 32, where he boasts of being "le premier des François" to sing "l'antique honneur du peuple à longue robbe." All citations of *Les Antiquitez* and *Les Regrets* are to *"Les Regrets" et autres oeuvres poétiques*, ed. J. Joliffe and M. A. Screech. There is, of course, a lovely irony in this sonnet, which echoes Horace's claim to have been the first ("princeps") to bring Aeolian song to Italy (*Carmina*, bk. III, ode 30).

30. See Ronsard's *Les Isles fortunées*, where he imagines a flight from Europe, presently blighted and poor, as if in an age of iron, across the Atlantic to the golden New World (*Oeuvres complètes*, 2: 409–14); Harry Levin discusses this poem in *The Myth of the Golden Age in the Renaissance*, chap. 3.

31. Cf. line 85 of his "Hymne Chrestien" (1552), which describes the Israelites among "les longues erreurs de ce desert sauvage" (*OP*, 4: 114). For Du Bellay's obsession with what might be called the phenomenology of exile, as an experience of endless wandering, see Michel Deguy's *Tombeau de Du Bellay*, especially pp. 49 ff.

32. See *Deffence*, p. 82, where Du Bellay remarks on the possibility that French may eventually "perish," as the ancient languages have, and be found, like them, to be great but lifeless, preserved in the "reliquary of books." For a useful discussion of this passage see Cave, *Cornucopian Text*, p. 69. See also Thomas Greene, "Petrarch and the Humanist Hermeneutic," in *Italian Literature: Roots and Branches*, for an analysis of the close link between humanist metaphors of rebirth and necromantic images of disinterment.

33. *Mythe et langage au seizième siècle*, p. 24.

34. On the many meanings of the word *copia* in ancient, medieval, and Renaissance theory, see Cave, *Cornucopian Text*, pp. 3 ff.; and Nancy Struever, *The Language of History in the Renaissance*, pp. 56–58.

35. The belief that there is a finite amount of representable matter in the world and that artists therefore cannot help repeating or resembling others appears, for instance, in the following passage from the second preface of the *Olive*: "Si deux peintres s'efforcent de representer au naturel quelque vyf protraict, il est impossible qu'ilz ne se rencontrent en mesmes traictz & lineamens, ayans mesme exemplaire devant eulx" (*OP*, 1: 20–21). Contrast this with Erasmus's statement, in his *De duplici verborum ac rerum copia*, that Nature's variety is so great that an artist who imitates Nature need never fall into repetition (see *Omnia Opera*, 1: 95; cited and translated in Cave, *Cornucopian Text*, pp. 22–23).

36. *Lineages*, p. 31.

37. On Du Bellay's unhappy relations with his brother René, see Chamard, *Joachim du Bellay*, pp. 21–24.

38. *Cornucopian Text*, p. 75. See also pp. 4–5, where Cave remarks on the paradoxically antithetical meanings of *copia*: from a term which signified, in classical Latin, a variety of "dynamically deployed energies," *copia* came to mean, in Medieval Latin, a "copy," a static product of endless repetition. Although Cave briefly notes that "the advent of printing, followed by other technologies of mass production, has assured the triumph of the word 'copy' and its modern [chiefly pejorative] range of meanings," he does not examine the specific historical and material factors which shape the contradictory concepts of *copia* in the Renaissance—the period Marx saw as the crucial transition, in the West, from feudalism to capitalism.

39. See chapter 19 of *Le Tiers Livre*, and François Rigolot, "Cratylisme et Pantagruelisme: Rabelais et le statut du signe."

40. Compare Du Bellay's text and Speroni's *Dialogo*, reprinted in the appendix of Villey's *Les Sources italiennes*. The passage on the conventional nature of language is on p. 138. All citations to Speroni's *Dialogo* refer to this edition.

41. See *De vulgari eloquentia*, 1. 7, where Dante presents Babel as the third historical instance of a fall caused by man's pride (the second is the lapse into evil punished by the flood): "tertio insurrexit ad verbera per superbiam suam et stultitiam praesumendo" (*Tutte le opere di Dante Alighieri*, p. 382). It is highly likely that Du Bellay knew Dante's *De vulgari*; he mentions Dante approvingly in the "Ode à Madame Marguerite, d'escrire en sa langue" (*OP*, 3: 99, l. 42), linking him with Bembo in a way that suggests Du Bellay is thinking, specifically, of the two Italians' contribution to their vernacular tongue. On the Tower of Babel *topos* in the Renaissance, see Dubois, *Mythe et langage*, p. 25; Cave, *Cornucopian Text*, p. 67, n. 41; and A. Borst, *Der Turnbau von Babel*, 4: 2.

42. See *Deffence*, pp. 11–12, quoted in full above, p. 28. Note that even the syntax of the first sentence suggests the problematic status of Nature; in the midst of a subjunctive statement about Nature, Du Bellay has a representative authority from ancient culture interrupt our perceptions, as it were, of Nature's workings: "Si la Nature (dont quelque personnaige de grand' renommée non sans rayson a douté si on la devoit appeller mere ou maratre) eust donné aux hommes. . . ." The parenthetical comment, which threatens to dominate the sentence, alludes to a text whose very title—*Historia naturalis*—highlights the issue of an unnatural Nature, seen here as a phenomenon which is inevitably and already part of culture and history. The phrase "mere ou maratre," which Du Bellay takes from Pliny and repeats often in later works (see p. 12, n. 1.), does not appear in Speroni's text, which Du Bellay otherwise follows closely here.

43. Rivalry between France and Italy is an important theme in *La Deffence* (see pp. 175, 184–85). See also Villey, *Les Sources italiennes*, pp. 3–7, for a discussion of the relation between Du Bellay and previous defenders of French such as Jean Lemaire de Belges, whose *Concorde des deux langues* (1511) seeks to prove that French is not inferior to Tuscan. Lemaire's *Illustrations de Gaule* (1510–13), which argues for the illustrious Trojan origins of the French people, is one of several texts (in a genre that we might call the "national family romance") that Du Bellay would have known and used in his own effort to restore to France that noble history he saw the Romans as having stolen from Gaul.

44. Sperone Speroni degli Alvarotti, born in Padua in 1500, was the son of a well-respected doctor. See Francesco Cammarosano, *La Vita e le opere di Sperone Speroni*, pp. 9 ff. For a good discussion of the *Dialogo*, see Giancarlo Mazzacurati, "Il 'cortegiano' (e lo 'scolare') nel *Dialogo delle lingue* di Sperone Speroni," in *Conflitti di culture nel cinquecento*, pp. 141–81.

45. *Lineages*, p. 31.

46. The phrase is from the *Deffence*, p. 33, where Du Bellay is discussing the means for acquiring "cete copie & richesse d'invention" which an orator, specifically, must possess. For other discussions of *copie*, see pp. 31, 48, 72 (where Du Bellay adds a praise of Plato's "divine copie" to the passage he is translating from Speroni [see Villey, *Les Sources italiennes*, pp. 58–59]). For Du Bellay's anxiety about the present poverty of French, in contrast to the copious ancient tongues, see Robert Griffen, *Coronation of the Poet*, pp. 49, 78.

47. See *Deffence*, pp. 168, 178–79, and above, note 10. One wonders how Rabelais—as physician to the Cardinal Jean du Bellay and as demystifier of aristocratic ideologies about purity of blood—would have glossed this passage.

48. For a discussion of Tasso's family romance, with specific reference to Freud's 1909 paper on that subject, see Chapter 3, below.

49. The origins of the historical theory of a westering movement of civilization, elaborated in the Carolingian period first with regard to the Holy Roman Empire (*translatio imperii*) and then with regard to learning (*translatio studii*), are discussed by E. R. Curtius, *European Literature and the Latin Middle Ages*, pp. 28–30. For the importance of these concepts to the Pléiade and Du Bellay in particular, see Françoise Joukovsky-Micha, *La Gloire dans la poésie française et néolatine du 16e siècle*, especially pp. 34 ff. and 215–16.

50. For examples of Du Bellay's emphasis on the Romans' debt to the Greeks, see *Deffence*, pp. 42, 48.

51. For the cyclical theory of history in the sixteenth century, see Peter Burke, *The Renaissance Sense of the Past*, pp. 89 ff; see also Joukovsky-Micha, *La Gloire*, pp. 33–34, for a useful discussion of the problems Renaissance authors encountered when they attempted to reconcile classical "cyclical" views with Christian "Providential" ones.

52. Du Bellay, like Ronsard, often articulates a view of history as a process of degeneration; see Du Bellay's poem to Bertran Bergier, which evokes the notion of a Golden Age of Greek literature and its subsequent decline (*OP*, 5: 119–20). Cf. Ronsard's similarly pessimistic view of (ancient) history in "Ode à Michel de l'Hospital," *Oeuvres complètes*, 1: 386–406.

53. For the relevant passage in Speroni's *Dialogo*, see Villey, *Les Sources italiennes*, p. 141.

Louis Le Roy echoed Du Bellay's argument against devoting time to learning ancient languages when in 1576 he delivered an address at the Collège Royale justifying the use of the vernacular for pedagogical purposes; see Brunot, *Histoire*, pp. 12–13.

54. For a provocative discussion of the sexual politics interwoven in historical debates about the relative merits of mother tongues—associated frequently with the ideal of a natural purity—and father tongues—forms of secondary speech, learned, written, foreign, and often the language of the conqueror—see Geoffrey Hartman, *Criticism in the Wilderness*, pp. 142 ff.

55. This sentence is virtually translated from Speroni; see Villey, *Les Sources italiennes*, p. 137. Cf. also *Deffence*, p. 72, where Du Bellay says that because knowledge has always been "en la puissance des Grecz & Romains . . . nous croyons que par eux seulement elles puyssent & doyvent estre traictées."

56. Deguy, *Tombeau*, p. 108.

57. Chamard's comment is in *La Deffence*, p. 103, n. 1; Aneau's, which goes on to accuse Du Bellay of using "figures where proper language [*proprieté*] would be more appropriate [*convenante*]," is quoted on p. 43, n. 2.

58. For a useful discussion of the innutrition metaphor, from Quintilian's influential formulation of it in the *Institutio oratoria* (bk. 10, chap. 1, sec. 19) to its use by Erasmus and Du Bellay, see Cave, *Cornucopian Text*, pp. 36–38, 71. See also Robert Griffin, *Coronation of the Poet*, pp. 79–84.

59. The peculiarity of Du Bellay's thought in this passage lies partly in his subversion of Quintilian. Du Bellay introduces his discussion of imitation here with an echo of Quintilian's statement, "Neque enim dubitari potest, quin artis pars magna contineatur imitatione" (*Institutio* 10. 2. 1; p. 74. All citations are to the Loeb Classical Library edition). Du Bellay follows the *Institutio* just to the point of mentioning Nature's failure to eradicate difference. Quintilian uses the fact of difference to emphasize the modern poet's need to invent, as well as imitate: the "mere follower" must "lag behind" the great originals because, as Nature herself has demonstrated, "there is nothing harder than to produce an exact likeness"; it is therefore "generally easier to make some advance than to repeat what has been done by others" (10. 2. 10; pp. 78–79). What Du Bellay does, then, is substitute a supra-natural concept of imitation for the invention Quintilian advocates in response to the natural law of difference.

60. For Quintilian's comments on "creative" paraphrase, see *Institutio* 10. 5. 5; pp. 114–15. Vida's discussion of an imitation that changes the original author by an act of graceful deceit is in *Ars poetica*, bk. 3, ll. 216–31. The "altra significazione che la lor propria" phrase is in *Il Cortegiano*, bk. 1, chap. 34. Cf. also the article on paraphrasis in Robert Estienne's *Dictionarium* (1531), where the paraphrast is defined as one who "does not transfer letter from letter, but sense from sense, as if he were speaking alongside his model" (cited in Cave, *Cornucopian Text*, pp. 38–39).

61. See, for example, *Les Antiquitez de Rome*, sonnet 6, where Du Bellay ironically plays on the distance between Virgil's historical perspective and his own by putting Virgil's prophecy of Rome's future greatness—"Imperium terris, animos aequabit Olympo"—into a past definite tense: "celle qui fit egale/Sa puissance à la terre, & son courage aux cieux."

62. Du Bellay's nostalgia for a natural eloquence—a concept linked, significantly, to the oral image of nurse's milk and evidently related to Du Bellay's tactile descriptions of a rich "mother tongue"—should be compared with his fantasy of returning to a golden age of nonverbal communication (see above, p. 39). A strong desire to escape the pain and labor of adult communication appears, as it were, in the interstices of Du Bellay's argument about the virtues of the industrious, proto-capitalist writer.

63. *Tombeau*, p. 33.

64. Cicero, *De oratore*, bk. 3, chap. 37, p. 118 of the Loeb Classical Library edition: "eis quae transferuntur et quasi alieno in loco collocantur."

65. For an account of Du Bellay's Roman journey see Chamard, *Joachim du Bellay*, part 2, chap. 1.

66. The four collections are *Les Antiquitez de Rome, Les Regrets, Les Divers Jeux Rustiques,* and *Poëmata*; there is, unfortunately, no readily available modern edition that prints all of Du Bellay's Roman poems together, though the Latin poems provide crucial glosses on the French ones and vice versa. It is an irony of literary history, and of the history of modern nation-states, that Du Bellay's French poems, particularly his patriotic sonnets, are so often anthologized whereas his Latin works are hard to find and for the most part unread. They have received some attention recently: Fred J. Nichols translates several in his *Anthology of Neo-Latin Poetry*; and I. D. McFarlane discusses some of the erotic poems in "Joachim du Bellay's *Liber Amorum,*" *L'Esprit créateur* 19 (1979): 56–65. The Latin poems are available in Etienne Courbet's edition of *Poésies françaises et latines de Joachim du Bellay* (1918).

67. The phrase "eternel exil," from *Les Regrets,* sonnet 50, echoes a line of Horace's Epode 16, where the poet enjoins his friends to choose eternal exile rather than stay in a Rome torn by civil war. The very fact of this echoic *translatio* dramatizes the metalinguistic dimension of Du Bellay's representation of exile as a condition of being separated not only from one's homeland (one's "proper ground") but also from one's mother tongue, which Du Bellay cannot use without awareness of the alienating and mediating presence of Latin precursors. The "Patriae desiderium," a poem which dramatizes the problem of linguistic exile, is in Courbet, *Poésies,* pp. 445–47, and also, with a translation, in Nichols's *Anthology of Neo-Latin Poetry*, pp. 525–27. In the "Patriae," Du Bellay laments his loss of French, echoing passages from the *Tristia* where Ovid laments his loss of Latin during his banishment from the very city to which Du Bellay has come.

68. In *Les Antiquitez* Du Bellay combines his attitude of reverent humility toward the "Divins Esprits" with a critical examination of Roman history. He frequently blames Roman hubris for causing the city's downfall and often alludes to the myth of genealogical warfare between the giants and the Olympian gods to portray Roman history as a series of violent struggles for supremacy. For poems concerned with genealogical strife, see sonnets 11, 12, 14, 17, 23, 24, 28, 30, 31. *Les Regrets* dramatizes an ambivalence toward the "demon du lieu" (sonnet 87) by portraying Rome as a lovely Siren or Circe capable of robbing the French poet not only of his hair but of his voice (see sonnets 72, 87, 88).

69. For an excellent discussion of Du Bellay's representation of oscillation between hope for a hypothetical future and regret for an idealized past, see François Rigolot, "Du Bellay et la poésie du refus," especially pp. 500–01.

70. Note that the text ends not only with the image of "Hercule Gallique" but with the word *langue,* meaning both "language" and "tongue." There are several fine ironies lurking in Du Bellay's final sentence, among them the fact that it adapts a comic story about Hercules originally told in Lucian's "Dialogues of the Dead" to new nationalistic purposes, "translating" (literally, "carrying across") the Greek text in order to advocate an act of pillaging Rome, the city to which Du Bellay himself was ambiguously linked by a chain attached, as it were, to his tongue. (For Chamard's discussion of the popularity of the "Hercule Gallique" figure in sixteenth-century French literature, see *Deffence,* p. 197, n. 4).

Chapter III

1. Often called the "Stacciata prima" ("first sifting") to distinguish it from later Cruscan attacks on Tasso, the pamphlet which provoked the *Apologia* was published in February 1585, with the title *Degli Accademici Della Crusca difesa dell'Orlando Furioso contra 'l dialogo dell'epica poesia di Cammillo Pellegrino* (reprinted in *Opere di Torquato Tasso colle controversie sulla "Gerusalemme,"* vol. 18). It was written, unbeknownst to Tasso, by an acquaintance

of his named Lionardo Salviati. For further details on its genesis and content, see below. See also Bernard Weinberg, *A History of Literary Criticism in the Italian Renaissance*, pp. 1004 ff. See also Angelo Solerti, *Vita di Torquato Tasso*, 1: 421–45, for a discussion of Tasso's reaction to the Cruscan pamphlet; in a letter dated 18 March 1585, he claims to have completed the *Apologia* in five days, without benefit of reference books. Solerti takes this letter as evidence that Tasso was not much upset by the Cruscan attack. I disagree, and would suggest, moreover, that while Tasso may well have written the pamphlet in a white heat, he may also have tinkered with it until at least the beginning of May, when he wrote to Lucio Scalabrini asking for money and aid in getting the *Apologia* printed. Despite another request, in June, for money and help in publishing the text, that event did not occur until 21 July, when a volume containing the *Apologia* and several other works pertaining to the quarrel appeared in Ferrara. For a description of that volume see Weinberg, *History of Literary Criticism*, 2: 1151–52; see also *Le Lettere di Torquato Tasso*, vol. 2, nos. 352, 367, 391. All references to Tasso's letters are to this edition. As pagination varies in different printings, I cite letter numbers and, whenever possible, dates.

2. The quoted phrase is from Bruno Maier's 1965 edition of the *Apologia*, in *Opere*, 5: 634. All quotations from the *Apologia* are from this edition, which reproduces the text established by Cesare Guasti for the *Prose Diverse* (1875) and slightly revised by Ettore Mazzali for his edition of Tasso's *Prose* (1959). For an excellent discussion of the early editions of the *Apologia* (the manuscript is lost), see *Prose*, ed. Mazzali, pp. 1145–46. In calling Ariosto's poem an "animal d'incerta natura," Tasso alludes to two passages beloved of sixteenth-century critics: Aristotle's *Poetics* 1450b–1451a, which compares a beautiful plot to a living creature which is neither tiny nor huge but rather of "a size to be taken in by the eye" (*The Basic Works of Aristotle*, ed. Richard McKeon, p. 1463); and the opening lines of Horace's *The Art of Poetry*, which compare a bad book to a picture of a monstrous creature. Although Tasso invokes such authoritative comments on formal decorum specifically to castigate Ariosto for having written a poem that is *between* epic and romance, the metaphor of the unclassifiable animal was, as Tasso knew, frequently used to describe the genre of romance itself. As David Quint suggests, Tasso's passage probably echoes Giovanni Battista Pigna's description of the romance as a "disproportionate animal," a monstrous creature like a giant. For the relevant citation from Pigna's *I Romanzi* (1554), see Quint's fine essay, "The Figure of Atlante: Ariosto and Boiardo's Poem," *MLN*, 94 (1979): 77–79.

3. The very existence of a distinction in kind between epic and romance is a matter of considerable theoretical dispute in Tasso's own works and in those of his contemporaries. When he states in the *Apologia* that those works called romances are not different "in kind" (*di specie*) from epic or heroic poems, (p. 633), he repeats an opinion already stated in the first version of his *Discorsi*; for the parallel passage see *Prose*, p. 375. (All quotations from the *Discorsi dell'arte poetica* and the later expanded *Discorsi del poema eroico* are from this edition.) Many passages, both in the *Apologia* and in the *Discorsi*, however, presuppose an essential rather than accidental distinction between epic and romance. For brief discussions of this locus of theoretical tension in the *Apologia* see Weinberg, *History of Literary Criticism*, 2: 1010; and Eugenio Donadoni, *Torquato Tasso: Saggio critico*, pp. 374–75.

4. On the theoretical critique of Ariostean romance implicit in the structure of Tasso's epic, see Andrew Fichter, "Tasso's Epic of Deliverance," *PMLA* 93 (March 1978): 265–74. See also Guido Baldassarri, *"Inferno" e "Cielo"*, especially pp. 49–70, on the ideological and formal problems Tasso attempts to solve with his paradoxical notion of the "marvelous verisimilar."

5. For an important discussion of these conflicts see Robert M. Durling's chapter on Tasso in *The Figure of the Poet in Renaissance Epic*, especially pp. 200–10; see also the section on Tasso in his essay "The Epic Ideal," in *Literature and Western Civilization: The Old World*. Durling comments astutely on passages in Tasso's prose which explicitly link theoretical and psychological problems; see, for example, pp. 204–05 of *The Figure of the Poet*, on Tasso's statement that the "diversity of goals" characteristic of romance plots causes "distraction in the

mind" of the author (*Discorsi dell'arte poetica*; omitted from the revised edition). See also the letter to Scipione Gonzaga of 15 April 1575 for an example of Tasso's habit of speaking of the *romanzo* as an independent genre. This letter is particularly interesting because in it Tasso criticizes himself for using, in canto 5 of *Gerusalemme Liberata*, a mode of linking episodes that belongs "più tosto da romanzo che da poema eroico," *Lettere*, vol. 1, no. 25).

6. For a detailed description of the quarrel between the "Ariostisti" and the "Tassisti," see Weinberg, *History of Literary Criticism*, 2: 954 ff. See also the "Bibliografia delle polemiche" in Angelo Solerti's *Appendice alle opere in prosa di Torquato Tasso*; and Donadoni's chapter on "Le polemiche sulla *Liberata*," *Torquato Tasso*, pp. 337–55.

7. See David George Hale, *The Body Politic*, p. 15. Hale gives a useful summary of the history of the metaphor in Greek, Roman, and medieval Christian thought; he rightly emphasizes the role of Paul's First Letter to the Corinthians in transforming the metaphor into an instrument of political theology that later Christian writers employed to justify both the institution of the papacy and the notion of a hierarchical social order in which the lower classes constitute the feet of the body, the nobility its hands, and the clergy its ruling head and eyes (pp. 28–38). Although the body analogy was widely used "in the conservative response to the literature of social and religious protest" which appeared in England and other European countries after 1350 (p. 35), it was also used, Hale observes, in ways which directly supported radical political and religious movements. Once the language of political theology had been appropriated by secular princes to support the idea that the king, rather than the pope, was the rightful "head" of a state, the body analogy became a double-edged sword. Not only were Renaissance writers highly aware that the conflicts between popes and secular rulers generated images of "monstrously two-headed or schizophrenic" states (p. 39); they also saw that the organic analogy could support an egalitarian conception of society as well as a hierarchical one. Indeed in both its original classical form and its original Christian one—the Aesopian fable of the belly and the Pauline image of a community of believers united in the *corpus mysticum* of Christ—the analogy offered Renaissance writers ammunition for their critiques of the political and economic *status quo*. Thomas More, for instance, relied heavily on the organic analogy in his depiction of a Utopian society free from the "disease" of private property, and Clement Armstrong mounted an attack on the policy of enclosure in England by asking why "oon hand" or "oon finger" should be given more food than another (quoted by Hale, p. 60). Italian writers seldom use the metaphor so explicitly for radical purposes, but they do frequently use it in ways which call attention to political problems. In *Il Cortegiano*, for instance, Castiglione's interlocutors refer at one point to the traditional idea of the prince as the "head" of the state; the reader remembers, however, that the prince was called the "heart" a few pages earlier and that the duke who should be occupying one or the other of these crucial roles is absent from the scene because of ill health (see *The Book of Courtier*, pp. 303, 315). By such ironies and metaphorical shifts, Castiglione obliquely diagnoses the parlous condition of his country, where princes, popes, and foreign monarchs vie for the position of "head" and where the body politic all too often looks like a dismembered object.

8. For the phrase "Vostra Paternità" and variations thereon, see, for example, the letters Tasso wrote to the Benedictine monk Don Angelo Grillo in 1585 (*Lettere*, vol. 2, nos. 348, 354, 362, 388); the first of these, written on 15 March is an anxiously jocular plea to the "rigido padre" to intercede on the poor prisoner's behalf both with God and with secular authorities, such as the emperor.

9. See Solerti, *Vita*, 1: 252–67 for a detailed account of Tasso's appeals for Inquisitorial absolution and the threat those appeals posed for Alfonso d'Este, whose mother, Renée, had been a Calvinist and who was anxious to avoid any conflict with Church authorities. In June 1577, Alfonso attempted to soothe Tasso by having him examined by the Ferrarese Inquisitor, who reported to the duke that Tasso was unsatisfied with the absolution granted him, since he wanted to be subjected to torture; moreover, the priest said that Tasso had made serious

accusations against a man named Montecatini—accusations Tasso later acknowledged to be the products of imaginative "transport." See *Lettere*, vol. 2, no. 123 (to Scipio Gonzaga), and also vol. 1, no. 101 (to Alfonso, apropos Tasso's relations with the Inquisition). For a succinct account, in English, of the events leading up to Tasso's imprisonment, and for a serious attempt to separate fact from fiction (a difficult task, since much of our information is provided by Tasso's letters), see C. P. Brand, *Torquato Tasso*, pp. 16–23.

10. See the letter written in 1578 to Francesco Maria della Rovere, Duke of Urbino, in which Tasso insists that he deliberately "dissimulated" in order to support Duke Alfonso's "false conception" of him as a madman. He did this, he writes, not from "viltà d'anima" but rather from "desiderio di renderlomi grazioso" as so to "open . . . a larger road to the duke's benevolence" (*Lettere*, vol. 1, no. 109). But in other letters he laments as genuine his physical and mental distress; see, for example, the plea for help "because I am desperate" which he addressed to Vincenzo Fantini on 18 March 1585 (*Lettere*, vol. 2, no. 350).

11. See *Apologia*, p. 644, where Tasso calls attention to his ignorance of his opponents' true identities by wondering whether those who hide under the "ugly name" of Crusca are like the images of gods hidden in the grotesque Silenus figures Plato mentions in the *Symposium*. Solerti (*Vita*, 1: 424–25) reads this passage as evidence that Tasso thought he had been attacked by members of the prestigious Florentine Academy, established forty years before the Cruscan Academy (1582). Tasso certainly did not know that the author of the pamphlet was Salviati, though he had discovered this by the next year, when Salviati wrote a response to the *Apologia* in which he mocked Tasso for thinking himself worthy of disputing with the dignitaries of the Accademia Fiorentina. For more details on Salviati's pseudonymous attacks (he called himself "L'Infarinato," "the flowered one"), see B. T. Sozzi, "Tasso contro Salviati con le postille inedite all'*Infarinato*," *Studi Tassiani* 1 (1951): 37–66. Since Salviati repeatedly accused Tasso of "irreligione," among other things, his attack undoubtedly revived the anxieties which had provoked Tasso to submit his epic to the severe criticism of his so-called Roman friends in 1575–76.

12. De Sanctis, *The History of Italian Literature*, 2: 628.

13. In his *Risposta a M. Giovambattista Pigna* (1554), for instance, Giraldi Cinthio praises Ariosto lavishly and defends the modern Italian poet's right to depart from classical models by means of an ideologically significant though linguistically dubious genealogical argument: Ariosto did not follow Virgil as closely as Virgil followed Homer, Giraldi asserts, because the Italian language does not descend as directly from the Latin as the Latin does from the Greek. Ariosto has created a new genre appropriate to its specific time and place, Giraldi says, by imitating authors "who wrote laudably in the languages from which ours derived its way of composing, such as French, Provençal, and Spanish romances" (quoted and translated in Weinberg, *History of Literary Criticism*, 2: 960).

14. Dante's poem was the subject of another major critical battle of the sixteenth century and was attacked, by Aristotelians, for many of the same faults they saw in Ariosto's poem; see ibid., pp. 831–33. The *Commedia* was defended, however, by Mazzoni and others, in terms that were clearly important to Tasso's definition of his own ideal of a Christian epic: it has "unity of action" and therefore deserves to be classed as an epic rather than a *romanzo*; and its representations of "marvels" serve theological truth (see ibid., pp. 835–36). By implicitly making Dante an ally in his battle against Ariosto, despite the fact that Dante's poem departs as boldly from classical norms as Ariosto's does, Tasso shows his desire to separate a good medieval heritage from a bad one, though to do so he must characterize the romance tradition as wickedly pagan. Two birds are thus killed by one stone: Ariosto's literary progenitors are devalued; and the charge of paganism is deflected from the ancients, who deserve it, to the authors of medieval romance, who do not.

15. See *Purgatorio* 30, ll. 40ff. and, on the significance of the idealized maternal figure, below, pp. 116–26.

16. In Tasso's writing, *fantasia* (from the Greek *phantasia*, literally "a making visible") is often used synonomously with the term *imaginazione*; see, for example, *Discorsi del poema eroico*, bk. 2, where he equates "la imaginazione intellettuale" with Dante's "alta fantasia" (*Prose*, p. 530). For the relation between Renaissance theories of fantasy (or fancy, in English) and Aristotelian psychology, see William Rossky, "Imagination in the English Renaissance," *Studies in the Renaissance* 5 (1958): 49–73; other useful studies include: E. Ruth Harvey, *The Inward Wits*; Harry Berger, Jr., "The Renaissance Imagination," *Centennial Review* 9 (1965): 36–78; and John D. Guillory, "The Genealogy of the Imagination," in "Poetry and Authority: Spenser, Milton, and Literary History," pp. 2–39.

17. In this passage from a letter of 30 December 1585 (*Lettere*, vol. 2, no. 456), Tasso alludes to Cicero's *Academica prior* 2. 29. 94: "etiam a certis et inlustrioribus cohibes adsensum." *Maninconia* was an alternative of *melanconia* or *malinconia* in sixteenth-century Italian; in a letter to the cardinals of the Roman Inquisition Tasso formally classifies himself as a "peccante di umor melanconico" (July 1577; *Lettere*, vol. 1, no. 98). Tasso's well-publicized case of madness contributed considerably to contemporary speculations about, and representations of, the psychic disorder said, by Aristotle, to be characteristic of geniuses. See Brand, *Torquato Tasso*, pp. 206 ff. for a discussion of works such as *Tasso's Melancholy*, a play, now lost, which was performed in London in 1594 and revived in 1602, the year *Hamlet* was first performed. The best general introduction to Renaissance theories of melancholy remains Erwin Panofsky's pages on Dürer's *Melancholia I* in *The Life and Art of Albrecht Dürer*, pp. 156 ff. For a fascinating analysis of the relation between melancholy and bourgeois social structures see Wolf Lepenies, *Melancholie und Gesellschaft*.

18. *Civilization and Its Discontents*, SE 21: 66–67; on the idea of God as an exalted father see ibid., p. 74; and *Totem and Taboo*, SE 13: 140–61.

19. This section (*Apologia*, pp. 628–44) is the only part of the treatise where Tasso uses a first-person narrative; it is as if he can write *in propria persona* only when his subject is another person—or ostensibly so. For as Eugenio Donadoni remarks, Tasso's defense of his father—a gesture of "filial piety" according to statements both in the *Apologia* and in a letter of 5 September 1585 (*Lettere*, vol. 2, no. 409)—was in truth "un espediente dialogico, più che un convincimento; era una copertura, dietro la quale il Tasso poteva introdursi a parlare di sè" (*Torquato Tasso*, p. 369).

20. See Weinberg's description (*History of Literary Criticism*, 1: 307 ff.) of the views held by Jesuit critics like Lorenzo Gambara and Francesco Panicarola. Gambara, in particular, seems important for Tasso; in his *Tractatio de perfectae poëseos ratione* (1576), he apologizes for writing profane poetry in his youth and condemns poets who mix sacred matters with profane ones. Moreover, he defines a Christian Republic of letters that will admit only those poems which deal with the holy crusades, the spreading of faith, and the conquest of Jerusalem.

21. Pellegrino, a canon of Capua, published his dialogue in November 1584, promising "to put an end, at least in part, to the question which occupies not only the multitude but even very serious men, as to which has achieved a greater degree of honor in epic poetry, Ludovico Ariosto or Torquato Tasso" (quoted in Weinberg, *History of Literary Criticism*, 2: 991). Far from ending what must have been, as Weinberg remarks, a sizable, if chiefly oral, quarrel, Pellegrino's dialogue precipitated a new phase in the controversy that lasted until the end of the century. Pellegrino renewed the war by collecting opinions about Ariosto that went back to the 1550s and juxtaposing them with opinions about Torquato and Bernardo Tasso that had been in the air since *Gerusalemme Liberata* was published in 1581. By expressing a clear preference for Tasso, Pellegrino offended the Cruscans and provoked them to publish Salviati's defense of the Florentine Ariosto. My quotations from both pamphlets—the latter of which was originally published as a so-called multiple text, in the form of glosses on the speeches of Pellegrino's two dialogic characters—are from Giorgio Rosini's 1827 edition of *Opere colle controversie*, vol. 18. In a challenge to the eye and the mind almost as great as that offered by the sixteenth-century

multiple texts themselves, Rosini prints sentences from Pellegrino's pamphlet at the top of each page and, beneath them, not only the glosses of the Cruscans but also replies by Pellegrino and, in turn, by Salviati. For a discussion of the "multiple" or "cumulative" text, see Weinberg, *History of Literary Criticism*, 2: 1004. This early phenomenon of the Gutenberg age, which allowed a critic like Salviati to reprint a precursor's text for his own purposes and thereby become, as Weinberg says, "a kind of additional interlocutor" in it, deserves more study, particularly in the light of Bakhtin's theoretical work on the phenomenon he calls *heteroglossia*. For the meaning of that term, see Michael Holquist's superb introduction to the collection of Bakhtin's essays called *The Dialogic Imagination*, especially pp. xvii-xx.

22. See *Apologia*, p. 630, where Tasso insists that he be allowed to defend his father not because such a defense is commanded "da le leggi ateniesi, come disse già Socrate, o da le romane, ma da quelle della natura, che sono eterne." The allusion to Socrates points obliquely to Tasso's doubts about his argument here, and about his entire project of defending a man who was not, as we shall see, wholly innocent in his son's eyes. For in a famous passage of the *Gorgias* (480b-d) Socrates argues that the philosopher's law of truth should take precedence over family loyalties. Tasso alludes to this passage in a dialogue about his father, *Il Gonzaga overo del piacere onesto* (to be discussed below), and also in Book 2 of the *Discorsi*; the latter passage provides a particularly interesting gloss on Tasso's defense of Bernardo and the ethical dilemmas which confront him as he tries to play the three somewhat incompatible roles of poet, orator, and philosopher devoted to the truth: "Si biasma il poeta che faccia nascere la compassione sovra persona che volontariamente abbia macchiate le mani nel sangue del padre . . . ma a l'oratore si concede la difesa del colpevole, come fu opinione di Quintiliano . . . non parlo de' filosofi: perché portaranno contraria opinione, essendo lecito (come si legge nel *Gorgia* di Platone) che l'amico accusi l'amico, o il parente il parente" (*Prose*, p. 517).

23. See *Opere colle controversie*, 18: 80.

24. For Bernardo's and Ariosto's "partial" perfection, see *Opere colle controversie*, 18: 54-55; for praise of Tasso, see pp. 193-94.

25. For the relevant passages on unity in both versions of the *Discorsi*, see *Prose*, pp. 372 ff. and 573 ff. See also Durling's fine discussion of Tasso's views on unity in *The Figure of the Poet*, pp. 200-10.

26. See *Apologia*, p. 634 and the comments on this passage in Quint, "Figure of Atlante," pp. 85-86; and Weinberg, *History of Literary Criticism*, 2: 1010-11.

27. In attempting to show the connections between the strands of autobiographical allegory in Tasso's epic and those in his prose works, I am building on the work of many critics in what might (broadly speaking) be called the Romantic tradition of Tasso interpretation. From Leopardi, Goethe, and Freud through Donadoni, Ulrich Leo, and, more recently, Robert Durling, and Giorgio Petrocchi (*I Fantasmi di Tancredi*), readers have sought "the figure(s) of the poet" in Tasso's writing. Such a search necessarily muddies the waters which Michael Murrin wants to purify in his provocative recent works of "historicist" criticism, *The Veil of Allegory* and *The Allegorical Epic*. See p. xi of the latter for Murrin's sweeping rejection of "the modern or romantic definition of allegory" which, following C. S. Lewis, Murrin polemically formulates as "the play of personifications which express our passions"; see also his informative but, in my view, finally unhistorical chapter on the enchanted woods episodes in *Gerusalemme Liberata* (pp. 87-127). Rather than consider the specific biographical and social circumstances which shape the allegorical meaning of these episodes, Murrin interprets them solely according to the set of abstract and doctrinally orthodox terms Tasso provided in the prose allegory he added to his epic—at least in part to avoid censorship—in 1575.

28. For a discussion of the scholarly debates on the meaning of *hamartia* see Gerald F. Else, *Aristotle's "Poetics,"* pp. 376-83. See also W. K. Wimsatt and Cleanth Brooks, *Literary Criticism*, pp. 39-44; as they point out, the etymological meaning of *hamartia* is "the missing of a mark with bow and arrow, an unskillful but not morally culpable act"; they also note, however,

that the term means "sin" in the New Testament. This meaning is obviously compatible with the "moral flaw" theory which some modern scholars maintain and which Else attacks in his commentary.

29. Maranta's *Lucullianae quaestiones*, a massive study of Virgil's epic plot and characterizations in the light of Aristotle's *Poetics*, is discussed in Weinberg, *History of Literary Criticism*, 1: 493-94; I quote (and translate) from a passage cited on p. 493.

30. For a particularly interesting example of the latter type of charge, see *Apologia*, p. 678, where Tasso criticizes as a "luogo sospetto" some lines from *Orlando Furioso* 41. 43; the objection, at once formal and doctrinal, is that Ariosto attributes Christian beliefs to the Muslim king Agramante.

31. Quoted from Mark Musa's bilingual edition of *The Prince*, pp. 144-45. Although *The Prince* was not published until 1532, manuscript copies of it circulated after its completion in 1513. It is therefore possible that Ariosto read it before publishing the 1516 edition of *Orlando Furioso*.

32. See *Orlando Furioso* 38. 83, where Charlemagne says: "io prometto subito la triegua/incominciar, che poi perpetua segua"; his words are echoed by Agramante in stanza 85: "e perpetua tra lor triegua saria." All quotations in Italian from *Orlando Furioso*, except for those taken directly from Tasso's text, are from the edition of Dino Provenzal (1955).

33. See, for example, the discussion of situations when promises are *not* to be kept in *De officiis* 1. 10, pp. 32-33 of the Loeb edition. Cicero's treatise, which takes the form of a letter from Cicero to his son Marcus and which uses the father-son relationship as the basis for many of its examples of ethical (and unethical) behavior, is an important influence not only on the *Apologia* but on Tasso's *Del piacere onesto* dialogue, discussed below. In his dialogue, Tasso alludes explicitly to Cicero's attempts to adjudicate the competing claims of the *utile* and the *onesto* (see *Dialoghi*, ed. Ezio Raimondi, 3: 217).

34. *De officiis* 1. 7, pp. 26-27. The fragment from Ennius comes, scholars speculate, from his lost tragedy *Thyestes*.

35. *Apologia*, p. 641. The lines Tasso omits are, "ch'oltre che si spera/di racquistar Belgrado, e soggiugarsi/ogni contrada che de' Bulgari era;/disegna." All translations are from Guido Waldman's excellent prose version of the *Orlando Furioso*. The passage quoted above is from p. 545.

36. See *Apologia*, p. 633, for Tasso's paradoxical use of the phrase "nuova gloria" to describe a poet who was older than Bernardo Tasso.

37. "Tasso's Epic," p. 266.

38. On the Tasso family see Solerti, *Vita*, 1: 1; and Williamson, *Bernardo Tasso*, pp. 1-3.

39. Bernardo, for instance, not only offended his patron the Prince of Salerno by refusing to live in Venice, where he could best further the Prince's dealings with French agents, but also wrote the Prince an extremely rude letter about the matter. See Brand, *Torquato Tasso* p. 25; and *Lettere inedite di Bernardo Tasso*, ed. G. Campori, no. 15.

40. See Williamson, *Bernardo Tasso*, pp. 7-8.

41. Ibid., p. 9.

42. On the origins of the suit, see ibid., p. 10; on Tasso's pursuit of it, see Solerti, *Vita*, 1: 584, 592-93, 752; and Torquato Tasso, *Lettere*, vol. 4, no. 944. Written in December 1587, to Filippo Spinelli, this letter provides a useful gloss on Tasso's theoretical concern with breaches of familial duty: the "nipoti di mia madre," he complains, care more for "la robba inguistamente e crudelmente posseduta, che del parentado e de l'amicizia."

43. Brand, *Torquato Tasso*, p. 27

44. Tasso's sister was born in 1536 or 1537; according to Solerti's pleasantly vague surmise (*Vita*, 1: 4), the brother also named Torquato arrived "dopo alquanto tempo" and died toward the end of 1542.

45. See *Gerusalemme Liberata* 12. 90, where Tasso gives an autobiographical resonance to

the traditional image of the plaining bird by making it lament not its beloved mate (the usual note on the stanza cites Virgil's *Georgics* 4. 465–66) but only its children, stolen by a "villan duro." See Bruno Maier's edition of *Gerusalemme Liberata*, *Opere*, 3: 424. All quotations from the epic are from this edition, which uses the same text (based on the B_2 MS) which Lanfranco Caretti uses for his critical edition of the poem, in *Tutte le poesie di Torquato Tasso* (Milan and Naples, 1963), vol. 1. Translations of *Gerusalemme Liberata* are usually taken from the Capricorn reprint of Edward Fairfax's *Jerusalem Delivered* (1600), though, when more precise renderings are necessary, I have supplied them.

46. Tasso's lyric description of the moment when he lost his mother ("me dal sen de la madre empia fortuna/pargoletto divelse") is in a canzone called "O del grand'Apennino," which is quoted and discussed below. For a brief account of Don Pedro's attempt to establish the Inquisition, see Williamson, *Bernardo Tasso*, pp. 14–15; see also G. A. Summonte, *Historia della città e regno di Napoli*, vol. 5, bk. 10, pp. 278–311; and Pietro Giannone, *Istoria civile del regno di Napoli*, vol. 4, bk. 32, ch. 5, pp. 88–99; and Henry Charles Lea, *The Inquisition in the Spanish Dependencies*, pp. 70 ff.

47. Rosario Villari comments on the earlier uprisings in Naples in his "The Insurrection in Naples of 1585," in *The Late Italian Renaissance*, ed. E. Cochrane pp. 305–30. For more details on the events of 1547, see Luigi Amabile, *Il Santo Officio della Inquisizione in Napoli*, 1: 200–11. Did Tasso know of the popular unrest in Naples, which was building throughout the spring of 1585, when he wrote the *Apologia*? It is possible, since he corresponded with a number of Neapolitans, including his sister; in April of 1585, moreover, he was attempting to find employment for his nephew Antonio, who had been banished from the kingdom for reasons scholars have not been able to determine; see Solerti, *Vita*, 2: 400–01; and Torquato Tasso, *Lettere*, vol. 2, no. 358. It is, however, equally possible that Tasso did not receive news in prison about the current political events in Naples; none of his letters from the period mentions those events.

48. Tasso's choice of the crusade as his epic topic was of course overdetermined: as Brand remarks, "the Christian-Turkish struggle was very much in people's minds following the expedition of Charles V against Tunis, in which Bernardo Tasso had taken part"; moreover, various histories of the crusades had recently been published, including William of Tyre's in 1549. Poems like Trissino's *Italia liberata dai Goti* and Bonsignori's *Liberazione di Terra Santa* also influenced Tasso's choice. See Brand's chapter, "The Epic: Preparation," *Torquato Tasso*, pp. 53–78.

49. Thomas Greene, *The Descent from Heaven*, p. 208.

50. See Donadoni's descriptions of Tasso as the "official moralist" of the Counter-Reformation and as a representative of "typical aristocratic and political ideas," *Torquato Tasso*, pp. 321, 489–90, 501.

51. For a useful survey of Tasso's critical comments on the *Aeneid*, see Giorgio Petrocchi, "Virgilio e la Poetica del Tasso," in *I Fantasmi di Tancredi*, pp. 83–117. I disagree, however, with Petrocchi's view that Tasso the "counter-reformationist" approved wholly of Aeneas's decision to kill Turnus "turbator de la pace e de la quiete pubblica" (ibid., p. 87). The man who had himself been imprisoned for disturbing the peace and who knew he was seen by many as a "ribello contro il principe mio signore" (*Lettere*, vol. 2, no. 123), was not incapable of questioning official judgments, whether they were Aeneas's or Alfonso d'Este's.

52. See Villari, "The Insurrection in Naples," p. 307.

53. For a discussion of the economic factors behind the insurrection see ibid., pp. 311–12.

54. Ibid., p. 308. See also Amabile's remark, in *Il Santo Officio* (1: 210), that the nobles spent the days fraternizing with the people and the nights paying homage to the viceroy. In his *Del piacere onesto* dialogue, Tasso has his father adopt an aristocratic perspective on the dangers of popular revolt and portray Sanseverino as a prince attempting to "quell the fury of the plebians" (*Dialoghi*, 3: 206).

55. *Il Santo Officio*, 1: 202.

56. See Williamson, *Bernardo Tasso*, p. 15; and Amabile, *Il Santo Officio*, 1: 204–05.

57. See Williamson, *Bernardo Tasso*, p. 16; and also C. Carucci, *Ferrante Sanseverino, Principe di Salerno*, pp. 87–93.

58. His decision to go to France was no doubt influenced by the fact that when he asked Charles for a safe conduct to Augsburg, Charles "replied that he was not accustomed to bargain with his vassals" (Williamson, *Bernardo Tasso*, p. 16; see also Brand, *Torquato Tasso*, p. 5). The threatened invasion of Naples by a French-Turkish force following a renegade Italian baron undoubtedly influenced Tasso's later representations of Turkish-Christian conflict. It is worth noting that in 1552 Bernardo Tasso actually went to Constantinople to enlist Soliman II in the plot to attack Naples (Williamson, *Bernardo Tasso*, p. 18).

59. Quoted from Brand, *Torquato Tasso*, p. 5 (the translation is mine); see also Williamson, *Bernardo Tasso*, p. 16; and Summonte, *Historia di Napoli*, 4: 243, which reprints the text of the sentence against Sanseverino.

60. Brand, *Torquato Tasso*, pp. 5–6; see also Williamson, *Bernardo Tasso*, pp. 16–17, on Bernardo's view of his actions as motivated solely by the code of honor.

61. See Sutherland, *On, Romanticism*, p. 264. For a discussion of the theory that Porzia's brothers poisoned her to get control of her dowry, see Solerti, *Vita*, 1: 21, and 2, pt. 2, no. 9, a letter from Bernardo stating his suspicions about his wife's death. Solerti thinks the suspicions are justified, but he draws no connection between them and Tasso's later fears—in effect, paranoid delusions—that he was being poisoned by his doctors. See Brand, *Torquato Tasso*, p. 19; and Torquato Tasso, *Lettere*, vol. 1, no. 97, especially pp. 253–54.

62. Quoted from Maier's edition of Tasso's *Rime*, in *Opere* 1: 582, ll. 27–28. Rachel Jacoff and David Quint kindly advised me on problems of translating this poem. For the legend of Parthenope, see G. Wissowa et al., eds., *Pauly's Real-Encyclopaedie der klassischen altertums Wissenschaft*, 18: 1934; the city of Naples itself originally bore Parthenope's name and was frequently characterized as sharing something of her personality: see *Metamorphoses*, 15. 711–12, where Ovid uses the phrase "in otia natam/Parthenopem" to describe the temptation that the city of Naples (like Dido's Carthage) represents for the Rome-bound hero Aeneas.

63. See ll. 29–30: "così avuto v'avessi o tomba o fossa/a la prima percossa!"

64. See Book 11 of the *Aeneid*, especially ll. 498–596.

65. Quoted from *New Introductory Lectures*, SE 22: 62; Freud goes on in this lecture ("Dissection of the Personality") to describe the superego as not merely the "successor" of the "parental agency" but "actually the legitimate heir of its body."

66. See *Gerusalemme Liberata* 13. 39. The detail of the hieroglyphic warning, which calls attention to the opacities of written language, is original with Tasso; previous treatments of the bleeding tree episode (in Virgil, Dante, Boccaccio, and Ariosto) focus on the issue of speech but not of writing.

67. The *Risposta del S. Torquato Tasso, Alla lettera di Bastian Rossi, Academico della Crusca, In difesa del suo Dialogo del piacere honesto* appeared in October, three months after the *Apologia* was published. As there is no modern edition of this text, I quote from the one in Rosini's edition of Tasso's *Opere colle controversie*, vol. 10. The passage quoted above is from p. 147.

68. For details about the battles analyzed in and provoked by the *Del piacere onesto* dialogue, see pp. 79–80 and notes 73 and 74, below.

69. Tasso's theory and practice of dialogue are deeply influenced by the fact that he was writing while imprisoned and ill with a disease that involved, among other symptoms, hearing voices he sometimes defines as products of his own imagination and, at other times, as demons invading his mind from outside. See, for an example of his ambiguous views on the "spirit" (*folletto*) whose conversations with him are described in the dialogue *Il Messagiero*, the letter of 30 December 1585 to Cataneo (*Lettere*, vol. 2, no. 456). See also in this connection Brand's

remarks on the relation between dialogue and "split personality" in *Torquato Tasso*, p. 181. *L'arte del dialogo*, written almost simultaneously with the *Apologia*, is available in *Prose*, pp. 331–46. For a useful discussion of the relation between this treatise and works like Speroni's *Apologia dei dialoghi* (ca. 1574–75) and Sigonio's *De dialogo liber* (1564), see Guido Baldassarri, "L'Arte del dialogo in Torquato Tasso," *Studi Tassiani* 20 (1970): 5–46.

70. See *Marxism and the Philosophy of Language*, chap. 2, "Exposition of the Problem of Reported Speech," especially pp. 116–17, where Voloshinov discusses the notion that "the real unit of language that is implemented in speech . . . is not the individual, isolated monologic utterance, but the interaction of at least two utterances, in a word, dialogue." Michael Holquist argues persuasively that this work was written by Bakhtin rather than by Voloshinov; see Holquist's introduction to *The Dialogic Imagination*, p. xxvi, and also pp. xx–xxi, on Bakhtin's general view of the radical alterity which characterizes language and makes it a phenomenon the individual can never fully appropriate.

71. See *Apologia*, p. 635, where Tasso personifies his father's poem as a hero like Cyrus, who having conquered Persia is fighting, now, with his brother (Pulci's *Morgante*). "Why do you contend with me?" Cyrus-Bernardo asks, in a truly bizarre instance of Tassesque ventriloquism. "Because I am richly dressed, and you poorly? Do you not know that these riches were acquired with valor, and will defend themselves with strength [*virtù*], and your poverty is certainly an argument for your small strength?"

72. The reason which triumphs here is a highly paradoxical phenomenon which is not at all the opposite of passion; insofar as Tasso uses words (*logoi*) to treat his psychic problems, however, he remains in the fragile realm which both philosophers and psychiatrists have traditionally defined in terms of restraint of passion. Consider, in this connection, Lacan's wry remark: "In itself, dialogue seems to involve a renunciation of aggressivity; from Socrates onwards, philosophy has always placed its hope in the triumph of reason. And yet ever since Thrasymachus made his stormy exit at the beginning of the *Republic*, verbal dialectic has all too often proved a failure" ("Aggressivity in Psycho-analysis," *Ecrits*, p. 11).

73. For a discussion of this complex compositional history and the problems which the various manuscripts of the dialogue pose for the modern editor, see Raimondi's introduction, *Dialoghi*, 1: 18–23, 80–102. I focus chiefly on the first version of the dialogue, the only one published in Tasso's lifetime, because it was written with less fear of offending either Florentine literary critics or a noble patron than later versions were. All quotations of *Del piacere onesto* are from Raimondi's critical edition in *Dialoghi*, 3: 169–296.

74. Rossi's letter (which is reprinted in *Opere colle controversie*, 10: 76–135) was evidently prompted not only by Florentine patriotism (what Freud calls "the narcissism of minor differences") but also by a desire to justify the Cruscan attack on Tasso's epic, an attack which had been widely criticized for its cruelty (see Solerti, *Vita*, 1: 423–425).

75. When the *Del piacere onesto* dialogue was published in 1583 (ironically, in a form that Tasso had not approved), it so offended the Florentine ambassador to Ferrara that a diplomatic incident was barely averted; see Solerti, *Vita*, 1: 423.

76. See Bibring's "The Conception of the Repetition Compulsion," *Psychoanalytic Quarterly* 12 (1943): 487 and, for the idea of "working-off mechanisms," p. 502. Daniel Lagache develops that idea in an article that attempts to mediate between the theories of American ego-psychologists and those of Jacques Lacan. Drawing a more subtle distinction between the ego and the id than Bibring does (and acknowledging, as Bibring does not, the concept of an "unconscious" portion of the ego), Lagache uses the notion of "working-off mechanisms" to account for the resolution of defensive conflict, especially in the therapeutic situation. See "La Psychanalyse et la structure de la personnalité," *La Psychanalyse* 6 (1961): 5–58.

77. In "Remembering, Repeating, and Working Through" (1914), Freud is relatively optimistic about the possibility of effecting a cure through the "transference neurosis" (see *SE* 12: 154). But in *Beyond the Pleasure Principle*, he is less sanguine as he considers the analyst's

endeavor to keep the transference neurosis "within the narrowest limits: to force as much as possible into the channel of memory and to allow as little as possible to emerge as repetition" (*SE* 18: 19). For a subtle analysis of the relation between Freud's concepts of "repeating" (*Wiederholen*) and "remembering" (*Erinnern*), see Jacques Lacan, *The Four Fundamental Concepts of Psycho-Analysis*, pp. 48–52 and passim.

78. These letters were evidently composed and circulated soon after the events of 1547, but they were not published until much later: Bernardo's were published posthumously in 1577 (Williamson, *Bernardo Tasso*, p. 15). See Bernardo's *Lettere di M. Bernardo Tasso*, ed. Anton-Federigo Seghezzi, nos. 307–08; and, for a relatively accessible reprint of Martelli's version of his speech, see Summonte, *Historia di Napoli*, vol. 5, bk. 10, chap. 1, pp. 293–96.

79. See Luther's "*Sendbrief vom Dolmetschen*" (1530), translated as "On Translating: An Open Letter" by C. M. Jacobs in the Philadelphia ed. of Luther's *Works* (5: 10–27); for Vasari's anecdote about Michelangelo's "sleeping Cupid" counterfeit, which concludes with Vasari rejecting the idea that either aesthetic or monetary value should depend on a work's being "antique" (in market terms, unreproducible), see *The Lives of the Artists*, trans. George Bull, p. 323.

80. The discussion of Glaucus begins when the interlocutors see a statue representing him in the garden: *Dialoghi*, 3: 266; Agostino discusses the "virtù imaginatrice" on p. 283.

81. See the letter to Giulio Caria of 7 June 1585 (*Lettere*, vol. 2, no. 387), where Tasso refers to his pride in his *patria*, then says he would glory in it even more if he called it *la mia cara matria*, following the "antique usage" of the Cretans (which Plutarch mentions in the *Moralia* 792F). It is important to Tasso that the linguistic substitution of *matria* for *patria* be sanctioned by an "antique" authority since he is attempting, throughout this letter, to justify verbal practices that have subversive political implications. These practices include the writing of vernacular poetry itself: the letter begins with Tasso insisting that his epic is written not only for "i dotti" (educated, mostly male, upper-class readers) but also for those common people who are in need of doctrinal instruction. As Protestantism had shown all too clearly, however, texts written in the mother tongue for lower-class people—even sacred texts—posed threats to the established order. Hence Tasso knows he is courting danger when he expresses a preference for *la matria*—as a term signifying a place, a language, or a member of the family who should be kept firmly in a subordinate place.

82. For the equation between Charles V and Caesar Augustus, see *Del piacere onesto* (p. 175) and the *Risposta* (p. 152); on p. 143 of the latter work Tasso discusses and ranks the "species of sedition."

83. This traditional use of the body politic metaphor occurs in *Risposta*, p. 144; see also *Del piacere onesto*, p. 206, on Sanseverino's duty (as defined by Bernardo) to bring "health and quiet" to the city.

84. See the essay "The Intellectuals" in *Selections from the Prison Notebooks*, especially pp. 12–13; see also the discussion of the status of intellectuals in A. Fiorato, "Bandello et le règne du Père," *Les Ecrivains et le pouvoir en Italie à l'epoque de la Renaissance*, 2: 77–154.

85. On the constraints of the patronage system see Lauro Martines, *Power and Imagination*, especially pp. 302 ff.

86. *Risposta*, p. 147; the phrase "victorious Emperor" places this passage squarely within a Machiavellian line of realistic vision: it is wrong to rebel against the emperor, not because he is good or because he is one's feudal overlord, but rather because he is, at the moment, Fortune's favorite.

87. Williamson, *Bernardo Tasso*, p. 15, n. 68.

88. A student of the Averroist Nicoletto Vernia at Padua, Nifo later wrote a refutation, at Pope Leo X's request, of Pomponazzi's arguments against the immortality of the soul. In an unpublished annotated translation of Tasso's *Nifo*, Carnes Lord observes that Nifo's change of philosophical position may have been due either to conviction or to ambition (n. 3). I have

benefited greatly from being able to see Lord's work on the *Nifo*. On Tasso's irregularities not only of belief but of behavior during his student days in Padua and Bologna, see Brand, *Torquato Tasso*, pp. 9–11; and Solerti, *Vita*, 1: 85–90. Solerti's account of Tasso's brush with the Bolognese police for reciting defamatory verses—an episode which resulted in Tasso's writing a self-defense and calling himself "Il Pentito" when he returned to Padua—suggests that the alternation between transgression and repentance that characterizes his later career began during that "età giovanile" he describes, in the *Apologia*, as a sinful period devoted to the "sweet food of the intellect" (p. 675).

89. On the epic narrator's sympathy for an erring hero like Tancredi, see pp. 128–29.

90. "Ma sì com'elli avvien, s'un cibo sazia/e d'un altro rimane ancor la gola,/che quel si chiede e di quel si ringrazia,/così fec' io con atto e con parola." (*Paradiso* 3. 91–94; quoted from *La Divina Commedia*, Charles H. Grandgent, p. 681. All quotations are from this edition; English translations are from the bilingual edition translated by John D. Sinclair.)

91. Ficino's translation of Plato's *Dialogues* (1484) included "Il Convito," which partly inspired the creation of the Florentine Platonic Academy. Many critics have seen that elegant setting for dialogue as inspired also by Cosimo and Lorenzo di Medici's desire to encourage intellectuals to adapt to oligarchical government, which drastically curtailed their chances of playing an active role in politics. See J. H. Plumb, *The Italian Renaissance*, pp. 56–57; and Eugenio Garin, *Italian Humanism*, p. 78.

92. See *Del piacere onesto*, p. 243, where Agostino suggests that the Sanseverino faction displeases the emperor in the same way that the German Protestants did when they refused to submit to imperial laws. Sanseverino did have Protestant sympathies; he fought on the side of the Huguenots in the French religious wars.

93. See ibid., pp. 243–44, for the fulsome praise of Gonzaga, an illustrious general who was in the Spanish service and hence, as Agostino remarks, not "inimico al viceré né sospetto all'imperatore." See also Tasso's poem, *La Genealogia della serenissima Casa Gonzaga*, in *Opere*, vol. 4, especially pp. 404–07, on Ferrante, his son Cesare (who died in 1575), and his grandson Ferrante (1563–1630). The references to the Gonzagas both in the dialogue and in the framing dedication create a strange counterpoint to Tasso's meditation on his own father. When he asks Ferrante for permission to "renovate the memory of your father as a young man" (in the dedication, *Dialoghi*, vol. 2, pt. 1, p. 157), we see that Ferrante has become an idealized double of Tasso himself; we also see that the Gonzaga family in general becomes a focus not only of Tasso's desires for patronage but also of his fantasies about belonging to a noble family superior to his natural one.

94. See *Il Nifo, overo del piacere*, in *Dialoghi*, 2: 159–245. Tasso replaces the debate about Glaucus in *Del piacere onesto* with a philosophical discussion (pp. 224–45).

95. I am indebted to Rachel Jacoff for calling the echo of *Inferno* 12 to my attention. Tasso marked the phrase "ove le due nature son consorti" in his copy of the *Commedia* (see *Postille di Torquato Tasso poste all'edizione del Sessa*, in *Opere colle controversie*, 30: 36); he also wrote a substantial marginal comment on line 12 of this canto which indicates his interest in defining the precise relation between the sins of violence, bestiality, and fraud. My hypothesis that Tasso links Chiron with Glaucus because he is particularly concerned with the poet's power to teach virtue or vice is supported by a passage in Benvenuto da Imola's commentary on *Paradiso* 1. Benvenuto draws an elaborate parallel between Dante the poet, who captures his readers with words, and Glaucus, who once captured fish. (Cited in Paget Toynbee, *A Dictionary of Proper Names and Notable Matters in the Works of Dante*, p. 329.)

96. The phrase occurs twice in the *Commedia*, in *Paradiso* 33. 142 and *Purgatorio* 17. 25–26; Tasso quotes both passages in Book 2 of the *Discorsi* (*Prose*, pp. 530–31) in a passage that provides a useful gloss on the defense of poetry Tasso implicitly conducts, with Dante's aid, in *Del piacere onesto*. In the *Discorsi*, Tasso cites Dante to prove that there exists such a thing as "la imaginazione intellectuale," a "high" form of imagination which Plato wrongly refused to

recognize in his attacks on poets and Sophists. For an excellent discussion of Renaissance theories of imagination (with a full bibliographical survey of work on the topic), see Guillory, "Poetry and Authority," chap. 1.

97. *Aminta* 1. 2. 680–81: quoted from the edition of Bruno Maier, *Opere*, 1: 125.

98. See Voloshinov [Bakhtin], *Marxism and the Philosophy of Language*, p. 121.

99. See *Discorsi del poema eroico*, Book 3, where Tasso grants that Ariosto's epic delights audiences more than Trissino's or even Homer's epics, but denies that a "multitude of actions" is inherently more apt to please than a "unified" plot (*Prose*, p. 587). See also Durling's discussion of Tasso's views on this issue in *The Figure of the Poet*, especially pp. 201, 205.

100. *Peregrino*, also spelled *pellegrino*, cannot easily be translated, since it means not only "pilgrim" but also "wanderer," "stranger," and "exile." Another facet of meaning is suggested by Tasso's later use of the phrase *nomi peregrini* to refer, specifically, to metaphorical terms, following Cicero's definition of such terms as "those which are transferred and placed, as it were, in an alien place" ("eis quae transferuntur et quasi alieno in loco collocantur" [*De oratore* 3. 37; Loeb ed. vol. 2, pp. 118–19]). See *Apologia*, pp. 691 and 707, where Tasso defends himself against various critical attacks on his use of *nomi peregrini*. Cf. also the discussion of *nomi peregrini* in *Discorsi del poema eroico*, bk. 4, in *Prose*, pp. 637 ff.

101. Cf. Tasso's discussion of the father's duty to prefer his family to his business in the dialogue *Il Padre di famiglia*, in *Prose*, pp. 116–18; Tasso is specifically concerned with the merchant's business, which involves the "unnatural" practice of usury and which often takes the man "to distant lands," making him "forget his house and children and wife." Not only is there a striking parallel between this passage and the one in the *Risposta* where Tasso laments his father's flight to France; there are also some interesting parallels between the merchant's mode of life, as Tasso describes it, and the courtier's: neither is a genuine "producer" according to the categories of Aristotle's *Economics* and both must be expert in the "correspondences that cities have with cities and provinces with provinces" (*Il padre*, p. 117). Neither, moreover, is tied to the land or to his family, and both—like the poet—make their living from the process Tasso calls *trasmutazione*.

102. For examples of Tasso's concern with his opponent's absence, see *Apologia*, pp. 647, 681, 684.

103. See *Lettere*, vol. 2, no. 532, and, for a discussion of Tasso's plans to revise his epic, Brand, *Torquato Tasso*, pp. 123–24. As Brand remarks, some of the changes in the *Conquistata* reflect statements of intention Tasso made as early as 1575 in letters to his Roman critics; but even if the 1581 edition of the *Liberata* did not accurately represent Tasso's intentions of 1575, it was not until 1585 that he contemplated a full-scale revision of the poem, prompted, perhaps, by the Cruscan attack.

104. For examples of such insults see *Apologia*, pp. 666–67, where Tasso quotes passages from Salviati describing the *Liberata* as "un poema asciutto e povero," an object that resembles one of those peasant huts built in modern Rome on the sites of once magnificent buildings like Diocletian's Baths. A useful summary of the charges against Tasso's poem appears in Orazio Lombardelli's *Discorso intorno a i contrasti che si fanno sopra la Gierusalemme Liberata* (published in October 1585); Weinberg, *History of Literary Criticism*, reprints Lombardelli's list of accusations (2: 1026).

105. Austin, "Plea for Excuses," p. 176.

106. Ibid., pp. 176–77.

107. See *Apologia*, pp. 670–71, for Tasso's effort to distinguish between the good and the bad type of marvel; see also the passages in bk. 2 of the *Discorsi* where Tasso alludes specifically to Plato's *Sophist* to refute Mazzoni's view that poetic imitation is "fantastic" (*Prose*, pp. 524–25). For a general discussion of Tasso's contribution to the debate about the "Christian marvelous," see Baxter Hathaway, *Marvels and Commonplaces*, especially chap. 4.

108. See *Apologia*, p. 644, for the moment where Tasso has the priest encourage and even

command him to respond to the critics. For a subtle discussion of features of Tasso's self-defensive style—his habit of using "concessive" interpolated phrases, for instance—see Ulrich Leo, *Torquato Tasso*, especially chapters 5 and 8.

109. Fantini's metaphor of clothing oneself in alien material reappears a few pages later in a formulation clearly based on Augustine's famous "accommodation" theory in the *De doctrina Christiana*; in bk. 2, chap. 40, of that work, Augustine sanctions the "use" of pagan literature by comparing Christians to the Israelites who legitimately stole Egyptian gold and clothing when fleeing to the Promised Land. Tasso has Fantini allude to this passage in *Apologia*, p. 697, where the priest remarks that "not only philosophers, but our Greek and Latin fathers have despoiled the gentiles of their beauties and riches, and clothed themselves quite gorgeously in those [stolen goods]."

110. On the link between the Sophists' theory and practice of rhetoric, on the one hand, and ethical relativism, on the other, see W. K. C. Guthrie, *The Sophists*, pp. 269–74 (on Gorgias) and passim. For a useful discussion of the issues at stake in the argument between Socrates and Gorgias on the question of self-defense—an argument of capital importance to Tasso, Sidney, and other Renaissance authors of defenses, including Milton—see James A. Coulter, "The Relation of the *Apology* of Socrates to Gorgias's *Defense of Palamedes* and Plato's Critique of Gorgianic Rhetoric," *Harvard Studies in Classical Philology* 68 (1964): 269–303.

111. Burke, *A Rhetoric of Motives*, p. 282. His definition of the "inferiority complex" differs strikingly, and no doubt deliberately, from that of Alfred Adler, whose "Individual Psychology" is based on the theory that neurosis arises from the perception of inferiority of an organic, morphological, or functional type, which appears in childhood. Freud too criticized Adler's view of inferiority, though not, as Burke implicitly does, for ignoring the *social* factors which cause it. See *SE* 22: 141–42 and, for further bibliographical references, the article on "Sense of Inferiority" in Laplanche and Pontalis, *Language of Psychoanalysis*.

112. It is an irony of Tasso's career that his work was never censored by the Inquisition which so frightened and fascinated him; indeed, persons like the Inquisitor of Ferrara seem not to have taken Tasso's religious beliefs seriously at all, worrying, instead, about the political embarrassment that his zeal for punishment might cause. See Solerti, *Vita*, 1: 260, for an account of the almost farcical episode in which the Ferrarese Inquisitor obliged Duke Alfonso by "feigning" a procedure which would acquit Tasso of the charges of heresy he had made against himself.

113. See the letter to Don Angelo Grillo of 15 March 1585, in which Tasso describes "la vena de l'usato ingegno" as "secca"; (*Lettere*, vol. 2, no. 348); see also his descriptions of himself as "smemorato" and incapable of writing (nos. 262 and 351).

114. There is a further ironic twist to the issue of freedom: Tasso never authorized the title *Gerusalemme Liberata*. When the printer Angelo Ingegneri took the liberty of giving the poem that title in 1581, Tasso was evidently considering naming the poem *Il Goffredo* (as early as 1570 he had referred to it as *Il Gotifredo*) or *Gerusalemme Racquistata*. Ingegneri justified his choice by referring to the model of Trissino's *Italia Liberata* (a model Tasso probably wished to forget) and by remarking—rightly—that the idea of liberating Jerusalem appears often in the epic. Ingegneri's preface is quoted in *Lettere*, vol. 2, no. 181, n. 1; for Tasso's objections to the printer's choice, see no. 220. Solerti, *Vita*, 1: 332–33 discusses the details of the title debates.

115. Greene, *Descent from Heaven*, p. 190. See also Giovanni Getto's chapter "Goffredo e il tema epico religioso," in *Nel mondo del "Gerusalemme*," pp. 9–71; and Ulrich Leo's useful discussion of Goffredo as the central figure, in *Ritterepos-Gottesepos*, pp. 31–40.

116. See Tasso's rather pathetic meditation on the charge that his poem is "sterile e smunto," and on the disturbing confirmation of that charge given by the critics themselves, who have clearly not been seduced by the charms of Tasso's epic: "là dov'egli dovrebbe aver prodotto amore e benevolenza negli animi . . . de' lettori, ha forsi generato in alcuni contraria passione" (*Apologia*, p. 675).

117. See *SE* 18: 16 and, for a survey of Freud's complex statements about the relation between the similar but not identical concepts of an "instinct to master" (*Bemächtigungstrieb*) and "aggressive instinct" (*Aggressionstrieb*), "destructive instinct" (*Destruktionstrieb*), and the (usually plural) "death instincts" (*Todestriebe*), Laplanche and Pontalis, *Language of Psychoanalysis*, pp. 217–19, 16–17, 116–17, 94–104. Jacques Derrida, in *La Carte postale*, and Jean Laplanche, in *Vie et mort en psychanalyse*, offer provocative and detailed commentaries on the pivotal role played by *Beyond the Pleasure Principle* in Freud's thinking about the problem of an aggressive instinct. See also the useful article by Leo Stone, "Reflections on the Psychoanalytic Concept of Aggression," *Psychoanalytic Quarterly* 40 (1971), 195–244.

118. Greene, *Descent from Heaven*, p. 189. Significantly, Tasso revises the first line of his epic to emphasize Goffredo's status as supreme commander. The *Liberata* opens with a Virgilian echo: "Canto l'arme pietose e 'l capitano." The *Conquistata* begins, "Io canto l'arme e 'l cavalier sovrano." The authorial "I" is more insistently present in the second version, as if Tasso's ability to take responsibility for his imaginative creation increases with Goffredo's exaltation. All quotations from the *Conquistata* are from the edition of Luigi Bonfigli.

119. Tasso's hostility toward Ariosto's popularity with princely patrons was caused, I suspect, not only by envy but by an obscure sense that the patronage system was itself a symptom of a larger social problem having to do with what Perry Anderson calls "the deadlock in Italian political development." The lords who usurped power in the republics of the peninsula, as Anderson remarks, "were frequently mercenaries, upstarts or adventurers, while others were elevated bankers or merchants. The sovereignty of the *signoria* was consequently always in a deep sense illegitimate: it rested on recent force and personal fraud, without any collective social sanction in aristocratic hierarchy or duty behind it" (*Lineages*, p. 162).

120. See *Opere colle controversie*, 12: 256, 258.

121. Although Tasso uses the pseudonym "Il Forestiero," usually with the adjective "Napolitano," in other dialogues (such as *Il Beltramo overo de la Cortesia*, and *Il Manso overo de l'Amicizia*), it seems a particularly complex verbal gesture in this text, where questions of personal identity are intimately tied to questions about the epistemological status of the poet's words, his *nomi peregrini*. For some shrewd comments on the significance of Tasso's proto-Romantic gesture of signaling his alienated self, see Donald Sutherland's chapter "Il Forestiero Napolitano," in *On, Romanticism*, pp. 257–301.

122. See the letter to Scipione Gonzaga of 14 May 1575 (*Lettere*, vol. 1, no. 29); note the masochism that colors Tasso's paradoxical phrasing here, as he insists that he will "willingly" force himself to cut words from his poem if Gonzaga commands him to do so: "io mi sforzerò di mitigarle; e ciò farò molto volentieri, perchè, comechè sempre abbia creduto poco al mio giudicio, ora vi credo meno che mai."

123. Ibid., vol. 5, no. 1452.

124. See the letter to Scipione Gonzaga of 1 October 1575 (ibid., vol. 1, no. 47), where Tasso mentions the "many stains" that remain in the last cantos of the *Liberata* and worries, in particular, about the "miracoli del bosco," the enchanted wood episodes, which "spiacerà, e moveranno quasi nausea."

125. *Opere colle controversie*, 12: 261.

126. Ibid., p. 255.

127. On Dante's theory of conversion and its Platonic and Augustinian sources, see the series of brilliant articles by John Freccero, "Dante's Prologue Scene," "Dante's Firm Foot and the Journey without a Guide," and "Infernal Inversion and Christian Conversion."

128. See *Purgatorio* 31. 59 and, for a survey of the scholarly debates about the *pargoletta*, Grandgent's headnote to the canto in his edition of the *Commedia*, pp. 612–14.

129. See *Purgatorio* 30. 43–45 for the simile comparing Virgil to a mother; in l. 50 he is called "dolcissimo patre." The rich play of family metaphors continues when Dante compares his tears at losing Virgil to those shed by "l'antica matre," Eden, at the time of the Fall.

130. In most examples of the metaphor of the book as a child, there is only one child, it is a boy, and the father unequivocally loves it; see E. R. Curtius's survey of the *topos* (which originates, he thinks, with Diotima's speech on Eros in Plato's *Symposium*) in *European Literature*, pp. 132–34. Curtius does mention a few authors who could fruitfully be compared with Tasso from the point of view of a "parental family romance"; one is Agrippa d'Aubigné, who in the prologue to *Les Tragiques* refers disapprovingly to his early work *Le Printemps*, calling it "un pire et plus heureux ainé" (quoted by Curtius, p. 133). None of the texts Curtius cites refer to a book as a female child, but in Henry James's Preface to *The Golden Bowl* there is a passage which strongly implies that the author's "progeny" are of different sexes and not altogether lovable. See *The Art of the Novel*, pp. 337–38, where the "uncanny brood" is described in terms that recall the terrifying children of *The Turn of the Screw*.

131. On Dante's invention of the name Eunoe, see Toynbee's *Dictionary*, pp. 254–55. On Dante's representation of a "gradual" rather than "sudden" type of conversion, and the Thomistic theological doctrine of a "conversion-by-stages," see Charles Singleton, "The Three Conversions," in *Journey to Beatrice*, pp. 39–56.

132. See *Purgatorio* 31. 88–90.

133. *Studies on Hysteria*, SE 2: 42.

134. The most searching study of such quasi-autobiographical, theoretical discourse I have read is Jacques Derrida's in the section of *La Carte postale* entitled "Spéculer—sur 'Freud,'" pp. 277–437. For an English version of this important essay, translated and abridged by James Hurlbert and entitled "Coming into One's Own," see *Psychoanalysis and the Question of the Text*, ed. G. H. Hartman, pp. 114–48.

135. The quotation is from *Apologia*, p. 672, where the secretary remarks, "Nella revisione del vostro poema . . . si aspettavano da voi cose mirabili e conformi a la dottrina delle sacre lettere." For a detailed discussion of the religious allegory which Tasso wrote to "explain" the *Liberata* and which he developed more fully in the *Conquistata*, see Murrin, *The Allegorical Epic*, pp. 87–127. The Prose Allegory is available in vol. 24 of Rosini's edition of the *Opere colle controversie*; an English translation, by Edward Fairfax, is in Henry Morley's edition of *Jerusalem Delivered* (1890). In the *Giudizio* Tasso explicitly defines religious allegory as a means of defense; he does not specify whether it defends the poet against his own tendencies to "vain thoughts" or against his readers' tendencies to discover "false" meanings in the poem: "l'allegoria co' sensi occulti può difendere il poeta dalla vanità, e dalla falsità similmente" (*Opere colle controversie*, 12: 258). On the nature and extent of Tasso's revisions in the *Conquistata*, see Brand, *Torquato Tasso*, pp. 125–32, and his article "Stylistic trends in the *Gerusalemme Conquistata*"; see also Mario Vailati, *Il Tormento artistico del Tasso dal "Liberata" alla "Conquistata,"* which argues (to my mind, unconvincingly) that Tasso's revisions were made chiefly for aesthetic reasons; and Fredi Chiappelli, *Studi sul linguaggio del Tasso epico*, pp. 186–200.

136. See *Aeneid* 6. 824–25: "Quin Decios Drusosque procul saevumque securi/aspice Torquatum." Anchises is showing Aeneas the line of his descendants. The immediate context is significant, for Anchises has just mentioned another man who welded a "cruel axe" in family battles, namely Lucius Junius Brutus; this Brutus is said to have put his sons to death when they attempted to restore the Tarquins to the throne (6. 819–22; pp. 564–65 of the Loeb ed.).

137. *De officiis* 3. 31: "At ille, ut ingressus est, confestim gladium destrinxit iuravitque se illum statim interfecturum, nisi ius iurandum sibi dedisset se patrem missum esse facturum" (pp. 392–93 of the Loeb ed.).

138. Laplanche and Pontalis define identification briefly as the "psychological process whereby the subject assimilates an aspect, property or attribute of the other and is transformed, wholly or partially, after the model the other provides." See *Language of Psychoanalysis*, pp. 205–07, for a discussion of the various shades of meaning which Freud and later psychoanalysts have given the term, and for its close relation to terms such as "imitation," "empathy" (*Einfühlung*), and "introjection." See also Anna Freud's chapter "Identification with the Aggressor" in

The Ego and the Mechanisms of Defense, pp. 109–21; and Robert Koff, "A Definition of Identification," *International Journal of Psychoanalysis* 42 (1961): 362–70.

139. See *SE* 22: 64, *New Introductory Lectures*: "In the course of development the super-ego also takes on the influences of those who have stepped into the place of parents—educators, teachers, people chosen as ideal models." For a discussion of Freud's concept of the superego's development, see Laplanche and Pontalis, *Language of Psychoanalysis*, p. 437.

140. See chapter 3 of *The Ego and the Id* (1923), where Freud discusses the "typical" process whereby an "object cathexis" is replaced by an identification: "It may be that this identification is the sole condition under which the id can give up its objects. At any rate the process, especially in the early phases of development, is a very frequent one, and it makes it possible to suppose that the character of the ego is a precipitate of abandoned object cathexes and that it contains the history of those object choices" (*SE* 19: 28–29).

141. For discussions of the origins of male homosexuality see chapter 7 ("Identification") of *Group Psychology*, *SE* 18: 108–09; chapter 3 of *Leonardo da Vinci* (1910); and the paper "Some Neurotic Mechanisms in Jealousy, Paranoia, and Homosexuality" (1922). In this connection it is worth citing C. P. Brand's opinion that the only signs of erotic attachment to be found in Tasso's letters are in those to the young Orazio Ariosto, nephew of the poet (*Torquato Tasso*, p. 370).

142. See the article "The Oedipus Complex" in Laplanche and Pontalis, *Language of Psychoanalysis*, pp. 282–87, and also the following passage from *The Ego and the Id*: "One gets an impression that the simple Oedipus complex is by no means its commonest form, but rather represents a simplification or schematization which, to be sure, is often enough justified for practical purposes. Closer study usually discloses the more complete Oedipus complex, which is twofold, positive and negative, and is due to the bisexuality originally present in children" (*SE* 19: 33).

143. The story of Sofronia and Olindo (canto 2) is cut, for instance, as is the episode where Erminia finds the wounded Tancredi (canto 19). For detailed descriptions of the changes Tasso made in the *Conquistata*, see Brand, *Torquato Tasso*, p. 125, and Leo, *Ritterepos-Gostesepos*, p. 43. The Bonfigli edition of the *Conquistata* prints Solerti's useful canto-by-canto comparison of the two epics on pp. 385–407 of volume 2.

144. Consider the following passage, from the *Giudizio*, where Tasso praises the quality of the *Conquistata* in terms of its quantity of episodes and characters: "non contento del numero dell'azioni e de' cavalieri contenuti nel primo poema, io ne ho voluto aggiunger molti altri, facendo in questa guisa la tessitura più ampia e più magnifica, siccome panno di seta e d'oro, in cui non solamente sono riguardati i ricami, o le figure maestrevolmente intessute per entro, ma si considera ancora, quanto egli sia lungo, e largo" (*Opere colle controversie*, 12: 324. Getto cites this passage in *Interpretazione del Tasso*, p. 417; he also observes that Tasso's additions include numerous representations of bloodthirsty cruelty, which supports my hypothesis that the *Conquistata* is to a remarkable degree a product of Tasso's superego.)

145. *Opere colle controversie*, 12: 297.

146. As Thomas Greene notes (*Descent from Heaven*, p. 209), Tasso refers to this etymological connection in *Il Messagiero* as if it were a fact; see *Prose*, p. 51.

147. See *Gerusalemme Liberata* 12. 91–93, and *Gerusalemme Conquistata* 15. 104–06 (hereafter abbreviated as *GL* and *GC*). The two versions of the dream are almost identical, which is significant in light of the fact that Tasso is concerned here with the problem of idolatry. Far from turning Tancredi's thoughts toward heaven, the vision of Clorinda in her "splendor celeste" leads him to remember her earthly beauty so intensely that he seeks to recreate it in a funerary statue (*GL* 12. 94; *GC* 15. 107). Like Tancredi, Tasso faces a temptation to idolatry: in revising his epic he may be exhibiting love for the "antica memoria" of his own earlier poem rather than serving God. See *GC* 15. 104: "ma lo splendor celeste/orna, e non toglie la memoria antica." The word *memoria* replaces the less autobiographically resonant *notizie* of *GL* 12. 91.

148. See *GL* 11 and *GC* 14.

149. On the significance of Freud's (mis)reading of the "picture," see p. 126 and n. 156, below.

150. *GL* 13. 42; *GC* 16. 46. I have given my own translation here because Fairfax misses the initial emphasis on excess by rendering the opening lines, "Enough, enough (the voice lamenting said)/Tancred, thou hast me hurt."

151. There are, to be sure, some significant changes in the later version of the bleeding tree episode; see Ulrich Leo's discussion of them in *Torquato Tasso*, pp. 72–76. He rightly observes that the revisions tend to replace highly specific and nuanced representations of mental doubt with abstract descriptions that have the effect of simplifying the hero's experience and distancing the reader from it. Tasso's search for stylistic sublimity and magnificence led him, in Leo's view, to sacrifice his concern with "individualistische Moralproblematik" (p. 75). The issue is not so simple, however, as we see when we note that many of Tasso's revisions seem designed to stress the non-Christian elements of the wood. In *GC* 16. 47, for instance, the phantasmic voice distinguishes between the spirits in the woods and those which await "il suon de la divina tromba"—a phrase absent from the corresponding stanza of the *Liberata* (43). While such changes serve to lessen the reader's initial uncertainty about the religious status of the phantasmic voice, they do not, it seems to me, in any way lessen the force of the epistemological and psychological questions raised in both versions of the episode; on the contrary, the question of what to believe and (for Tancredi) how to act is, if anything, further complicated in the later version by the fact that the phantasm there pays lip service to Christian concepts like the Last Judgment. The truth value of all the phantasm's words is in doubt as soon as she announces her identity—"Clorinda fui"—and thereby contradicts the inference that the Christian reader, like Tancredi, should have drawn from the fact of her deathbed baptism, namely that the "real" Clorinda is in heaven.

152. See *Aeneid* 3, *Inferno* 13, and *Orlando Furioso* 7. Tasso would also have known Boccaccio's version of the story in Book 5 of *Il Filocolo*, although this source is less important for him than the other three.

153. "Deh! se non sei crudel quanto sei forte, / deh! non turbar questa secreta sede" (*GL* 13, 39; *GC* 16. 43). Although it is cumbrous, I shall continue to cite both versions of the poem, since it is important to remind the reader graphically that the quotations appear in two different texts. I shall, however, quote from the text of the *Liberata*, noting any substantive differences between the texts when they occur.

154. "Spiar di novo le cagioni ascose" (*GL* 13. 47; *GC* 16. 51).

155. The quoted phrase is Fairfax's free but inspired interpretation of Peter's doctrinal position when he chides Tancredi for indulging in the *folle colpa* ("mad sin") of loving Clorinda excessively and desiring to commit suicide after her death (*GL* 12. 86–88; *GC* 15. 99–101). Even though Peter classifies the sin as a type of madness, he clearly sees it as a phenomenon that the individual willfully indulges, like a passion, "refusing" the gift of grace God offers: "Rifiuti dunque, ahi sconoscente!, il dono/del Ciel salubre . . ./Misero, dove corri in abbandono/a i tuoi sfrenati e rapidi martiri?" The harshness of Peter's perspective here is underscored by the fact that he has just suggested that God's gift takes the form of a scourge; the death of Clorinda, he says, is a *sciagura* designed to recall Tancredi from his erring ways.

156. On this point see Neil Hertz's brilliant article "Freud and the Sandman," in *Textual Strategies*, pp. 296–321. Hertz begins with a meditation on Freud's remark, "I invented psychoanalysis because it had no literature"—a joke, Hertz suggests, "about what is now lugubriously known as The Burden of the Past or The Anxiety of Influence" (p. 296). Freud's allusion to Tasso is, I believe, inscribed squarely within this "lugubrious" theoretical territory. By mentioning the rhetorical power of Tasso's poem (which provides a "most moving picture"), while at the same time failing to mention those aspects of its theoretical inquiry which most directly relate to his own activity as a writer (Clorinda's status as a phantasm, the simile comparing Tancredi to a sick man), Freud forces us to wonder whether Tasso's poem serves,

here, simply as an *illustration* of a phenomenon which the psychoanalyst discovers and accounts for "scientifically." Moreover, the literary example, the last in a series which offers a rich field for autobiographical speculation, highlights the way in which Freud, like Tasso, is implicated in the phenomena he would somehow control and explain. Among the examples of "normal" people whose lives exhibit the compulsion to repeat, Freud mentions "the benefactor who is abandoned in anger after a time by each of his protégés . . . or the man who time after time in the course of his life raises someone else into a position of great private or public authority and then, after a certain interval, himself upsets that authority and replaces him by a new one" (*SE* 18: 22). It seems fair to surmise that Freud is here speculating indirectly on his own case—and he continues to do so when he borrows a later example of the repetition compulsion from Jung, his most famous erstwhile protégé, and in a laconic footnote refers the reader to Jung's "apt remarks" on the subject (p. 22, n. 1). Freud, I would suggest, is no less concerned than Tasso is about the difficulty of distinguishing a "simulacrum" from an "original" in the competitive arena of literary authority.

157. *Le Tiers Livre*, chap. 44: "soy deffiant de son sçavoir et capacité, congnoissant les antinomies et contrarietez des loix, des edictz, des coustumes et ordonnances; entendent la fraulde du Calumniateur infernal, lequel souvent se transfigure en messagier de lumiere . . . [et] tourne le noir en blanc." *Oeuvres complètes*, ed. Pierre Jourda, 1: 586; English translation from *Gargantua and Pantagruel*, trans. J. M. Cohen, pp. 410–11.

158. It is no accident that Orlando goes mad in canto 23 of a 46-canto epic; the number symbolizes the idea of a whole split in half, like the original beings in Aristophanes' fable in the *Symposium*. The moment when Orlando, enraged, tears trees from their roots and shows that his wits have flown to heaven is anticipated in 23. 82, which describes the shattering of the lances in Orlando's duel with Mandricardo: "Parveno l'aste, al rompersi, di gielo;/e in mille scheggie andàr volando al cielo." For an excellent discussion of canto 23 as the "center of meaning" in the *Furioso*, see A. Bartlett Giamatti, "Headlong Horses, Headless Horsemen: An Essay on the Chivalric Epics of Pulci, Boiardo, and Ariosto," in *Italian Literature*; pp. 265–307.

159. The loss of self signaled in the phrase "va fuor di sé" seems a nightmare version of religious ecstasy (*ec-stasis*). For Tasso, however, the phrase evidently points as well to a condition particularly dangerous for the artist, who must be "self-collected" in order to exercise his imaginative powers. When Tancredi first enters the enchanted woods, he is "in sé ristretto" (*GL* 13. 33; *GC* 16. 37); the phrase recalls the "in sé raccolto" Ariosto uses to describe Orlando before he loses his reason (*Orlando Furioso* 23. 86). Although Tancredi's self-containment here does not preclude spiritual error (he is obsessed with an inner grief for Clorinda), it does allow him to withstand Ismeno's magic creations. Taking Tancredi as a figure of the artist, we see that he loses his "virtù imaginatrice" at the moment when other texts or voices penetrate his consciousness and partly win his belief. Cf. the passage in *Il Messagiero* where Tasso writes that "le forze della virtù imaginatrice sono incredibili; e sebben pare che allora ella sia più possente, quando l'animo non occupata in essercitare i sensi esteriori in sé stessa si raccoglie" (quoted in B. T. Sozzi, *Studi sul Tasso*, p. 320.)

160. *GL* 13. 45; the corresponding lines in *GC* 16. 49 are slightly revised: "va fuor di sé; presente, e quasi in viso,/vede la donna sua che plori e gema."

161. There is another significant echo of the autobiographical lyric in *GL* 12. 57 and *GC* 15. 71, which describe Tancredi's night battle with Clorinda: "Tre volte il cavalier la donna stringe/con le robuste braccia; ed altrettante/da que' nodi tenaci ella si scinge,/nodi di fier nemico e non d'amante." Clorinda here looks very like the mother Tasso laments in the canzone: "oh'io non doveu giunger piu volto a volto/fra quelle braccia accolto/con nodi così stretti e sì tenaci." The scene also recalls the one in *Purgatorio* 2 where Dante thrice attempts to embrace the shade of Casella (79–81). The Dantesque echo is particularly rich, since it implicitly equates both Clorinda and Tasso's mother with the soul who sang to Dante a song from his past—a song he himself had written—and caused him momentarily to forget his

journey, prompting the stern Cato to rebuke him. Tasso alludes again to Casella in *GL* 14. 6, in the description of Goffredo's dream encounter with his dead friend Ugone; the passage is cut from the *Conquistata*, perhaps because it presents Goffredo as being, like Tancredi, too vulnerable to human affections.

162. See *Orlando Furioso* 34. 57, where the old man reveals himself to be "colui che l'evangelio scrisse"; and stanza 86, where he is described as "lo scrittor de l'oscura Apocalisse." The idea that the Gospel of John and Revelation were written by the same person—the Apostle John, son of Zebedee—dates back to the second century A.D. For a discussion of this idea, generally rejected by modern biblical scholars, see *The Interpreter's Bible*, 12: 356–59.

163. As Hannah Arendt observes, the "elaborate system of rewards and punishments for deeds and misdeeds that did not find their just retribution on earth" was not elevated "to the rank of dogmatic certitude" until the fifth century, "when the earlier teachings of the redemption of all sinners, even of Satan himself (as taught by Origen and still held by Gregory of Nyssa), and the spiritualizing interpretation of the torments of hell as torments of conscience (also taught by Origen) were declared to be heretical." This change, she adds, "coincided with the downfall of Rome, the disappearance of an assured secular order . . . and the emergence of the papacy as a temporal power" ("What is Authority?" in *Between Past and Future*, pp. 128–29). Origen was one of the early church fathers most avidly read by Pico della Mirandola and other Renaissance humanists. For an account of the heterodox ideas about salvation which may have influenced Ariosto, see D. P. Walker, *The Decline of Hell*, pp. 11–18.

164. Note the resemblance between John's words and those spoken by Tasso's Peter in *GL* 12. 86 and (with a slight variation of phrasing) in *GC* 15. 99: "non odi i detti suoi,/che ti sgrida e richiama a la smarrita/strada che pria segnasti e te l'addita?" Both authors are of course following not only God's road here but the path signaled in a graphic way by Dante. The difficulty of staying faithfully in the road laid down by someone else's text is, however, dramatized throughout Ariosto's episode, which follows the *Commedia* and the New Testament in the mode of parody ("a song sung beside").

165. See, for instance, *Orlando Furioso* 35. 1, where the narrator asks, "Chi salirà per me, madonna, in cielo/a riportarne il mio perduto ingegno?" Such assertions of human fallibility on the part of the narrator are part of a complex joke, of course, since Ariosto repeatedly calls our attention to the God-like powers he wields as controller of his textual universe. But as Robert Durling rightly observes, Ariosto develops the analogy between God and the poet in a way that dramatizes "his deep sense of the limits of human endeavor"; "if he is a god he is, to use Cusanus's term, a *deus occasionatus*, a contingent god" (*The Figure of the Poet*, p. 132).

166. For a fine and witty analysis of how Ariosto's narrative technique works to train the reader in the art of bearing frustration, see Daniel Javitch, "Cantus Interruptus in the Orlando Furioso," *Modern Language Notes* 95 (1980): 66–80.

167. For this eclectic cure, which alludes to the Antaeus myth and also involves a parodic baptismal ceremony, see *Orlando Furioso* 39. 47–57. Woven into the broad humor of the scene is a serious reflection on the poem itself, as a work of art that in several ways resembles the "arte di risanarlo" Astolfo seeks for Orlando. When the hero is brought under control by ropes with slip knots (*nodi correnti*), we are invited to recall the narrator's famous description of the *varie fila* which make the *varie tele* of his story (2. 30).

168. "L'Ariosto, il quale, lasciando le vestigia de gli antiqui scrittori e le regole d'Aristotele, ha molte e diverse azioni nel suo poema abbracciate, è letto e riletto da tutte l'età, da tutti i sessi, noto a tutte le lingue, piace a tutti, tutti lo lodano, vive e ringiovenisce sempre nella sua fama, e vola glorioso per le lingue de' mortali, ove il Trissino all'incontro, che i poemi d'Omero religiosamente si pensò d'imitare e d'osservare i precetti d'Aristotele, mentovato da pochi, letto da pochissimi, muto nel teatro del mondo e morto alla luce, sepolto a pena ne le librerie e ne lo studio d'alcun letterato si ritrova" (quoted in Getto, *Interpretazione*, p. 422).

169. I am thinking here not only of the *Conquistata* but of *Le Sette giornate del mondo*

creato, which Tasso began in 1592 and completed in the year of his death, 1594. Du Bartas's hexameral poem *La Sepmaine ou création du monde* had appeared in 1578 and Tasso probably knew it, though there is little evidence of direct imitation (see Brand, *Torquato Tasso*, p. 189). *Del Mondo creato* is not a magnificent failure; it is just a failure, a confused amalgam of a host of authorities and a sad commentary on the atrophying of Tasso's creative powers. Milton admired Tasso but he must have quietly rejoiced that his Catholic predecessor had not made great poetry from the subject of God's creation.

170. See *GL* 11. 46 and *GC* 14. 67, where the "most sublime of [Goffredo's] machines" is described as a moving tower "grave d'uomini ed armata." Cf. Virgil's description of the Trojan Horse in *Aeneid* 2. 235–38; his phrase "machina feta armis" seems a direct source for Tasso's passage. This parallel has not to my knowledge been noted, perhaps because critics do not expect Tasso's "virtuous" Christians to resemble Virgil's treacherous Greeks.

171. See *New Introductory Lectures*, *SE* 22: 62, for the superego as the "legitimate heir," and p. 67 of the same work for one of Freud's most interesting attempts to formulate his disagreement with "materialistic views of history," which err, he argues, by "underestimating" the role of the superego in perpetuating tradition. Freud's attack on a vulgar Marxist error in the definition of ideology is worth quoting if only because recent theorists like Fredric Jameson have begun to change our views of psychoanalysis itself by considering it from a sophisticated Marxist perspective which—building on the work of Lacan and Althusser—by no means "underestimates" the role of the unconscious in the formation of ideological structures. Criticizing those who consider ideologies to be "nothing other than the product and superstructure of their contemporary economic conditions," Freud writes that "the past, the tradition of the race and of the people, lives on in the ideologies of the super-ego, and yields only slowly to the influences of the present and to new changes." See Jameson's discussions of psychoanalysis in *The Political Unconscious*, especially pp. 62–68; and see also his article, "Imaginary and Symbolic in Lacan," in *Literature and Psychoanalysis*, pp. 338–95.

172. *Gerusalemme Conquistata* 14. 43. The passage is a striking gloss on Tasso's ironic reference to himself as a "cultore furioso" in *Apologia*, p. 699.

173. See *Discorsi*, bk. 3, for Tasso's argument that Boiardo's and Ariosto's poems may be considered "non come due libri distinti, ma come un poema solo cominciato da l'uno e con le medesime fila, benché meglio annodate e meglio colorite, da l'altro poeta condotto al fine" (*Prose*, p. 569).

174. The full passage about Ariosto and Trissino is quoted above, n. 168.

175. For a discussion of the fate of Tasso's works in England, see Brand, *Torquato Tasso*, pp. 226–308. Tasso's enormous fame in the Romantic period rested almost entirely on the *Liberata*, though the *Aminta* and the lyrics were also admired. This of course represents a critical judgment directly opposed to the one Tasso hoped to win by his argument in the *Giudizio*.

176. Ibid., p. 130.

Chapter IV

1. For a good discussion of the trial scene at the end of the *Old Arcadia* and the critical controversy it has provoked, see Richard McCoy, *Sir Philip Sidney: Rebellion in Arcadia*, pp. 124–37. See also D. M. Anderson, "The Trial of the Princes in the *Arcadia*, Book V," *RES* 8 (1957): 409–12; and Elizabeth Dipple, " 'Unjust Justice' in the *Old Arcadia*," *SEL* 10 (1970): 83–101.

2. The two publishers were Henry Olney, who used the title terms "apologie" and "poetrie," and William Ponsonby, who used the terms "defence" and "poesie." For a description of the edition cited in this chapter, which uses a hybrid title (*A Defence of Poetry*) although it is based on Ponsonby's rather than Olney's text, see below, n. 9.

3. See, for example, Musidorus's address to the judge in *The Countess of Pembroke's*

Arcadia, pp. 402-03; the prince's speech of defense vacillates, as McCoy observes, between "a blustering assertion of his virtue, honor, and services and a grudging admission of 'a venial tresspass' and 'human error'" (*Rebellion in Arcadia*, p. 126). McCoy's chapter "The Pattern of Conflict" draws instructive parallels between the situations of the heroes in *The Lady of May*, *Astrophil and Stella*, and the *Old Arcadia*.

4. *Jerusalem*, chap. 2, plate 49, ll. 21-23; quoted from *The Poetry and Prose of William Blake*, p. 196.

5. The quotations are from: L. C. Wolfley, "Sidney's Visual Didactic Poetic," *Journal of Medieval and Renaissance Studies* 6 (Fall 1966): 220; David Daiches, *Critical Approaches to Literature* (Englewood Cliffs, N.J., 1956), p. 67; Catherine Barnes, "The Hidden Persuader," *PMLA* 86 (May 1971): 422; and Walter Ong, *Rhetoric, Romance, and Technology*, pp. 94-95. The quotations are not, of course, selected without bias. Barnes's subtle analysis of Sidney's ironic rhetorical style highlights the ironic dimension of her own unwillingness to entertain the idea that rhetorical style may affect "intellectual arguments." There is a Borgesian similarity between Barnes's and Ong's descriptions of Sidney's text and Sidney's description of a speech by the horseman Pugliano, whose "strong affection and weak arguments" Sidney observes before going on (apologetically) to imitate them.

6. Hugh Kenner, *The Counterfeiters*, p. 19. One critic who has analyzed Sidney's talents as a counterfeiter very well is Ronald Levao; see his article, "Sidney's Feigned *Apology*," *PMLA* 94 (March 1979): 223-33. See also Arthur Barker's discussion of Sidney's text as "a paradoxical fiction, a praise of lying, in which the speaker adopts . . . the persona or mask of one who does not know clearly what he is talking about, in order to induce us to figure it out" ("An Apology for the Study of Renaissance Poetry," in *Literary Views: Critical and Historical Essays*, p. 39).

7. J. L. Austin, a "Plea for Excuses," p. 177; see also Paul de Man's discussion of the excuse as a "belated" mode of discourse that occurs in "an epistemological twilight zone" (*Allegories of Reading*, p. 286).

8. Sidney's letter to his brother is printed in *The Correspondence of Philip Sidney and Hubert Languet*, pp. 214-15.

9. Quoted from *A Defence of Poetry*, in *Miscellaneous Prose of Sir Philip Sidney*, pp. 104, 77. All citations to the *Defence* refer to this excellent critical edition, which is based on the De L'Isle MS 1226 and the text printed for William Ponsonby (1595). This edition usefully notes variants that occur in the other surviving manuscript and early text, the Norwich MS and the text printed for Henry Olney (1595). Stephen Gosson's *The Schoole of Abuse* (1579) was dedicated to Sidney and is thought by many critics to have provoked the *Defence*. For a discussion of Sidney's parodic replies to Gosson's attack on poetry, see Arthur F. Kinney, "Parody and its Implications in Sidney's *Defence of Poetry*," *SEL* 12 (Winter 1972): 1-19.

10. For a good discussion of the epistemological paradox Erasmus creates by making Folly both the subject and the object of her discourse, see Walter Kaiser, "The Ironic Mock Encomium," in *Praisers of Folly*, pp. 36 ff. On I. A. Richards's critical project as a "defense of poetry," see Geoffrey Hartman, "I. A. Richards and the Dream of Communication," in *The Fate of Reading*, pp. 20-40.

11. On the *Defence* as an imitation of the classical forensic oration, see Kenneth Myrick, *Sir Philip Sidney as a Literary Craftsman*, pp. 46-83. Critics have not paid enough attention to the ways in which an imitation of a forensic speech is already an instance of epideictic oratory—the "oratory of display." See chapter 1, above, for a discussion of Kenneth Burke's useful remarks on the relation between epideictic oratory and poetry. See also Rosalie Colie's comments on "the defense as epideixis" in *Paradoxia Epidemica*, pp. 3 ff. She has some particularly astute comments on the speculative and metalinguistic tendencies of rhetorical works like Sidney's, in which a "member of a class" makes statements about his own class and thereby plays with the Cretan liar paradox.

12. For the "affinity" between poetry and oratory in "the wordish consideration," see *Defence*, p. 119. Although Sidney is here discussing errors of style shared by English "versifiers"

and "prose printers," the distinction between poetry and oratory does not coincide with that between verse and prose "eloquence," since Sidney, unlike other critics (e.g., Scaliger), considers verse "but an ornament and no cause to poetry" (p. 81). Early in the *Defence* Sidney distinguishes the poet from the rhetorician in terms of the former's superior freedom of invention (p. 78). Clearly the "affinity" between poetry and oratory is, in Sidney's text, a complex issue, one which is dialectically examined from several perspectives. Daniel Javitch, in *Poetry and Courtliness in Renaissance England*, argues astutely that for Sidney, as for other courtly writers, the poet subtly "usurps" the cultural role previously expected of the orator (see especially pp. 100–04). But he overstates his case, I think, when he mentions the striking "absence of any discussion of oratory" in Sidney's argument, and his reading of Sidney's description of Menenius Agrippa, the "excellent orator" who behaves "like a homely and familiar poet," differs from my reading of the passage as an ambivalent expression of the poet's desire for a kind of oratorical power (and social role) unavailable to the Elizabethan courtier.

13. Neil Rudenstine, *Sidney's Poetic Development*, p. 152.

14. See Aristotle's *Rhetoric*. 1. 1 (1355a-b); and Sidney, *Defence*, pp. 104–05; I discuss the "double-edged sword" defense later in this chapter. Sidney translated the first two books of Aristotle's *Rhetoric* and was, I think, more deeply interested in the questions raised in the *Rhetoric* about language as power than he was in the formal justification of poetry offered in the *Poetics*. Most critics have focused on Sidney's borrowings from the latter rather than the former work.

15. See, for example, the essays by Walter Ong and O. B. Hardison, Jr., discussed in Chapter 1 and cited in nn. 37 and 38.

16. See *The Ego and the Id*, SE 19: 55–56; and Ricoeur's *Freud and Philosophy*, pp. 278–79.

17. See Plutarch's "Life of Coriolanus," in *Lives*, trans. Thomas North, vol. 2, 177–78.

18. See Gosson's remark in *The Schoole of Abuse*, pp. 10–11: "No merveyle though Plato shut them [the poets] out of his schoole, and banished them quite from his commonwealth, as effeminate writers, unprofitable members, and utter enemies to virtue." For a discussion of the relation between economic and moral notions of profit in sixteenth-century attacks on poetry and the stage, see Russell Fraser, *The War against Poetry*.

19. "Plea for Excuses," pp. 179–80.

20. Walter Davis, *Idea and Act in Elizabethan Fiction*, p. 35, mentions Sidney's use of the singing match convention. The quotation from the *Rhetoric* (1. 9 [1368a]) is from the translation by Richard McKeon, *The Basic Works of Aristotle*, p. 1358. All citations to Aristotle refer to this edition.

21. See Sidney's praise of David's "notable *prosopopeias*" in the Psalms (*Defence*, p. 77). Although *prosopopeia* sometimes refers specifically to personifying inanimate objects, it can also mean giving voice to an absent or imaginary person.

22. Paul Alpers, *The Poetry of the Faerie Queene*, p. 282. Once one grants Sidney the wit of Shaw's gentleman, who never gives offense unintentionally, one sees that Sidney's examples in the *Defence* frequently serve to complicate or undermine the points they are supposed to prove. Here, for instance, the questioning of the distinction between true and feigned discourse, of historians, poets, or Sidney's own text, is carried into the realm of intertextual allusion. Sidney was, I suspect, perfectly aware that the feigned example of Abradates's superior feigning is not to be found in Xenophon at all. In his notes to his edition of *An Apology for Poetry*, Geoffrey Shepherd suggests that Sidney has confused Abradates with two other figures who appear in the *Cyropaedia* (p. 178). F. J. Levy might well have used this passage to extend his interesting argument that Sidney contributed to the sixteenth-century debate about whether history was a "branch of moral philosophy" or a "branch of politics" ("Sir Philip Sidney and the Idea of History," *Bibliothèque d'humanisme et de renaissance* 26 [September 1964]: 608–17). See also Elizabeth Story Donno's comments on Sidney's complex views of history in "Old Mouse-Eaten Records," *Studies in Philology* 72 (July 1975): 275–98.

23. Forrest G. Robinson, *Sidney's "Apology" in Its Philosophical Tradition*, argues that

Sidney was deeply influenced by Ramist thought and accepted the Ramist distinction between form (ornament) and matter (see p. 111). While there are indeed moments in the *Defence* which sound Ramistical (that adjective's meaning is disputed by scholars like Walter Ong and Rosemond Tuve), notably the discussion of the "outside" of poetry (which is words [p. 117]), Sidney's attitude toward Ramus, like his attitude toward other authorities, is hard to pin down; see J. P. Thorne's discussion of William Temple's Ramist critique of the *Defence* ("A Ramistical Commentary on Sidney's *An Apologie for Poetrie*," *Modern Philology* 54 [February 1957]: 158–64).

24. "Lectures on the age of Elizabeth," in *The Complete Works of William Hazlitt*, p. 322.

25. The political drama of usurpation staged metaphorically in the *confirmatio* is in fact a revenge play whose traces are dispersed through the text. The places the poet "usurps" here were rightfully his: early in the *Defence* Sidney writes that the historians "either stale or usurped of poetry their passionate describing of the passions" (p. 75); and later he compares the philosophers to "ungrateful prentices, [who] were not content to set up shops for themselves, but sought by all means to discredit their masters; which by the force of delight being barred them, the less they could overthrow them, the more they hated them" (p. 107).

26. Shepherd, ed., *An Apology for Poetry*, p. 40.

27. *Republic* 10. 607e (p. 291).

28. *The Poems of Sir Philip Sidney*, p. 202.

29. Plutarch's "How the Young Man Should Study Poetry" is in the *Moralia*; my references are to the Loeb Classical Library bilingual edition, trans. Frank Cole Babbitt, 1: 74–197. Plutarch writes that "it may be said, as it seems, not only of the land of the Egyptians but also of poetry, that it yields 'Drugs, and some are good when mixed and others baneful to those who cultivate it'" (p. 79).

30. Since Plutarch views the reading of poetry as a way to *introduce* the young man to philosophy ("Young Man," p. 81), his argument is somewhat circular; the young man who presumably does not yet understand philosophical ethics is advised to protect himself from the poets' errors by imitating the philosophers who freely "amended" lines of poetry with which they disagreed; for instance, Zeno revised the second line of a supposedly subversive Sophoclean fragment ("Whoever comes to traffic with a king / To him is slave however free he come") thus: "Is not a slave if only free he come" (p. 175). If the student is to "disobey" the poets with the help of the philosophers, he is also, Plutarch later says, "to foster and amplify" any "edifying sentiment" he meets in poets "by means of proofs and testimonies from the philosophers, at the same time crediting these with the discovery" (p. 189). Clearly Sidney had ample reason to disobey Plutarch's text and to admire its complex politics.

31. See Part 2 of Plutarch's essay, "Young Man," pp. 81–91.

32. "Amiot to the Readers," reprinted in Thomas North's translation of Plutarch's *Lives*, p. xvi. For a useful discussion of Sidney's transformation of Amiot's arguments for history into his own arguments for poetry, see Donno, "Old Mouse-Eaten Records," p. 293.

33. Hardison, "The Two Voices of Sidney's *Apology for Poetry*," *ELR* 2 (Winter 1972): 94.

34. There has been much scholarly debate about the dating of the *Defence* (for a summary of opinions and, I think, a convincing argument for early 1580, soon after Sidney wrote his "Letter to the Queen," see Jan Van Dorsten's introduction, *Miscellaneous Prose*, pp. 59–63). Hardison's argument that Sidney wrote the *Defence* in two phases, the second after reading Italian neo-Aristotelian criticism, and never had time to "harmonize" the two parts seems tenuous, especially since the "contradiction" between freedom and fettering is a dialectical one woven into the text from beginning to end.

35. *The Ego and the Id, SE* 19: 56.

36. *The Language of the Self*, p. 9.

37. Catherine Barnes, "Hidden Persuader," shows the structural parallels between Puglia-

no's praise of horsemen and Sidney's praise of poetry: Sidney's oration "first establishes poetry as man's noblest, most ancient estate, then amplifies on its uses and value. Next, it demonstrates the serviceableness of poetry to the Prince, and concludes by praising the beauty of poetry itself" (p. 425). Kenneth Myrick, *Sidney as a Literary Craftsman*, notes that Sidney's play on the themes of "exercise" and "contemplation" anticipates his later concern with "praxis" and "gnosis" (p. 56).

38. Voloshinov [or Bakhtin], *Marxism and the Philosophy of Language*, p. 121. Voloshinov adds that the "pictorial style" "involves a severe debilitation of both the authoritarian and the rationalistic dogma of utterance."

39. The preposition "into" appears only in Ponsonby's version of the *Defence*. In light of the great amount of commentary the "another nature" sentence has provoked, it is worth noting that the textual variant "into" gives additional support to those critics who think Sidney's "another nature" refers chiefly to human nature rather than to the poem as a "heterocosmic" object. See Davis, *Idea and Act*, p. 42.

40. Bacon's comment is in *The Proficiencie and Advancement of Learning*, bk. 2, paragraph 43; its dry skepticism ("Poetry was ever thought to have some participation in divinesse") is, I think, a useful gloss on an aspect of Sidney's theory of imaginative power that is not often discussed. Precisely because the imagination can "lift up the mind from the dungeon of the body to the enjoying his own divine essence" (*Defence*, p. 82), it has the potential to lift the mind in a secularly dangerous way: "ambition, like love, can abide no lingering and ever urges on his own successes," as Sidney writes in the *Arcadia*.

41. The "Letter of Advice," whose authenticity has been doubted, is nevertheless printed in *The Prose Works of Jonathan Swift*, 9: 327–45. Sidney's friend Fulke Greville describes his own use of irony as a defensive strategy in his work the "Declination of Monarchy": "A new counsell rose up in me, to take away all opinion of seriousness from these perplexed pedigrees, and to this end carelessly cast them in that hypocriticall figure *Ironia*, wherein men commonly (to keep above their workes) seeme to make toies of the utmost they can do" (*Life of Sidney*, p. 239).

42. See Voloshinov's discussion of texts which develop dynamic relations between "authorial" and "reported" speech (*čužaja reč*, literally, "other's speech"), *Marxism and the Philosophy of Language*, pp. 115–23. See Barnes, "Hidden Persuader," for a discussion of the contradictions between the *peroratio's* claims for poetry and arguments made earlier in Sidney's text. Barnes also notes that "the speaker asks his audience to believe 'with Aristotle' a statement that is actually Boccaccio's interpretation of Aristotle" (p. 426).

43. See *The Praise of Folly*, p. 73; the poets, says Folly, are "a race of free souls . . . all of whose efforts tend to no other end than soothing the ears of fools with vapid trifles and silly stories. And yet they so rely on these things, strange to say, that they not only promise themselves immortality . . . but they also assure as much to others. Philautia and Kolakia are more intimate with this fraternity than with others." For the Latin text of this passage, see *Ausgewählte Schriften*, 2: 120–22.

44. Quoted from the chapter "Excuses," in *Allegories of Reading*, p. 300.

45. Emerson, "Uses of Great Men," in *Representative Men*, p. 11. In this essay Emerson also writes that "you are you and I am I and so we remain."

46. "Moving and Teaching," in *Sir Philip Sidney and the Poetics of Protestantism*, p. 38. Weiner argues that the *Defence* is "largely based on Calvinist theology"; for strong counterarguments, see Frank B. Evans, "The Concept of the Fall in Sidney's *Apologie*," *Renaissance Papers* (1969): 9–14, and D. H. Craig, "A Hybrid Growth: Sidney's Theory of Poetry in *An Apology*," *ELR* 10 (1980): 183–201. These essays suggest that Sidney's religious views are as dialectical as his literary ones. In any case, the strictest Calvinist would not grant a man the power Weiner grants Sidney's conception of the "right poet"—the power to abrogate others' freedom to choose evil. Although the question of the audience's free will is certainly a problem

for Sidney (his ideal of oratorical power necessarily involves a desire that the audience relinquish its ability to resist the poet's will), he is too aware of the poet's own "infected will" to approach the question without wariness.

47. Schlegel's comment is from "Über die Unverständlichkeit," cited by Douglas Muecke, *The Compass of Irony*, p. 201.

48. See A. C. Hamilton, "Sidney and Agrippa," *Review of English Studies* 7, no. 26 (1956): 151–57; Hamilton shows that Agrippa's work was read both as an orthodox Christian attack on "vain learning" and as an "elaborate joke whose whole point is that 'a demi-god in omnisufficiency of knowledge, a devell in the practice of horrible Artes' (as Gabriel Harvey calls him), can use immense knowledge to denounce the use of knowledge."

49. See p. 109 of the *Defence*, where Sidney calls attention to his own virtuosity in the oratorical game: whatever "dispraise may be set upon it [poetry], is either easily overcome, or transformed into just commendation." As Kenneth Burke remarks, epideictic rhetoric was often "aimed at praise, not as an attempt to win an audience's praise for the subject discussed, but as an attempt to win praise for the oratory itself" (*Rhetoric of Motives*, p. 70).

50. Shepherd, ed., *Apology*, p. 195. The "replacing" of *vitium* by *virtus* may, of course, be read as a graphic indication of the Christian allegorist's moral intentions.

51. Quoted from *The Art of Love and Other Poems*, pp. 110–11. Ovid is here describing the rhetorical trope *paradiastole*, which Peacham, in his *Garden of Eloquence* (1577), associates with the art of excusing one's own or others' vices, and which Puttenham, in the *Arte of English Poesie* (1589), terms "Curry-favell" (see Daniel Javitch's interesting discussion of this trope and its relation to the courtier's style of life in *Poetry and Courtliness*, pp. 62–63). Sidney would have seen the trope's implications for the whole project of verbal self-defense; Ovid's apology for his own poetry in Book 2 of the *Tristia* is an extended effort to curry favor with Augustus.

52. See *Tristia*, bk. 2, ll. 273–74, for Ovid's comparison of poetry to a sword that may be used for both criminal and virtuous purposes; in ll. 275–76 he argues that poetry can harm no one who reads "with an upright mind." (Loeb Classical Library edition of the *Tristia*, pp. 74–75.)

53. *Validity in Interpretation*, p. 31. Hirsch revised his intentional theory to include the interpreter's share in "Three Dimensions of Hermeneutics," *New Literary History* 3 (Winter 1972): 245–62.

54. *The Vanity of Arts and Sciences*, p. 364.

55. *Self-Consuming Artifacts*, p. 69.

56. See *Defence*, p. 76, where Sidney describes poetry's power to "soften" and "sharpen" the readers' "dull wits"; "for until they find a pleasure in the exercises of the mind, great promises of much knowledge will little persuade them that know not the fruits of knowledge." The "labour" of turning the mind "inward for thorough self-examination" is mentioned in Sidney's letter to Hubert Languet of 1 March 1578 (*Correspondence*, p. 160). See A. C. Hamilton, *Sir Philip Sidney*, p. 32, on the importance of the Platonic injunction "know thyself" in the *Defence* and in Sidney's other writing.

57. See *Rhetoric* 1. 1 (1355b). Sidney would, I think, have been struck by the fact that Aristotle justifies rhetoric in the context of a general discussion of self-defense; he would also have noted Aristotle's silence about the possible defensive motivations of his own discourse. Aristotle evidently regards his project in the *Rhetoric* as a dialectical examination of an "art"; but his second paragraph is an attack on previous "treatises on rhetoric" and hence his discourse is rhetorical by his own initial definition of a universal phenomenon: "all men make use, more or less, of both [dialectic and rhetoric]; for to a certain extent all men attempt to discuss statements and to maintain them, to defend themselves and to attack others" (p. 1325 of McKeon's translation). Sidney's self-reflexivity constitutes an implicit critique of all philosophical discourses which assume a "disinterested" stance toward an object of inquiry.

58. Wimsatt and Brooks, *Literary Criticism*, p. 68.

59. This biblical story (2 Samuel 12) has been used by post-Freudian analysts to describe a psychic defense known as the "King David Reaction." Involving the "mutual interaction of Repression, Projection, and Identification," the defense operates when "approved or disapproved aspects of the self, which are not consciously recognized," are nevertheless perceived in another person who serves as a double or mirror for the self. Such a perception, according to Henry Loughlin, characteristically produces strong positive or negative feelings; the latter type of reaction, which he illustrates with reference to Claudius's response to the play-within-a-play in *Hamlet*, is known as "King David's anger." See Loughlin's chapter "The King David Reaction" in *The Ego and Its Defenses*, pp. 236–49; my quotations are from p. 238.

60. See Hunter's excellent essay, "Humanism and Courtship," reprinted from his book *John Lyly* (1962), in *Elizabethan Poetry*, pp. 3–40. See also the chapter on power in Lawrence Stone, *The Crisis of the Aristocracy*, pp. 199–270, and George O'Brian's fine book, *Renaissance Poetics and the Problem of Power*.

61. For Sidney's ironic reflection on his unfulfilled "great expectation," see *Astrophil and Stella*, sonnet 21. His complaint about his inability to find "fit employments" is from a letter to Edward Denny, cited by Hamilton, *Sir Philip Sidney*, p. 31. Hamilton's first chapter gives a concise account of the political and financial frustrations which Sidney experienced in his position of "dependency" on the Queen. One effect of Elizabeth's "unnoble" policy toward her nobles was to turn them into "a set of shameless mendicants," as Lawrence Stone puts it, quoting Sidney's own remark that "Need obeys no law and forgets blushing" (*Crisis of the Aristocracy*, p. 477). When in the *Defence* Sidney describes poets as "makers of themselves, not takers of others" (p. 110), the statement is resonant with irony. Indeed critics have not sufficiently explored the economic and political context that shapes not only Sidney's subtly personified "*poor* poetry" but also his poetic theory; his belief that the "fruit" of virtue is "not gnosis but praxis" should be read in the light of his complaint to Languet: "For to what purpose should our thoughts be directed to various kinds of knowledge, unless room be afforded for putting it into practice, so that public advantage may be the result, which in a corrupt age we cannot hope for?" (*Correspondence*, p. 159).

62. *Correspondence*, p. 163. Sidney adds, "I am now meditating with myself some Indian project"; a "voyage of exploration" would be his romantic solution to the frustrations caused by Elizabeth's unwillingness to be "persuaded" to wage war.

63. See Jan Van Dorsten's introduction to the *Defence* (in *Miscellaneous Prose*), pp. 59–63. The quotation from Seneca's *Oedipus* appears on p. 96 of the *Defence* and on p. 56 of the same volume's edition of the "Letter." Van Dorsten does not mention that both texts also develop the metaphor of the body politic (with Sidney implicitly playing the role of "defender of the state"), but that parallel would further support his argument that the *Defence* was written soon after the "Letter," during the months when Elizabeth's policy toward her Protestant lords in general and toward Sidney in particular was making the notion of "tyranny's self-destructiveness" a pressing concern (p. 69).

64. Quoted from the edition of the "Letter" in *Miscellaneous Prose*, pp. 46, 53. Katherine Duncan-Jones suggests that Sidney's letter did not offend Elizabeth greatly; it was certainly more tactful than other criticisms of the marriage plan. Hubert Languet, however, worried that the letter might hurt Sidney: "I admire your courage in freely admonishing the Queen and your countrymen of that which is to the state's advantage," Languet writes, "but you must take care not to go so far that the unpopularity of your conduct be more than you can bear. . . . For I do not doubt there will be many who will run to the safe side of the vessel, when they find you are unsuccessful in resisting the Queen's will, or that she is seriously offended at your opposition" (30 January 1580; *Correspondence*, pp. 187–88). And Hamilton remarks, apropos of Sidney's general career, that "instead of being content to serve the Queen's will," he "sought to impose his will—or what he saw as God's will—upon her. Inevitably, he lost her favour and was left to languish or retire from the court" (*Sir Philip Sidney*, p. 28). One could say that Sidney acted out

the ambiguities of the courtier's role as Castiglione defines it in Book 4 of *Il Cortegiano*, where Ottaviano insists that the courtier's duty is "to bring or help one's prince toward what is right and to frighten him away from what is wrong" but admits, ruefully, that "if I had the favor of some of the princes I know, and if I were to tell them freely what I think, I fear I should soon lose that favor" (*The Book of the Courtier*, pp. 290–310).

65. See *Defence*, pp. 110–11; Sidney explicitly mentions England's "overfaint quietness" as "a piece of a reason" why poets "are less grateful to idle England." The pointed repetition takes us back to the initial paradox of Sidney's project, undertaken "(I know not by what mischance) in these my not old years and idlest times": he is defending his *unelected* vocation and in so doing he is covertly attacking the injustice which prevents him from acting in deed as well as in word.

66. Puttenham, *The Arte of English Poesie*, p. 196. Puttenham later elaborates on the use of the trope he alternately terms "false semblant" and "faire semblant": the poet should "so wisely and discreetly behave himselfe as he may worthily retaine the credit of his place, and profession of a very courtier, which is in plaine termes, cunningly to be able to dissemble" (p. 305). In *Poetry and Courtliness* Daniel Javitch usefully comments on the ways in which Puttenham's theory of figures departs from earlier humanistic theories that emphasized the norm of "clarity" (see especially pp. 50–75).

67. Quoted from Sidney's letter to Leicester (2 August 1580), in *The Prose Works of Sir Philip Sidney*, 3: 129. Sidney is literally referring to a head cold which "keepes me from the cowrte," but the cold metaphorically describes the Queen's attitude toward her courtier; Sidney asks Leicester to remind Elizabeth that "necessity did even banishe mee" and he bitterly remarks that "so longe as she sees a silk doublett upon me her Highness will thinke me in good cace."

68. The phrase "so unprofitable a spender," which signals the allegorical relation between poetry and the belly in Sidney's version of Plutarch's fable, also alludes, I think, to the parable of the talents which Sidney uses in other works to express his fears of failure. See, for instance, *Astrophil and Stella*, sonnet 18, which is, like Milton's sonnet "How Soon Hath Time," a meditation on the poet's "bad stewardship" of his talents. For an excellent discussion of this autobiographical theme in the *Old Arcadia* (where a son is judged "unworthy" by a stern father), see McCoy, *Rebellion in Arcadia*, pp. 53–68 and passim. The word "ungratefully" hints at the parallel between the "adulterous" David and Sidney's Queen by echoing the epithet applied to poetry's "enemies" elsewhere in the *Defence* (see p. 74, where Sidney describes the "ungratefulness" of poetry's accusers as a metaphorical violation of social and familial "sacred bonds." See also p. 107, where Plato is compared to an "ungrateful" apprentice).

69. *Literary Criticism*, p. 169.

Conclusion

1. For an excellent discussion of medieval retractions and their relation to the ancient convention of the palinode, see Wesley Trimpi, "The Quality of Fiction," *Traditio* 33 (1974): 1–118; see especially p. 83, n. 96, on the palinode "as a prayer for the withdrawal of what had been granted to a previous prayer imprudently made," and Appendix A.

2. "Video vos epilogum exspectare, sed nimium desipitis, siquidem arbitramini, me quid dixerim etiam dum meminisse, cum tantam verborum farraginem effuderim." Erasmus, *Ausgewählte Schriften* 2: 210; *Praise of Folly*, trans. Hudson, p. 125.

3. In 1933, as Bruce F. Pauley observes, "the proportion of academicians in the Austrian Nazi party was even higher than in Germany" (*Hitler and the Forgotten Nazis*, p. 94). Anti-Semitism was certainly a major cause of Freud's strained relations with the University of Vienna and the Austrian Ministry of Education. But as Ronald W. Clark suggests (*Freud: The Man and the Cause*, p. 210), other factors were also at work, including, probably, Freud's own

social aloofness. Clark gives a good account of Freud's repeatedly foiled efforts to be promoted to a professorship and gain "official recognition" for his work; see pp. 208–09 and, for comments on the "grudging" recognition Freud eventually won in 1920, when he was appointed full professor but without a seat on the board of the faculty, p. 424.

4. This is the fourth definition of the term given by the *OED*.

5. *The Ordeal of Civility*, p. 7.

6. For a useful discussion of Boccaccio's theory of poetry and of allegorical interpretation, see Trimpi, "Quality of Fiction," pp. 98–100; and Millicent Marcus, "The Accommodating Frate Alberto," *Italica* 56 (Spring 1979): 3–21. See also Charles Osgood's introduction and notes to *Boccaccio on Poetry*, a translation of the Preface and Books 14 and 15 of the *Genealogia*. Osgood's translation is the text cited throughout this chapter, though I shall, when necessary, refer to the Latin text of the *Genealogie deorum gentilium libri*, edited by Vincenzo Romano.

7. *Ordeal of Civility*, p. 37.

8. On Freud's interest in deliberately offending "the reticent manners and morals of the cultivated classes of the nineteenth century," see Philip Rieff, *Freud: The Mind of the Moralist*, pp. 315–17. Cuddihy quotes Rieff and also Freud's remark to Joseph Wortis: "An analysis is not a place for polite exchanges" (*Ordeal of Civility*, pp. 32, 35).

9. As Osgood notes (p. 168, n. 1), Boccaccio's portrait of the poet as a solitary being alludes to Petrarch's *De vita solitaria* and to his *Invective contra medicum*, a text which contains Petrarch's most extended defense of poetry. For Boccaccio as for Tasso, there is an important connection between the figure of the poet as a solitary wanderer and the poet's need to use figurative language. Cf. Tasso's meditations on *nomi peregrini* (discussed in Chapter 3, above) with Boccaccio's definition of allegory in *Genealogia* 1. 3: "Nam allegoria dicitur ab allon, quod alienum latine significat, sive diversum." (quoted from Romano's ed., p. 19). Millicent Marcus observes that Boccaccio draws in this passage on Isidore of Seville's famous *Etymologiarum sive originum* 1. 37. 22; see her "Accommodating Frate Alberto," p. 4.

10. For a discussion of this passage from Sidney's letter to the Queen, see Chapter 4, above; and see below, n. 24, for a parallel passage in Shelley's *Defense*.

11. *SE* 18: 60. This passage, in which Freud comments on his own figurative language, has become a touchstone in literary critical discussions of psychoanalysis as "a science of tropes." In his important essay "Freud and Literature" (1950), Lionel Trilling refers to this passage as a "kind of defiant apology" for metaphorical discourse, and goes on to compare Freud to Vico, another student of the ways in which we necessarily "feel and think in figurative formations"; quoted from *Freud: A Collection of Critical Essays*, ed. Perry Meisel, p. 108. Psychoanalysts continue to discuss the problematic status of figurative language in their science; in "Metaphor and the Psychoanalytic Situation," Jacob Arlow quotes Bernfeld's description of psychoanalysis as a "science of traces" (*Psychoanalytic Quarterly* 48 [1979]: 363–85); and Leon Wurmson offers "A Defense of the Use of Metaphor in Analytic Theory Formation," *Psychoanalytic Quarterly* 46 [1977]: 466–98. For literary critical discussions of the questions about figurative language Freud raises in the key passage of *Beyond the Pleasure Principle*, see Neil Hertz, "Freud and the Sandman," in *Textual Strategies*, p. 300; Meredith Skura, *The Literary Uses of the Psychoanalytic Process*, p. 20; and Harold Bloom, "Freud and the Poetic Sublime," *Antaeus* (Spring 1978): 355–77.

12. *Allegory*, p. 295.

13. Adler's "Theory of the 'Individual Psychologists [sic],'" Freud remarks later in the lecture, contains "*something* correct": "a small particle is taken for the whole" (*SE* 22: 142). For an account of Adler's and Jung's defections, see Ernest Jones, *The Life and Works of Sigmund Freud*, 2: 126–51. Adler broke with Freud in 1911 and Jung began to show signs of rebellion in 1912, the year Freud wrote *Totem and Taboo*. Freud wrote that he didn't "really want a split; I should prefer him [Jung] to leave on his own accord. Perhaps my *Totem* work will hasten the break against my will" (letter to Ferenczi; quoted in Jones, *Life*, 2: 354).

14. See Freud's letter to Abraham of 11 June 1908: "There are still so few of us that disagreements, based perhaps on personal 'complexes,' ought to be excluded among us," Freud writes, and goes on to mention Jung's particular value as a member of the group: "As a Christian and a pastor's son he finds his way to me only against great inner resistances. His association with us is more valuable for that. I nearly said that it was only because of his appearance on the scene that psychoanalysis escaped the danger of becoming a Jewish National affair" (*A Psycho-Analytic Dialogue: The Letters of Sigmund Freud and Karl Abraham 1907-1926*, p. 34. Cited in Clark, *Freud: The Man and the Cause*, p. 252.) Clark gives a thorough account of the vicissitudes of Freud's relations with Jung, "the Gentile" and "official psychiatrist" Freud had once hoped to make "permanent president" of the International Psychoanalytic Association. See pp. 296–97, 252–53, and passim.

15. The quotation is from a letter of 23 March 1900, in *The Origins of Psychoanalysis*, p. 315.

16. Ibid.

17. *Letters of Sigmund Freud*, p. 376.

18. See Bakhtin's *Problems of Dostoevsky's Poetics* (1929), trans. R. W. Rostel, pp. 4–5; and, for a further discussion of the concept of monologic discourse, *Marxism and the Philosophy of Language*, pp. 72–73. In Bakhtin's dialectical style, the term monologic refers sometimes to a text or utterance but more often to the critic's or linguist's erroneous mode of perceiving a verbal object, as if it were "isolated, finished . . . divorced from its verbal and actual context."

19. Quoted from *A Defense of Poetry* (written 1821, first published 1839), ed. John E. Jordan, p. 71. All quotations of Shelley's *Defense* are from this edition, which also contains Peacock's *The Four Ages of Poetry*.

20. As Jonathan Arac points out, Shelley explicitly criticizes the traditional notion of the "individual subject" in the essay "On Life." To support his skeptical argument about "the existence of distinct individual minds," Shelley cites the linguistic example of the personal pronoun: "the words *I* and *you* and *they*," he writes, are "merely marks," "grammatical devices . . . totally devoid of the intense and exclusive sense usually attached to them" (quoted in Arac, "To Regress from the Rigors of Shelley: Figures of History in American Deconstructionist Criticism," *Boundary* 2, 8 [Spring 1980]: 241–57). Shelley's meditation on the status of the personal pronoun anticipates Jakobson's famous discussion of "the shifter" in "Shifters, Verbal Categories, and the Russian Verb" (1956), in *Selected Writings* 2: 130–47.

21. *The Four Ages of Poetry*, printed with Shelley's *Defense* in the edition by John E. Jordan cited in n. 19; the quotation is from p. 20.

22. The quotation is from a letter of 15 February 1821, cited by Jordan in *Defense*, p. ix.

23. See Paul Ricoeur's discussion of a "quest for recognition" which also extends into "a quest for mutual esteem or approval" (*Freud and Philosophy*, p. 523.) See also Meredith Skura's comments on "the fundamental wishes which seem to be both the ground and the end of communication—the wish for 'recognition' . . . or the wish for 'presence,' for relationship" (*Literary Uses*, p. 174).

24. See *Defense*, p. 46, where Shelley explains this problem of self-recognition in terms that recall Sidney's image of the eye blind to itself in his letter to Elizabeth: "Neither the eye nor the mind can see itself," Shelley writes, "unless reflected upon that which it resembles."

25. Quoted from *The Poems of Shelley*, p. 440. I am grateful to Jonathan Arac for drawing this passage to my attention.

26. See *SE* 4: 142, n. 1, for references to the other places where Freud quotes these lines from *Faust*, part 1, scene 4.

27. See ibid., p. 144, for the discussion of the censoring agency's effect on the "sense organ" of consciousness; the censor's function resembles that of the "protective shield" as described in *Beyond The Pleasure Principle*, except for the fact that the former filters internal data whereas the latter filters stimuli from the "external world."

28. See the last paragraph of Boccaccio's Preface (p. 13) for the passage where he compares himself to Aesculapius. The story of Hippolytus's miraculous resurrection was an important *topos* of early humanist thought. Writers like Poggio and Salutati followed Boccaccio in applying the myth to their own secular project of restoring ancient texts; they thereby radically changed the allegorical interpretation of the myth set forth by Saint Jerome and later medieval writers who took Hippolytus as a figure for the resurrected Christian. For this tradition of interpretation, see Marguerite Mills Chiarenza, "Hippolytus' Exile," *Dante Studies* 84 (1966): 65-68. A. Bartlett Giamatti discussed the humanist reading of the myth in a lecture at Yale on 28 November 1978: "Hippolytus Among the Humanists: Exile in the Early Renaissance."

29. "Now that everything has been taken from them, I had to go and take their best man," Freud wrote in a letter to Stefan Zweig soon after *Moses and Monotheism* was published. The letter is quoted in Clark, *Freud*, pp. 423-24. See pp. 420-24 of Clark's book for a general discussion of Freud's doubts about publishing a text which would, he thought, offend not only Jews but also Catholic authorities in Austria. See also Humphrey Morris's fine discussion of *Moses and Monotheism* in "The Need to Connect," in *The Literary Freud*, ed. J. Smith, pp. 338-43.

30. *Astrophil and Stella*, sonnet 72.

Appendix

1. See "The Neuro-Psychoses of Defence," *SE* 3: 45-47 and, for a useful account of Freud's early uses of the term "defence," Peter Madison, *Freud's Concept of Repression and Defense*, pp. 17-18.

2. *Language of Psychoanalysis*, p. 108.

3. "Freud's Concepts of Defense and Poetic Will," in *The Literary Freud*, ed. J. Smith, pp. 5-6. Cf. Laplanche and Pontalis, *Language of Psychoanalysis*, p. 106: "Defence cannot be adequately accounted for by *homeostasis of the organism.*"

4. Freud in fact used the term "repressed" (*verdrängt*) in 1893, in the famous "Preliminary Communication" he wrote with Breuer and later republished as Chapter 1 of *Studies on Hysteria*. See *SE* 2: 10, and Peter Madison's comment on the passage in *Repression and Defense*, p. 16. Madison gives a useful survey of Freud's early uses of both terms, which often occur in formulations where they appear to be synonymous: e.g., "Thus it comes about that we are only able to produce very incomplete evidence in favor of our view that sexuality seems to play a principal part in the pathogenesis of hysteria as a source of psychical traumas and as a motive for 'defence'—that is, for repressing ideas from consciousness" (*SE* 2: xxix). See, however, the evidence cited by the editors of the Standard Edition for the idea that there was "some discrimination" between Freud's use of the two terms: " 'repression' seems to have described the actual process, and 'defence' the motive for it" (Appendix A to *Inhibitions, Symptoms and Anxiety*, *SE* 20: 173). See also Laplanche and Pontalis, *Language of Psychoanalysis*, p. 391, for an argument that Freud rarely employed the two terms "as if they were interchangeable."

5. Wollheim, *Sigmund Freud*, p. 17.

6. The editors say Freud's account is "perhaps a little misleading," *SE* 20:173.

7. My attention was initially caught by this addendum because it seemed a remarkable instance of defensive discourse which is, like Austin's "A Plea for Excuses," a metacommentary on its own rhetorical mode. Cf. Freud's statement that "Even a purely terminological innovation ought to justify its adoption" (p. 163).

8. See the editors' Appendix A, *SE* 20: 173; and, for a fuller survey of Freud's use of the term *Abwehr* and its cognate forms in works between 1896 and 1926, see Madison, *Repression and Defense*, pp. 18-21. He questions Charles Brenner's view that "Freud in 1915 no longer considered 'defense' and 'repression' to be synonymous" ("The Nature and Development of the

Concept of Repression in Freud's Writings" [1957], cited by Madison, p. 21). I think Brenner is right, but I disagree with the notion that Freud ever did think the two terms were "interchangeable," which is what both Brenner and Madison seem to mean by "synonymous." Madison is in any case right to note that, even in his 1915 papers, Freud continued to use "repression" to designate a general category of defensive processes, as well as to designate one process among others; see Madison's citations, pp. 19–21.

9. See the *Oxford Dictionary of the Christian Church*, ed. F. L. Cross, p. 759. Freud's interest in Josephus was evidently sparked by a book by Robert Eisler, to whom Freud alludes at the beginning of his analogy. In 1929 Eisler published his *Iesous Basileus ou Basileusas*, which discusses Josephus and the Christological passage interpolated into the *Antiquities*.

10. The German original of this sentence is: "Hier weist uns die Idee den Weg, dass die Abwehr eines unerwünschten Vorganges im Inneren nach dem Muster der Abwehr gegen einen äusseren Reiz geschehen dürfte, dass das Ich den gleichen weg der verteidigung gegen die innere wie gegen die äussere Gefahr einschlägt" (*Gesammelte Werke* 14: 119).

11. *Language of Psychoanalysis*, p. 105.

12. *Language of Psychoanalysis*, p. 105. Laplanche and Pontalis do not of course deny that the motives of defense lie in the external world, but they do maintain that by "defence" Freud means to designate only an interpsychic process. Cf. Otto Fenichel's view that conflicts between the ego and the outside world merely "reflect" conflicts between the ego and the id (*The Psychoanalytic Theory of Neurosis*, p. 131).

Selected Bibliography

The following list contains all the book-length studies and some of the articles directly cited in the text or the notes. Included under "Works of Reference" are several volumes I have found useful but have not had occasion to cite.

Primary Sources

Agrippa, Henry Cornelius. *The Vanity of Arts and Sciences*. Trans. James Sanford, 1569. Reprint. London, 1694.

Aneau, Barthélemy. *Quintil Horatian*. 1549. Reprinted in *La Deffense et illustration de la langue françoyse*. Ed. Henri Chamard. Paris, 1966.

Apuleius. *The Works of Apuleius*. London, 1889.

Ariosto, Ludovico. *Orlando Furioso*. Ed. Dino Provenzal. 4 vols. Milan, 1955.

_____. *Orlando Furioso*. Trans. Guido Waldman. London, 1974.

Aristotle. *The Basic Works of Aristotle*. Ed. Richard McKeon. New York, 1941.

Augustine. *De doctrina christiana*. Trans. D. W. Robertson, Jr. New York, 1958.

Bacon, Francis. *The Works of Francis Bacon*. Popular ed. New York, 1878. Vol 1, *The Advancement of Learning*, pp. 79–412.

Blake, William. *The Poetry and Prose of William Blake*. Ed. David V. Erdman, with a commentary by Harold Bloom. 1965. Reprint, with revisions. Garden City, N.Y., 1970.

Boccaccio, Giovanni. *Boccaccio on Poetry, Being the Preface and the Fourteenth and Fifteenth Books of Boccaccio's "Genealogia Deorum Gentilium."* Ed. and trans. Charles G. Osgood. 1930. Reprint. New York, 1956.

_____. *Genealogie deorum gentilium libri*. 2 vols. Ed. Vincenzo Romano. Bari, 1951.

Castiglione, Baldesar. *The Book of the Courtier*. Trans. Charles Singleton. Garden City, N.Y., 1959.

_____. *Il Cortegiano*. Ed. Silvano del Messier. Novara, 1968.

Cicero. *De officiis*. Trans. Walter Miller. Loeb Classical Library. 1913. Reprint. London, 1908.

_____. *De oratore*. Trans. H. Rackham. Loeb Classical Library. 2 vols. London, 1942.

Dante. *De vulgari eloquentia.* In *Tutte le opere di Dante Alighieri.* Ed. E. Moore. Oxford, 1894.

———. *La Divina Commedia.* Ed. Charles H. Grandgent. Rev. ed. Boston, 1933.

———. *Inferno, Purgatorio, Paradiso.* Trans. John D. Sinclair. 3 vols. New York, 1961.

Defoe, Daniel. *Moll Flanders.* Ed. James Sutherland. New York, 1959.

Du Bellay, Joachim. *La Deffence et illustration de la langue françoyse.* Ed. Henri Chamard. 1948. Reprint. Paris, 1966.

———. *Oeuvres poétiques.* Ed. Henri Chamard, 6 vols. Paris, 1908–31.

———. *Poésies françaises et latines du Joachim du Bellay.* Ed. Etienne Courbet. Paris, 1918.

———. *"Les Regrets" et autres oeuvres poétiques.* Ed. J. Joliffe and M. A. Screech. Geneva, 1966.

Emerson, R. W. E. *Representative Men.* Ed. E. W. Emerson. Boston, 1903.

Erasmus, Desiderius. *Ausgewählte Schriften.* 3 vols. Darmstadt, 1967. Vol. 2, *Laus Stultitiae,* pp. 1–211. Vol. 3, *Apologia,* pp. 78–115.

———. *Opera Omnia.* Basle, 1540–41.

———. *The Praise of Folly.* Trans. Hoyt Hopewell Hudson. 1941. Reprint. New York, n.d.

Estienne, Robert. *Dictionarium Latinae linguae thesaurus . . . cum galica fere interpretatione.* 2 vols. Paris, 1531.

Gosson, Stephen. *The Schoole of Abuse.* 1579. Reprint. London, 1841.

Greville, Fulke. *Life of Sidney.* Ed. Nowell Smith. Oxford, 1907.

Hazlitt, William. *The Complete Works of William Hazlitt.* Ed. P. P. Howe. London, 1931.

Horace. *Satires, Epistles and Ars Poetica.* Trans. H. R. Fairclough. Loeb Classical Library. Rev. ed. 1929. Reprint. London, 1970.

Luther, Martin. *Sämmtliche Schriften.* St. Louis, 1907. Vol. 5, *Sendbrief vom Dolmetschen,* pp. 968–85.

———. *Works.* Vol. 5, "On Translating: An Open Letter," pp. 10–27. Trans. C. M. Jacobs. Philadelphia, 1931.

Machiavelli, Niccoló. *The Prince.* Ed. and trans. Mark Musa. New York, 1964.

Milton, John. *Complete Poems and Major Prose.* Ed. Merritt Hughes. New York, 1957.

Nichols, Fred J., ed. *An Anthology of Neo-Latin Poetry.* New Haven, 1979.

Ovid. *The Art of Love and Other Poems.* Trans. J. H. Mozley. Loeb Classical Library. London, 1969.

———. *Metamorphoses.* Trans. F. J. Miller. Loeb Classical Library. 2 vols. 3rd rev. ed., revised by G. P. Goold. London, 1977.

———. *Tristia, Ex Ponto.* Trans. A. L. Wheeler. Loeb Classical Library. 1924. Reprint. London, 1965.

Peacock, Thomas. *The Four Ages of Poetry.* Ed. John E. Jordan. New York, 1965.

Pellegrino, Camillo. *Il Carrafa o vero della poesia epica.* Florence, 1584. Reprinted in *Opere di Torquato Tasso colle controversie sulla "Gerusalemme,"* vol. 18. Ed. Giorgio Rosini. Pisa, 1827.

Plato. *Euthyphro, Apology, Crito, Phaedo, Phaedrus.* Trans. Harold North Fowler. Loeb Classical Library. 1914. Reprint. London, 1977.

———. *Lysias, Symposium, Gorgias*. Trans. W. R. M. Lamb. Loeb Classical Library. 1925. Reprint. London, 1975.

———. *The Republic*. Trans. and with commentary by Allan Bloom. New York, 1968.

Plutarch. *Lives of the Noble Grecians and Romans*. Trans. Thomas North. 3 vols. 1579. Reprint. Oxford, 1928.

———. *Moralia*. Trans. Frank Cole Babbitt. Loeb Classical Library. 16 vols. 1927. Reprint. Cambridge, Mass., 1969. Vol. 1, "How the Young Man Should Study Poetry."

Puttenham, George. *The Arte of English Poesie*. Introduction by Baxter Hathaway. Facsimile of the 1906 edition of Edward Arbor. Kent, Ohio, 1970.

Quintilian. *Institutio oratoria*. Trans. H. E. Butler. Loeb Classical Library. 4 vols. London, 1921.

Rabelais, François. *Gargantua and Pantagruel*. Trans. J. M. Cohen. 1955. Reprint. Baltimore, 1967.

———. *Oeuvres complètes*. Ed. Pierre Jourda. 2 vols. Paris, 1962.

Ronsard, Pierre. *Oeuvres complètes*. Ed. Gustave Cohen. 2 vols. Paris, 1950.

Salviati, Lionardo ("L'Infarinato"). *Degli Accademici della Crusca difesa dell'Ariosto. Contra'l dialogo dell'epica poesia di Cammillo Pellegrino. Stacciata Prima.* Florence, 1584. Reprinted in *Opere di Torquato Tasso colle controversie sulla "Gerusalemme,"* vol. 18. Ed. Giorgio Rosini. Pisa, 1827.

Shelley, P. B. *A Defense of Poetry*. Ed. J. E. Jordan. New York, 1965.

———. *The Poems of Shelley*. Ed. Thomas Hutchinson. 1907. Reprint. London, 1961.

Sidney, Philip. *An Apology for Poetry*. Ed. Geoffrey Shepherd. London, 1965.

———. *The Correspondence of Philip Sidney and Hubert Languet*. Ed. William Aspenwall Bradley. Boston, 1912.

———. *The Countess of Pembroke's Arcadia: The Old Arcadia*. Ed. Jean Robinson. Oxford, 1973.

———. *Miscellaneous Prose of Sir Philip Sidney*. Ed. Katherine Duncan-Jones and Jan Van Dorsten. Oxford, 1973. [Includes *A Defence of Poetry*.]

———. *The Poems of Sir Philip Sidney*. Ed. William A. Ringler, Jr. Oxford, 1962.

———. *The Prose Works of Sir Philip Sidney*. Ed. Albert Feuillerat. 4 vols. 1912. Reprint. Cambridge, 1962.

Speroni, Sperone. *Dialogo delle Lingue*. Reprinted, with Gruget's French translation, in Pierre Villey, *Les Sources italiennes de la "Deffense et illustration de la langue françoise."* Paris, 1908.

Swift, Jonathan. *The Prose Works of Jonathan Swift*. Ed. Herbert Davis. Vol. 9, "Letter of Advice," pp. 327–45. Oxford, 1963.

Tasso, Bernardo. *Lettere di M. Bernardo Tasso accresciute, corrette e illustrate*. Vols. 1 and 2 ed. Anton-Federigo Seghezzi, vol. 3 ed. Pier Antonio Serassi. Padua, 1733–51.

———. *Lettere inedite di Bernardo Tasso precedute dalle notizie intorno la vita del medesimo*. Ed. G. Campori. Bologna, 1869.

Tasso, Torquato. *Dialoghi*. Ed. Ezio Raimondi. 5 vols. Florence, 1958.

———. *Discourses on the Heroic Poem*. Trans. Mariella Cavalchini and Irene Samuels. Oxford, 1973.

_____. *Gerusalemme Conquistata*. Ed. Luigi Bonfigli. 2 vols. Bari, 1934.
_____. *Jerusalem Delivered*. Trans. Edward Fairfax (1600). Reprinted with an introduction by John Charles Nelson. New York, 1963.
_____. *Le Lettere di Torquato Tasso*. Ed. Cesare Guasti. 5 vols. Florence, 1853–55.
_____. *Opere*. Ed. Bruno Maier. 5 vols. Milan, 1965. Vol. 3, *Gerusalemme Liberata*. Vol. 5, *Apologia in difesa della "Gerusalemme Liberata."*
_____. *Opere di Torquato Tasso colle controversie sulla "Gerusalemme."* Ed. Giorgio Rosini. 33 vols. Pisa, 1824–32.
_____. *Prose*. Ed. Ettore Mazzali. Introduction by Francesco Flora. Milan and Naples, 1959.
Vasari, Giorgio. *The Lives of the Artists: A Selection*. Trans. George Bull. London, 1965.
Vida. *Ars Poetica*. Ed. Albert S. Cook, with a translation by Pitt. Boston, 1892.
Virgil. *Eclogues, Georgics, and Aeneid*. Trans. H. R. Fairclough. Loeb Classical Library. 2 vols. Rev. ed. London, 1935.

Secondary Sources

Works of Reference

Battaglia, Salvatore. *Grande Dizionario della lingua italiana*. 10 vols. Turin, 1961–.
Bloch, O., and W. Von Wartburg. *Dictionnaire etymologique de la langue française*. 23 vols. Basel, 1968.
Cotgrave, R. *A Dictionarie of the French and English Tongues*. Facsimile of the first ed. (1611). New York, 1950.
Cross, F. L., ed. *The Oxford Dictionary of the Christian Church*. 2nd ed. Oxford, 1974.
Huguet, E. *Dictionnaire de la langue française au seizième siècle*. 7 vols. Paris, 1925–67.
The Interpreter's Bible. 12 vols. New York, 1952–57.
Lausburg, H. *Handbuch der literarischen Rhetorik*. 2 vols. Munich, 1973.
The Oxford English Dictionary, being a corrected re-issue of *A New English Dictionary on Historical Principles*, ed. J. A. H. Murray. 12 vols. 1933. Reprint. Oxford, 1961.
Pauly's Real-Encyclopaedie der klassischen altertums Wissenschaft, ed. G. Wissowa et al. Vol. 18. Stuttgart, 1949.
Toynbee, Paget. *A Dictionary of Proper Names and Notable Matters in the Works of Dante*. 1898. Revised and edited by Charles Singleton. Reprint. Oxford, 1968.
Vocabulario degli Accademici della Crusca. 7 vols. (incomplete). Florence, 1863–93.

Works on Du Bellay

Bakhtin, Mikhail. *Rabelais and His World*. Trans. Helene Iswolsky from the 1965 original edition. Cambridge, Mass., 1968.
Borst, A. *Der Turmbau von Babel: Geschichte der Meinungen über Ursprung und Vielfalt der Sprachen und Völker*. 6 vols. Stuttgart, 1957–63.

Brunot, Ferdinand. *Histoire de la langue française des origines à nos jours.* Vol. 2, *Le XVIe Siècle.* Paris, 1967.

Cammarosano, Francesco. *La Vita e le opere di Sperone Speroni.* Empoli, 1920.

Castor, Grahame. *Pléiade Poetics: A Study in 16th Century Thought and Terminology.* Cambridge: Cambridge University Press, 1964.

Cave, Terence. *The Cornucopian Text: Problems of Writing in the French Renaissance.* Oxford, 1979.

Chamard, Henri. *Histoire de la Pléiade.* 4 vols. Paris, 1939–49.

———. *Joachim du Bellay, 1522–1560.* 1900. Reprint. Geneva, 1969.

Clements, Robert J. *Critical Theory and Practice of the Pléiade.* Cambridge, Mass., 1942.

Dassonville, Michel. "De l'unité de *La Deffense et illustration de la langue françoyse.*" *Bibliothèque d'humanisme et de Renaissance* 27 (1965): 96–107.

Deguy, Michel. *Tombeau de Du Bellay.* Paris, 1973.

Dubois, Claude-Gilbert. *Mythe et langage au seizième siècle.* Paris, 1970.

Griffin, Robert. *Coronation of the Poet: Du Bellay's Debt to the Trivium.* University of California Publications in Modern Philology, no. 96. Berkeley and Los Angeles, 1969.

Joukovsky-Micha, Françoise. *La Gloire dans la poésie française et néolatine du 16e siècle.* Geneva, 1969.

Mandrou, Robert. *Introduction to Modern France, 1500–1640: An Essay in Historical Psychology.* Trans. R. E. Hallmark from the 1961 ed. London, 1975.

Rigolot, François. "Du Bellay et la poésie du refus." *Bibliothèque d'Humanisme et de Renaissance* 36 (1974): 489–502.

———. "Cratylisme et Pantagruélisme: Rabelais et le statut du signe." *Etudes Rabelaisiennes* 13 (1976): 115–32.

Salmon, J. H. M. *Society in Crisis: France in the Sixteenth Century.* New York, 1975.

Saulnier, V. L. *Du Bellay.* 1951. Rev. ed. Paris, 1968.

Stone, Donald. *France in the Sixteenth Century: A Medieval Society Transformed.* Englewood Cliffs, N. J., 1969.

Struever, Nancy. *The Language of History in the Renaissance.* Princeton, 1970.

Tilley, Arthur. *Studies in the French Renaissance.* New York, 1968.

Vianey, Joseph. *"Les Regrets" de Joachim du Bellay.* 1930. Reprint. Paris, 1967.

Villey, Pierre. *Les Sources italiennes de la "Deffense et illustration de la langue françoise."* Paris, 1908.

Weber, Henri. *La Création poétique au XVIe siècle en France.* Paris, 1956.

Works on Tasso

Amabile, Luigi. *Il Santo Officio della Inquisizione in Napoli.* 2 vols. Castello, 1892.

Baldassarri, Guido. "L'Arte del dialogo in Torquato Tasso." *Studi Tassiani* 20 (1970): 5–46.

———. *"Inferno" e "Cielo": Tipologia e funzione del "Meraviglioso" nella "Liberata."* Rome, 1977.

Brand, C. P. "Stylistic Trends in the *Gerusalemme Conquistata.*" *Italian Studies Presented to E. R. Vincent.* Cambridge, 1962.

———. *Torquato Tasso: A Study of the Poet and of His Contributions to English Literature.* Cambridge, 1965.

Carucci, C. *Ferrante Sanseverino, Principe di Salerno.* Salerno, 1899.

Chiappelli, Fredi. *Studi sul linguaggio del Tasso epico.* Florence, 1957.

De Sanctis, Francesco. *The History of Italian Literature.* Trans. Joan Redfern. 2 vols. New York, [1931].

Donadoni, Eugenio. *Torquato Tasso: Saggio critico.* 4th ed. Florence, 1952.

Durling, Robert M. "The Epic Ideal." In *Literature and Western Civilization. The Old World: Discovery and Rebirth.* Ed. David Daiches and Anthony Thorlby. London, 1964, pp. 105–46.

———. *The Figure of the Poet in Renaissance Epic.* Cambridge, Mass., 1965.

Fichter, Andrew. "Tasso's Epic of Deliverance." *Publications of the Modern Language Association* 93 (March 1978): 265–74.

Fiorato, A. "Bandello et le règne du Père." *Les Ecrivains et le pouvoir en Italie à l'epoque de la Renaissance,* vol. 2. Paris, 1973.

Garin, Eugenio. *Italian Humanism: Philosophy and Civic Life in the Renaissance.* Trans. Peter Munz. 1965. Reprint. New York, 1975.

Getto, Giovanni. *Interpretazione del Tasso.* Naples, 1967.

———. *Nel Mondo della "Gerusalemme."* 2nd ed. Rome, 1977.

Giamatti, A. Bartlett. "Headlong Horsemen: An Essay on the Chivalric Epics of Pulci, Boiardo, and Ariosto." *Italian Literature: Roots and Branches.* Ed. G. Rimanelli and K. Atchity. New Haven, 1976.

Giannone, Pietro. *Istoria civile del regno di Napoli.* 4 vols. 3rd ed. Palmyra, 1763.

Greene, Thomas. *The Descent from Heaven: A Study in Epic Continuity.* New Haven and London, 1963.

Hathaway, Baxter. *Marvels and Commonplaces.* New York, 1968.

Lea, Henry Charles. *The Inquisition in the Spanish Dependencies.* New York, 1908.

Leo, Ulrich. *Ritterepos-Gottesepos: Torquato Tasso's Weg Als Dichter.* Studi Italiani, no. 2. Cologne, 1958.

———. *Torquato Tasso: Studien Zur Vorgeschichte des Secentismo.* Bern, 1951.

Martines, Lauro. *Power and Imagination: City States in Renaissance Italy.* New York, 1979.

Murrin, Michael. *The Allegorical Epic: Essays in Its Rise and Decline.* Chicago and London, 1980.

———. *The Veil of Allegory: Some Notes Toward a Theory of Allegorical Rhetoric in the English Renaissance.* Chicago, 1969.

Patterson, Annabel M. "Tasso and Neoplatonism: The Growth of His Epic Theory." *Studies in the Renaissance* 18 (1971): 105–33.

Petrocchi, Giorgio. *I Fantasmi di Tancredi: Saggi sul Tasso e sul Rinascimento.* Rome, 1972.

Plumb, J. H. *The Italian Renaissance: A Concise Survey of Its History and Culture.* 1961. Reprint. New York, 1965.

Quint, David. "The Figure of Atlante: Ariosto and Boiardo's Poem." *Modern Language Notes* 94 (1979): 77–91.

Solerti, Angelo, ed. *Appendice alle opere in prosa di Torquato Tasso.* Florence, 1892.

———. *Vita di Torquato Tasso.* 3 vols. Turin, 1895.

Sozzi, B. T. *Nuovi Studi sul Tasso.* Bergamo, 1963.

———. *Studi sul Tasso.* Pisa, 1954.

_____. "Tasso contro Salviati, con le postille inedite all'*Infarinato.*" *Studi Tassiani* 1 (1951): 37–66.

Summonte, G. A. *Historia della città e regno di Napoli.* 6 vols. 3rd ed. Naples, 1769.

Sutherland, Donald. *On, Romanticism.* New York, 1971.

Vailati, M. *Il Tormento artistico del Tasso dal "Liberata" alla "Conquistata."* Milan, 1950.

Villari, Rosario. "The Insurrection in Naples of 1585." *The Late Italian Renaissance.* Ed. E. Cochrane. New York, 1970.

Weinberg, Bernard. *A History of Literary Criticism in the Italian Renaissance.* 2 vols. Chicago, 1961.

Williamson, Edward. *Bernardo Tasso.* Rome, 1951.

Works on Sidney

Alpers, Paul. *The Poetry of the Faerie Queene.* Princeton, 1967.

Anderson, D. M. "The Trial of the Princes in the *Arcadia*, Book V." *Review of English Studies* 8 (1957): 409–12.

Barker, Arthur E. "An Apology for the Study of Renaissance Poetry." In *Literary Views: Critical and Historical Essays.* Ed. C. C. Camden. Chicago, 1964.

Barnes, Catherine. "The Hidden Persuader: The Complex Speaking Voice of Sidney's *Defense of Poetry.*" *PMLA* 86 (May 1971): 422–27.

Craig, D. H. "A Hybrid Growth: Sidney's Theory of Poetry in the *Apology.*" *English Literary Renaissance* 10 (1980): 183–200.

Davis, Walter. *Idea and Act in Elizabethan Literature.* Princeton, 1969.

Dipple, Elizabeth. "'Unjust Justice' in the *Old Arcadia.*" *Studies in English Literature, 1500–1900* 10 (1970): 83–101.

Donno, Elizabeth Story. "Old Mouse-Eaten Records: History in Sidney's *Apology.*" *Studies in Philology* 72 (1975): 275–98.

Fish, Stanley. *Self-Consuming Artifacts: The Experience of Seventeenth-Century Literature.* Berkeley, 1972.

Fraser, Russell. *The War against Poetry.* Princeton, 1970.

Greville, Fulke. *Life of Sidney.* Ed. Nowell Smith. Oxford, 1907.

Hamilton, A. C. *Sir Philip Sidney: A Study of His Life and Works.* Cambridge, 1977.

Hardison, O. B., Jr. "The Two Voices of Sidney's *Apology for Poetry.*" *English Literary Renaissance* 2 (Winter 1972): 83–99.

Hunter, George K. "Humanism and Courtship." *Elizabethan Poetry: Modern Essays in Criticism.* Ed. Paul J. Alpers. London, 1967.

Javitch, Daniel. *Poetry and Courtliness in Renaissance England.* Princeton, 1978.

Kinney, Arthur F. "Parody and Its Implications in Sidney's *Defence of Poetry.*" *Studies in English Literature, 1500–1900* 12 (Winter 1972): 1–19.

Lanham, Richard. "*Astrophil and Stella*: Pure and Impure Persuasion." *English Literary Renaissance* 2, no. 1 (1972): 100–15.

Levao, Ronald. "Sidney's Feigned Apology." *Publications of the Modern Language Association* 94 (March 1979): 223–33.

Levy, F. J. "Sir Philip Sidney and the Idea of History." *Bibliothèque d'humanisme et de renaissance* 26 (September 1964): 208–17.

McCoy, Richard. *Sir Philip Sidney: Rebellion in Arcadia.* New Brunswick, N. J., 1979.

Myrick, Kenneth. *Sir Philip Sidney as a Literary Craftsman.* Lincoln, Nebraska, 1935.

Ong, Walter J. "The Province of Rhetoric and Poetic." In *The Province of Rhetoric,* ed. Joseph Schwartz and John A. Rycenga. New York, 1965.

Robinson, Forrest G. *Sidney's "Apology" in Its Philosophical Tradition.* Cambridge, Mass., 1973.

Rudenstine, Neil. *Sidney's Poetic Development.* Cambridge, Mass., 1967.

Stone, Lawrence. *The Crisis of the Aristocracy: 1558–1641.* Oxford, 1965.

Weiner, Andrew. *Sir Philip Sidney and the Poetics of Protestantism: A Study of Contexts.* Minneapolis, 1978.

Wolfley, L. C. "Sidney's Visual Didactic Poetic: Some Complexities and Limitations." *Journal of Medieval and Renaissance Studies* 6 (Fall 1966): 217–42.

Psychoanalytic Material

Abraham, Hilda C. and Ernst L. Freud, eds. *A Psychoanalytic Dialogue: The Letters of Sigmund Freud and Karl Abraham, 1907–1926.* Trans. Bernard Marsh and Hilda Abraham. London, 1965.

Arlow, Jacob A. "Metaphor and the Psychoanalytic Situation." *Psychoanalytic Quarterly* 48 (1979): 363–85.

Bibring, Edward. "The Conception of the Repetition Compulsion." *Psychoanalytic Quarterly* 12 (1943): 486–519.

Brenner, Charles. "Metapsychology and Psychoanalytic Theory." *Psychoanalytic Quarterly* 39 (1980): 189–214.

———. "The Nature and Development of the Concept of Repression in Freud's Writings." *The Psychoanalytic Study of the Child* 12 (1957): 19–46.

Clark, Ronald. *Freud: The Man and the Cause.* New York, 1980.

Cuddihy, John Murray. *The Ordeal of Civility: Freud, Marx, Levi-Strauss, and the Jewish Struggle with Modernity.* New York, 1974.

Derrida, Jacques. *La Carte postale.* Paris, 1980.

Felman, Shoshana, ed. *Literature and Psychoanalysis: The Question of Reading.* Yale French Studies, nos. 55–56. New Haven, 1977.

Fenichel, Otto. *The Psychoanalytic Theory of Neurosis.* New York, 1945.

Freud, Anna. *The Ego and the Mechanisms of Defense.* 1937. Rev. ed. 1966. Reprint. New York, 1977.

Freud, Sigmund. *The Letters of Sigmund Freud.* Selected and ed. Ernst Freud; trans. Tania and James Stern. 1960. Reprint. New York, n.d.

———. *The Origins of Psychoanalysis: Letters to Wilhelm Fliess.* Trans. Eric Mosbacker and James Strachey. 1954. Reprint. New York, 1977.

———. *The Standard Edition of the Complete Psychological Works of Sigmund Freud.* Ed. James Strachey et al. 24 vols. London, 1953–73. Cited as *SE.*

———. *Gesammelte Werke.* Ed. A. Freud, E. Bibring, W. Hoffer, E. Kris, O. Isakowers. 18 vols. Vols. 1–17: London, 1940–52. Vol 18: Frankfurt am Main, 1968.

Glover, Edward. "The Therapeutic Effect of Inexact Interpretation: A Contribution to the Theory of Suggestion." *International Journal of Psychoanalysis* 12 (1931): 397–411.

Hartman, Geoffrey H., ed. *Psychoanalysis and the Question of the Text. Selected papers from the English Institute, 1976–77.* Baltimore, 1978.

Hertz, Neil. "Freud and the Sandman." *Textual Strategies: Perspectives in Post-Structuralist Criticism.* Ed. Joseph Harari. Ithaca, 1979.

Jones, Ernest. *The Life and Works of Sigmund Freud.* 3 vols. New York, 1955.

Koff, Robert H. "A Definition of Identification: A Review of the Literature." *International Journal of Psychoanalysis* 42 (1961): 362–370.

Lacan, Jacques. *Ecrits: A Selection.* Trans. Alan Sheridan. London, 1977.

———. *The Four Fundamental Concepts of Psycho-analysis.* Ed. Jacques Alain-Miller. Trans. Alan Sheridan. 1977. Reprint. New York, 1981.

———. *The Language of the Self: The Function of Language in Psychoanalysis.* Trans. Anthony Wilden. New York, 1968.

Lagache, Daniel. "La Psychanalyse et la structure de la personnalité." *La Psychanalyse* 6 (1961): 5–58.

Laplanche, J. "La Défense et l'interdit." *La Nef,* no. 31 (1967): 43–55.

———. *Vie et mort en psychanalyse.* Paris, 1970. Trans. J. Mehlman as *Life and Death in Psychoanalysis.* Baltimore, 1976.

Laplanche, J., and J.-B. Pontalis. *The Language of Psychoanalysis.* Trans. Donald Nicholson-Smith, with an introduction by Daniel Lagache. New York, 1973.

Leavy, Stan. "Psychoanalytic Interpretation." *The Psychoanalytic Study of the Child* 28 (1973): 305–30.

Loewenstein, R. M. "Some Thoughts on Interpretation in the Theory and Practice of Psychoanalysis." *The Psychoanalytic Study of the Child* 12 (1957): 127–50.

Loughlin, Henry. *The Ego and Its Defenses.* New York, 1970.

Madison, Peter. *Freud's Concept of Repression and Defense: Its Theoretical and Observational Language.* Minneapolis, 1961.

Meisel, Perry, ed. *Freud: A Collection of Critical Essays.* Englewood Cliffs, N. J., 1981.

Ricoeur, Paul. *Freud and Philosophy: An Essay in Interpretation.* Trans. Denis Savage. New Haven, 1970.

Rieff, Philip. *Freud: The Mind of the Moralist.* New York, 1959.

Shafer, Roy. "The Mechanisms of Defence." *International Journal of Psychoanalysis* 49 (1968): 49–62.

Skura, Meredith Anne. *The Literary Uses of the Psychoanalytic Process.* New Haven, 1981.

Smith, Joseph H., ed. *The Literary Freud: Mechanisms of Defense and the Poetic Will.* Psychiatry and the Humanities, vol. 4. New Haven, 1980.

Stone, Leo. "Reflections on the Psychoanalytic Concept of Aggression." *Psychoanalytic Quarterly* 40 (1971): 195–244.

Wollheim, Richard. *Sigmund Freud.* New York, 1971.

Wurmson, Leon. "A Defense of the Use of Metaphor in Analytic Theory Formation." *Psychoanalytic Quarterly* 46 (1977): 466–98.

General Works

Abrams, M. H. "Belief and the Suspension of Disbelief." *Literature and Belief: English Institute Essays, 1957.* Cambridge, Mass., 1958.

Anderson, Perry. *Lineages of the Absolutist State*. London, 1974.

Arac, Jonathan. "To Regress from the Rigors of Shelley: Figures of History in American Deconstructionist Criticism." *Boundary 2*, 8 (Spring 1980): 241–57.

Arendt, Hannah. *Between Past and Future: Six Exercises in Political Thought*. New York, 1961.

Austin, J. L. *Philosophical Papers*. Ed. J. O. Urmson and G. J. Warnock. 3rd ed. Oxford, 1979.

Bakhtin, Mikhail. *The Dialogic Imagination. Four Essays*. Ed. Michael Holquist. Trans. Caryl Emerson and M. Holquist. Austin and London, 1981.

———. *Problems of Dostoevsky's Poetics*. Trans. R. W. Rotsel. Ann Arbor, 1973.

Berger, Harry, Jr. "The Renaissance Imagination: Second World and Green World." *Centennial Review* 9 (1965): 36–78.

Burke, Kenneth. *A Rhetoric of Motives*. Berkeley and Los Angeles, 1969.

Burke, Peter. *The Renaissance Sense of the Past*. 1969. Reprint. New York, 1970.

Chiarenza, Marguerite Mills. "Hippolytus' Exile: *Paradiso* XVII, vv. 46–48." *Dante Studies* 84 (1966): 65–68.

Colie, Rosalie. *Paradoxia Epidemica*. Princeton, 1966.

Coulter, J. A. "The Relation of the *Apology* of Socrates to Gorgias's *Defense of Palamedes* and Plato's Critique of Gorgianic Rhetoric." *Harvard Studies in Classical Philology* 68 (1964): 269–303.

Curtius, E. R. *European Literature and the Latin Middle Ages*. Trans. Willard R. Trask from the 1948 original. 1953. Reprint. New York, 1963.

De Man, Paul. *Allegories of Reading: Figural Language in Rousseau, Nietzsche, Rilke, and Proust*. New Haven and London, 1979.

Derrida, Jacques. *La Dissémination*. Paris, 1972.

Diels, Hermann, and Walter Kranz. *Fragmente der Vorsokratiker*. 3 vols. 6th ed. Berlin, 1952.

Else, Gerald F. *Aristotle's "Poetics": The Argument*. Cambridge, Mass., 1967.

Fletcher, Angus. *Allegory: The Theory of a Symbolic Mode*. Ithaca and London, 1964.

Freccero, John. "Dante's Firm Foot and the Journey without a Guide." *Harvard Theological Review* 52 (1959): 245–81.

———. "Dante's Prologue Scene." *Dante Studies* 84 (1966): 1–25.

———. "Infernal Inversion and Christian Conversion: *Inferno* XXXIV." *Italica* 42 (1965): 35–41.

Freeman, Kathleen. *Ancilla to the Pre-Socratic Philosophers: A Complete Translation of the Fragments in Diels "Fragmente der Vorsokratiker."* Cambridge, Mass., 1956.

Gramsci, Antonio. *Selections from the Prison Notebooks*. Ed. and trans. Quintin Hoare and Geoffrey Norwell-Smith. New York, 1971.

Greene, Thomas. "Petrarch and the Humanist Hermeneutic." *Italian Literature: Roots and Branches*. Ed. G. Rimanelli and K. Atchity. New Haven, 1976.

Guillory, John D. "Poetry and Authority: Spenser, Milton and Literary History." Ph.D. dissertation. Yale University, 1979.

Guthrie, W. K. C. *The Sophists*. Cambridge, 1971.

Habermas, Jürgen. *Knowledge and Human Interests*. Trans. from the 1968 German ed. by Jeremy J. Shapiro. London, 1972.

Hale, David George. *The Body Politic: A Political Metaphor in Renaissance English Literature*. Paris and The Hague, 1971.

Hartman, Geoffrey. *Beyond Formalism*. New Haven, 1970.

————. *Criticism in the Wilderness: The Study of Literature Today*. New Haven, 1980.

————. *The Fate of Reading and Other Essays*. Chicago, 1975.

Harvey, E. Ruth, *The Inward Wits: Psychological Theory in the Middle Ages and the Renaissance*. Warburg Institute Surveys, 6. London, 1975.

Havelock, Eric A. *Preface to Plato*. 1963. Reprint. New York, 1967.

Hirsch, E. D. *Validity in Interpretation*. New Haven, 1967.

Jakobsen, Roman. *Selected Writings*, vol 2. "Shifters, Verbal Categories, and the Russian Verb," pp. 130-47. The Hague, 1971.

James, Henry. *The Art of the Novel: Critical Prefaces*. Introduction by Richard P. Blackmur. New York, [1962].

Jameson, Fredric. *The Political Unconscious: Narrative as a Socially Symbolic Act*. Ithaca, 1981.

————. "Imaginary and Symbolic in Lacan: Marxism, Psychoanalytic Criticism, and The Problem of the Subject." *Literature and Psychoanalysis: The Question of Reading*. Ed. Shoshana Felman. Yale French Studies, nos. 55-56. New Haven, 1977.

Kaiser, Walter. *Praisers of Folly: Erasmus, Rabelais, Shakespeare*. Cambridge, Mass., 1963.

Kennedy, George. *The Art of Persuasion in Greece*. Princeton, 1963.

Kenner, Hugh. *The Counterfeiters*. New York, 1973.

Kermode, Frank. *The Genesis of Secrecy: On the Interpretation of Narrative*. Cambridge, Mass., 1979.

Lepenies, Wolf. *Melancholie und Gesellschaft*. Frankfurt am Main, 1969.

Levin, Harry. *The Myth of the Golden Age in the Renaissance*. New York, 1969.

Manley, Lawrence. *Convention: 1500-1750*. Cambridge, Mass., 1980.

Marcus, Millicent. "The Accommodating Frate Alberto: A Gloss on *Decameron* IV. 2." *Italica* 56 (Spring 1979): 3-21.

Mazzacurati, Giancarlo. *Conflitti di culture nel cinquecento*. Naples, 1977.

Mendelsohn-Martone, Beatrice. "Benedetto Varche's 'Due Lezione': Paragoni and Cinquecento Art Theory." Ph.D. dissertation, Institute of Fine Arts, New York, 1978.

Muecke, Douglas C. *The Compass of Irony*. London, 1969.

Mukařovský, Jan. *Structure, Sign and Function*. Trans. and ed. John Burbank and Peter Steiner. New Haven and London, 1978.

O'Brian, George. *Renaissance Poetics and The Problem of Power*. Chicago, 1951.

Ong, Walter J. *Rhetoric, Romance, and Technology: Studies in the Interaction of Expression and Culture*. Ithaca, 1971.

Panofsky, Erwin. *Galileo as a Critic of the Arts*. The Hague, 1954.

————. *The Life and Art of Albrecht Dürer*. Princeton, 1955.

Pauley, Bruce. *Hitler and the Forgotten Nazis: A History of Austrian National Socialism*. Chapel Hill, 1981.

Pepe, M. "Il 'paragone' tra pittura e scultura nella letteratura artistica rinascimentale." *Culture e scuola* 8 (1969): 120-31.

Poggioli, Renato. *The Poets of Russia, 1890–1930*. Cambridge, Mass., 1960.

————*The Theory of the Avant-Garde*. Trans. from the 1962 Italian ed. by Gerald Fitzgerald. Cambridge, Mass. 1968.

Ricoeur, Paul. *The Conflict of Interpretations: Essays in Hermeneutics*. Ed. Don Ihde. Evanston, Illinois, 1974.

Rossky, William. "Imagination in the English Renaissance: Psychology and Poetic." *Studies in the Renaissance* 5 (1958): 49–73.

Singleton, Charles. *Journey to Beatrice*. Dante Studies, 2. Cambridge, Mass., 1967.

Spitzer, Leo. *Essays in Historical Semantics*. New York, [1948].

Tollemache, Lionel A. *Benjamin Jowett, Master of Balliol*. London and New York, 1895.

Trimpi, Wesley. "The Quality of Fiction: The Rhetorical Transmission of Literary Theory." *Traditio* 30 (1974): 1–118.

Untersteiner, Mario. *The Sophists*. Trans. from the 1948 Italian ed. by Kathleen Freeman. Oxford, 1954.

Uspensakij, B. A., Ivanov, V. V., and other members of the Tartu Group. "Theses on the Semiotic Study of Cultures (as applied to Slavic Texts)." *Structure of Texts and Semiotics of Culture*. Ed. Jan van der Eng and Mojmír Grygar. The Hague, 1973.

Versény, Laszlo. *Socratic Humanism*. New Haven, 1963.

Voloshinov, V. N. (M. M. Bakhtin). *Marxism and the Philosophy of Language*. Trans. Ladislav Matejka and I. R. Titunik. New York, 1973.

Walker, D. P. *The Decline of Hell: Seventeenth-Century Discussions of Eternal Torment*. Chicago, [1964].

Ward, Philip. *Apuleius on Trial at Sabratha*. London, 1968.

Wimsatt, W. K., and Brooks, Cleanth. *Literary Criticism: A Short History*. New York, 1957.

Wittgenstein, Ludwig. *Philosophical Investigations*. Trans. G. E. M. Anscombe. 3rd ed. New York, 1958.

Index